Teaching Children about Life and Earth Sciences

Also by Elaine Levenson

Teaching Children About Physical Science:
Ideas and Activities Every Teacher and Parent Can Use

Teaching Children about Life and Earth Sciences

Ideas and Activities Every … r and Parent Can Use

Elaine Levenson

…trations by Debra Ellinger

… Mary Budd Rowe, Past-President … Science Teachers Association

The Four Seasons
Divide paper into four sections by folding (draw line dividing 4 sections)
In corner of each section write season names (Fall, Winter, Spring, Summer)
-Clockwise-
Have class draw a picture for each season describing weather
(30-35)

TAB Books

…sion of McGraw-Hill, Inc.

…rancisco Washington, D.C. Auckland Bogotá …bon London Madrid Mexico City Milan …al New Delhi San Juan Singapore Sydney Tokyo Toronto

Published by TAB Books, a division of McGraw-Hill, Inc.

This book is printed on recycled, acid-free paper containing a minimum of 50% total recycled fiber with 10% post-consumer de-inked fiber.

1 2 3 4 5 6 7 8 9 0 MAL/MAL 9 9 8 7 6 5 4

Library of Congress Cataloging-in-Publication Data
Levenson, Elaine.
Teaching children about life and earth sciences : ideas and activities every teacher and parent can use / by Elaine Levenson; foreword by Mary Budd Rowe.
p. cm.
Includes index.
ISBN 0-07-037655-7 (pbk.)
1. Biology—Study and teaching. 2. Earth sciences—Study and teaching. I. Rowe, Mary Budd. II. Title.
QH315.L39 1994
372.3'5—dc20 93-40784
CIP

Acquisitions editor: Kimberly Tabor
Editorial team: Robert E. Ostrander, Executive Editor
Sally Anne Glover, Book Editor
Production team: Katherine G. Brown, Director
Wanda S. Ditch, Desktop Operator
Brenda Wilhide, Computer Artist
Joan Wieland, Proofreading
Jodi L. Tyler, Indexer
Design team: Jaclyn J. Boone, Designer
Brian Allison, Associate Designer
Cover design and illustration: Sandra Blair Design, Harrisburg, Pa.

GEN2
0376557

Dedication

In loving memory of Julia Pearce, a special friend whose beauty of spirit, energy, and good cheer were always contagious.

I dedicate this book to my mother (Sadie Moss), to parents and teachers who feel insecure about teaching science subjects, to the young children they teach, who ask, "why?" and "how come?" and to my own very special children, William and Emily, whose curiosity and thoughts helped inspire many of the ideas put forth in this book, as well as to Jean Harlan whom I have never met, but whose book greatly influenced me.

"Teaching Children About Science *is a good resource for persons in both school and nonschool settings who are helping children learn science ... much more functional than other activity-oriented books.*"

— *Curriculum Review*

"*An excellent source of ideas presented in a simple, sound format. It belongs in the library of every science curriculum lab, school, and teacher .... Levenson's work could be the key to running an exciting, effective science program.*"

— *Science and Children*

"*This author knows what scientific information children need and how that information is successfully transferred to the child .... She is involved in improving the quality of science instruction on a grand scale with this wonderful book.*"

— *Science Activities*

"*Highly recommended.*"

— *Science Books & Films*
Children's Science Booklist (Education)

"*One of the best teacher reference books I have found. Her approach is so well structured that a parent, novice teacher or seasoned science teacher would have no difficulty bringing science education into the home or classroom. The hands on and interdisciplinary approach fit right into our Montessori classroom.*"

— Terry Cook, Educational Director
Montessori Elementary School of Blacksburg, VA

"*If a parent or a teacher could buy only one book about exploring science with children, there is no doubt that* TEACHING CHILDREN ABOUT SCIENCE *is absolutely, wholeheartedly the book I would recommend.*"

— Julie Fudge Smith
Volunteer scientist for the Boston Museum of Science, Science-by-Mail program, Science Curriculum Consultant and science writer for parents and children.

"*We highly recommend this book for teachers, home-schooling families, and parents who want to stimulate and enrich their children's view and understanding of their world.*"

— Harriet Eskridge, Lead Teacher
Faith Christian Academy

Contents

Foreword

One afternoon I went to a rural first-grade classroom, invited by the young teacher who was doing the "career education" part of the curriculum in that district. The program called for a visiting scientist (me) to whom the children were to ask a set of questions about careers in science. They sat on tiny chairs in a semi-circle around me. Finally, in dutiful fashion the questions began. No children in first grade would ever have thought of them: "Do you have career satisfaction? How many years of training did you have? Are you satisfied with your job? Would you advise others to go into science?" There were ten questions. It took five minutes to answer them. Then we sat facing each other. I finally said, "Are there any questions you always wanted to ask a scientist? I can't promise to answer all of them—maybe there are no answers yet. We keep learning new things every day. What I can't answer I will try to find out by asking other scientists."

They sat for a moment in silence. Then the first hand went up and a small boy said, "Why is it that every time just before I start a fight, I sweat?" I answered that, and the next question was, "I watch preying mantises eat some leaves and he looks like it's good. But when I try chewing those leaves I get sick. Why is that?" Another asked, "Are we sort of a sack of blood? It seems like any place you get cut blood pours out. What good is that?" And so the questions came—for nearly two hours.

There is a great drive on the part of children to know, to get answers. They have to learn, however, that the way we explain things today might change tomorrow. New discoveries lead to new ways of thinking about the facts. As the children themselves mature, their conceptions of the world and their ability to deal with abstraction expands, just as science does. We need to nurture the ability of children to ask questions, seek answers, compare competing ideas, and learn strategies for finding out which explanations are more likely. It is characteristic of scientists to ask questions, to continually challenge ideas. Children start life that way, but somewhere many of them appear to lose it. (Actually, we now know they go "underground"; they get answers, sometimes from undesirable sources. The questions do not stop.)

Once during a trip to China I met a history teacher who was teaching science. He knew very little science and a great deal of history, but he preferred to teach the science because, "They keep changing the version of history to be taught. But science doesn't change. You can count on it," he said wistfully.

He is wrong, of course. Science is always changing. Someone challenges an interpretation; that prompts a basketful of questions, and these are usually followed by experiments meant to provide evidence that favors one of the competing interpretations. Our explanations are continually subject to new interpretations. Science thrives on argument, on resolving conflicting views through experiment and observation, on exploration, and on asking questions. That is one thing little children do with great gusto if anyone will listen—they ask questions!

This book provides three things to adults who work with young children: a large set of science activities that do not require any sophisticated equipment, guidance about how to conduct the activities, and some relevant science content to help answer questions.

Be careful in using the information provided. The temptation is to tell it all before its pertinence ever occurs to students. One second grader in a class I was visiting sat without doing anything during a science class, despite the fact that he had materials on his desk. When I asked him why, he shrugged, "What's the use. They don't care what I think or what we find out ourselves—just what they think. They always tell you what that is, whether you believe it or not. I have lots of questions, but who cares?"

For very young children, nothing is ordinary. Everything is worthy of their attention. They have no hard-and-fast rules about priorities, about what is important and what is not. They have a million questions for anyone who will listen. Remember that about the questions; listen to their questions as you start to use this book. There is a host of simple activities and little explorations in this book that you can use to provide occasions for children to do some "sciencing." Warning: Do not turn these occasions into inquisitions. Let the questions come from the children. Answer them when you can; encourage them to find answers on occasion by asking other people; and help them plan activities that will produce both answers and more questions. If you do not know answers, do not worry about it. Let them help you find out.

Use this book as the valuable resource it is. Listen to the questions and the observations of children—that will show them you care. Besides, it's great fun. They do see the world in a different way. One young child gazed up at the contrail of a jet and said, "Look how that plane is scratching up the sky." She needed no comment, just someone to see it, too.

Enjoy using this book. Science ought to be fun and adventure. More learning takes place when we are having fun, when we feel compelled to find out something or to make something work. Once, while doing some science problem-solving activities with a small group of first graders, I asked if they wanted to come back for another session. One of them said, "I had a good time and I learned how to make that system work the way I wanted it to. But my mother didn't send me to school to have a good time. I'm supposed to get into Stanford and I have no time for fun in school." (First grade!) This mother did not understand that there is a close connection between what information people have and how they learn it. We all know people who are virtually walking encyclopedias but who cannot seem to do anything with the information. The ability to solve problems is closely related to what you know and how you came to know it. Science is best learned through involvement, by talking over what happened, by arguing and experimenting until some satisfactory explanation emerges—and by holding on to ideas tentatively until something better comes along. Science is fun, and the bonus is that it is the most successful device we know of for developing language comprehension.

Mary Budd Rowe

About the second edition

While in the process of writing a revision of *Teaching Children about Science*, it seemed that I included so many new activities that the publisher decided it would be best to divide it into two books. That meant two new titles needed to be created for what I had envisioned would be a single book. Thus, we decided on the titles: *Teaching Children about Physical Science* and *Teaching Children about Life and Earth Sciences*.

I did not feel entirely comfortable with these titles because I was concerned that some might find the titles to be misleading. So, I am writing this note to the reader to clarify what this book contains and what it does not contain. *Teaching Children about Life and Earth Sciences: Ideas and Activities Every Teacher and Parent Can Use* does not include extensive coverage of the following topics: cells, organ systems, earth in space, the solar system.

This book about life and earth sciences covers:

- Weather, which includes activities on: temperature, currents, air pressure, the water cycle (clouds, weather formation, and measurement).
- Volcanoes, rocks, and erosion, which includes activities on: the crust and interior of the earth, distinguishing rocks from one another, distinguishing the three classes of rocks, observing erosion and the formation of rocks.
- Animals, which includes activities on: small creatures, observing how small creatures develop and grow, learning to classify small creatures, becoming aware of the classification scheme of the animal kingdom, and becoming aware of the classification system of vertebrates/animals with backbones.
- All about seed-bearing plants, which includes activities on: seeds; the parts of green plants; leaves; roots and stems; flowers and fruits; experimenting with seeds; experimenting with leaves, stems, and roots; investigating flowers and fruits.
- Ecology, which includes activities on: observing our environment, observing populations, observing adaptations, observing how environments differ, becoming aware of food chains and webs, becoming aware of pollution and its causes.

Both *Teaching Children about Life and Earth Sciences* and *Teaching Children about Physical Science* have the same introductory chapters. When I found out that this new, original manuscript was to be divided, I felt that these chapters were a necessary part of each book, as they explain my philosophy of how to do science with children.

The first three chapters deal with the concepts that integrate physical, life, and earth sciences. Please know that, in everyday life, sciences do overlap. They are not isolated subject areas. There is an interrelationship between the sciences. It is important for children as well as adults to become aware that systems and measurements can and do connect the sciences. Both books contain an introduction to science, a chapter on models, and a chapter on the five senses. (Developing quality observation skills by using our appropriate senses is an essential skill when doing a scientific investigation, and/or a science experiment.) Each book is now a complete entity, and I believe your experience of each will be a thorough one.

Preface

To a young child, the unexplainable is magic. Experiments and activities that help explain physical phenomena help children understand their environment better and help them to have a sense of mastery over it. Children should be encouraged to observe and to compare, to predict and test their ideas. They should be encouraged to repeat an experience or an activity several times to see if the results are always the same or if they vary. In learning about the process of inquiry, you can encourage children to question their results and to try varying their experiences or "experiments" to find out if their results change. You can encourage children to devise ways to measure, record, and arrange their findings in an orderly way, and to think in a logical way when they try to find answers or try to set up experiments.

When science ideas are presented to young children, the experiences need to be real, concrete, tangible experiences with real materials. The ideas and experiences need to be presented in a way that will allow children to feel a connection to them. Avoid presenting information, ideas, or activities in isolation. Try to tie them to a child's life so that the child will feel a desire to know.

As adults, we often become carried away with content and facts. Try to remember that, for a young child, less is more. It is more important for young children to be actively involved in science experiences than for them to learn all of the facts. They will learn and remember what they choose to and that for which they are ready.

My goal is that, through the activities in this book, children will see that learning about and understanding science is simply a matter of looking at the world a bit differently. Science is thinking about the world in terms of how and why. It is seeing relationships between common occurrences and looking for patterns in these common occurrences to help make the world make sense. Science helps young children learn to control their world and to develop a better understanding of natural and physical phenomena. It is exciting for young children to understand that some things are yet to be discovered and understood—and that someday, when they are older, they themselves might be the very ones who find the answers to today's mysteries.

During the past ten years, there has been a boom in the development—and the availability—of useful and innovative science books filled with science activities and experiences for young children. Most of the newer children's books have beautiful, life-size, colorful photographs, and/or wonderful diagrams. With that in mind, I have decided to update this book to include some of the newer ideas that I have discovered, and also to share with the reader some of the more current quality science books now available.

In general, a high-quality science book is one in which: the author is reliable; the science content is accurate and interesting; the sequence is logical; the format is attractive; the illustrations enhance the text and are accurate; the safety precautions and pertinent background information are included in the text; and, finally, the materials used are readily available. Often, thought-provoking questions are included in the text, as well as suggested ways or places to find the answers. Usually, an outstanding science book has received a "very good" or higher rating from a science specialist, or a librarian, who has written a published review in a respected periodical.

Please be aware that when a publisher prints a suggested age of reader or audience in a book, it is merely a "suggested" age. When you visit the libraries and book stores, do not be influenced by the suggested age. Picture books with labels can be of great value to both adults and children to increase their understanding or awareness of a system, a structure and its function, a cycle, a pattern, and sometimes properties of an object.

Because the primary audience for this book is adults who use it as a resource book for young children, I have included Additional Selected Resource Books for Parents and Teachers, as well as Additional Science Books for Children and Their Parents at the end of each chapter. Another list of generic titles for adults and for children appears at the end of the book.

A bibliography of Suggested Literature Connections has been added to the end of most of the chapter bibliographies. These particular fiction books have been listed because when they are read to children, their contents and their illustrations can be used by parents and teachers as a resource to spark interest in and/or discussion about science topics. The list of books in the Suggested Literature Connections are merely a sample of some of the beautiful trade books that are in existence today.

It is not my intention to overwhelm the reader, so I have not attempted to make the lists in the appendices or the bibliographies complete. They are merely a sample of the possibilities. As this book goes to print, other new books will be "emerging." The only books that appear in this book's bibliographies are the ones I have actually been able to put my hands on and have opened, or books that I have not seen but have been highly recommended by other respected sources.

Workshops at your school

The author offers hands-on workshops and seminars for teachers and parent groups, and parents-with-their-children groups, on the activities written about in this book, as well as other topics. She can be reached at Levenson Communications, First Colonial Professional Building, 921 First Colonial Road, Suite 1805, Virginia Beach, Virginia 23454, or telephone (804) 496-0745. FAX (804) 491-0389.

A special note to parents

In the past ten years since I first wrote this book, I have been pleasantly surprised to find out that it has been used as a supplementary methods text in many college courses to train both pre-service and in-service teachers who plan to teach kindergarten through third-grade children, as well as in graduate classes to train special education teachers. I have also learned that it has been a useful source book for sixth-grade children who are able to read this book on their own.

Ten years ago, I had intended that this book would be used by parents, and perhaps a few teachers. It has been my hope that more parents would begin to take a more active role in the education of their children. My own view is that science is intellectually stimulating and can be so much fun. It presents a wonderful opportunity to share your own knowledge of the world, rediscover the world through the eyes of your child, slow down from your own hectic pace, and observe what your child observes.

Parents have a great opportunity to spend special "awareness-time" and "story-time" with their children. As a practical matter, the school and the child's teacher cannot provide children the same kind of science experiences that their own parents can. Often, in a school setting, children do not get that "special time" to be alone with their teacher in a one-to-one experience for longer periods of time.

Unfortunately, in most schools, because of the necessary push for literacy, science activities are neglected or fit in only at the end of the day. Although I love to do science with children, I am as guilty as other teachers are of not devoting more class time to science. Perhaps, if children come into our classrooms more enthused about science, teachers might make the time for more science activities.

As for literacy, as your children are learning to read, or even having difficulty, the experiences with science that you share together can surely enhance their interest in wanting to read "to find out more." Your children can easily make the connection that reading is of value because it allows them to become independent and to try out science experiences for themselves. Science activity books contain exhilarating activities and interesting information with which to play. Science observation skills can enhance auditory discrimination (which is important for repeating sounds with phonics), as well as perceptual discrimination skills (being able to distinguish letters and words).

Please remember that collecting exact measurement and data is for older children. Younger children should be encouraged to keep a journal of their science experiences. For younger children, the journal of their science experiences can be pictures that they draw of what they "did" or "found out," with a caption they dictate to their parent or teacher about their observation or their results. Such a journal of their observations is called recording. Scientists who are serious about their work always record what they do. It helps them to remember what happened, and what they attempted. If you copy down your children's exact words, later the child will be able to review and read back their own captions. This will encourage the development of their reading skills. Older children who are more capable can do their own writing. Their journal entries can be written about:

- What they already think they know about a science concept.
- What they would like to find out.
- What they learned or found out from having done "some things."

Some of the reasons hands-on science activities are often omitted in schools include:

- It takes a good deal of teacher preparation time—let alone storage area—to gather materials for a class to have ongoing science experiences. A teacher might need to gather twelve of everything, so that children could work, say, in twelve pairs; in contrast, the parent only needs to gather one of everything.
- When children do science activities at school, they often become excited and loud, and sometimes they are difficult to bring back to order. When such chaos results, teachers feel uncomfortable, losing momentary control of their class. The more time it takes to settle children down, the more time is wasted from doing other important school activities. Parents need only to deal with the excitement elicited from one or two children.
- Science activities usually result in making a "mess." For a parent, cleaning up one mess is less time-consuming than cleaning up a mess created by twelve pairs of children.
- Often a complete science experience takes time. Observation of events or changes do not always occur rapidly; some take "awhile" to occur. It is easier for a parent and child to leave something on display for "awhile," to observe a change without worrying that the custodian or another child might shift or inadvertently move materials that were being observed. When a parent engages in science activities with their children, the parent has more space to store materials and more control over the environment.
- Sometimes teachers neglect science because they feel intimidated and uncertain about their knowledge of science, and they prefer to teach units of study with which they are more familiar. Teachers have lots of pressure on their time and, although their intentions are good, the time is not always available to them to read or study about specific areas they know they will need to learn

more about. As a parent, you can afford the time to learn with your child and have an enjoyable time in your "second childhood" discovering what you missed the first time around. It's a great opportunity for you to experience what you missed.

I am a kindergarten teacher, not a scientist. I happen to enjoy doing science with children. As a student in high school, I did not have an extensive science background. My math skills were inadequate to continue taking "serious science" classes. I avoided science courses in college in that I was too concerned about a grade-point average. Looking back on my earlier years, it seems rather dim-witted to be more concerned about grades than with obtaining knowledge. Fortunately for me, I had an opportunity to take several graduate-level science classes in a noncompetitive setting through the National Science Foundation and to enjoy learning about all the wonders I missed the first time around.

Of course, we are never too old to learn. As we grow older, we realize that there are many things we do not know. If we stop learning, we stop growing. We are all living entities, and when living entities stop growing, they die. Eleanor Roosevelt, whom I have always greatly admired, is said to have written in her daily column: "Living is learning, and learning is living. When we stop learning, we stop living a vital life."

This book is a result of my having a chance to have a "second childhood" (in league with my own children), who are now quite grown up and in their twenties. This book is filled with happy memories; it is my journal of my own science experiences.

Enjoy your children while they are still young and while they "believe everything you say," but please let them make their own discoveries. Your knowledge will help guide them.

Happy "sciencing!"

About the Icons

Whenever you see this icon, it is meant to be a safety tip.

This icon indicates that this information is meant as an additional piece of information. It is not necessarily meant for the children. Most of this information is too abstract and too complicated for young children to understand or comprehend. It is included to enhance parent or teacher background.

Other respected sources

Appraisal: Science Books for Young Children, Boston University, School of Education, Science Education Program, 605 Commonwealth Ave., Boston, MA 02215.

Brainard, Audrey. A bibliography of children's literature connections that she compiled.

Butzow, C.M. and Butzow, J.W. *Science through Children's Literature*. Englewood, CA: Teachers Ideas Press, 1989.

Cordel, Betty, A bibliography of children's science books that she compiled.

Harwayne, Shelly. *Lasting Impressions: Weaving Literature into the Writing Workshop*. Portsmouth, NH: Heinemann Educational, 1993.

Kramer, Pamela A. and Smith, Gail. Presentation entitled, Science and Literature: Linking and Loving Them. Eighth Annual STS Meeting/Technological Literacy Conference, Arlington, VA, Jan. 1993.

National Science Resource Center. *Science for Children: Resources for Teachers*. National Academy Press, Washington, DC, 1988.

Paula, Nancy and Margery Martin. *Helping Your Child Learn Science*. Office of Educational Research and Improvement, U.S. Dept. of Ed.: Washington, DC, September, 1992.

Science and Children, March issue, published annually by National Science Teachers Association (NSTA), lists outstanding trade books for children, NSTA, 1742 Connecticut Avenue, Washington, DC 20009.

Teachers' Clearinghouse for Science and Society Education Newsletter, edited by Irma Jarcho at 1 West 88th Street, New York, NY 10024

The Korbin Letter, Concerning Children's Books about real people, places and things, 732 Greer Road, Palo Alto, California 94303.

The Science Book List for Children, published by the American Association for the Advancement of Science (AAAS), 1515 Massachusetts Ave., Washington, DC 20005.

Acknowledgments

For this second edition, I wish to acknowledge the following people for their assistance and help in the preparation of this book.

I am greatly indebted to Ralph Brainard, Ph.D., for helping me better understand the nature of atoms, static electricity, weather, sugar crystals, and glaciers, and above all for taking his time to explain concepts to me and to clarify my thinking; I also thank him for editing and helping me to clarify my text so that it would be scientifically accurate; to Audrey Brainard for sharing her knowledge of "literature connections" to science activities and for her guidance and support, for regularly lending me so many great publications, and for the science activities and experiences she was so willing to share at her Hands-On-Science seminars, as well as her Literature-And-Science seminars; to Marco DiCapua, Ph.D. for assisting me to better understand the use of models; to Edward E. Jones, Ph.D., Miami University, Ohio for helping me define density more accurately, for his suggestions on ways to improve this book, and for offering me moral support and encouragement; to Dianne Q. Robinson, Ph.D., Director of the Interdisciplinary Science Center, Hampton University, for her guidance. I am also indebted to my special friend Estelle Feit, a terrific editor, for willingly volunteering to edit this second edition as well as the first one.

I am grateful to my special friends and colleagues from Virginia Beach Public Schools: Sarina Coffin, from Thoroughgood Elementary School, for her patience, suggestions, and words of encouragement; Judy Lewis, Ph.D, Principal, Trantwood Elementary School; Melanie Malbon, Julie Hallberg, Lynn Gibson, Kim La Ferriere, and Alice Walsh, from Linkhorn Park Elementary School, for their support as well as my supervisors at Linkhorn Park Elementary School: Carroll W. Monger (Principal), Julie Rishey (Assistant Principal). I am also grateful for having many special friends who provided me with needed breaks: Julia and Harvey Pearce, Marie Biggers, Rose and Manny Meyer, Nat and Georgia Kramer, to Eileen Bengston, CESI President, for listening to me and helping me come to a decision about staying a kindergarten teacher, to Kay Kent, an AIMS workshop leader for taking her time during her workshop to answer my many questions, to Debbie Deyer, Ph.D. for her contagious energy, to Shalini Perumpral, Ph.D., (my son William's accounting professor) from Radford University for sharing the first edition of *Teaching Children About Science* with her child's Montessori teacher, to educators across the country who reached out for me and gave me "warm-fuzzies," in particular: Beverly Perna, from Boston, Mass; Julie Fudge Smith from Columbus, Ohio; Kathleen Green, Ph.D., Director of Science Education, Beloit College, Beloit, Wisconsin; Terry Cook, Educational Director Montessori Elementary School of Blacksburg, VA; Sandi Schlichting, Educational Director of the Idea Factory, Riverview, Florida; Nancy Jones, Director of Resource Center, Wheelock College, Boston, Mass; Harriet

Eskridge, Lead Teacher, Faith Christian Academy, Cheraw, S.C; and to Mary Kennan Herbert for helping connect me to Kim Tabor at TAB Books; to Kim Tabor for her patience with me, and for keeping this book "alive," to Andrea Sykora, an instructor at Electronic Systems in Virginia Beach and the support people at WordPerfect who answered so many of my questions about word processing procedures.

My greatest acknowledgment goes to my family for their love, understanding, and support. I am especially indebted to my daughter, Emily, who is currently in her junior year at James Madison University, for researching the bibliographies from the first edition to find out if the books listed were still in print (to my surprise most of them were not) and for assisting me with the preparation of this manuscript, and from whom I have learned so much over the years; to my son William, who graduated from Radford University this past year, and who has always been helpful at assisting me in organizing my thoughts; most of my thanks goes to my husband of thirty years, Hal, for giving me the space and time to work on this revision, for his insights, support, encouragement, understanding, and above all his ability in the last decade to cope with being neglected for long periods of time.

1
Introduction to science

How to use this book

At the beginning of each topic, you will find "Objectives," followed by "General Background Information for Parents and Teachers" about the science content and concepts.

The chapters are divided into several concepts for each science topic. The concepts are further broken down into numerous sequential activities. In the "Activities and Procedures" section of chapters 3–13, you will find numbered sequential activities. They progress from simple, concrete experiences to more complicated, abstract ideas. I suggest that this sequence be followed. The activities have been arranged to progress from simple ideas to more complicated ones in a sequential order. Try to present the activities in order, even if you skip some.

Materials

Materials are listed at the beginning of each procedure.

Procedure

Each procedure in an activity begins with a bullet (•).

Questions

All suggested questions are italicized.

( )

Items inside of a parenthesis after a question or a suggested discussion indicate to adults a possible answer or a direction in which to lead children. These answers are provided more for your benefit, rather than for the children. Children should be encouraged to discover their own answers. They also need to know that there can be more than one answer.

Vocabulary

Suggested vocabulary to use with children is included in the suggested possible answers and in the explanations.

Fine points to discuss with children

These suggestions are introduced occasionally when it will enrich an activity. They are usually meant to be discussed with older or more sophisticated younger students who are better able or ready to think and analyze on a higher level.

Going further

These are suggestions for further investigations usually meant for older children. They are the ideas I have come across that I have found to be especially good or innovative, that would extend the activity.

Older children

By older children I mean children in the third grade and up. The activities in this book are intended for children between the ages of four and ten.

You will notice that I have acknowledged the sources of "unique" ideas that I have not found to be redundant in other source books. This book is really a "science sampler" and a synthesis or "anthology" of science activities from many sources that I have found useful in helping young children to better understand science ideas.

An important note to teachers and parents about using this book

As you read this book, you will notice that many of the procedures have long explanations. These explanations to children have been included more for your benefit than for the children's. They are provided in the event that a child asks a question that you might not be able to answer. But, primarily, the explanations are included so that you, as adults, will understand the content of a procedure.

It is wise, if the children are intellectually able, to have them reason on their own and not to "tell them everything." Allow the children to come up with their own explanations whenever possible. Have children do the experiments or do research in age-appropriate reference books such as those listed in the bibliographies at the end of each chapter. Many of the explanations are included so that you, as an adult, will know whether a child is on the right track or needs to be guided to use more reason and systematic logic to solve a problem.

With older children or those who are able intellectually, show them the materials and let the children devise ways to use them, rather than telling them how to use everything.

The content of science is a wonderful tool for helping children develop their reasoning and thinking skills. Reasoning is the fourth "R," along with reading, writing, and 'rithmetic. Help children develop themselves by allowing them the freedom to think problems out on their own and to test out their ideas.

To do many of the procedures in the book, you will need to assist many of the children, but remember not to over-assist.

Science journal

1-2 Science journal.

Do encourage all children to keep a science journal. A science journal is a personal log written by and about what each child is experiencing.

Younger children can draw pictures, and adults can take down the children's dictations. Keeping a journal will help children remember what they did. It will encourage children to take a closer look and to think more carefully about what they see.

Children should be encouraged to write or draw a picture of anything that catches their attention and that they personally find interesting. When they write in their science journals encourage them to ask themselves:

"What do I already think I know about this?"

"What do I think will happen?"

"What did I do?"

"What did I really see?"

"What really happened?"

"What else would I like to find out?"

For a mnemonic device for assisting a child to make a journal entry, see Table 1-1.

Table 1-1 Science journal entry

Encourage children to write or draw a TT-DD-K in their journal.

T –	1. What I THINK I know.
T –	2. What I THINK will happen.
D –	3. What I DID.
D –	4. What I DISCOVERED.
K –	5. What I now KNOW I know.

Answers

Please be aware that when you do activities with children and ask questions of children during an activity, there are no wrong answers. Every answer a child volunteers or that you yourself think of should be considered and investigated. Creativity should be encouraged.

Questions

All questions in this book that are meant to be asked of children are usually italicized. When you begin any new activity, it is usually good to review what knowledge your child(ren) already has by asking a few simple questions to recall previous information.

When you formulate your own questions during a science activity, try to ask questions that start with "How" or "Why." "How do you know" questions help children to focus and assist them to give a logical explanation of their observations and encourage them to see the need for taking or recording measurements, either formally with a measuring device or informally by sight, sound, touch, or smell. "Why" questions are more open-ended and lead to more creative answers, but not necessarily logical ones.

When you are almost finished with an activity that your child(ren) or you have especially enjoyed, encourage your child (ren) to go further by asking some questions that start with:

"What if ......?"

"What do you think might happen if we (change a part of the procedure [that was just done] or use different materials) [other than the ones suggested by the author]?"

Demonstrations

Some activities in this book need to be demonstrated by an adult. When an activity is demonstrated, it should be followed up by encouraging children to repeat the demonstrated procedure on their own. In general, more demonstrations might be needed for younger children than for older children. (Older children usually have better hand-eye coordination, more control of their larger body muscles, a longer attention span, and more logic from experience about how to go about accomplishing a task.) As you read the directions in this book, use your own good judgment as to the appropriate approach to use. Whatever approach you decide to use, do remember to encourage children to repeat their procedures several times to find out if their results are always the same or similar and to discuss their results and the differences that they might notice in their results.

How to teach science

Young children (and those who have not been exposed to science) should learn about science through a multitude of hands-on experiences with real physical objects or models* or real things. The objects, ideas, and concepts presented should be placed in a meaningful context, so that a need is created within the child to want to know more. If a question or

*Models are representations of real things and can be much smaller or much larger than the objects' real-life size. A more detailed description of what is meant by models is presented in chapter 2.

problem can be created, the experience becomes more relevant and significant to the child's life. The information learned from the experience is more likely to be remembered.

Many adults feel insecure about their knowledge of science and, therefore, are uncomfortable teaching content areas with which they feel a lack of familiarity. In reality, most adults understand much more than they give themselves credit for. The basic problem is that of not knowing how to organize the science knowledge they already possess.

Science is "everything" and "everywhere." Just zero in on what you already understand and know a little about, or choose something you are already interested in and want to know more about. As parents and early childhood educators, you have the freedom to choose what areas to study in science and what you want to expose your children to. You have the total world to choose from; the natural world, the physical world, the ancient world, and the universe. The study of most science subjects at the early stages is merely a matter of looking at the content in a methodological way and organizing the content into classes and subsets so that a meaningful context and relevance can be set up for the information.

Teaching by contrasts and similarities

The easiest way to help children understand or learn something new is to expose them to sharp contrasts, so that differences will be obvious. Then they can try to find the similarities between objects that are different. For example, if you are looking at mammals, you might ask if the cat and the horse look alike: How are they different? How are they alike? How are their bodies like our bodies? How are they different? What special features do horses have in their anatomy that help them run faster than we can? What does a cat have on its feet that helps it climb a tree faster than we can, if we can at all? How do cats and horses stay warm? When we run, what part of our body starts to perspire first?

Teaching with a topic and a sequential plan in mind

Avoid a flamboyant "magic-show" style, one that creates mystery and awe. For example: one day presenting magnets, the next day making a cloud appear in a glass, and the next day taking a flower apart. It is difficult to connect these three experiences. Instead, a more formal plan should be implemented. For example, decide on a science unit you or the children would like to investigate, and then spend a week or two doing activities related to the topic being studied so that a relevant context for the experiences can be created and built upon.

Teaching systems for categorizing

Help children develop a system for categorizing and classifying, so that they will be able to break down a large area of study into its smaller parts. Then create an order out of the chaos by grouping, sorting, matching, and positioning materials.

Teaching to discriminate among details

Help children develop their ability to discriminate among details by looking for attributes held in common. Compare likenesses and differences of size, color, shape, texture, age, sound, smell, and if possible, taste.

Teaching by helping children think and make discoveries

Ask children a lot of questions, rather than giving them information. Try to make them find the answers and think. Allow children the opportunity to feel, manipulate, and discover on their own, and then encourage them to share their thoughts. As an adult, help children make predictions, and help them design experiments to test out their hypotheses. Allow yourself and the children to make mistakes; then try to analyze the mistakes together. Stress the importance of testing something several times before drawing conclusions.

Teaching by using logic

Science is logical. Categories and sets need to make sense. Things are included or excluded for reasons, and sometimes sets can overlap and form a union or intersection of two sets. For example, animals can be categorized by two sets: those with backbones and those without backbones. An intersection can occur, however, between the two sets that consists of all animals with jointed legs. Allow children to form a classification system thought out by themselves. Question the child's logic. Ask, "Why is this included and why is that not included?" Ask if there is another way of sorting the items. "Can you make more piles or fewer piles that would make sense?" There is no right or wrong way, as long as there is a logical reason for inclusion or exclusion. All categories are artificial and arbitrary.

Teaching abstract thinking skills by discussing familiar objects

Discuss things around you that can be observed for likenesses and differences. For example:

Are tables and chairs alike?

How are they alike?

How are they different?

Are the floor and the ceiling alike?

How are they alike?

How are they different?

Are people and flowers alike?

How are they alike?

How are they different?

Then progress to:

What is like a pencil?

What is like a ball?

Scientific behaviors

While doing science activities with children, try to keep in mind that there are scientific behaviors that you should attempt to make your child(ren) aware of and to encourage.

- Encourage your children to use their observation skills by using their five senses to observe properties and to notice inconsistencies, (what a scientist would call a "discrepant event," then see if the discrepant event can be repeated).
- Encourage further investigation by asking—"What would happen if?"—by changing a variable (see glossary).
- Encourage your children to always find and use safe available resources or materials to find out answers to questions they might think about after making an observation; discourage them from ever tasting anything unless they know it is absolutely harmless to themselves.
- Encourage the development of logical thinking by asking questions about possible outcomes, making predictions about what might happen, and by carefully observing what does happen.
- Encourage your children's ability to develop and make inferences about his/her observations and the results.
- After your children have had many repetitious experiences and observations with various materials, encourage your child(ren) to think up new situations to see if a generalization he/she is creating can be formulated about a "phenomenon" or event.
- Encourage the refinement and enrichment of your children's logic by discussing: what happened, what worked, what did not work, why or why not, creating new problems to solve and then doing further investigations to find out possible answers or solutions to the problems.
- Encourage your children to construct models to represent or simulate a phenomenon.

I hope that, eventually, when children are doing science activities they will become aware of the importance of creating and doing investigations that can be replicated and repeated by another person, so that a generalization can be formed about an event they have discovered.

The big conceptual pictures

While doing science activities with your children, try to put your experience into a conceptual context. There are nine big conceptual pictures that the The National Center for Improving Science Education has recommended. Most science experiences you do with your children can fit into the framework of one or more of these nine large concepts.

Organization

Encourage your children to classify by: color, size, shape, kind, similar properties. Can they find patterns in the objects they have classified?

Changes

Encourage your children to observe and talk about changes. Is there an observable or measurable change? Has the change occurred rapidly or slowly? Has there been an observable change in any of the objects' properties (color, size, shape, odor, texture) position, (movement/position). Any change is an "event." Events take time to occur. Time is measured from one change until the next. Have your child observe repeatable patterns, cycles in nature: water cycle, lunar cycle, seasonal cycle, day/night cycle, growth cycle of a seed into a plant.

Systems

Make your children aware of systems. A *system* is a whole that is composed of many parts. Usually a hierarchy of interdependence between many systems exists. The "parts" of a system can be systems in their own right. A system occurs when two or more objects or parts of a system or systems interact in some way with each other.

For example: A wolf has many systems operating inside of its body in order to function (skeletal, digestive, reproductive, nervous-sensory, etc.). The wolf is part of a larger system and is part of a food chain. A food chain is part of another system called a food web. The food web is part of an ecosystem, which is part of a biome system. All of the biome systems are part of a still larger system. A change of energy or a "breakdown" in one part of a system over a period of time will have an effect on other parts of the system.

Cause and effect

Encourage your children to test their inferences to see if there is a predictable pattern. Have them observe and record repeatable patterns; predict; experiment; and record. Do they notice that there is a repeatable experience? Can a prediction be made based on repeated experiences with similar results?

Models

Models represent something real. They can be exaggerated in scale-size to be larger than life, smaller than life, or exact replicas of objects in size. Models can be created for things we have never seen. Examples of real things of which we often make models are: the solar system, buildings, cars, and insects. Models can help us look closely at objects or systems that are too big, or too small, to see. They also allow us to create images of what we see by drawing pictures of our observation. All illustrations, diagrams, maps, and pictures are models that are representative of reality. Encourage your children to construct models of what they observe or do by drawing pictures or by creating a three-dimensional representation out of paper, plasticine clay, construction toys, etc. (See chapter 2.)

Structure and function

All living things consist of many parts. These parts make up a system. Each part or structure in the system has a function. By observing skulls, we can observe the kind of teeth an animal had, and infer the kind of food it ate. By observing the placement of the eyes on the skull, we can infer whether the animal was a predator or prey. We can observe a bird's feet and infer its preferred habitat. Encourage your children to make inferences about the function of structures he/she (they) observe.

Variations

There are no living things that are exactly identical. Two leaves from the same tree might look identical, but a closer look at their vein pattern will show distinctions. The same is true of our fingerprints. There are many similarities, but there are also distinct and subtle differences. Even amoeba have different shapes. Identical twins are very different to the discerning eye. Their mothers and close acquaintances can easily tell them apart. Encourage your child to observe, verbalize, and record variations.

Diversity

The natural world is filled with diversity. The world consists of innumerable kinds of animals, plants, and objects. The diverse creatures, plants, germs, protista, monera, and nonliving objects interact with themselves and with each other due to changes in systems. Rocks wear away due to the force of water, wind, and weather. Seeds fall into cracks in boulders and the roots of new plants can either "cement" the boulder together or force the boulder apart, allowing water to enter, freeze, expand, and break the boulder apart. Most events do not occur in isolation. In a laboratory setting, diversity (variables) can usually be controlled if we are aware of all of the variables. There are usually so many variables that it is difficult to isolate and control all of them. Encourage your children to observe, verbalize and record the diversity in nature that surrounds us.

Scales and measurement

Measurements and scales are relative. For measurement or scale to have meaning, there needs to be a context for a comparison to be made. For example: How big is big? Is an elephant big? If an elephant is big, what would you call the size of a brontosaurus? Yet, the word you choose to describe the brontosaurus' size is meaningless in comparison to the size of the solar system, or to the universe. What does big mean? Absolutely nothing unless it is placed into a context. The same is true of our perception. Our perception of what we observe and choose to measure is relative to our position. For example, a room full of children might seem noisy to a teacher who is in the room. A bystander outside of the building, observing the same classroom looking in through a window, might not notice the noise level at all. Encourage your children to talk about objects in comparison to other objects when they describe a property. For example: It was as dark as; it was as small as; it was as shiny as. Making comparisons will enhance your children's vocabulary, and improve their observation skills.

How to organize a science unit

When introducing a new unit, it is necessary to establish a context for the unit. Children understand new ideas better if they can relate them to a context. It also helps them remember what they learn. There are three basic approaches to organizing a science unit:

Moving from the familiar to the less familiar

Children are familiar with their own bodies but are less familiar with the structure of other organisms. For example, if you decide to investigate trees, you might want to compare our human body to the tree's "body:" Both, humans and trees, are alive. Both, humans and trees, become taller and wider as they grow. We have feet; trees have roots. We have skeletons; trees have trunks. We need to eat food and cannot make our own food; trees are able to make their own food. We have veins and tubes going through our bodies; trees also have veins and tubes going through their "bodies." Veins and tubes carry liquids. Liquids can flow.

Or you could compare our bodies to an insect's body: We both have eyes, jointed legs, and are able to walk. Our skeleton is on the inside of our body; the insect has an exoskeleton on the outside of its body. We are unable to fly unless we take an airplane ride. We have senses in our ears and noses that an insect has on its antennae.

Another choice might be to compare our human body processes to that of an exploding volcano. If we hold our breath, we, too, will need to let the air (which is a form of gas) out of our body. Like a volcano we cannot hold it in. Eventually, our body will force air out, just as a volcano must ventilate its accumulated gases.

Moving from the beginning of a process to a result with a tangent or two

Children are familiar with many things that are made from lumber, but they might not understand where the lumber comes from, or how something is constructed. For example, you might want to investigate how wooden boats are made by examining the building process in detail. Trace a boat's origin from forest to log to mill to factory. Then go on a tangent and investigate the properties of wood, metals, and rocks. Try hammering a nail into wood, metal, and rock. Which is the easiest to penetrate? Which weighs the least and is the easiest to carry?

Or, take another tangent. Try to design a wooden boat that will float. Experiment with different designs. Add a sail. Find out if the sail can catch wind. Find out what kind of sail design is most efficient.

Or, you might want to find out where paper comes from by tracing its origin. As with boats, you might examine other kinds of materials from which books could be made, and determine which material is easiest to find and lightest to carry. Also, which would be the easiest to inscribe or mark?

Arranging information in chronological order

Children are familiar with life as it is today. They take it for granted that life has always existed as it does now. It is revealing and fun for children to think about how life might have been during prehistoric times or to think about how electricity might have been discovered. It is possible to trace the steps in human knowledge that eventually led to the discovery of electricity. It was not until the 1900s that electric companies came into existence. There was a long series of events, and much experimentation took place before electricity was harnessed. Many of those experiments can be duplicated. Especially easy are the Oersted and Faraday experiments dealing with electromagnetism.

There are many possibilities and ways to cover topics. The important thing is to design a cognitive structure that makes all the pieces of new information stick together. Moving from the familiar to the less familiar, following a process and/or a chronological order establishes a direction, a focus, and a relevancy, so that a context can be provided.

Skills to be nurtured and developed through teaching science

- Observation skills. Learning to use our five senses.
- Learning to classify. Identifying, matching, sorting, naming, comparing, contrasting, grouping, and distinguishing likenesses and differences.
- Learning to measure. Arranging objects in sequence by: length (shortest to longest); weight (lightest to heaviest); volume (least to greatest); chronologically (beginning to end); numerically (in ordinal order).
- Learning to communicate. By identifying, matching, sorting, naming, comparing, contrasting, grouping, and distinguishing likenesses and differences by verbalizing descriptions, asking questions, relating observations, and using words accurately.
- Learning to make predictions. By developing skills of thinking systematically and logically about what might happen next, and beginning to think about planning ahead.

In summary, an easy acronym to remember when doing science with children is the word NOTICE. (See Table 1-2.)

Role of parent or teacher in exposing young children to beginning science experiences

We as adults can greatly influence children's interests. Most children have a vast untapped potential. It is our responsibility to tap that potential and to expose children's curiosity to new and stimulating topics and to help them organize their knowledge. Knowledge that is not categorized, sorted, and classified in some internal way is not helpful. The knowledge is out of reach. It is useless trivia, meaning-

Table 1-2 NOTICE

Adult's role:	Begin a science activity by: finding out what a child already knows, helping the child name their observations and organizing what they know.
	N – Naming observations **O** – Organizing observations with adult assistance
Child's role with adult guidance:	
	To do the play or "tic" part of notice.
Find out what makes something "tic"	**T** – Take apart and analyze what you observe **I** – Investigate your (child's) questions **C** – Change something and observe it
Adult's role:	**E** – Extend and Enrich a child's observations, to create Accelerated Learning and correct any misconceptions.
Guide child's observations and help child place the observations into a meaningful context.	

less facts, and unconnected thoughts, like the information on a television game show. The ability to generalize is based on our past experiences and the significance those experiences hold for us. If we can convey our enthusiasm about the topics we are interested in to our children, then we can arouse their curiosity and interest in those areas of science to which we expose them. Children's interests are acquired. If they are stimulated and exposed to "something," they become curious about the "something" and acquire an interest in it. It is easier for children to build future cognitive bridges* with ideas and topics with which they are familiar.

Try to see the world through a child's eyes, but try to add structure and organization to observations that are made. Children are experts at observing, but they lack analytical skills.

Our job as early-childhood educators is not to give an intense course in science, but rather to open doors and plant seeds of knowledge that will grow and will continue to excite children about the wonders of their environment. We want to encourage them to delve and be curious, to ask questions, to experiment, to learn, and to integrate knowledge from their own experiences.

* Cognitive bridge: When two seemingly unrelated ideas fit together to form a broader concept. For example: A young child learns the names of the basic colors. Later the child learns that by mixing and combining two colors, he/she will form a new color with a new name. A cognitive bridge is built. The idea forms that materials can be mixed and combined to form new colors and/or new substances.

Selected professional science resource books for parents and teachers

(Dewey Decimal Number, 372.3)

**Abrucato, Joseph. *Teaching Children About Science, 2nd ed.* Englewood Cliffs, NJ: Prentice-Hall, 1988.

**Blough, Glenn, and Julius Schwartz. *Elementary School Science and How to Teach It*, 8th edition. New York: Harcourt, Brace, Jonovich, 1990.

**Carin, Arthur A. *Teaching Science Through Discovery*. New York: Macmillan, 1993.

*Claitt, Mary Jo Puckett and Shaw Jean M. *Helping Children Explore Science: A Source Book for Teachers of Young Children.* New York: Macmillan, 1992.

**Esler, William and Mary. *Teaching Elementary Science, 5th ed.* Bellmont, CA: Wadsworth, 1989.

**Gega, Peter C. *Science in Elementary Education, 6th ed.* New York: Macmillan, 1990.

*Harlan, Jean. *Science Experiences for the Early Childhood Years.* NY: Macmillan, 1992.

**Lorbeer, George C. and Nelson, Leslie W. *Science Activities for Children, 9th ed.* Dubuque, IA: Wm. C. Brown, 1992.

*Taylor, Barbara J. *Science Everywhere: Opportunities for Very Young Children.* New York: HBJ, 1993.

**Victor, Edward. *Science for the Elementary School, 7th ed.* New York: Macmillan, 1993.

**Zeitler, William R. and Barufaldi, James P. *Elementary School Science: A Perspective for Teachers.* New York: Longman, 1988.

Selected further resources

Hauser, Bernice. "Educating Parents About Educating Children," Teachers' Clearing House for Science and Society Education Newsletter, Vol. XII, No.2., Spring 1993.

*Kamii, C. and DeVries, R. *Physical Knowledge in Preschool Education: Implications of Piaget's Theory.* Englewood Cliffs, NJ: Prentice-Hall, 1978.

*McIntyre, M. *Early Childhood and Science: A Collection of Articles.* Washington, D.C.: National Science Teachers Association, 1984.

*Denotes adult resource books for younger children.

**Denotes that these books can be ordered from Science Supply Catalogue Companies, or your local book store. (College and university book stores often stock a few of them depending on which text is a required book for their science methods courses.)

*Pade, Alyson. *Science at the Sensory Table*. Early Education Materials, Denver, CO, 1991.

*Paula, Nancy and Margery Martin. *Helping Your Child Learn Science*. Office of Educational Research and Improvement, U.S. Dept. of Ed.: Washington, D.C. September, 1992. (A short, helpful guide for parents. Filled with great ideas.)

Petroski, Henry. *The Evolution of Useful Things: How Everyday Artifacts—from Forks and Pins to Paper Clips and Zippers—Came to Be as They Are*. N.Y.: Knopf, 1992.

Rowe, Mary Budd. *Teaching Science as Continuous Inquiry: A Basic, 2nd ed.* New York: McGraw-Hill, 1978.

Rowe, Mary Budd. "Wait-Time: Slowing Down May Be a Way of Speeding Up," American Educator, Vol.11, No.1, pp. 38–47, Spring, 1987.

The National Center for Improving Science Education. *Getting Started in Science: A Blueprint for Elementary School Science Education*. The NETWORK, Inc. Andover, Mass., and Washington, D.C.; and Biological Sciences Curriculum Study, Colorado Springs, Colorado. 1989.

UNESCO Source Book for Science Teaching. New York: UNESCO, 1976. (This book is a classic. It suggests inexpensive easy to find materials. It has been used in third world countries where materials are hard to come by.)

Weber, Robert J. *Forks, Phonographs and Hot Air Balloons—A Field Guide to Inventive Thinking*. N.Y.: Oxford University Press, 1993

*Wilkes, Angela. *My First Nature Book*. New York: Knopf, 1990. (Contains beautiful, life-size drawings and activities appropriate for pre-schoolers as well as older children.)

*Williams, Robert A., Rockwell, Robert E., and Sherwood, Elizabeth A. *Mudpies to Magnets*. Mt. Rainer, MD: Gryphon House, 1987. (Contains activities that do not require special equipment.)

Young, Ed. *Seven Blind Mice*. New York: Scholastic Books, 1993. A beautifully illustrated children's book about the importance of seeing the whole before making conclusions about the parts. Seven blind mice observe different parts of an elephant, and each mouse comes to a different conclusion about what the elephant is.

2 Models

Objectives

The objectives of this chapter are for children to develop an awareness of the following:

- What models are.
- How and why models are used.
- What the words "science" and "observe" mean.
- That some events continually reoccur in cyclical patterns in nature.
- That living things have many parts to them, and each "part" is important to the "whole."
- That a "whole" that has more than one part is called a system.
- That objects and models can be arranged in an orderly way.
- That objects and models can be sorted or classified into groups.

General background information for parents and teachers

Models are representations of real things. They can be much smaller or much larger than the object's real-life size. Scientists and engineers build models or replicas of large and small objects to see if the objects or "things" are constructed well. They test, study, and observe working models close up. Many children's art projects are models they have constructed of real things in their world. Most toys are models of real things. Toy cars, trucks, houses, dolls, etc., are miniature models that represent reality. Many toys are models of the real things that children might not be allowed to touch and manipulate. For example, a child can "drive" a play truck, or play "parent" to a doll, "cook" dinner for the dollhouse people, or "mow" the lawn with a model of a lawn mower.

The wonderful part about introducing and using the word "model" with children is that it helps train them to think abstractly. They can learn to picture something in their minds that they are familiar with without having to touch it. When children do have a model to look at and to touch, they can study and observe the model to compare it to reality. How is the model like the real thing? How is it different? For example:

Does a real fire truck have only two doors and six windows like the toy model? (It depends on the model design of the real fire truck we are comparing it to.)

Does a real frog have four front toes as the rubber model shows? (Yes.)

How is the frog's body different from our bodies?

How is the frog's body like ours?

What body parts do frogs and people have on their heads?

Do frogs have ears? Where?

How can you find out?

Do the little wooden people found inside of commercial toys look like real people? What part of them is missing? (All of their joints are missing, including their arms, legs, fingers, and toes.)

Why are joints important?

Do all animals have joints?

Some models are much larger than reality, like rubber spiders and rubber insects. Their large size allows us to examine and observe things we might not have discovered if the creatures were moving or were too small to see. Some models are built in exact proportion to their real-life size, like silk flowers. A silk flower is a model representing reality. Usually it contains the stamen, pistil, calyx, stem, and leaves along with the flower petals to make it look real. Pictures are also models. A picture of a flower or a house can be seen as a model of the flower or the house. The picture helps us visualize what something looks like when we cannot touch it. Likewise, a cross-section diagram is a model of reality. It is a model representing a splitting open of a surface. It allows us to use our imaginations, and gives us the ability to think abstractly. We can look at a model and imagine that it has been cut open. A globe is also a model. A map is a flat representation or "model" of a globe (or part of a globe). Maps are models of models. They are flat representations of a curved surface.

A good reason to encourage children to use or construct models is that, as children grow older, their ability to construct abstract models will allow them to use their imaginations to visualize or to create tangible models of theories or systems that no one has ever thought of or seen before.

The television program Star Trek is based on a fantasy model of our world and the universe as it could exist in the distant future. The world of the starship U.S.S. Enterprise is a model. The stage-set represents a model of that fantasy. Does Star Trek exist in reality? No, but perhaps it could exist. It is a world that exists in the imagination of Star Trek fans and of the writer who has created it.

If children can be trained to visualize or think abstractly about a model of a theory, it will be easier for them to solve problems by finding up solutions or developing theories to test.

Albert Einstein visualized an imaginary model of a person riding on a light beam, and that image or mental model helped him to develop the General Theory of Relativity.[1]

When children are encouraged to predict (hypothesize or guess) what will happen if a variable is changed, they are actually generating a model based on a set of assumptions. It is through experimenting or testing their thoughts (models) that they are able to refine their thinking and their model to fit the features of the known data collected from their observations and to reach a conclusion or generalization.

As new information is gathered, models are altered and refined to be compatible with the more current information. The theory of what the model of an atom would look like has been modified many times since "scientists" first began to discuss it in ancient Greece.

Likewise, the model of the solar system has also changed periodically. In ancient days "scientists" believed the earth was the center of the universe and that the

[1] Please note: Atomic physics is beyond the scope of this book. However, if children become aware that their observations are based on their own relative position, perhaps, when they are older it might be easier for them to comprehend the relativity theory. What is observed depends on the observer's relative position to what is being seen. Terms such as: slow/fast; above/below; east/west are relative to the position of the observer in relation to what is being observed. Observations are meaningless without a frame of reference.

earth was flat. As "new" information was gathered or discovered over the centuries, the model did not account for that data, so the model was modified until it was able to represent the features of the known data. In the future, as more discoveries are made, the model will continue to evolve.

As models evolve, they change to include new features to explain data. Models are valuable tools because they give us the freedom to think abstractly, and to use our imagination to construct mental images. In the most general sense, practically anything that is not "real"* but a representation of something real can be called a model.

Note: As you do these activities with your children, do try to encourage them to keep a science journal of their observations and their thoughts.

Definitions of frequently used terms

Concept

A *concept* is a general idea or understanding, derived from specific instances or occurrences. It is important to try to establish the concept of what "model" means. It is a goal to be worked on all year. When children understand the concept of what a model is, they are free to develop their abstract thinking skills and to use their minds more effectively. They will not be constricted by needing concrete materials in order to think.

The concept of a model is a way of thinking about something. It allows children and adults to paint in their minds pictures of real things when the real things or objects are not available to touch.

Models in play

When children use their imaginations in playing house, building with blocks, and constructing in sand, they are creating models of things they are thinking about. Art activities and play activities are chances for young children to role-play, act out, build or construct, "pretend" play, and manipulate reality. They provide an opportunity to discover a problem or create a challenge and to try to solve the problem or meet the challenge.

*"Real" in this sense means an object or thing that is tangible and three-dimensional, something that we are able to touch physically as a whole that is not a representation or model of "something" else.

Science

Science is the art of studying. It is also the study of observation, identification, description, experimental investigation, and theoretical explanation of those (observable) events. It is a methodological activity that attempts to answer and discover "why, when, and how" observable natural and physical events occur as they do.

The five senses

Seeing, hearing, smelling, tasting, and feeling. All five senses are located in our faces. Our senses help us make observations. (See chapter 3 for activities that develop an awareness of our five senses.)

Cycle

A phenomenon or event that repeats itself predictably.

Classification

The systematic grouping of objects or organisms into categories based on shared characteristics or traits.

Attribute

A quality or characteristic belonging to an object or thing. It is a distinctive feature that results in an object or thing belonging to a set or group.

Sort

Grouping similar objects together. Ordering objects according to some characteristic such as: size, weight, or alphanumeric designation.

Group

The assembling of objects or things into a set.

The short lessons that follow represent a "model" of how to present a science idea or concept to young children. Each mini-lesson takes about five or ten minutes to present. The model lessons include the kinds of questions you might want to ask, the kinds of comparisons you might want to make to induce a child to want to inquire further on his/her own, and the kinds of explanations you might give to children about a particular topic.

The model lessons have been included in this chapter on models to set the tone and to be a "model" or an example of how to present ideas. The model lessons do not need to be followed. However, the tone of "acceptance" the lessons try to demonstrate does need to be followed. Please feel free to develop your own style. Do remember to have a direction or a focus. Your focus or direction could simply be to develop observation skills, to heighten awareness and curiosity, and to help children develop an inquiring attitude.

The experiences and information gained by the children from individual science units and from the activities described in the chapters are important. However, they are not nearly as important as nurturing children to develop a desire and a need to know more about natural and physical phenomena, so that they will develop a positive attitude toward inquiry.

Eight model lessons

Lesson one: What is science?

Science is the art of studying. It includes everything around us: living, nonliving, and not living now.

Objective

For children to become aware of what the words "science" and "observe" mean.

Materials needed

The word "science."

Procedure

1 Hold up the word "science."

Does anyone know what this word says? (It says science.)

Does anyone know what the word "science" means?

2 *Explain*: The word science means the art of studying. It is a way of looking at everything around us that is living, nonliving, and not living now. It is also the study of how things work and why things happen.

2-2 *What is science? Science is everything around us (living, nonliving, and extinct).*

Are dinosaurs alive today? (No.)

How do we know they existed?

3 *Explain*: Scientists study and observe everything. They study and observe things that were never alive, like rocks and sound. They study and observe things that are alive, like plants and animals. And they study and observe things that are no longer living, like dinosaurs and other things that have died. Scientists also study subjects such as: why shadows are formed, how to make jobs feel easier, and why volcanoes erupt. Scientists try to answer why, how, and when things happen. The first thing a scientist does is observe.

What does observe mean? (To study carefully.)

What parts of our body do we use when we observe? (Our eyes help us see. Our ears help us hear. Our nose helps us smell. Our skin helps us feel. Our tongue helps us taste.)

4 *Explain*: We use our senses—eyes, ears, nose, skin, and tongue—to find out about things. Our senses help us observe. Sometimes we need to use all of our senses.

Conclusion

(See chapter 3, "The five senses," for activities and ideas on what to do with the children to make them aware of their five senses.)

Vocabulary

Science, living, alive, nonliving, once living, observe.

Evaluation

After this discussion, see if a child can name or point to something that is alive or was once alive and then to something that was never alive. Also, see if the children can point to a part of their body that helps them observe and to explain how that part enables them to observe: Eyes—see, ears —hear, nose—smells, etc.

Note: In most cases, italic type indicates questions to ask children. Material in parentheses indicates a possible answer.

Lesson two: Identifying natural and human-made objects

Objective

For children to develop an awareness that all materials and things can be classified.

Materials needed

Assorted natural objects, such as: seeds, leaves, flowers, rocks, soil, bark, feathers, and chicken bones; Assorted human-made objects, such as: nails, bottle caps, paper, pencil, scissors, paper clips, and rubber bands.

Procedure 1

1 Place all of the objects in a container and then spill the objects out onto the floor.

2 Ask the children to find objects that grow on plants or can be found in the soil, and to place all of these objects in a pile.

What kinds of things are not in the pile?

3 *Explain*: All of the objects in the pile are called natural things. The materials not in the pile are things people have made with the help of machines.

Procedure 2

1 Ask the following questions:

Can you name something that is living? (We are living.)

What is something that we can find on the ground outside that is not alive and never has been? (A rock.)

Note: If children say "picnic table" or "chair" and the picnic table or chair are made out of wood, then ask them to explain from where the wood for the picnic table and the chair came. (From a tree.)

2 *Explain*: Even though the picnic table and the chair are not alive now, the materials they are made from were once alive. They have been made into a table and chair by people and machines. They are made by humans. Tables and chairs are often made from natural materials but would not be found in nature unless people made them.

3 Ask children to name on their own some things that are made by people and some other things that are natural or found in nature.

Conclusion

Take a nature walk with the children so they can collect natural and human-made objects. After the nature walk, ask the children to observe their collection and sort it into two piles: human-made and natural. Most human-made things that are found on a nature walk are called litter: bottle caps, paper, empty containers, nails, wire, etc.

Vocabulary

Nature, natural, human-made, machine-made, pile, litter, sort.

Evaluation

Ask children to sort all of the objects found in nature into three piles: See if children can separate the pile of natural objects into:

- Things that are still alive now.
- Things that are not alive now.
- Things that were never alive.

Lesson three: Awareness of cycles

Objective

For children to develop an awareness that some events continually reoccur in cyclical patterns in nature.

Materials needed

Fresh flowers, dead flowers, full seedpods, one paper plate labeled "seeds," one paper plate labeled "petals."

Procedure

1 Bring fresh flowers to class. (Marigolds are easy to study. They grow in abundance.)

Are these flowers alive now? (The children will probably say: "No, they have been picked and they can no longer grow.")

2 Hold up some dead flowers.

3 *Explain*: Even when flowers stay on a plant, they eventually die. They do not stay alive forever. If the flowers are not picked, they might look pretty longer, but eventually the flowers will die.

Are these dead flowers really dead? (The children will probably say, "Yes.")

4 *Explain*: The flower has died, but it has produced seeds that are very much alive. The seeds can create whole new plants that will flower again. The new flowers from the new plants will create seeds all over again for new plants.

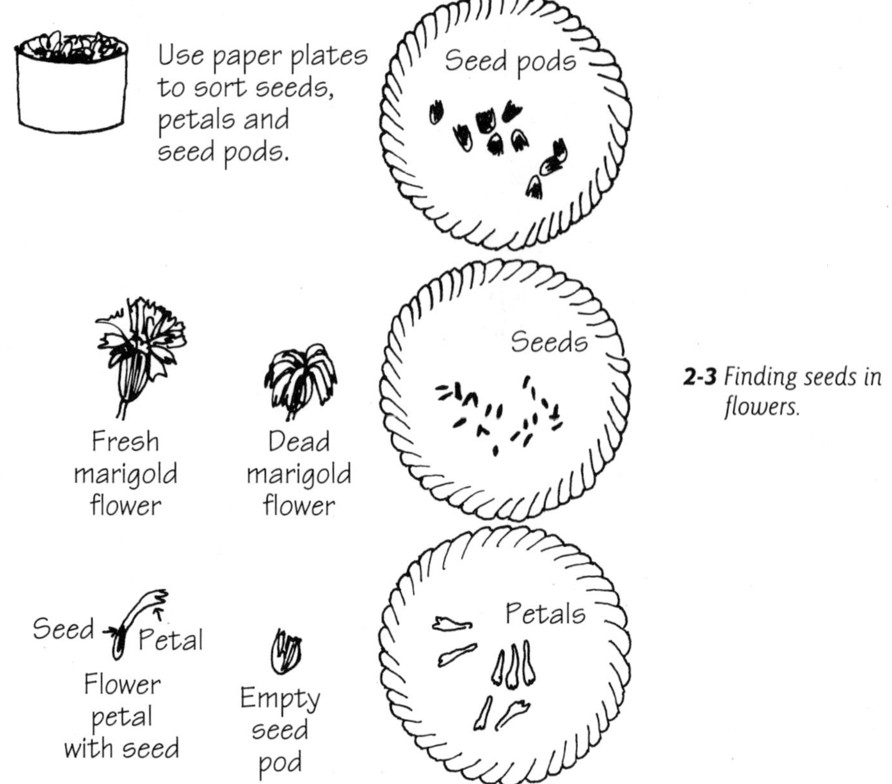

2-3 *Finding seeds in flowers.*

Why do plants grow flowers? (To make seeds.)

Where do we look to find the seeds on a marigold flower? (In the seed pod at the bottom of the petals.)

5 Have each child open up a seed pod.

6 Pass out a petal with a seed attached to it to each child.

7 Ask children to find a similar petal with a seed attached from their opened seed pod.

8 *Explain*: The petal is the yellow part. The seed is the black part. Hold the petal with one hand and the seed with your other hand and pull.

What happens? (The petal separates from the seed.)

9 Set up two paper plates—one labeled "seeds" and one labeled "petals."

10 Ask the children to drop some of their seeds into the "seed" plate.

11 Ask them to drop some petals into the "petal" plate.

12 Have children check the placement and correct the placement of any misplaced seeds or petals.

Are the seeds alive now? (Yes.)

Are the petals alive now? (No.)

13 *Explain*: The plant grows flowers to make seeds so it can flower again next year. The seeds grow into new plants with flowers. When events or things occur or happen in a pattern over and over again, it is called a *cycle*. A cycle is like a bicycle wheel: it goes around and around and has no beginning or end.

Do all of the flower seeds become plants? (No.)

Why not? And what happens to them? (Some seeds are eaten by small insects and birds, and some decay. Many animals eat plant seeds for food.)

What kinds of seeds do you eat?

Note: The topic of seeds can be expanded. Various edible nuts and seeds can be tasted: peanuts, almonds, sesame seeds, poppy seeds, caraway seeds, sunflower seeds, etc. The diets of animals like squirrels and other small rodents can be discussed to see the relationship and interdependence that exists between plants and animals for food, and seed dispersal of plants by animals. (See chapter 12 for activities to do with seeds.)

Conclusion

Ask children to explain what is inside a dead flower. Show them another kind of dead flower like a dandelion or a zinnia. (Ask them if they find a seed and separate it from the petal). *Note*: Different species of plants vary in the length of time that it takes to produce seeds from flowers.

Vocabulary

Alive, dead, plant, seed(s), flowers, marigold, seed pod, petal, cycle.

Evaluation

Find out if children can think of other re-occurring cycles, (day/night, seasons, days of the week). Have children find other dead flowers in their yards or at school and open them up to look for the seeds.

Lesson four: The marigold plant

Objective

For children to develop an awareness that living things have many parts to them and that each "part" is important to the "whole."

Materials needed

Marigolds with leaves, buds, flowers, and stems; Styrofoam tray labeled for flower parts (see Fig. 2-4).

Procedure

1 Give each child or group of children a flower stalk with leaves and buds and a Styrofoam tray (labeled with plant parts).
2 Examine the parts of a marigold plant (or other kind of plant).

Does it have leaves? (Yes.)

Who can show me a leaf? (Have child show and then tear a leaf off for the Styrofoam tray. Point to the stem. Break one off and add it to the labeled Styrofoam tray.)

Does anyone know what this long part underneath the flower is called? (Stem.)

3 Point to a bud. Break off and add to tray.
4 *Explain*: This is a baby flower that has not opened yet. It is called a bud. When it blossoms, it will be a flower.
5 Point to a smaller bud without a stem.
6 *Explain*: This bud is so small it is hard to see.

Which of these buds do you think will open first? (The larger one on the longer stem.)

Why? (The larger bud has a longer stem and the petals look larger.)

What part of the plant is missing from this plant? (The roots.)

Why is that part important to the plant?

7 *Explain*: The roots grow under the ground. If the plant had roots, and the roots were in the ground, it would still be growing.

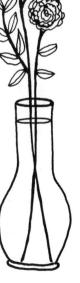

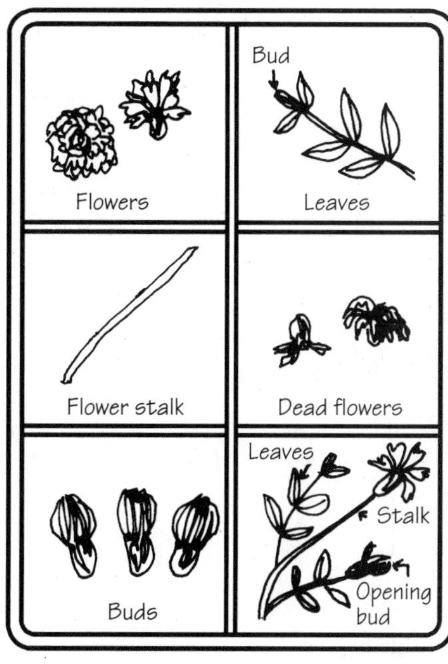

2-4 *Dissecting a flower.*

8 Finish adding appropriate parts of the marigold plant to the labeled Styrofoam tray. Discuss how each part of the plant is important to it.

9 Try to elicit from the children what they think the various parts of the plant do and why each part is important to the working system of the plant. Ask questions to find out what they know.

10 *Explain*: The leaves help make food for the plant, the stem helps the plant stand tall, the bud helps protect the baby flower until it is ready to bloom, the dried-out old flower contains a seed pod that holds new seeds to make new plants and food for animals. The roots help anchor the plant and help the plant get water.

Conclusion

Display several small potted flowering plants or take a walk outside to locate flowering plants. Have children name and point to: the stem, buds, leaves, and flower of the plant they look at.

Vocabulary

Marigold plant, bud(s), stem(s), flower parts, leaf, large, small, dried, roots.

Evaluation

If children are young and not very verbal, see if they can point to the parts of the plant as you name them. If the children are older and have better verbal ability, see if they can name the parts of the plant as you point to them, and/or see if they can find a very tiny bud hidden in the leaves.

Lesson five: Bubbles

2-5 *Bubble making.*

Objectives

For children to develop an awareness of how they can control the size of a bubble.

Materials

For indoor bubble making (for each child or group of children): a small container to contain the soapy solution (see recipe), Styrofoam cups, drinking straws, brownie baking pan, table, and goggles.

For outside bubble making (for each child or group of children): empty berry baskets, strainers, empty frozen juice cans made of cardboard with top and bottom removed, hose washers, plastic 6-pack holders, string, some sponges for easier clean up, goggles.

Table 2-1
Recipe for making a soapy solution

1 You will need: *Joy or *Dawn liquid detergent, water, a clean empty bucket, a measuring cup.

2 Mix one cup of liquid detergent with 8 cups of cold water.

3 Optional, add three tablespoons of glycerine. (Glycerine can be purchased at a local pharmacy. Glycerine makes bubbles last longer, so that they will not evaporate as quickly.)

4 Stir up the solution, but not too much. Avoid creating a froth on top. If one develops, skim it off the top.

5 For best results, make the bubble solution the night before you plan to use it to allow the ingredients to stabilize.

Note: Bubbles will last longer on humid days.

* John Cassidy, author of *The Unbelievable Bubble Book* has stated in his book that for the purpose of bubble making, these two brands do seem to work better than the less expensive brands.

Procedure

1 Show children the goggles. Discuss why they will need to be wearing them.

2 *Explain*: Sometimes people need to protect parts of their body from possible harm. You might want to discuss other items that people wear for safety: safety belts in cars, hard hats, fireman's protective garb, chin guards, teeth guards, etc.

Have children put on their goggles. Be sure all children that are investigating bubbles are wearing goggles. When large bubbles burst, particles of the bubbles often hit the eye, which causes a burning sensation and is extremely uncomfortable to little children. It frightens them when their eyes feel like they are burning.

3 Tell children to scoop up some bubble solution into their cup and to use their drinking straw to blow into the bubble mixture.

Bubble solution is poisonous. Warn the children not to suck up the solution, but to blow out. The solution will taste pretty awful if it gets into their mouth. However, if they do not swallow the solution, it will not harm them.

4 Discuss what happens. See who can blow the biggest mound of bubbles.

What happens to the bubbles when they pile up high? (They pour over the side of the cup onto the table.)

What color is your bubble? (Clear with a swirling rainbow.)

5 Instruct children to pierce a Styrofoam cup with a pencil to make a hole. Then stick a drinking straw into the cup to create a bubble pipe. Dip the pipe into the solution so that the rim of the cup has a film over it. Gently blow through the straw. Observe how much larger a bubble can be made.

6 Pour some soapy solution into a baking pan. Dip some of the listed indoor materials into the solution one at a time. Have children experience the different materials by blowing through them.

What is inside a bubble? (Air.)

What happens when you blow through these materials? (You stretch the soapy solution and fill the solution with air to create a bubble.)

Why do the bubbles burst? (The soapy film dries out or evaporates.)

How can you pet or touch a bubble so it will not pop? (Wet your hand in the bubble solution before you touch the bubble.)

Can you blow a bubble inside of a bubble? (Pierce a bubble with a drinking straw and blow inside the bubble.)

Can you make a small bubble bigger?

Can you blow a bubble through your hands or between your closed index finger and thumb?

What are other things you can use to blow bubbles?

What does a bubble blowing device need to have? (A hole to blow through, or for wind to blow through.)

Conclusion

How can you make gigantic bubbles? Listen to their suggestions. Go outside to try out their ideas. If they do not suggest using two straws and a string to create a bubble frame, then show them how to create a collapsible bubble blowing frame and demonstrate it for them outside. (Zubrowski, 1979.)

Vocabulary

Bubble, solution, air, wind, evaporate, poisonous, film, air stream, collapsible frame.

Evaluation

Ask children to explain to you the kind of devices they need to use to create large or small bubbles.

How is the size of a bubble controlled? (By a steady stream of air.)

Lesson six: What are models?

Objective

For children to develop an awareness of models.

Materials needed

Rubber frog, toy model car or truck, picture of a flower, real flower, silk flower.

Procedure

1 *Explain*: Sometimes scientists use models to look at or study things. Sometimes real objects are too big to bring to class, or too small to see. So big things are sometimes made to look small and sometimes small things are made to look big.

2 Display a model toy car or truck, rubber frog, and a picture of a flower.

3 Hold up the toy truck.

Is this a real truck that we could ride in? (No.)

4 *Explain*: This is a model of a nonliving thing. We can count the windows, the tires, and the doors.

Do real trucks have four windows too? (It depends on the truck, since trucks vary.)

5 *Explain*: Some models are built exactly like the real thing. Some models are not very real looking.

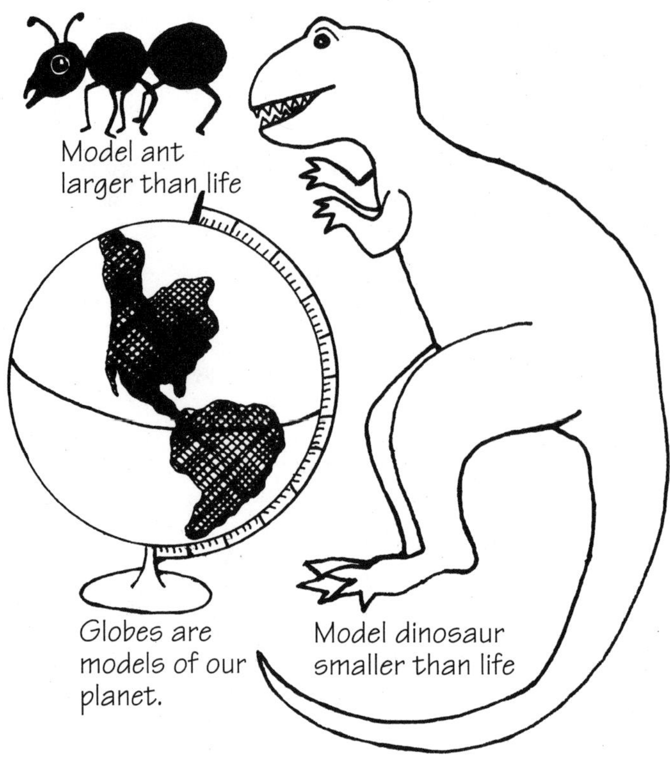
Model ant
larger than life
Globes are
models of our
planet.
Model dinosaur
smaller than life

2-6 Models can be larger or smaller than life size.

6 Hold up the rubber frog.

Is this frog real? (Yes, it is a real* model of a frog.)

Is this frog alive? (No, it is the model of something that is alive.)

7 *Explain*: The rubber frog is a model of a living thing.

8 Hold up a picture of a flower.

Is this flower real? (Yes, it is real, but it is a picture of a flower.)

9 *Explain*: The picture is real. The flower in the picture is a model. The picture is a model of a real living thing.

Conclusion

Have children draw a model of their favorite toy, their room, their house, their car, their family. Ask children to explain why we can't have a real dinosaur visit our classroom or house and how a model helps us to understand better what a dinosaur might have looked like.

Vocabulary

Model(s), exactly, compare, different, alike, real.

Evaluation

Find out if children can point to a picture or a model of "something" and then name what "it" is a model of. Have children explain whether the model is: the exact size, smaller or bigger than the "real" thing? Find out if the children can find something that is not a model but is "real," like a pair of scissors or a crayon.

*Real in this context means not make-believe—something tangible that we can touch and see.

Lesson seven: Sorting objects into sets

Objectives

For children to become aware:

- Of how objects can be arranged in an orderly way.
- Of what it means to sort or classify objects and models into groups by a common attribute or property.

Materials needed

About 15 assorted buttons, about 5 pencils of different lengths, some coins, 4 models of people, 4 models of cars, 6 fat crayons in assorted colors and lengths, 6 rocks and pebbles, 6 thin crayons in colors that match the fat crayons.

Procedure

1 Give each child or group of children a small box with assorted materials.

2 Ask them to spill out the assorted materials onto the floor.

3 *Explain* to the children that there are sets of things in the big, messy pile, but it is hard to make sense of what is in

Use yarn circles to make sets and intersecting sets with picture cards of living and non-living things
Living
Non-living
Both living and non-living

2-7 *Sorting picture cards.*

the pile because everything is mixed together.

4 Ask the children if they can find groups of "things" in the big pile that look alike and to name those "things." (Pencils, buttons, crayons, coins, toy cars, toy people, rocks, etc.)

5 Ask the children to make a pile or sort each group of "things" they find. (There will be a set of pencils, a set of crayons, a set of rocks, etc.)

How many ways can a set be organized? (Sets can be organized many different ways, as long as the objects in the set have at least one attribute or property in common.)

6 After the big messy pile is sorted into several sets of "things" that look alike, ask the children if they can think of ways to arrange each set in an orderly way so that each set can be observed more closely. For example, pencils can be arranged from largest to shortest. Fat crayons can be color-matched to thin crayons. Toy cars can be lined up so that all the headlights are facing in the same direction and so they all have their wheels on the floor. The pebbles can be separated from the rocks, etc.

7 Discuss with children how sorting and order help us observe and find "things" more easily. Ask them to think about how food is organized into an order at the grocery store, books in a library, furniture in a house, clothes in dresser drawers.

8 Discuss the human-made order of material things in general and why order is helpful for finding "things" quickly.

Conclusion

Have the children sort a deck of playing cards into groups and subgroups. For example: reds and blacks, pictures and numbers, or matching sets of numbers or pictures into sets of four or into suits.

Vocabulary

Order, mess, arrange, separate, alike, different, match, "line-up," longest, shortest, rough, smooth, organize, sort, group, set.

Evaluation

Find out if children can arrange a messy pile of assorted "things" into several sets of objects that have something in common. If not, ask them if they see a way that the sets of objects can be arranged in an order:

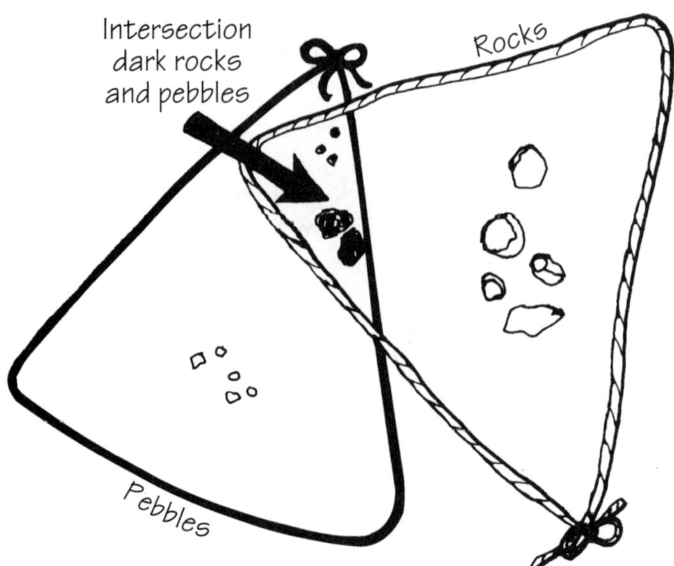

2-8 *Sets of rocks and pebbles.*

by size, color, texture, and/or the same directional orientation.

Lesson eight: Creating sets and intersecting sets

Objective

For children to develop an awareness that objects can be classified and grouped.

A. Sets of rocks and pebbles

Objective

For each child or group of children: rocks, pebbles, yarn circles.

Procedure

1 *Explain*: We can place things that are alike into a group. When we put things together into groups that are alike. We can observe them more closely and look for things that make the things that look alike look different from each other.

2 Have children look at their rocks and pebbles.

Do all of these rocks look alike? (No.)

How are they different? (Some are round and smooth, some are rough and sharp, some are very small, some are darker than others.)

Are they all rocks? (Yes.)

Which ones can be called pebbles? (The round smooth ones.)

Are all the pebbles rocks? (Yes.)

Are all rocks pebbles? (No.)

Why not? Elicit from children what the differences are between rocks and pebbles.

3 *Explain*: Pebbles are a special kind of rock. They are rocks that have been worn down by water or by rubbing to become smooth. Let's see if we can sort the pebbles from the rocks. We can place all of the pebbles into this yarn circle. We can place all of the rocks that are not pebbles into this other yarn circle.

Is there anything about the rocks and pebbles that makes them look alike? (Some of the rocks and some of the pebbles are dark.)

Can we form an intersection to put all of the darker-colored rocks and pebbles together? (Yes.)

Are all of the darker rocks the same color? (Probably not. Some might be tinted yellow or brown or red; some might be striped or spotted. If you look closely enough, you will be able to see differences.)

4 Ask the children to suggest other ways to sort the rocks into groups or sets. (Possible ways: large from small, broken from whole, speckled and striped from solids.)

Conclusion

Find out if children can group the rocks and pebbles and then have other children in your class guess how the rocks and pebbles were grouped.

Vocabulary

Rock, pebble, smooth, rough, round, sharp, light(er), dark(er), worn, striped, spotted, alike, different, broken, whole, group(s), attribute.

Evaluation

With a younger child, see if he/she can form a group of rocks and a group of pebbles. With an older child, see if he/she can form those groups plus an intersection of rocks and pebbles that are the same color or speckled and striped.

B. Creating sets with pictures

Materials needed

For each child or group of children: yarn circles, a deck of marked picture cards (made from an old book or children's picture dictionary that has been cut up).

Procedure

1 Ask the children the following questions:

Can you name some things that are alive in our classroom?

Can you name some things that are not alive in our classroom?

2 *Explain*: Scientists have divided the world into two large groups. One group is made up of all the things in the world that are alive, were once alive . . . all the plants and animals. The other group of things is made up of all the things in the world that are not or were never alive, like rocks and mountains.

3 Place two yarn loops into the shape of a circle. The loops should be different colors. Place one of the yarn circles so that it is intersecting the other circle.

4 Show the children that there are three spaces or areas that are enclosed inside the circles. Point out the space in the middle. This space is a special area called an intersection. Both of the circles overlap and meet here. You might want to compare this meaning of intersection with a street intersection—the area in the middle of all the crosswalks where the streets join and blend together.

5 Hold up a deck of adult-made, marked picture cards that have symbols or a color code depicting pictures as being living, nonliving, or both on their nonpicture side.

Are these cards alive? (No, they are nonliving.)

6 *Explain*: Each card has a picture on it. The picture is a model of something real. It is a model of something living, nonliving, or both. For example:
   Living = A tree, flower, person, animal
   Nonliving = House, car, furniture
   Both = A house with a yard and flowers; a person wearing clothes

7 Show the children each picture and ask:

Is it a model of something living or nonliving?

Does the model (picture) contain some objects that are alive and some objects that are not alive?

Where should we place pictures that show some objects that are alive and some objects that are not alive? (In the intersection space.)

8 After the children have sorted the cards, see if they can describe why and how the symbol or color code helps you to know if you separated the cards the way they have been marked.

9 *Explain* that the code is there to help you in case you do not feel sure of where to place a picture card. You can peek on the back. It is better to try to think first and then to look, or to wait until the end and to check all of the picture cards in the sets together.

Conclusion

Have children make and mark a set of their own cards from magazine pictures or from old workbooks to show pictures that represent both living things and nonliving things.

Vocabulary

Living, nonliving, both, group, divided, intersection, space, model, code, set.

Evaluation

With a younger child, find out if the child can sort out the deck of cards into "living" and "nonliving" sets. With an older child, see if he/she can sort the deck of cards out and form an intersection of sets.

Selected resource books for adults and older children

Cassidy, John. *The Unbelievable Bubble Book*. Palo Alto, CA: Klutz Press, 1987.

Preuss, Paul, editor. *Bubbles*. San Francisco: The Exploratorium, 1986.

Zubrowski, Bernie. *Bubbles: A Children's Museum Activity Book*. Boston: Little Brown and Company, 1979.

Selected literature connections for younger children

Steig, William. *Sylvester and the Magic Pebble*. New York: Simon & Schuster, 1988. (Good introduction for classifying and sorting a collection.)

Young, Ed. *Seven Blind Mice*. New York: Scholastic Books, 1993. A beautifully illustrated children's story about the importance of seeing the whole before making conclusions about the parts. Seven blind mice observe different parts of an elephant, and each mouse comes to a different conclusion about what the elephant is.

3
The five senses

Objective

To help children develop a heightened awareness of their five senses and to improve their observation skills.

General background information for parents and teachers

As adults, we are quite familiar with our ability to see, hear, smell, taste, and touch. We often take these abilities and skills for granted. We have learned how to integrate the knowledge and information gained from our senses. However, most children and many adults do not fully appreciate all of the information available to them through thoughtful and systematic use of their senses. If we use our senses fully and perceive all we can from them, they will communicate to us in a way that words do not.

If our senses are not fully developed, we can train ourselves and our children to become more observant. When we slow down from our usual pace and when we are patient about what we are observing, we begin to notice and observe "happenings" we were not aware of before. For example, if we play ball with our children in the park or jog with them along a path, we are absorbed in the physical activity of moving our body. We tend to notice our surroundings on a superficial level. However, when we walk slowly in the same park or on the same path with the purpose of observing, we begin to sense more "happenings." If we choose to stop and stay very still, we can use all of our senses. We can choose to concentrate on one sense at a time, or on many at once. Often our senses do not get used unless we concentrate on using them. If we are very still when we are outside, we can hear things that we cannot hear when we are moving. If we stop to touch "things," we can feel textures that we might not have been able to sense physically unless we stopped to touch the "things." We can smell aromas on our hands of objects we have touched or rubbed. We can even taste objects and spit out those things that might taste bitter.

Becoming fully aware of our five senses and the subtle differences that our senses can communicate to us helps us to develop the techniques of observing, comparing, matching, identifying, sorting, classifying, sequencing, and measuring. The development of these skills provides the framework for enjoying and understanding scientific phenomena as well as enriching readiness activities in reading and math.

When children become more aware of these senses, they often enjoy hypothesizing or predicting, and testing their ideas. It gives them reasons for wanting to communicate and to investigate things they are curious about. Children acquire a feeling of mastery over their world when they are allowed and encouraged to study, observe, and investigate materials that are part of their everyday life.

The child's five senses can be stimulated by familiar items. Young children absorb experiences through their bodies. They are extremely egocentric. Experiences that can be felt by them or that can be related to their own bodies are experiences they internalize and remember. For example, the word "hot" has meaning when one is burned. If a child is burned, he/she will avoid things that are called "hot." "Hot" will become an abstract idea that he/she will understand without continuing to need the "hands-on" experience of being burned.

3-2 *Hot.*

Young children learn through such experiences. The senses can be used as tools for enhancing these learning experiences. Not only will children be learning about their five senses, but their heightened awareness of their senses will help them become more aware of the world around them.

It is easy to recall and name all of our sense organs. All of them are located on our face: eyes see; ears hear; nose smells; tongue tastes; and skin surfaces sense touch. Our face is crucial to our identity because it houses all these senses, and because it contains the features by which other people know us.

Our hands serve us as a second set of eyes and ears. Our fingers are very sensitive to touch. If our eyes are closed, our fingers can become our "eyes." If we cannot hear, our fingers are able to sense sound vibrations. They can be trained to pick up vibrations caused by sound waves. Most of us do not need to train our fingers to read braille or to "hear" throats vibrate, but we are all capable of training and developing our fingers to become highly sensitive to the sensations felt by touch.

The list of activities in Table 3-1 is only a partial list. It has been written to entice you into thinking of your own activities. Our senses are constantly bombarded by stimuli. The important idea is to become more aware of what our senses can do for us, and to develop our senses more fully so that we can all enjoy our surroundings and our lives to their fullest. *Note*: As you do these activities with your children, try to encourage them to keep a science journal of their observations and their thoughts.

Table 3-1 Useful sense words

Sight		
dazzle	dull	bright
dingy	sparkle	wavy
shiny	knotted	gnarled
transparent	opaque	clear
cloudy	dark	narrow
shady	crooked	wrinkled
glowing	flashing	
Sound		
crunch	whisper	shriek
crash	fizz	snap
boom	singing	ping
splash	squeak	squeal
gasp	rattle	drip
creaking	buzz	chirp
croak		
Smell		
smoky	damp	acrid
sour	sweet	musty
woodsy	grassy	fresh
antiseptic	pungent	decaying
sweaty	moldy	spicy
Taste		
crunchy	sweet	fresh
hearty	rich	tasty
sour	salty	bitter
spiced	cool	fizzy
peppy	creamy	juicy
savory		
Touch		
sticky	silken	soft/hard
firm	cool/cold	freezing
shivery	slimy	furry
crisp	refreshing	parched
bumpy	tickle	rough
prickly	wet/dry	jagged
sharp	crisp	crunchy
juicy	smooth	heavy
light	warm/hot	scalding

Activities and procedures

I. Sound

1. Locate a ringing bell

Material

A small brass bell.

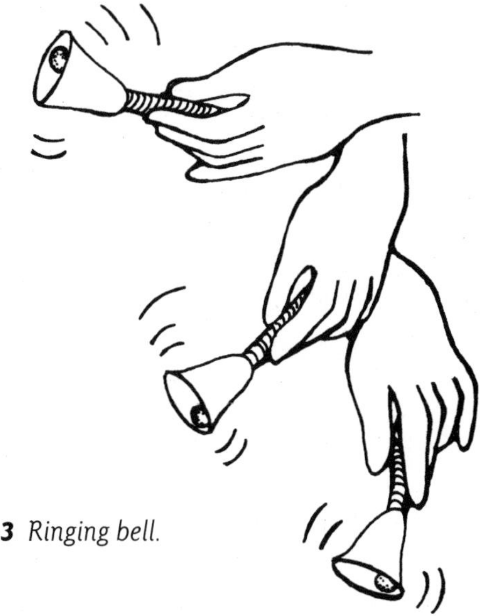

3-3 *Ringing bell.*

Procedure

Have a child sitting in a chair close his/her eyes and guess which direction the sound came from: up, down, behind, in front of, to the left, right, or middle. *Note*: This activity helps reinforce positional and spatial terms.

Going further

- Cover one ear.

Can you still tell the position or direction from which a sound is coming? (Probably not.)

- *Explain*: We usually need two ears to receive clues to tell us from which direction a sound is coming.

Margaret Kenda in *Science Wizardry for Kids*, gave a wonderful explanation for this phenomenon as follows:

With two ears, you get a clue to the direction a sound comes when the sound vibration hits one ear a split second before it hits the other ear. And you get another clue about direction when the sound is very slightly louder in one ear than in the other. (pg. 302)

2. Guessing objects by the sounds they make

Materials

Various objects, i.e., coins, comb, ruler, rubber band, tinfoil.

Procedure

Parent or teacher shows child various objects. Child closes his/her eyes. Parent or teacher drops one of the objects. Child tries to guess which object was dropped.

Going further

- Save empty film canisters. Put different materials or objects in each closed container (rice, sand, beans, cotton, paper clips, marbles, etc.). Have children predict what might be in the closed containers without letting them know or see the possibilities.

3. Tape-recorded sounds

3-4 *Tape-recorded sounds.*

Material

A tape recorder.

Procedure 1

Tape-record individual children's voices and familiar adult voices. See if the children can recognize each others' voices as well as their own voices.

Procedure 2

Tape-record sounds of familiar "things." For example: garbage truck, fire engine, dishwasher filling up, dog barking, telephone ringing, bird chirping, ball bouncing, airplane overhead, ice-cream truck, cricket chirping, door slamming, baby crying. Have child try to identify the sounds heard, and to decide whether the sound is made by something that is alive, or something that is not alive but mechanical or human-made.

Going further

- Discuss with children what the last thing was that they heard before they went to sleep last night, or what was the first thing they heard when they woke up this morning.

What kinds of sounds were they? (Soft, harsh, mechanical, pleasant.)

Fine points to discuss

How are natural sounds different from mechanical sounds?

What are the qualities that make them different?

What kinds of sounds appear to last longer, and to be more monotonous? (Sounds with little variety to them.)

When do sounds become monotonous and boring? (When we can no longer "hear" them because they blend into everything else. We often do not hear traffic on a busy street, or a machine that is humming, or the motor in a car, because the sound is constant.)

What are the sounds we cannot hear? (Quiet "happenings" in nature. See Fig. 3-5.)

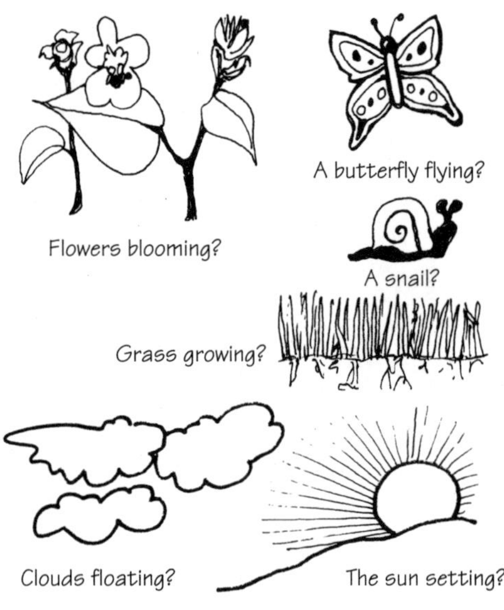
can you hear...
Flowers blooming?
A butterfly flying?
A snail?
Grass growing?
Clouds floating?
The sun setting?

3-5 *Can you hear these things?*

Does the rainbow make a sound?

Does the sunrise make a sound?

Do butterflies make noise when they flutter?

Can we hear a bud opening up to blossom?

Can we hear clouds moving in the sky?

Can we hear an ant walk?

Why do animals make sounds? (To communicate.)

What do animal sounds communicate to us? (Hunger, fear, happiness, hurt, pain, warning.)

Why do cats purr?

Why do babies cry?

Why do dogs growl?

Why does a rattlesnake rattle its tail?

Do humming birds hum? (No, their fast vibrating wings create a humming sound.)

What are other animal sounds?

What does laughter mean?

What does a scream mean?

How can sounds be a valuable source of information about our environment?

What are some safety sounds that let us know we need to pay attention? (Police car, car horn, elevator buzzer, electric door closing on a train, school fire alarm, ambulance.)

What are some of the things you can hear before you see them? (Mosquitoes, fire engines, cars, child screaming, jet.)

Questions for older children to think about

Why do elephants have such large ears? (Probably to help keep them cool, and to swat away flies.)

Do fish have ears? (No, but most have a lateral line along their side that receives vibrations.)

*Do snakes have ears?** (No. Their bodies can sense vibrations through the ground. They cannot hear sound waves traveling in the air.)

Do insects have ears? (No. Their antennae assist them to pick up vibrations.)

How do animals that do not have ears hear?

Note: For more activities on sound, see chapter 6, which gives a more detailed description of what sounds are and how sounds travel.

II. Sight

1. Take a closer look

Materials

A magnifying glass for each child, and/or a pocket microscope.

INFORMATION Pocket microscopes can be purchased at Radio Shack or from science supply houses. They need two AA batteries. They usually have a power of 40×. In order to see things through them, the object has to be touching the lens.

Procedure

1 Take the children outside, turn over a rock, or a log. Take a closer look with a magnifying glass or a pocket microscope.

* Audrey Brainard Hands-On-Science workshop.

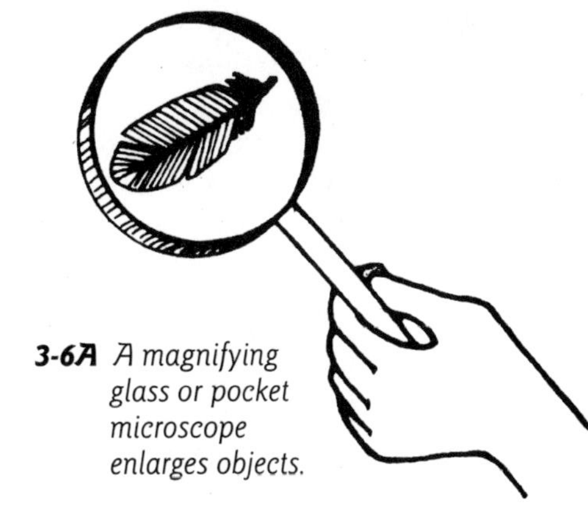

3-6A *A magnifying glass or pocket microscope enlarges objects.*

What do you see?

2 Use a magnifying glass or pocket microscope to observe a dead insect. Dead insects can often be found after a rain or on a window sill.

What can you see with the magnifying glass or microscope that you didn't see before? (Perhaps the veins in the wings, or the hair on the legs.)

3 Use a magnifying glass or pocket microscope to observe a bird's feather or a leaf or any other object that children bring to class or find outside. Discuss with them what they can see with the magnification that they could not see with their naked eye.

2. Find matching objects outside

Materials

Leaves, rocks, or other objects easily found outside.

Procedure

1 Collect a few leaves and rocks that are in great abundance on the ground.

2 Show the items to your children.

3 Ask them to find objects that appear the same. For example, leaves from the same kind of tree that your leaf came from; rocks that are made up of the same colors (granite, blacktop, white pebbles) as the rock or pebble you show them.

4 Have them compare what they find to what you had.

Do the objects look exactly alike? (If they look closely enough, no.)

5 *Explain*: All living things are unique. No two living things are ever exactly

alike. Only some human-made things can look exactly alike.

6 Discuss what makes the found objects look different and what makes the found objects look alike. Try to help children observe details and attributes.

Going further

Children might enjoy using a magnifying glass or pocket microscope to observe the objects for more details.

3. Depth perception

Materials

None

Procedure

1 Tell children to look at something in the distance across the room or outside.

2 Ask them to cover one eye and to look at the object again.

Do you notice anything different about what you see? (It is difficult to gauge what is in front of what. Objects lose their three dimensional quality.)

3 *Explain*: We need two eyes to see depth. When we use one eye it is hard to judge distance, and to figure out what object is in front and what object is in back. Most things appear to be on a flat surface with no depth or distance between them. When only one eye is opened, moving about helps to restore a sense of depth perception.

III. Touch

1. Barefoot touch

3-6B *Barefoot touch.*

Materials

A collection of materials such as sandpaper, cellophane, bath towel, jacks, chalkboard, chalk eraser, inflated balloon, animal cage, wet sponge, dry sponge, baseball, and paintbrush.

Procedure

Show the children the materials. Have a child remove his/her shoes and socks. Choose three items from the collection. Then have the child close his/her eyes. Let the child touch an object from the three objects chosen with his/her bare feet and then try to guess which object is being touched. Have the child describe how the object feels. Later, advance to not showing the child which three objects you will choose, as this will increase the difficulty of the activity.

2. Feeling weight

Materials

Three to five empty half-gallon milk cartons. Fill each of the cartons with a different amount of sand.

Procedure

Have the children arrange the sand-filled milk cartons in order from the lightest in weight to the heaviest while blindfolded or with their eyes closed. (See Fig. 3-7A.)

Note: This activity reinforces the need to have more than one object when comparing weights. An object cannot feel "heavier" or "lighter." In order to feel weight, we have to compare the object to something else.

3. Feeling height

Materials

Cut the top off empty half-gallon milk cartons to create three to five different heights.

Procedure

While blindfolded or with their eyes closed, have the children sort the cartons according to their height. *Note*: This activity reinforces the need to have more than one object when comparing heights. An object cannot look or feel "taller" or "shorter." In order for the object to look or feel tall or short, it has to be compared to something else.

3-7A *Feeling weight.*

4. Describing touch

Materials

Samples of assorted textured fabrics: burlap, felt, satin, velvet, lace, corduroy, and tweed. Samples of assorted household products: wax paper, butcher paper, brown paper bag, plastic grocery bag, aluminum foil, coffee filter, paper towel, toilet paper, wet sponge, dry sponge, cotton balls, and sand paper.

Procedure

Ask children to feel the assorted materials and try to describe how the assorted materials feel.

What other familiar things do the materials feel like? (For example, velvet might feel like skin.)

Which material feels the roughest? Smoothest?

Which feels the softest? Hardest?

Which material feels sticky? Heavy? Light? Sharp? Wet? Bumpy? Hot? Cold?

Going further

- Collect similar looking sets of objects like small balls or coins: penny, nickel, dime, quarter.
- Have children close their eyes and try to describe the differences in touch between each of the coins.

Which coin has a smooth, thick side?

Which coin has ridges going around its edge?

5. Is touch the same all over your body?

Materials

Toothpicks.

Procedure

1 Divide children into pairs.

2 Instruct children to experiment with the toothpicks.

3 Have them touch their partner's skin with one or two toothpicks held between their fingers.

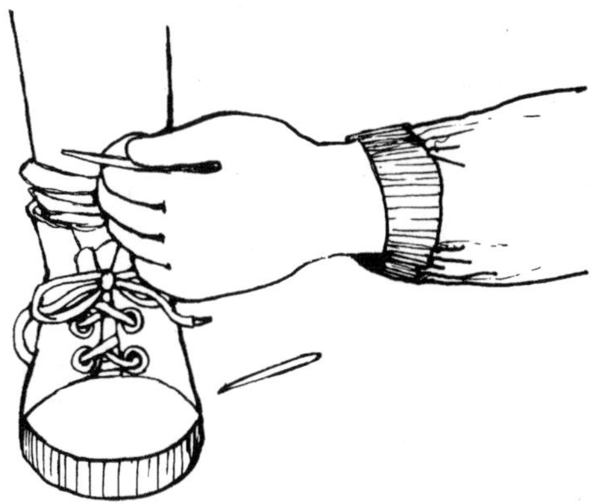
3-7B *How sensitive is your skin?*

4 Tell them to gently touch different parts of their partner's body with one or two toothpicks. See if their partner can feel whether one or two toothpicks are touching their body.

Which parts of your body are most sensitive to touch? (Tip of tongue, finger tips, and tip of nose.)

Which areas of your body are least sensitive to touch? (Back of the shoulders and legs.)

IV. Smell

1. Spices

Materials

An assortment of aromatic spices: mint, tarragon, onion, basil, parsley, thyme, marjoram, bay leaves, and garlic. Paper napkins or cheesecloth to wrap the individual crushed spices. One whole leaf of each spice left uncrushed and unwrapped.

Procedure

Children have to sniff and match the smell of the spice wrapped in cheesecloth to the smell of the unwrapped whole-leaf spice.

3-8 *Smelling spices.*

"Nerve cells of the nose recognize four odors:

1 Burnt (toast, fire).
2 Rancid (moldy bread).
3 Acrid (sour like vinegar).
4 Fragrant (sweet).

A continual exposure to one odor causes nerve cells to become insensitive to that odor." (Gega, pg. 433)

2. Mystery box

Materials

Make a "feely box" (call it a "mystery box") that you can "feel through" without peeking. Either hang a piece of cloth in front of a small open cardboard box, or cut out holes on the two sides of a small cardboard box; a slice of fruit peel; crayons in the colors of fruit.

Procedure

Hide a slice of fruit peel in the "mystery box." Have children sniff and try to identify what the odor is. (Suggestions of fruit peels to hide: lemon, orange, apple, banana, cantaloupe, watermelon.) Have the children draw a circle using the color of crayon that the fruit peel smells like:

Yellow—banana, lemon.

Red—apple, watermelon.

Orange—orange, cantaloupe.

Note: This coloring activity reinforces the names of colors and the names of common foods, and develops children's awareness

3-9 *Mystery box.*

of how color symbols can be used to represent ideas.

3. Smelling flowers

Materials

An assortment of fresh flowers: carnation, rose, marigold, dandelion, violet, zinnia, daisy. A flower identification guidebook, or flower and seed catalog.

Procedure

Smell all the flowers. Sort out which ones have an aroma and which ones have very little scent. Look through the flower identification guidebook. Match the real flowers to models of flowers in the book. Discuss how the model does not have the aroma that the real flower has.

Note: This activity reinforces the idea that books can be used as a reference aid for identifying specimens, and that books contain useful and interesting information.

4. Take a nature walk

Materials

Gathering a variety of leaves, rocks, tree bark, and soil.

Table 3-2
Some other observations that can be made on a nature walk

See	Feel	Smell	Hear
clouds	soil	soil	birds singing
birds flying	mud	pond water	animals playing
hole in a tree	sand	tree bark	voices
holes in leaves	moss	leaves	cricket chirp
holes in ground	tree bark	flowers	dog barking
insects	thorns	seeds	your footsteps
a spider web	leaves	mushroom	wind
bird nest	wind	rotting log	leaves moving
an ant hill	sun	litter	water flowing
shadows	texture/shapes	animals	machines

Procedure

Take a walk. Gather things that smell. Compare the different aromas of leaves, tree bark, and soil odors. Which things smell earthy? (See Table 3-2.)

V. Taste

1. Salt and sugar

Materials

Salt, sugar, two cups.

Procedure

Pour some sugar into one cup and some salt into another cup. Discuss with your child the difficulty of telling the difference between these two "white powders." They both look alike.

What is an easy way to tell which is which? (By tasting them.)

2. Lemon juice, vinegar, and water

Materials

Lemon juice, vinegar, water, and sugar.

Procedure

Have the child taste each liquid. Discuss how each tastes. Add sugar and water to the lemon juice.

Does the lemon juice still taste sour?

Do sugar and water change the taste of the vinegar?

3. Skull and crossbones

Materials

A poison label with a skull and crossbones, ammonia.

Procedure

Show the children the poison label. Discuss with them what it means and why we should avoid ever tasting something from a bottle with this kind of label. Let the child take a whiff of ammonia to smell how bad poison would taste. Discuss how odors often tell us when something is dangerous to swallow.

Note: It is important to emphasize with children that it is not always smart to taste unknown things because they might be dangerous to us. If we taste something unknown and it tastes awful, it is wise to spit it out and not swallow it. Sometimes things taste awful, like cod liver oil, but they are good for us. It is okay to swallow something that tastes awful if we know what it is and know that it is not poisonous.

4. How we taste

Materials

A tongue chart showing where our taste buds are located. (See Fig. 3-10.)

Procedure

Experiment by tasting foods that are bitter, sweet, salty, and sour. Experiment by touching different parts of your tongue as you taste the foods.

Do foods taste different on different parts of our tongues?

Does candy taste better on the front tip of our tongue than in the rear of our tongue near our throat?

5. Use food color

Materials

Food color, mashed potatoes, and rice.

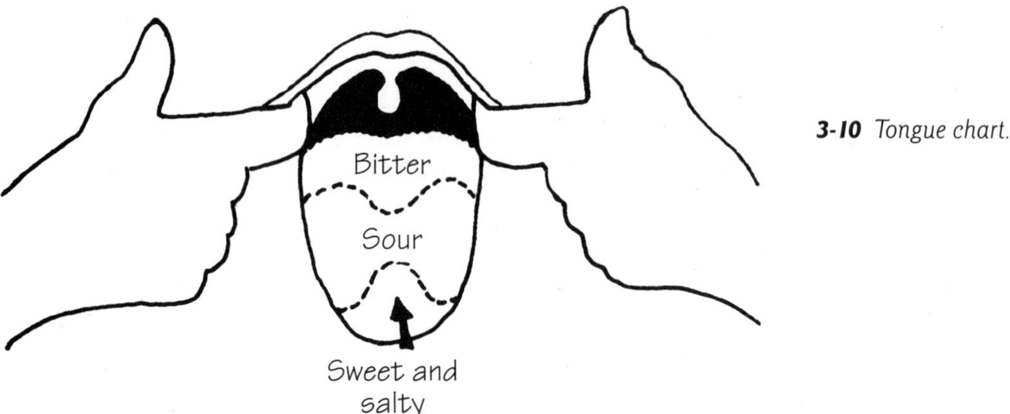
How We Taste!
Tongues have taste buds for tasting bitter, sour, sweet and salty things.
Bitter
Sour
Sweet and salty

3-10 *Tongue chart.*

Procedure

Have the child taste the mashed potatoes and the rice. Then add blue food color to the rice and to the potatoes.

Does the color affect the taste of the food?

Fine points to discuss

Discuss how the color of the food we eat affects the way we think it will taste.

Can we taste the color?

Discuss how important it is to smell foods when we eat them. Smell enhances the taste of food. It is often difficult to distinguish taste from smell. Hold your nose while you taste a food.

Does the food taste as good as it does when you can smell the food as you taste it?

Going further

Taste different textured foods and describe how they feel on your tongue and what sounds they make. For example: crunchy/noisy foods—carrots, celery, crackers, pretzels; soft/quiet foods—mayonnaise, banana, cream cheese

VI. Going further with sight and touch

1. Describing attributes of sets

Materials

Attribute set. A commercially prepared attribute set can be used, or you can prepare an attribute set yourself. If you make it yourself, it should consist of at least 12 pieces for touching and sorting.

Circles: 2 large circles, 2 small circles.

Rectangles: 2 large rectangles, 2 small rectangles.

Squares: 2 large squares, 2 small squares.

One set of each of the two matching pieces should have a rough texture (sandpaper finish), and the other set of six pieces should have a smooth texture. All of the pieces in the set of 12 should be one color. Otherwise, color will become an attribute and more pieces will need to be added to the set. (If color is going to be an attribute, then each additional color set will consist of 12 additional pieces. Each set of shapes and sizes will have to be made in each additional color.)

Procedure

Children play with the 12 pieces. They describe what piece they are touching. For example:

"I am holding a large, smooth circle."

"I am holding a small, rough square."

Note: This activity helps increase a child's verbal abilities and his/her ability to clarify and distinguish.

2. Finding pieces or objects by sight or touch

Materials

Attribute set (refer to materials listed in II.1, the Describing section).

Procedure 1

Divide the 12 pieces into sets by shape, size, or texture.

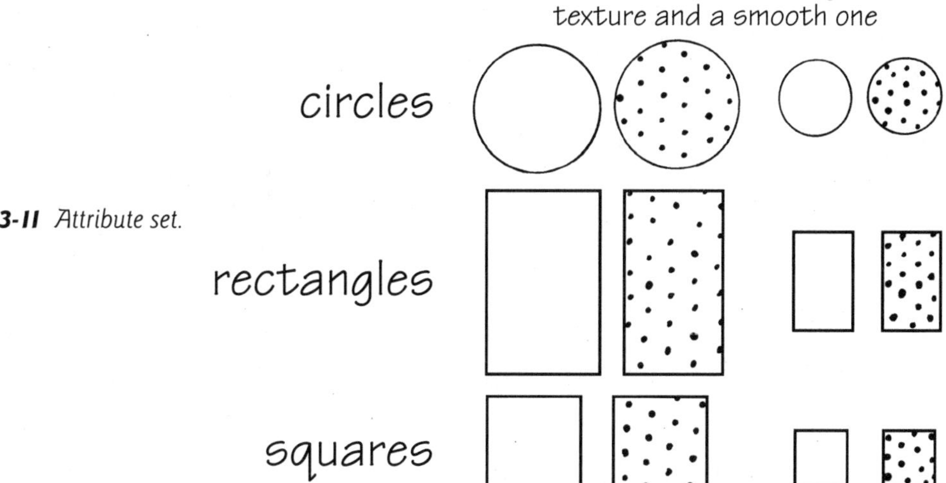
Each size has a rough
texture and a smooth one
circles
rectangles
squares

3-11 *Attribute set.*

Procedure 2

Try the same activity blindfolded.

3. Which piece is missing?

Materials

Attribute set (refer to materials listed in II.1, the Describing section of this chapter).

Procedure

Lay out all of the pieces to the attribute set. Remove one piece from the set while the child has his/her eyes closed. Have child open his/her eyes and guess which piece of the set is missing, or feel which piece of the set is missing.

4. Mystery box

Materials

Mystery box (refer to Activity IV. 2., "Smell," in this chapter).

Procedure

Place an object inside the box. Children feel the object with their fingers and try to guess what the object is without peeking inside. Suggested items to hide in the box: a pencil, a shoelace, a ball of yarn, a sea shell, a marble, and a crayon.

5. Construction

Materials

Mystery box or "feely box" and colored wooden blocks, each block shape a different color, i.e., rectangle, green; square, red; cylinder, purple. Two of each block shape in matching colors.

Procedure

One set of blocks is inside the feely box, and the other set is outside the box. The child constructs an "arrangement" of the blocks that are outside the box in an order. Then, without peeking, the child tries to reconstruct the same arrangement of the blocks with the blocks that are inside the feely box.

3-12 *"Seeing" with our hands.*

Note: This activity takes a certain level of skill on the part of our fingers, since our fingers have to "see" for us. The activity can be made more difficult by adding more wooden blocks, or by trying to duplicate pictures of block formations by only looking at a "picture" of the formation and not looking at three-dimensional blocks.

VII. Fooling your senses

1. Fooling your sense of hearing*

Materials

Two 2-foot pieces of an old garden hose, or rubber tubing; two kitchen funnels.

Procedure

1 Place a funnel on each end of the garden hose. Secure with masking tape if it does not stay on.

3-13 *Fooling your sense of hearing.*

2 Have a child place the end of a hose in each of his/her ears.

3 Twist the hose around the child's body so that the opened funnel end of the hose from the left ear is near the child's right ear, and the funnel end of the hose from the right ear is near the child's left ear.

4 Tell the child with the two hoses in his/her ears to close his/her eyes. Make noises. See if the child can figure out which direction the noise comes from.

2. Fooling your sense of sight—optical illusions

A. Seeing tunnels on and in a spinning top

Materials

Several tops, marking pens, pencils, white paper circles. (The circles can be cut to be the size of the top or slightly larger.)

Procedure

1 Use one color of marking pen to create a spiral design.

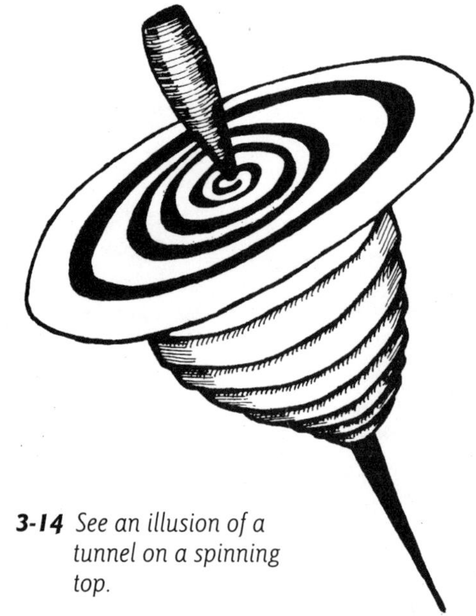

3-14 *See an illusion of a tunnel on a spinning top.*

2 Poke a hole through the center of the circle with a pencil

3 Place the spiral design on the top.

4 Observe what happens.

What happens to the spiral design when the top spins? (You will see the illusion of a tunnel.)

How does the speed of the top affect the illusion? (When the speed is very fast, you will not see a tunneling illusion.)

What happens if you change the direction of the spinning top? (When the top spins in one direction, it will look like the tunnel is pushing out at you. When the top spins in the opposite direction, it will appear as though the tunnel is taking you into it.)

Note: This phenomenon occurs because the rotation on the spinning top occurs so quickly that our eyes cannot stop the rotation. Our eyes integrate what they see. Our brains cannot process the information as quickly as the rotation of the top. Therefore, when we look at the spirals spinning or other designs that might be spinning on the spinning top, an optical illusion is created because we have fooled our brain.

Going further

Experiment by making different designs and colors on the disk and observing the illusions.

B. Seeing a floating finger tip

Materials

None.

* Adapted from Gega, page 295.

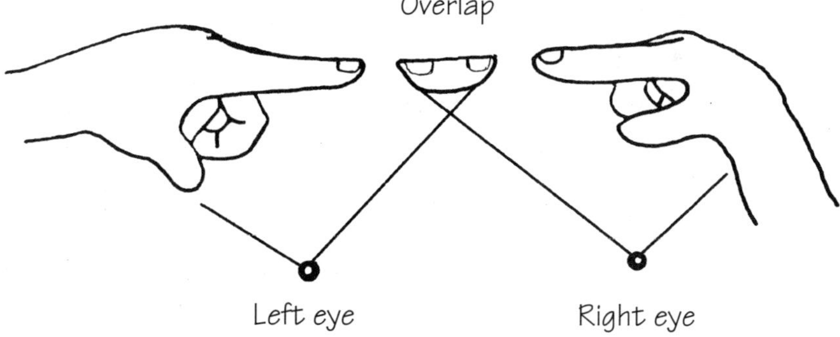

3-15 *Keep both of your eyes open and focus on a far point.*

Procedure

Instruct children to:

1 Touch your index fingers together.
2 Stretch your arms out in front of you with your index fingers still touching at eye level.
3 Keep both eyes opened.
4 Look straight ahead and focus on a far point.
5 Slowly bring your touching index fingers closer in toward the bridge of your nose.

What do you see? (It will appear that you grew a sausage between your index finger tips.)

If you focus both of your eyes on to your "touching" index fingers instead of on a far away object, what do you see? (Two fingers and no "sausage" because you are only able to perceive depth when both of your eyes are opened.

INFORMATION This activity is written about in many science activity books. However, Tik L. Liem, in his book, *Invitation to Science Inquiry*, explains the reason for our eyes perceiving this strange vision of a "floating sausage" in understandable terms.

"Even though the eyes are focused on a far point, we still see objects that are closer to the eyes . . .. This is the reason why we see only a piece of the finger. Whatever image overlaps is seen more clearly." (pg. 441)

6 *Explain*: Optical illusions are the result of our brains following reasoning to what would appear to be a logical conclusion. The image of the two eye retinas have to correspond. Our visual system attempts to do the best it can, which is sometimes wrong.

3. Fooling your sense of touch—feeling temperature

Materials

Arrange three water basins on a table together. Fill one basin half full with warm water, another basin half full with hot water, and the third basin half full with cold water. Place the basin filled with warm water between the other two basins.

Procedure

Blindfold a child and have the child dip his/her hand into the hot, cold, and warm water. The child is to identify what the temperature of the water feels like. Take the blindfold off and place one hand in hot water and the other hand in cold water at the same time. After a minute, place both hands into the warm water. The warm water will feel cold to the hand that was in hot water and hot to the hand that was in cold water. (See Fig. 3-17.)

Note: This activity helps children understand the relative nature of temperature. Warm can feel both hot and cold. It depends on what our body temperature was before.

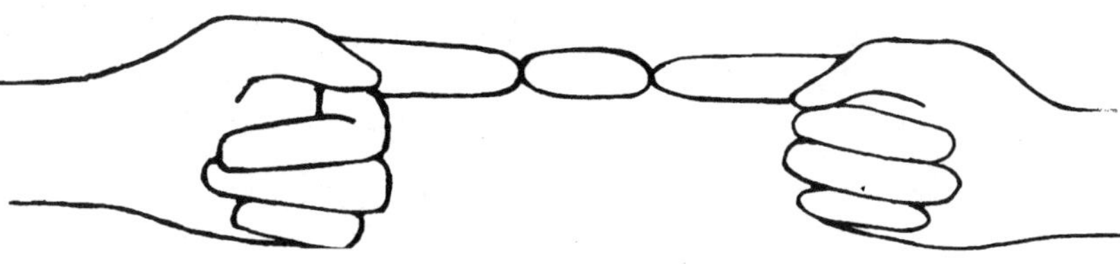

3-16 *An overlap occurs.*

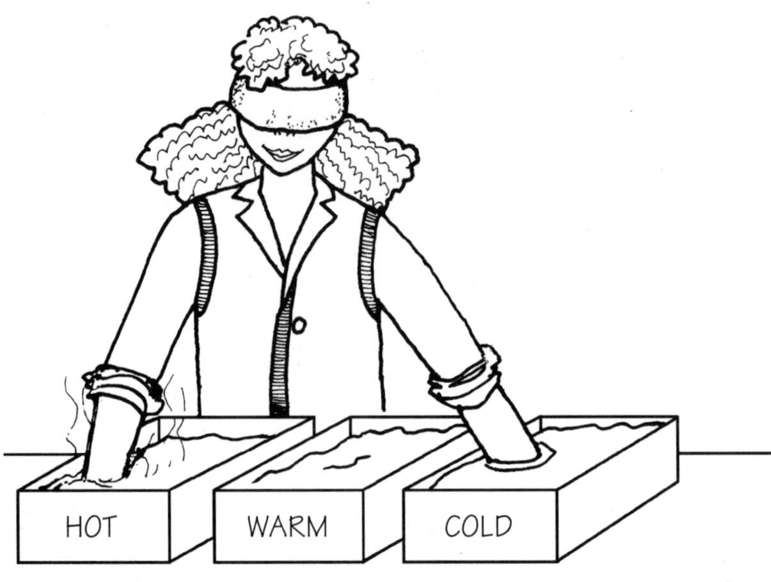

3-17 *Both hands will feel a different temperature.*

4. Fooling your sense of taste*

Materials

Slices of: raw potato, apple, and onion.

Procedure

1 Blindfold the child who is doing the tasting.
2 Pinch his/her nose closed with a clothespin, or let him/her hold his/her own nose. Place a small slice of each food: apple, potato, and onion, one at a time, on the child's tongue. The child is to try to guess what the food is by the taste, without chewing on it.
3 *Explain*: The texture of each of the foods and the sounds it made when it was chewed would be a clue as to what the food was.
4 Let all of the children have a turn.
5 Keep a record by making a graph of how often the children were able to guess the correct food when they were not given a chance to see it or to smell it. Discuss the results.

Further resources

Dewey Decimal Classification Numbers for the human body and five senses are: 372.3, 516.22, 531.6, 541.3, 591.4, 612, and 641.1.

Selected books for children

Aliki. *My Five Senses*. New York: Harper and Row. 1989.

* Adapted from Vicki Cobb, pg. 45, How to Really Fool Yourself.

Ardley, Neil. *The Science Book of the Senses*. Gulliver Books (HBJ): New York. 1992.

Ball, J.A. and Hardy, A.D. *What Can It Be? : Riddles About Our Senses*. Morristown, NJ: Silver Burdett, 1989.

Brandt, Keith. *My Five Senses*. Mahwah, NJ: Troll Associates, 1985. (K–3).

Brenner, Barbara, *Bodies*. New York: Dutton, 1973. (Photographs that tell a story. Shows how our body is like a machine.)

Catherall, Ed. *Touch*. Wayland Publishers Limited, East Sussex, England. 1982. (Suggested investigative activities to be done with the sense of touch.)

Davis, Kay and Oilfield, Wendy. *My Balloon: Simple Science*. New York: Doubleday, 1990. (Beautiful color photos make this an easy book for young children to use on their own.)

Evans, David and Williams, Claudette. *Let's Explore Science: Make It Change*. New York: Dorling Kindersley, 1992.

Evans, David and Williams, Claudette. *Let's Explore Science: Make It Go*. New York: Dorling Kindersley, 1992.

Evans, David and Williams, Claudette. *Let's Explore Science: Me and My Body*. Dorling Kindersley, New York. 1992.

Evans, David and Williams, Claudette. *Let's Explore Science: Make It Balance*. Dorling Kindersley, New York. 1992.

Hoban, Tana. Circles, *Triangles and Squares*. New York: Macmillan, 1974. (Black-and-white photographs of a city environment. The photos emphasize the shapes of things. There are no words, just photos. Good for a discussion about shapes we see around us and for the development of observation skills.)

Hoban, Tana. *Is It Larger? Is It Smaller?* New York: Greenwillow, 1985.

Hoban, Tana. *Look! Look! Look!* New York: Greenwillow, 1985.

Hulme, Joy. *Sea Squares*. Hyperion. 1991. (Beautifully illustrated underwater scenes. Helps give meaning to the concept of square numbers.)

Marzollo, Jean. *I Spy a Book of Picture Riddles*. New York: Scholastic, 1992.

Ogle, Lucille, and Tina Thoburn. *The Golden Picture Dictionary*. Racine, WI: Western Publishing, Golden Books, 1989. (A good preschool and kindergarten book. The book helps develop vocabulary and sight words.)

Orii, Eiji. *Simple Science Experiments with Optical Illusions*. Milwaukee: Garth Stevens Children's Books, 1989.

Ruis, M., Parramon, J. and Puig, J. *The Five Senses Series: Sight, Smell; Taste; Touch; Hearing*. Woodbury, N.Y.: Barron's, 1985.

Waring, Jane Main. *My Feather: Simple Science*. New York: Doubleday, 1990. (Beautiful color photos make this an easy book for young children to use on their own.)

Wilson, April. *Look! The Ultimate Spot the Difference Book*. New York: Trumpet Club, 1990.

Resource books for more ideas

Brown, Robert J. *333 Science Tricks and Experiments*. TAB Books, 1984. (See chapter 5, Biology and Psychology.)

Brown, Sam Ed. *One, Two, Buckle My Shoe: Math Activities for Young Children*. Mt. Rainier, Maryland: Gryphon House, 1982. (Presents ideas for pre-school–Kindergarten.)

Cobb, Vicki. *How to Really Fool Yourself: Illusions for All Your Senses*. NY: Lipincott, 1981.

Cobb, Vicki. *Science Experiences You Can Eat*. New York: Lippincott, 1972. (Describes cooking experiences to develop the senses.)

Discover the World of Science. Special Issue. The Mystery of Sense: How We Manage to Touch, See, Hear, Smell and Taste the World. June, 1993, Vol. 14, number 6.

Forte, Imogene, and Marjorie Frank. *Paddles and Wings and Grapevine Swings*. Nashville, Tennessee: Incentive Publications, 1982. (Things to do with nature's treasures.)

Frank, Marjorie. *I Can Make a Rainbow*. Nashville, Tennessee: Incentive Publications, 1976. (Describes art activities that help develop the senses.)

Furth, Hans G., and Harry Wach. *Thinking Goes to School: Piaget's Theory in Practice*. New York: Oxford University Press, 1974. (Describes thinking activities to make us more aware of our senses.)

Gega, Peter. *Science in Elementary Education*. 6th ed., New York: Macmillan, 1990. (See chapter 16, The Nervous System.)

Goodwin, M.T. and Pollen, G. *Creative Food Experiences for Children*. Washington, DC: Center for Science in the Public Interest, 1980.

Grady, Denise. "The Vision Thing: Mainly in the Brain". Discover the World of Science, June, 1993, Vol. 14, number 6, pg. 56–66. (Helps explain how the brain processes information obtained from our eyes.)

Hibner, Liz and Dixie Cromwell. *Explore and Create*. Livonia, Michigan: Partner Press, 1979. [Distributed by Gryphon House, Mt. Rainier, Maryland.] (Describes various activities which develop the senses.)

Hoover, Rosalie and Barbara Murphy. *Learning About Our Five Senses*. Carthage, IL: Good Apple, 1981. (Songs, fingerplays, and games for developing awareness of the five senses.)

Kenda, Margaret and Phyllis S. Williams. *Science Wizardry for Kids: Safe Scientific Experiments Kids Can Perform*. Haupapauge, N.Y.: Barrons Educational Series, 1992. (This book is full of great innovative ideas and new ways to do familiar activities.)

Knapp, Clifford, "Exploring the Outdoors with Young People," Science and Children, October, 1979.

Liem, Tik L. *Invitation to Science Inquiry. 2nd ed.* Chino Hills, CA: Science Inquiry Enterprises, 1987.

Ontario Science Center. *Foodworks—Over 100 Science Activities and Fascinating Facts that Explore the Magic of Food.* Reading, MA: Addison-Wesley, 1987.

Rasmussen, Greta. *Discover*. Stanwood, WA: Tin Man Press, 1987. (Encourages creative thinking skills, Grades K–6.)

Rasmussen, Greta. *Nifty Fifty*. Stanwood, Washington: Tin Man Press, 1987. (A book of creative questions about familiar topics; possible answers are also provided. Grades K–6.)

Williams, R.B., Rockwell, Robert E. and Sherwood, Elizabeth A. *Everybody Has a Body*. Mt. Rainier, MD: Gryphon House, 1992.

Williams, R.B., Rockwell, Robert E. and Sherwood, Elizabeth A. *Hug A Tree, and Other Things to do Outdoors with Young Children*. Gryphon House, 1986.

Williams, R.B., Rockwell, Robert E. and Sherwood, Elizabeth A. *More Mudpies to Magnets: Science for Young Children*. Gryphon House, 1990.

Warren, Jean. *Learning Games*. Palo Alto, California: Monday Morning Books, 1983. (Describes activities to reinforce sorting, observing, and counting. Grades K–2.)

Selected literature connection for younger children

Carlson, Nancy. *Harriet's Halloween Candy*. New York: Puffin Books, 1984. (A story about classification.)

Community enrichment activities

Post office For experiencing sorting and classifying the mail, listening to sounds of the mailroom.

Car wash For observing the sequence of events that occur during a car wash.

Grocery store For observing the orderly arrangement of categories of food and nonfood items. All five senses can be used at the grocery store, especially in the produce section.

Bakery For observing odors and tasting samples. Seeing the sequential process of baking take place.

Florist For observing variety and colors of flowers, plants, and their scents.

Library For observiing how books are classified.

Circus For observing the sights and sounds and smells.

4
Weather

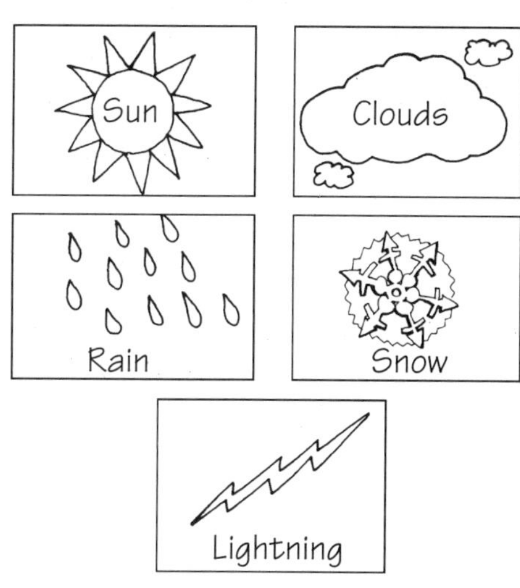

Objectives

The objectives of this chapter are for children to develop an awareness of the following:

- That weather is the result of interactions among air, water, earth (or land), and heat from the sun.
- That air can be cooled by water and heated by the sun.
- That wind is fast-moving air.
- That when two different air masses with different temperatures meet, a wind occurs.
- That when temperatures change, so does air pressure.
- How water is recycled by nature.
- The meaning of the terms associated with the water cycle: water vapor, evaporation, condensation, precipitation.
- The various kinds of clouds and how they form.
- How air masses form, and why their temperatures are different.
- Some of the instruments used to measure and predict weather.
- What weather data means, and why weather data records are kept.

General background information for parents and teachers

Weather Weather is created or caused by a combination of air, water, land, and the sun's heat. Weather involves changes in air pressure and temperature, wind speed and direction, and the amount of moisture in the air. When these factors change, they affect the movement of air masses, which creates the short-term changes in the atmosphere that is called weather.

Climate Climate is the predominant weather in a particular region.

Temperature Temperature is a measure or degree of warmth or coldness.

Thermometer An instrument that measures temperature.

Air pressure The amount of weight or force that air exerts on a surface per square inch.

Warm air Warm air has a relatively low air pressure. Warm air tends to rise and expand because it is lighter in weight per cubic inch than cool air. Warm air has energetic molecules that bang against each other and disperse or bang apart. This results in reducing the air density. (See Fig. 4-2.)

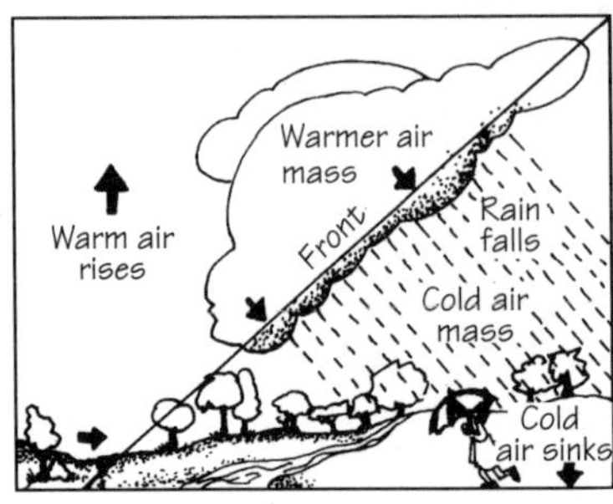

4-2 *When warm and cold air meet, turbulence occurs.*

Cool air Cool air has a relatively high air pressure. Cool air tends to sink and contract because it is heavy in weight per cubic inch. It has a higher density than warm air. (See Fig. 4-2.)

Density Weight per cubic inch.

Moist, warm air Warm, moist air has less pressure than warm air. It takes up a lot of space. Moist air contains water (molecules) and is therefore denser than dry air. In turn, the atmospheric pressure of moist air is higher than that of dry air at the same temperature. (See Fig. 4-2.)

Dry, cool air Dry, cool air has less pressure than cool air. It contracts more than cool air. (See Fig. 4-2.)

Ice Ice is water in the "solid" state. When water freezes, it turns into ice. Ice is able to float because it is lighter than water. The process of expansion makes ice lighter in weight than an equal amount of water before it freezes. When ice forms, it crystallizes on exposed surfaces first and in the center last.

Land Refers to continents and islands of the earth. During the day, the air above continents and islands warms up. At night, the air above them cools off. (See Fig. 4-3.)

Water Refers to the large and small bodies of water on the earth: oceans, lakes, rivers, and streams. During the day, water tends to absorb the heat from the sun slowly. At night, water tends to slowly lose the heat it absorbed. At night, the air above water bodies tends to feel warmer than the air above land areas. (See Fig. 4-4.)

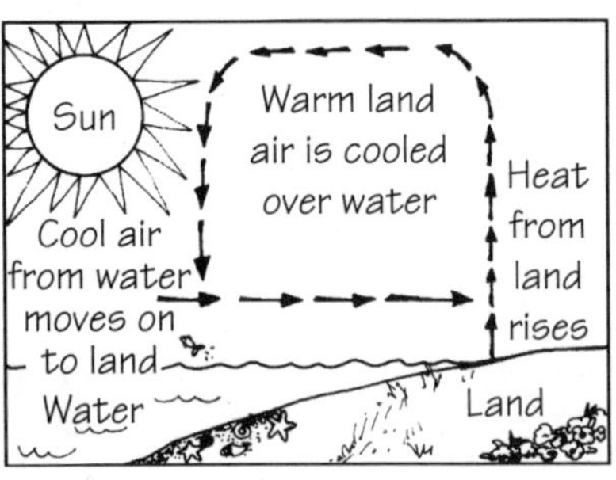

4-3 *Daytime sea breeze.*

Land breeze A breeze that blows from the land to the water. It tends to happen at night. (See Fig. 4-4.)

Sea breeze A breeze that blows from the water to the land. It tends to happen during the day. (See Fig. 4-3.)

Low air pressure Warm air has low air pressure.

High air pressure Cool air has high air pressure.

Winds and currents Changes in air temperature bring about changes in air pressure. Air tends to move from an area of high pressure to an area of low pressure. When air moves, it is called a wind or an air current.

Wind Air that moves parallel to the ground.

Current Air that moves up or down.

Direct sun rays Sunlight that shines directly down on the earth.

Indirect sun rays Sunlight that shines down at a slant so that a given quantity of sunlight is spread over a larger area than if it shines directly down.

Water cycle The process by which water is recycled into the atmosphere over and over again. Water evaporates from the earth and becomes water vapor. Then it condenses and forms a cloud or dew. When the air in the cloud becomes saturated, precipitation occurs, which starts the whole cycle over again.

Water vapor The form water takes when it is diffused as a gas. It is invisible.

Evaporation The process of liquid water disappearing as it diffuses and changes into water vapor.

Condensation The process whereby water changes from a gas back into a liquid.

4-4 *When the sun sets, both the land and the water become cooler. The land becomes cool quicker than the water. The warm air from the water rises. Cooler air from the land moves onto the water.*

Precipitation Condensed water that falls from clouds as rain, hail, sleet, or snow.

Acid rain Neutral and pure raindrops that become polluted (mixed with acid) as they fall through the atmosphere.

Saturated Air that is filled with water. When air is 100 percent saturated, it rains.

Humidity The amount of moisture in the air relative to how much it can hold.

Moisture The amount of water vapor in the air.

Dew point The temperature at which condensation occurs.

Droplets Minuscule drops of water. Droplets are extremely light in weight.

Cloud A large mass of moist air containing tiny suspended water droplets or ice particles. Clouds can be categorized by their appearance. They can also form at different altitudes in the sky.

Fog A very low cloud that touches the ground.

Dew A condensation that can be seen on surfaces as little water droplets. It occurs when air temperatures drop below the dew point.

Frost A condensation that can be seen on surfaces as small ice crystals. It occurs for the same reason dew does, but the water vapor freezes when the temperature is at freezing point or below.

Stratus clouds Clouds that look long, flat, and thin. When they are dark looking, they are called nimbostratus. Nimbostratus are rain clouds.

Cumulus clouds Can be seen on sunny days. They look like puffs of cotton. Cumulonimbus clouds form when the air cools off dramatically. They are big, vertical rain clouds, and they hold a lot of water.

Cirrus clouds They appear at a high altitude in the sky and look like thin, wispy curls. They indicate that the weather might change.

Air mass A large body of air that forms over the land or the water and that has a fairly consistent temperature and moisture level.

Tropical air mass A tropical air mass will have warm, moist air if the air mass formed over water, and warm dry air if the air mass formed over land.

Polar air mass A polar air mass will have cool, dry air if the air mass formed over land, and cool, moist air if the air mass formed over water.

Turbulence Occurs when two air masses with different temperatures collide. A "battle" over air space ensues, and the weather changes.

Front The boundary line between two air masses with different temperatures.

Warm front A warm front is a warm air mass that overtakes a cold air mass. A warm front brings about a slow and gradual change in the weather that lasts several days.

Cold front A cold front is a cold air mass that overpowers or invades the air space occupied by a warm air mass. A cold front brings about a sudden change in weather and lasts for a few hours. Thunderstorms occur when a cold front moves in. The air becomes very turbulent and violent during a thunderstorm. The cold air is denser than the warm air. It rushes in and pushes a warm mass of air up quickly. The warm air cools off fast as the cool air pushes against it and the warm air condenses, causing precipitation to occur. Then the sky clears and it is sunny.

Stationary front The boundary between two non-moving masses of air. (See Fig. 4-2.)

Meteorologist A weather scientist. Meteorologists study and record weather data and make predictions about the weather.

Weather data Information about the weather: temperature, air pressure, wind speed, wind direction, relative humidity, etc.

Weather instruments Instruments that help measure weather data: thermometer, wind vane, anemometer, barometer, rain gauge.

Wind vane Tells you from which direction the wind is blowing.

Anemometer Tells you how fast the wind is blowing.

Barometer Tells you the air pressure.

Rain gauge Tells you how much rain fell.

Hurricane A tropical low-pressure storm that forms at sea near the equator. The low pressure creates a vortex or whirlwind of strong, powerful winds that often move a hurricane toward a continent or island. If a hurricane does not blow out to sea, it arrives on land and can be quite destructive.

Tornado A funnel-shaped low-pressure storm with very powerful winds resulting from the low pressure induced by a vortex or whirlwind. A tornado forms over land. It brings much destruction as it passes over a small area of land for a short time.

Vortex A strong flow involving rotation about an axis, resulting in a whirlwind or whirlpool.

Note: As you do these activities with your children, try to encourage them to keep a science journal of their observations and their thoughts.

Activities and procedures

I. Air plus sun plus water plus land make weather

1. What is weather?

Materials

The word "weather" written on a card or blackboard; teacher or parent-made pictures of each of the following: sun, raindrops, snowflakes, clouds, lightning. (See Fig. 4-5.)

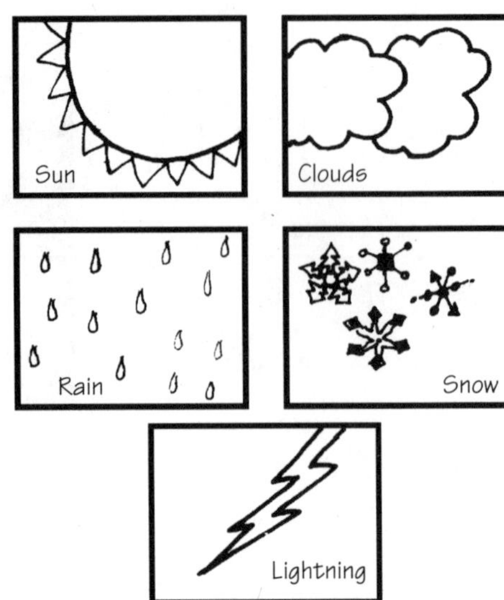

4-5 *Types of weather.*

Procedure

1 Show children the word "weather." Ask them if they can tell you what weather is. Ask them if they can name different kinds of weather.

2 Hold up the teacher- or parent-made pictures one at a time. Explain to the children that the pictures are models or symbols of different kinds of weather. Ask them to describe the kinds of weather each picture represents.

3 Ask the following kinds of questions:

Why isn't every day sunny or rainy? (Weather changes.)

Why does weather change? (Wind blows in new kinds of weather and/or the temperature changes after it rains.)

Where is the sun on a cloudy or rainy day? (The clouds are between the sun and the earth.)

Where do rain and snow fall from? (The clouds.)

When do we see lightning? (Sometimes during or before a storm.)

4 *Explain*: We are surrounded by an ocean of air. Tell children to make a swimming motion with their arms or to flap their arms like a flying bird. (They will feel the air being pushed away.)

2. Wind is moving air

Materials

A paper fan folded accordion style, a deflated balloon.

Procedure

1 Wave the paper fan in front of each child's face. Ask the children what they feel as the fan moves quickly in front of them. (Wind.)

What is wind? (Moving air.)

2 Inflate the balloon. Hold the neck between your fingers. Tell the children you are going to let go of the balloon. Ask the children what will happen to the balloon. (It will fly around.)

3 Let go of the balloon. Observe what happens. Ask the children the following kinds of questions:

What came out of the balloon? (Fast-moving air or wind.)

What caused the balloon to move or "fly"? (The reaction to the fast-moving air or wind coming out of the balloon.)

4 *Explain*: Wind can make things move. When large masses of air move, weather changes.

3. Water cools air

Materials

A sunny day, a bucket filled with water at room temperature.

Procedure

1 Take the children outside. Have the children dip their hands into the water. When their hands hit the outside air, their hands will feel cool, especially if there is a gentle breeze. The water and breeze from moving air will cool the air before it touches their skin. (If there is no breeze, the children can move their hands around to create a breeze.)

2 Spill some water onto a cemented or blacktopped area. Have the children feel the blacktop and/or cement after some water has been poured on it. Have the children compare the difference in heat or temperature their hands feel from the wet area and the area that is still dry. *Note*: Be sure the wet and the dry area are either both in the sun or both in the shade.

4. The sun heats air and water

Materials

A sunny day, a shade tree, two dark-colored basins, water.

Procedure

1 Take the children outside. Stand with them in the sun and then in the shade of a tree or a building. Discuss the difference in temperature.

Where does the air feel warmer? (In the sun.)

Where does the air feel cooler? (In the shade.)

2 Fill each basin with one inch of water. *Note*: If you begin with the water at a shallow level in a dark-colored basin, it will absorb more heat. The final results will be more dramatic.

3 Place one basin in the shade and the other basin in the sun. Wait about an hour. Then observe the temperature in both basins by feeling the water in each basin.

4 Discuss the differences. (Results will differ according to the season. On a warm day, the water left in the sun might evaporate. On a freezing day, the water left in the sun might turn into ice. But in any event, the temperature of the water in the basins should feel different.)

II. Temperature, currents, and air pressure

1. Thermometer

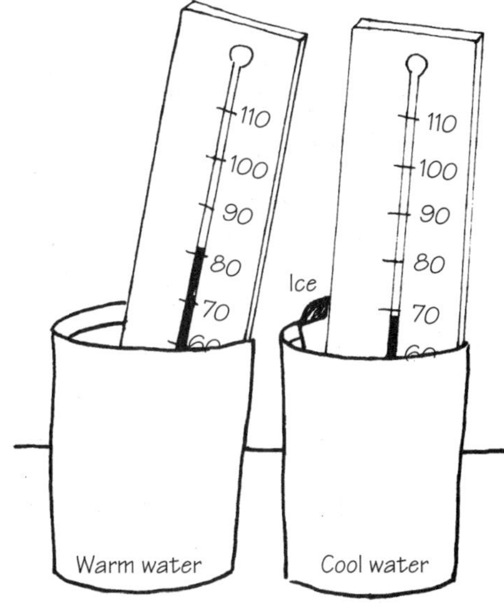

4-6 Thermometers measure the air temperature.

Materials

Two identical weather thermometers, two cups of warm water, ice cubes, paper towel, newspaper to absorb possible mess.

Procedure

1 Show children a thermometer. Ask them the following kinds of questions:

What is this tool or instrument called? (A thermometer.)

What is it used for? (Measuring temperature.)

What is temperature? (How hot or cold something is.)

How does it work? (The temperature makes the liquid inside of the tube go up or down.)

2 Have the children try to see the liquid column.

3 Fill both cups with warm water. Place the thermometer into one of the cups. Have the children compare that temperature reading to the temperature on the other thermometer, which should be at room temperature.

Which thermometer has a longer line? (The one in the warm water.)

4 Place an ice cube in the other cup of warm water.

What will happen to the ice cube? (It will melt.)

5 Place one ice cube on the paper towel.

Which ice cube will melt faster, the one on the paper towel or the one in the water? (The one in the water.)

Why? (The water is warmer so the ice will melt faster.)

There is also better heat transfer from water to ice than from air to ice.

When the ice melts in the warm water, how will the water feel, warmer or colder? (Colder.)

How can you find out if that is so? (By feeling the water, and by measuring the temperature of the water with the thermometer.)

Will the column of liquid in the thermometer be higher and longer, or lower and shorter after it measures the warm water with melted ice? (Shorter than the other thermometer.)

Does the liquid in the thermometer go up or down when the air is cold? (Down.)

Where does the liquid move when the air is warm? (Up.)

2. Balloon on a soda bottle

Materials

Small, empty glass soda bottle; a small, deflated balloon; bucket of hot water; bucket of ice water.

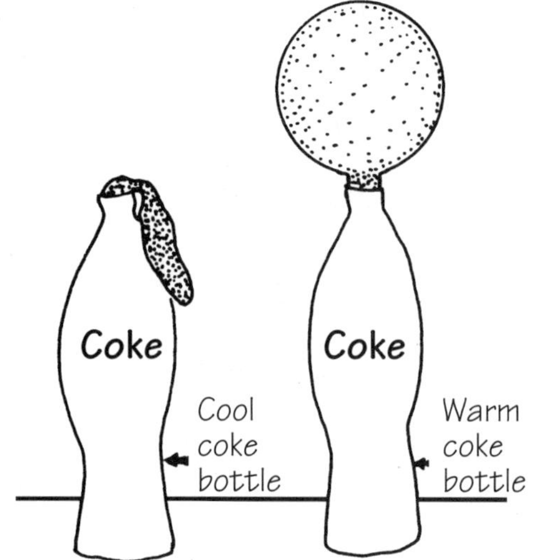

4-7 *Cool air takes up less space; warm air takes up more space.*

Procedure

1 Pass an empty soda bottle around for the children to feel. Then place the bottle in the bucket of ice water. Leave it in the bucket for a few minutes.

How do you think the bottle will feel when I take it out of the ice water? (The bottle will feel cool. The air inside of the bottle will be cool.)

2 Stretch the neck of a deflated balloon around the neck of the cooled bottle. (See Fig. 4-7.)

3 Pass the cooled bottle with the balloon on its neck around for the children to feel again. Have them hold the bottle with both hands for a few seconds.

How does the bottle feel? (At first, it will feel cool. After it passes through a few sets of hands, the air in the bottle will become warmer.)

4 As the bottle is passed from one child's hands to another, tell them to observe the balloon. (As the air in the bottle becomes warmer, the balloon will start to inflate as the warm air moves up or rises.)

5 Place the warmed bottle back into the bucket of ice water. Have the children observe what happens to the balloon. (It will deflate. If the water is very cold, the balloon might become inverted inside of the bottle.)

6 After the balloon deflates, place the cooled bottle into the bucket of hot water.

7 Have the children predict what will happen to the balloon when the bottle

is placed in the bucket of hot water. (The balloon will expand or fill with air again.)

8 *Explain*: A special kind of wind has been created in the bottle. It is called a current. Currents are winds that move up or down.

What happens when the air in the bottle warms up? (The balloon inflates.)

What happens when the air in the bottle cools down? (The balloon deflates.)

Fine points to discuss

How is the balloon on a bottle like a thermometer? (Warm air goes up. Cold air sinks.)

Why does the balloon fill with air? (Warm air takes up more space and rises.)

Why does the balloon lose its air? (Cold air takes up less space and is heavier than warm air, so there is less air pressure.)

How does the temperature of the water affect the air? (The temperature of the water changes the temperature of the air.)

What current direction is caused when air cools off? (Downward movement.)

What current direction is caused when air warms up? (Upward movement.)

What is wind? (Wind is moving air.)

Going further

What do you think would happen to an inflated balloon if it were placed inside of a freezer overnight? Why?

After children make and record their predictions in their science journals, have them inflate a balloon and place it in a freezer overnight. Then ask children to observe and compare the actual results with their predictions.

3. Collapsing a plastic bottle

Materials

An empty plastic liter bottle with a cap, access to a freezer or outside temperature below freezing, a bucket of hot water.

Procedure

1 Place an empty bottle into a bucket of hot water. Allow the air inside the bottle to become warm. Cap the bottle and allow the children to feel its warmth with their hands. Tell the children you are going to place the bottle filled with warm air into a place where the temperature is below freezing.

What do you think will happen to the bottle ? (It will cave in or collapse.)

2 Place the bottle with warm air capped tightly in the freezing air. Tell the children to observe what happens to it.

3 *Explain*: Warm air takes up a lot of space. When the warm air inside of the bottle cooled off, it took up less space. This caused the bottle to cave in.

Fine points to discuss

When the air in the bottle cooled off, where was the force of air pressure greater, on the inside or the outside of the bottle? (On the outside of the bottle, so the bottle caved in.)

What happened to the air inside of the bottle? (The warm air cooled off and took up less space.)

Which air takes up more space, warm air or cool air? (Warm air.)

Which air has more air pressure, warm air or cool air? (Cool air.)

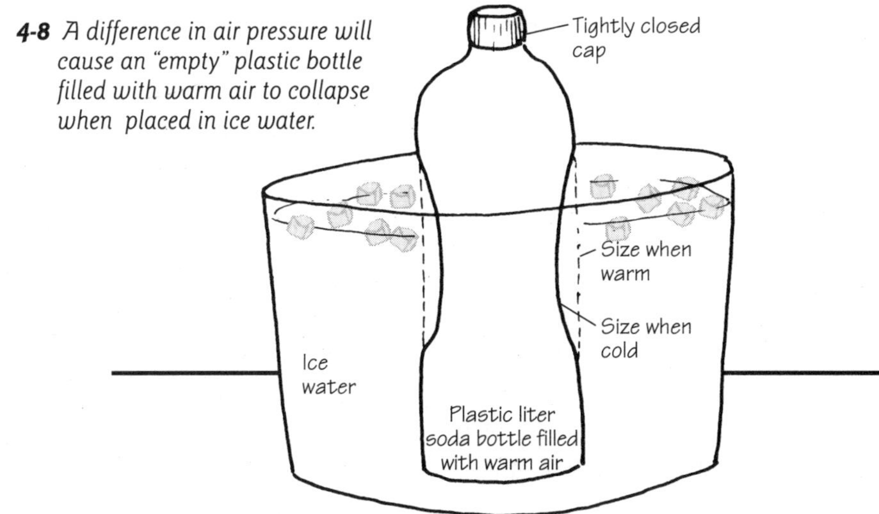

4-8 *A difference in air pressure will cause an "empty" plastic bottle filled with warm air to collapse when placed in ice water.*

4. Hot and cold water

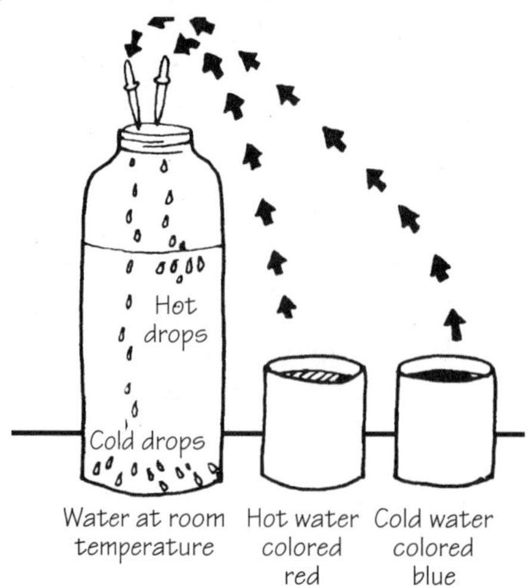

4-9 Observe where colored water of different temperatures settles.

Materials

Two colors of food coloring, large two-quart clear glass or plastic bottle, two eye droppers, water, two small containers, hot water, ice cubes, water at room temperature, newspaper to absorb possible mess from water.

Procedure

1 Fill a two-quart bottle with water at room temperature. Pour some water into a container and add ice cubes. Pour some hot water into another container. Ask the children if they can tell by looking at the water whether it is hot or cold. (They will probably say that the water with the ice cubes is colder.)

When the ice cubes melt, will they be able to tell by just looking, which water is hot and which water is cold? (Yes, condensation will occur on the outside of the colder container, but it will be harder to tell which is which by just looking at the surface of the water.)

2 Show children two different food colors. Tell them you are going to add one color to the cold water and the other color to the warm water.

Will the food color make the cold water colder or the warm water warmer? (No.)

Will color added to the water make it easier to tell, by just looking, which water is warm and which water is cool? (Yes.)

3 Add several drops of food color to each container of water so that the color is fairly dark. Have the children observe the drops as they enter the water and spread or diffuse into the water.

Does the food color spread (diffuse) faster in the hot water or the cold water? (The hot water.)

Does the color spread out faster in still water or turbulent water? (Turbulent water.)

4 Use two eye droppers, one for each container of colored water. Draw some warm colored water up with the eye dropper. Drop the warm colored water from the eye dropper into the large two-quart bottle filled with water at room temperature. Have the children observe where the drops go after they enter the bottle. They will observe that the colored warm drops of water from the eye dropper will float to the surface of the water in the bottle.

5 Tell the children you are going to use the eye dropper to draw some cool colored water and that you will drop the cool colored water into the large bottle.

Will the cool drops of water float to the surface or will they go to the bottom? (They will go to the bottom.)

Which kind of water (hot or cold) stays in the shape of a ring or a doughnut? (The cold water.)

If the hot colored water is sent far down in the water, will it still come up to the surface? (Yes.)

6 Let the children continue to do this experiment on their own using eye droppers to drop colored water at different temperatures into a bottle filled with water.

Fine points to discuss

How do the hot and cold water behave? (Hot water moves up and cold water moves down.)

5. Ice floats

Materials

A bucket of water, ice cubes, a milk carton, a can filled to the brim with water and then frozen, newspaper to absorb possible mess from water.

Procedure

1 We have found out that cold air and cold water sink and that hot air and hot water float.

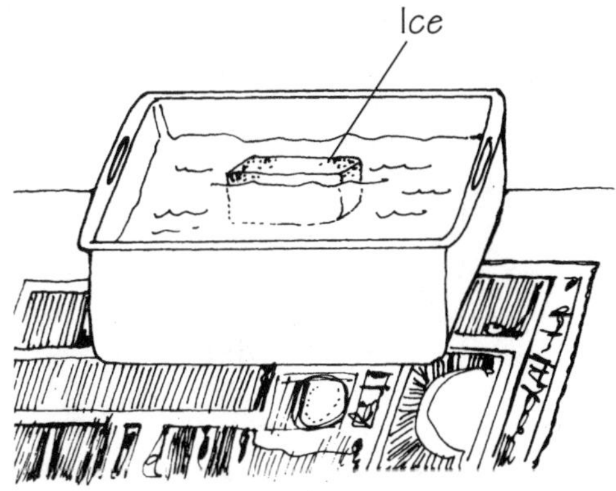

4-10 *Ice floats low.*

What does ice do when it is in the water? (It floats.)

2 Place some ice cubes in the bucket of water and tell the children to observe what the ice cubes do.

Does the entire ice cube float above the water? (Only part of the ice cube floats above the water.)

3 Have children observe a can of frozen water and a milk carton filled with water and frozen. (They will notice the ice has a bump, and/or that it is taking up more space than the container. The frozen water has expanded.)

Fine points to discuss

If ice is cold, why does it float? (Ice floats because it is less dense than water. When water freezes, it expands and it takes up more space. It also becomes less dense than water, so it is able to float in water.)

Note: See Chapter 8, Air and water, Activity IX, Boats and buoyancy, Procedure 6, Making a clay ball float, Fine points to discuss.

How much of a floating iceberg can we see? (About one-ninth is above the water, and eight-ninths is hidden beneath the water.)

6. The center freezes last

Materials

A bucket of water, a semi-frozen block of ice (use an empty half-gallon milk container as a mold for the block of ice), newspaper to absorb possible mess from water.

Procedure

1 Unmold the block of ice.

2 Allow it to float in the bucket of water. Have the children observe the center of the block. (It will still be filled with water. The water can be emptied out of the center, and the center will be hollow.)

What shape was the frozen block? (The same shape as the container it was frozen in.)

What appears to be the last part of the block that froze? (The center.)

What appears to be the first part of the block that froze? (The sides.)

Why is it important to know how something freezes? (It helps us understand how living things can live in water in the winter.)

Where do fish swim in the winter when the lake they live in freezes over? (They live underneath the ice. The lake freezes on the top before it freezes in the center. This allows plant and animal life to continue during the winter in a pond or lake.)

Does the water move underneath the ice? (Yes, there is a current that continually turns water over in a circular pattern. The water near the ice becomes cold and more dense. It falls toward the bottom. When water falls below 4 degrees centigrade, it expands as it is cooled, so colder water rises. That is why ice forms at the surface of the water.)

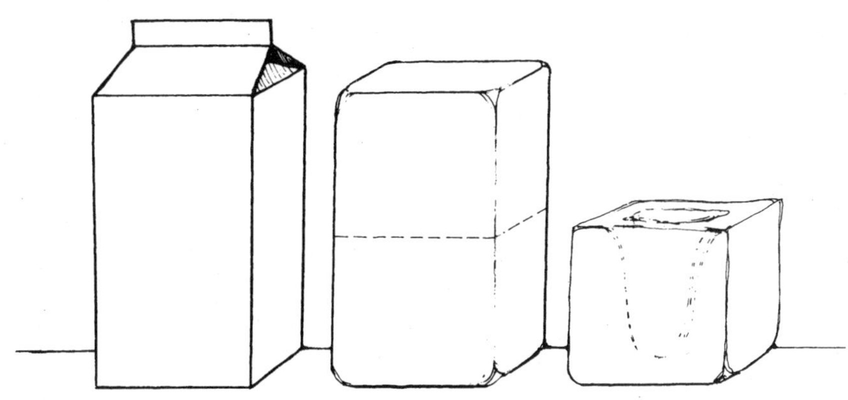

4-11 *Make an ice "brick;" unmold it; break it open.*

7. Land and water

4-12 *Air temperature varies between the shade and the sun.*

Materials

Dark brown paper; light blue paper; two basins, one filled with topsoil, the other filled with water; two thermometers.

Procedure

1 *Explain*: In order to understand weather better, we are going to conduct an experiment to observe how land and water absorb heat or become warmer from the sun. Show the children the two basins. The basin with topsoil will represent a "piece of land." The basin with water will represent a water area like an ocean or lake. Show the children the colors of construction paper.

Which color of construction paper might represent land and which color could represent water? (Land, dark brown; water, light blue.)

2 Place the two basins in the sun, either outside or inside on a windowsill. Allow the basins to absorb sunlight for about one hour or more.

Do you think the temperature will be the same in each basin?

3 Check and record the temperature at the beginning of the experiment and again after several hours to find out if there has been a change in the temperature. (The soil should become warmer than the water.)

4 *Explain*: The dark color of the soil should absorb more heat from the sunlight. *Note*: Have older children record the temperatures in their science journals. Explain to them that it is important to record this kind of data because it is easy to forget the exact numbers. Ask older children to calculate how much the temperature changed.

5 Place the two basins in the shade or away from sunlight. Have the children check and record the temperature of each basin, then let each basin sit in the shady area for about 15 minutes or more. Have the children check and record the temperature again. (The water should stay at a fairly constant or even temperature, whereas the soil will lose a lot of its heat.) *Note*: Ask older children to calculate how much the temperature changed.

6 Place the pieces of colored paper in the sunlight. After about 30 minutes, have the children check the way the papers feel.

Does one color feel warmer than the other color? (The dark brown paper will most likely feel warmer than the light blue paper.)

7 Discuss observations and results of the experiments with the children. You might want to ask the following kinds of questions:

What happens to the soil and to the water when the sun shines on them? (They become warmer.)

Which becomes hotter in the sun, the "piece of land" or the water? (The soil or "piece of land.")

During the night when the sun is not shining on the land or the water, which cools off faster? (The "piece of land" or soil cools off faster because it does not retain heat. Soil heats up and cools off faster than water.)

Fine points to discuss

How does the temperature of the land and the water affect the air and the weather? (The different temperatures of the air from land and water create a breeze or gentle wind near water.)

Explain: In the daytime when the sun shines, the air above the land warms up faster than the air above the water. The warmer air is very light and tends to rise. As the warm air rises, a low-pressure area is created and the cooler air from above the water rushes in to take the place of the warm air above the land that has floated upward. Cool air is heavy and has a higher pressure than warm air. When the cool, high-pressure air rushes into the low-pressure area vacated by the warm air, a sea breeze or wind is created. The reverse happens at night.

INFORMATION Land in general is a good insulator. The sun warms the surface and the heat travels very slowly to whatever is below the surface. Therefore, the surface heats up faster. At night, all of the heat is at the surface and escapes quickly into the air. Water, on the other hand, is somewhat transparent to the sun's rays. The sun's rays are absorbed deep into the water as well as at the surface. All the water is heated some but not a lot. At night the surface of the water temperature quickly cools. The water temperature differences cause some water underneath the surface to replace the surface water and, therefore, it takes a longer time for the "surface water" to cool down. (Ralph Brainard.)

Why does a sea breeze become a land breeze at night? (When the sun goes down, the land cools off quickly and loses its heat. The water stays warm. It cools off much more slowly than the land. At night the air above the water is warmer than the air above the land, so a cool breeze comes from the land toward the water to replace the warm air that has floated upward.)

Note: With older children you might want to review the results of this experiment again:

- Water takes a longer time to heat up, but once it is warm it stays warm a longer time.
- Land warms up quickly and cools off quickly.
- You might also want to discuss and review with the children the results of the soda bottle and balloon experiment or the hot and cold water experiment described earlier in this section, so that they will better understand how and why air currents occur.

Going further

- You might want to look at a globe with older children and discuss the land and water formations on the globe. Land breezes and sea breezes occur on and from the continents and on and from the oceans. These "breezes" affect our weather. Sometimes major storms begin as little winds.
- Ask older children to find out more information about where the prevailing winds are formed and in what direction they blow.

8. Direct and indirect rays from the sun

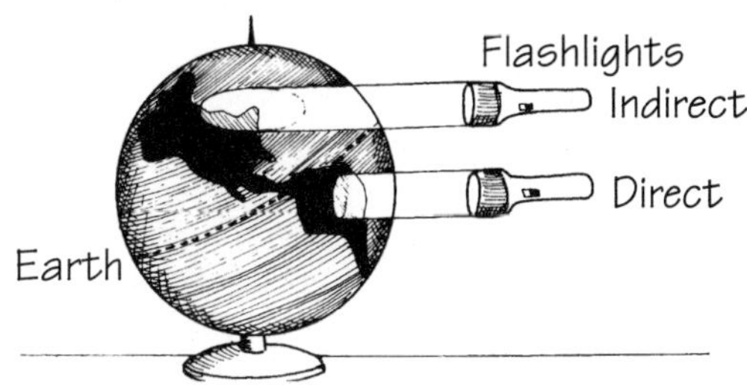

4-13 *Model of direct and indirect sunlight.*

Materials

A globe on an axis; a flashlight or projection light.

Procedure

1 Show children the globe and rotate the globe on its axis. Shine the light from a flashlight or projector on to the equator of the globe as it spins.

2 *Explain*: The globe is a model of the earth. It rotates or spins on its axis. The flashlight or projector is a model of the sun's light. The sun stays still. Half of the earth faces the sun and has daylight, while the other half of the earth is in darkness and has night. Every twenty-four hours, the earth rotates on its axis and a day is completed. The sun shines directly over the equator. Point to the equator area on the globe. This area of the earth is always very warm. The rays from the sun shine directly on the equator in a straight line. The sunlight is very strong at the equator and warms the water and the land. The sunlight is not as strong at the top and bottom of the earth. The top and bottom of the earth are called the North Pole and the South Pole. It is very cold at both the North Pole and the South Pole because the earth is round and curved. The sunlight does not shine directly on the poles. The poles receive indirect rays from the sun. The equator receives direct rays from the sun. The sun's heat and light are not as strong at the poles as they are at the equator. This difference in heating at different places on the earth causes winds to occur

when the air masses from the equator and the poles meet.

Going further: for older children

- Esler (pg. 400–401) suggests placing two boxes with soil in the sun. Tilt one box toward the sun's rays, and place the other box flat. After an hour, measure the temperature in each box filled with soil to see if there is a difference in temperature between the box of soil that has direct sunlight and the one that does not.
- Gega (pg. 571) suggests creating two black paper pockets with a stapler, then placing a thermometer inside of each of the black paper pockets. Lay one thermometer flat and tilt the other one on some books so that the sun will strike it directly. After a few minutes, read both thermometers to find out if there is a difference in temperature between the two thermometers.

Fine point to discuss

How can you be sure the tilted box or tilted thermometer inside of the black paper pocket is receiving a direct ray from the sun? (Adjust the tilt until there is almost no shadow. When there is almost no shadow, the object will be receiving direct sunlight.)

Explain: When the sun is directly overhead, our shadow is quite short. (If possible, allow children to play shadow tag at different times of the day, including when the sun is directly overhead to experience the effect of direct sunlight on shadows for themselves.)

II. Water cycle

1. Seeing water vapor

Materials

A mirror or eyeglasses.

Procedure

1 Have the children breathe through their mouths onto a mirror or eyeglasses. The moist air that has come from their lungs will cloud the surface of the mirror or eyeglasses. The cloud will then evaporate or disappear.

2 *Explain*: The cloud on the mirror or eyeglasses from their own warm, moist breath is called water vapor. The water vapor disappears before their eyes because it evaporates or goes into the air. Warm, moist air floats up or rises because it is lighter than cool, dry, heavy air.

Water vapor is invisible. When the air is cooled to a temperature below the dew point, water will condense in small droplets. The droplets start most easily on "something." In breathing on the mirror, that is the "something." The water vapor becomes small droplets that we can see. Our exhaled breath has higher humidity from the water added in our lungs. The water on the mirror eventually evaporates and becomes invisible water vapor again. (Ralph Brainard.)

2. Feeling water vapor

Materials

None.

Procedure

Tell the children to put their hand up to their mouth and to breathe on it. Ask them how their breath feels on their palm. It will feel warm and moist.

Where does the moisture they feel on their hand go? (Into the air.)

What is the moisture they feel on their hand called? (Condensed water vapor.)

3. Evaporation

Materials

A blackboard, two sponges, water.

Procedure

1 Wipe a blackboard with a wet sponge. Ask the children how long they think the blackboard will stay wet. Ask the following kinds of questions:

Will the blackboard dry by itself, or does it have to be wiped dry? (It can dry by itself.)

Where will the water go that was on the blackboard? (Into the air.)

Will the wet sponge dry by itself? (Yes.)

Where will the water go that was in the sponge? (Into the air.)

2 Wet two sponges. Place one sponge in the sunlight or over a heating vent and the other sponge in a shaded and cool area.

Which of these two sponges do you think will become dry faster?

Where will the water go? (Into the air.)

Can they see the water as it leaves the sponge? (No.)

3 *Explain*: When the water goes into the air, it is called water vapor. Water vapor is invisible. The process of water

4-14A A wet blackboard.

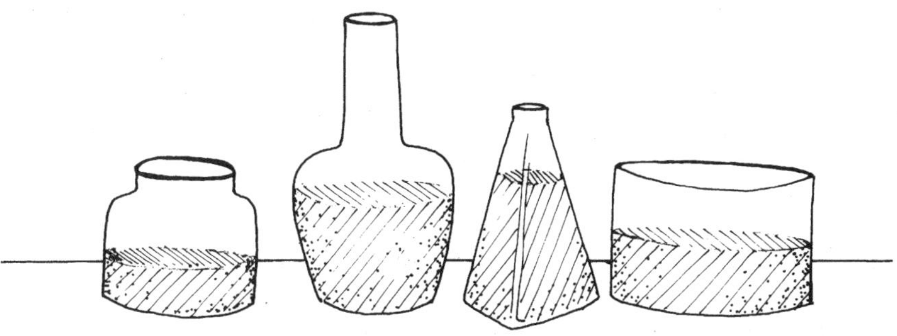

4-14B Which jar will lose water faster to evaporation?

going into the air is called evaporation.

Can you think of other things that are affected by evaporation? (Suggested things to discuss might be: where the water from puddles goes after a rain; how wet clothes become dry; how wet paint becomes dry; how dishes dry on a drain-board; how Play-Doh dries in the air; how a wet body becomes dry after swimming; where does the morning dew go; etc.)

Going Further

You might want to do experiments to find out which kind of container shape and container opening will make water evaporate faster. If you color the water with food color, it will leave a residue when the water evaporates and the children will be able to see the water mark left by the water that evaporated.

Does the same amount of water evaporate faster from a shallow pan or a deep pan? (A shallow pan or area.)

Does the size of a jar opening or the length and size of a jar's neck affect how much water evaporates? (The larger-size jar opening has faster evaporation; the shorter-necked jar also has faster evaporation.)

4. Condensation on a glass of water

Materials

A glass or an empty tin can, ice cubes, water, newspaper to absorb possible mess from water.

Procedure

1 Place several ice cubes into a glass or an empty tin can. Add some water so that the glass or can is about three-quarters full. Let it stand for about ten minutes.

2 Observe what happens to the outside of the glass or tin can. (At first, the outside is dry, but after about ten minutes, tiny water droplets begin to form like beads of sweat and cling to the outside of the glass or can. Ask the children where the water came from.)

3 *Explain*: The beads of water on the outside of the glass or can came from the air. Air contains a lot of water or moisture that we cannot see. It is called water vapor. Water vapor is like

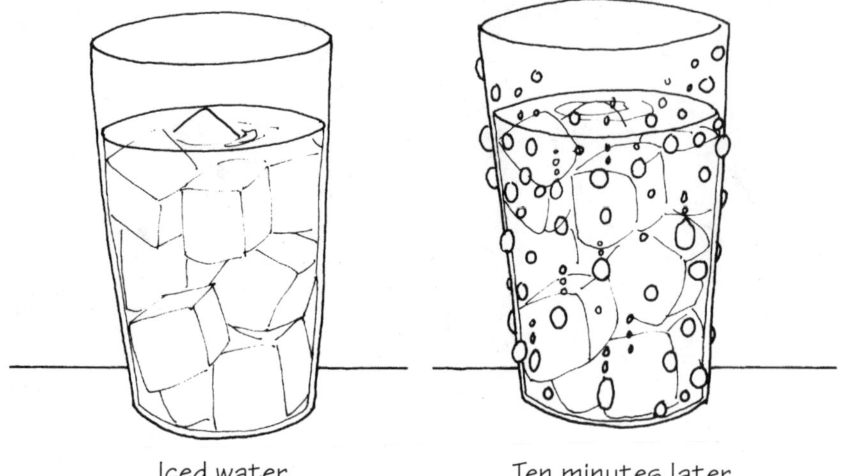
Iced water
Ten minutes later

4-15 *On a hot day, a glass with ice cubes will appear to "sweat."*

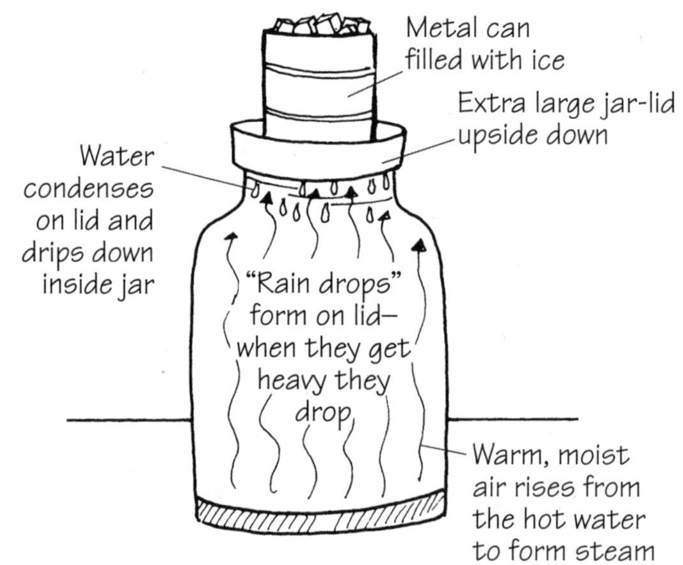
Metal can filled with ice
Extra large jar-lid upside down
Water condenses on lid and drips down inside jar
"Rain drops" form on lid— when they get heavy they drop
Warm, moist air rises from the hot water to form steam

4-16 *Make "rain" inside a jar.*

air. We cannot see it, but sometimes when water vapor condenses into droplets we can see the condensed water vapor.

The air surrounding the outside of the cold glass or tin can filled with ice water became cooler. Cool air cannot hold as much water vapor as warm air. The extra water vapor came out of the surrounding air that cooled off. The extra water vapor condensed or turned into water and clung to the outside of the glass or tin can. When a gas changes into a liquid, it is called condensation. *Note*: With older children, you might want to introduce the three states of water to the children: ice/solid, water/liquid, water vapor/gas.

5. Making it "rain" inside a jar

Materials

A large, empty Pyrex jar; very hot water; a tin lid for the jar; an empty tin can filled with ice cubes; a flashlight.

Procedure

1 Tell the children that you are going to create a cloud in a jar from water vapor and that the cloud will become very heavy with moisture and will condense. The condensation will fall as large water drops. (You're going to make rain!)

2 *Explain*: When a cloud's droplets become large enough, they fall. This is called precipitation. Precipitation can be in the form of rain, snow, hail, dew, drizzle, or sleet.

3 Pour some very hot water into a large empty Pyrex jar. (About half a cup of water will do—just enough to form a lot of steam inside of the Pyrex jar.) Cover the jar with a lid. Place an empty tin can filled with ice cubes on top of the jar lid. (See Fig. 4-16.)

4 Notice what happens inside the jar.
- The heat inside the jar from the hot water warms the air.
- The warm, moist air in the jar begins to look steamy.
- The steamy, moist warm air condenses and turns into water vapor.
- The water vapor condenses on bits of dust and forms droplets that we see as a cloud. The cloud will look white, especially if you shine a flashlight through the jar. (The flashlight is like sunlight.)
- As the small, light droplets of water in the steam become larger and heavier droplets, the white steam will appear grayer in color.
- The warm, moist air mass inside of the jar becomes cooler when it hits the cool lid of the jar, which has been cooled by the ice cubes (that are filling the tin can on top of the lid of the jar).
- When the warm, moist air becomes cooler, the cloud inside the jar becomes darker because the large water droplets form shadows and block the light of the sun or flashlight from shining through.
- Large water drops begin to form on the lid of the jar. The water vapor has changed back to water. This is called condensation. If you lift the lid off the jar, you will be able to see the large water droplets forming.
- When the condensed water droplets fall, many will roll down the side of the jar or just drop. When they fall, it is called precipitation. Precipitation means that water or moisture is falling out of the clouds onto the land or water below.

6. Water cycle chart

Materials

A teacher- or parent-made chart of the water cycle. (See Fig. 4-17.)

Procedure

1 Show the children the water cycle chart. Ask them to explain what the chart is showing a picture of or trying to represent.

2 Ask the following kinds of questions:

Where do the arrows begin? (They do not begin. They continue in a circle over and over again. There is no beginning.)

What is a cycle? (Something that continues to happen over and over again with no beginning or end.)

Note: You might want to use a bicycle chain as an example of a cycle. The links on the bicycle chain turn or move around continuously as the bike is pedaled. As long as the wheels are in motion, the chain continues in motion until it is stopped, but there is no real beginning or end to the circular motion. Each section or link of the continuous chain is necessary for the system to be complete and whole. If a link of the chain were missing, the pedals would not be able to move the wheels, and the system would not work.

What happens to the water in the ocean? (The heat from the sun and air evaporates some of the water. When it evaporates, the water turns or changes into water vapor.)

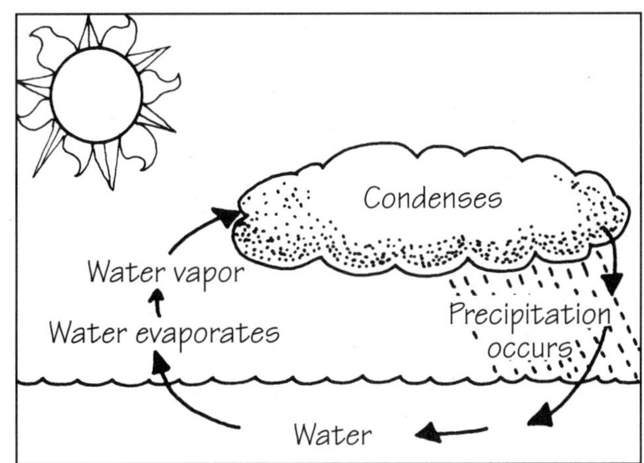

4-17 *Water cycle. Heat from the sun causes water to evaporate. Water that evaporates turns into a gas called water vapor. Water vapor rises and forms a cloud. When the water vapor becomes heavy, the vapor condenses and forms large water droplets. When water droplets fall it is called rain or precipitation.*

Where does the water in the ocean come from? (Some of the water from rain flows into streams, which flow into rivers, which flow into the ocean.)

What happens after the water from the oceans and lakes and our yards evaporates? (The warm water vapor floats up and forms clouds.)

What happens when the clouds become large and cool off? (They become heavy and the water vapor in them changes back into water again. This is called condensation. When condensation occurs, precipitation sometimes follows. Precipitation means water or moisture falls into the ocean, lakes, or rivers and onto the land.)

Does new water fall from the sky or is it the same water that fell before? (It is the same water that fell before. Since the time of the dinosaurs or earlier, the water on our earth has been continuously recycled—that is, used over and over again. The water cycle has no beginning or end.)

Note: You might want to discuss: what "recycled" means; how aluminum cans can be melted down and reused; how paper products can be turned into pulp again and reprocessed, etc.

How does dirty and polluted water become clean? (When water evaporates, only the water turns into vapor. The other things that were in the water remain behind. When water falls from clouds, it is pure water unless it falls through polluted air; then it becomes acid rain.)

What is acid rain? (When rain falls from the clouds, sometimes it comes in contact with pollution in the air. The rain clings to the pollutants and brings the pollution in the air down with it to the ground and water below when it falls. Acid rain is harmful to living things. Our government has a special agency called the Environmental Protection Agency (EPA), which tries to protect our country's environment from pollutants.)

7. Pure water evaporates

Materials

For each child or group of children: a Styrofoam meat tray or a jar lid, different food colors, water, a cup, a tablespoon.

Procedure

1 Tell children to mix several drops of food color into three tablespoons of

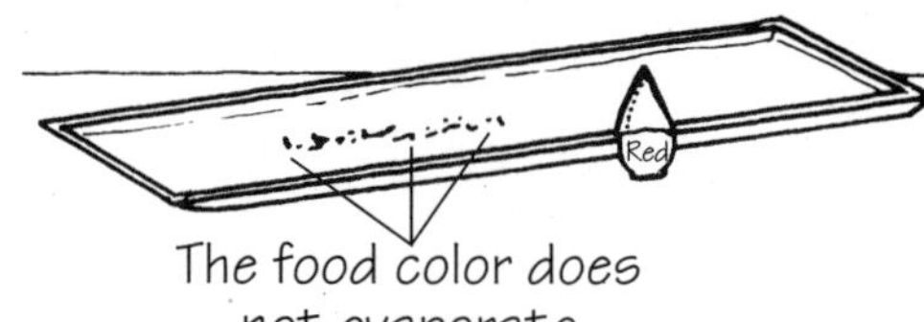

4-18 *When water evaporates, the debris in the water does not.*

water. Then pour the colored water mixture into the Styrofoam meat tray or into the jar lid.

What do you think will happen to the colored water mixture if you let it sit on a sunny surface in the room? (It will evaporate.)

Do you think the color will evaporate too? (It will not.)

2 Have the children check back in a few days to see if the water evaporated.

3 Discuss the results.

(The color remained behind. Only the water evaporated.)

How does this experiment show us that when water evaporates, it is pure and not dirty? (The dirt or color stays behind; only the water disappears.)

What will happen to the color if you add water to it? (It will mix with the water.)

4 Add the color and let the children see the mixture form again and allow the water to evaporate again.

Note: The color is like a pollutant. It does not disappear. It remains and spreads when the water mixes with it.

IV. Clouds

1. Water vapor

Materials

Deflated balloon marked with a thick water-soluble marking pen.

Procedure

1 Show the children the balloon with the black mark on it. Tell them you will be inflating or blowing the balloon up with warm air from your lungs.

What do you think will happen to the black spot on the balloon when the balloon is filled with warm air? (They might suggest that the black spot will become much larger. Actually, the black spot will become so much larger that the spot will appear to have disappeared. It will be stretched out so much that it will become very light in color.)

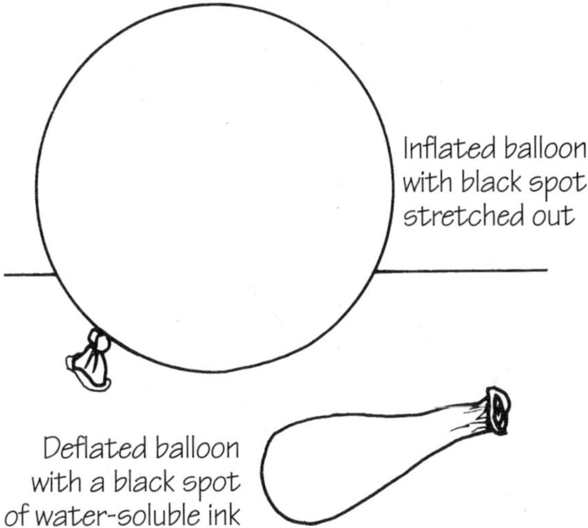

4-19 *A tangible model of water vapor.*

2 Proceed to inflate the balloon and discuss the results.

Is the black spot still there? (It seems to have disappeared.)

3 Allow the air to escape from the balloon. The black spot will reappear. Ask the following kinds of questions:

Did the black spot really disappear? (No, it was there all the time. It seemed to disappear because the molecules of ink from the marking pen were spread apart so far on the surface of the balloon that the mark appeared not to be there anymore.)

How is the black spot on the balloon like hot air? (Hot air takes up a lot of space and spreads out. It becomes very thin and light like the black spot on the balloon.)

How is the black spot on the blown-up balloon like water vapor? (Water vapor is in the air. It is invisible and cannot be seen. When the balloon is inflated, the black spot is like water vapor. It is difficult to see. Although the black spot seems to disappear, it is really still there. Water vapor seems to disappear when it evaporates, but it does not disappear. It floats up or rises and forms a cloud with other particles or molecules of water that have also floated up.)

Why does water vapor float up or rise? (Like air, water vapor is a gas. It is very light in weight. It is the temperature of air.)

INFORMATION

Gases act independently. When water evaporates, the water molecules separate from each other and spread all around, including up. Water vapor can float on itself. We refer to air being moist if the humidity is high. Air is a mixture of gases; water vapor is one of the gases in our air. Water vapor can make up approximately 1 percent of air. (Ralph Brainard.)

2. Clouds float

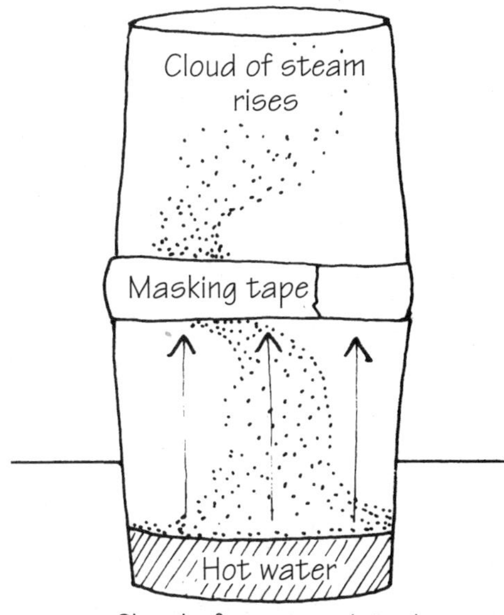

4-20 *Moist air moves up to form a cloud.*

Materials

Two clear plastic glasses the same size, masking tape, very hot water, newspaper to absorb possible mess.

Procedure

1 Pour a small amount of very hot water into a plastic glass. Quickly place another plastic glass upside-down on top of the first glass so that the lips of the two glasses are touching. Secure the two glasses (with the small amount of hot water inside) with masking tape so that the container is sealed and the

water will not be able to run out. (See Fig. 4-20.)

2 Have the children observe the steam or water vapor forming above the water. Discuss the children's observations. You might want to ask the following kinds of questions:

Where is the cloud forming? (On top of the container, above the warm water.)

Why is the cloud forming? (The air is warm and moist. Moist, warm air moves up or rises. It is lighter than cool, dry air.)

If the container is turned upside-down, what will happen to the cloud? (It will form on top of the container again.)

3 Turn the container upside-down and observe what happens to the cloud of steam.

Why does the steam rise to the top again? (The steam is filled with warm, moist air. Warm, moist air is lighter than cooler air, so it rises or floats up.)

Fine points to discuss

What are clouds made of? (Clouds are made of tiny water droplets and ice crystals. When warm, moist air evaporates and turns into water vapor, it expands and cools as it rises. Cool air cannot hold as much water vapor as warm air. When the warm, rising air cools off, it begins to condense and change into very tiny water droplets. Sometimes the temperature in the air above is so cold, it is freezing. If the temperature above is freezing, the water droplets change into crystals of ice.)

Why do clouds float? (Clouds float because they are made up of very tiny water droplets or ice crystals. These tiny droplets of water and crystals of ice are so small and light that the force of warm, rising air keeps the tiny water droplets and ice crystals that form clouds from falling to the earth. When the tiny water droplets and ice crystals become heavier and larger, they fall out of the cloud. The cloud then loses its moisture and becomes smaller or blows away.)

As a mass of warm air rises, it has reduced pressure and expands. The expansion cools the air. Eventually, and depending on its humidity, the water vapor will start to condense and form droplets. If the air in the cloud is warmed again, the droplets will evaporate and the cloud will disappear. Sometimes when the conditions are right, a cloud will form at the surface of the land or water. When this happens, it is called fog. Fog is a cloud that occurs on the surface of water or land. (Ralph Brainard.)

3. Colliding water drops

Materials

An eye dropper, water, food color, a piece of waxed paper, a paper cup to mix water and food color together.

Procedure

1 With an eye dropper, drop some water drops colored with food color onto a piece of waxed paper. Have the children notice how the water forms little beads on the waxed paper. The beads stay separate unless they touch. When the drops or beads of water touch, they collide and the small drops become bigger.

2 Lift the waxed paper up at one of the corners or edges. Have the children observe the speed at which a larger drop of water rolls in comparison to a smaller drop of water. The larger drop rolls much faster. When water drops roll and collide or touch, they become much larger. All of the little drops can be rolled to touch each other and can be made to form one large drop on the paper.

Note: One of water's properties is its ability to stick to itself. This property is called cohesion.

How does this experiment help us understand how small water droplets in a cloud can become large water droplets? (Water droplets in a cloud collide. The more activity or turbulence there is in a cloud from wind or air currents caused by differing air temperatures mixed together, the more collisions take place between water droplets. As water droplets become larger, they become heavier and move faster. If they become too heavy, they drop from the cloud.)

3 Let the children continue to experiment with the eye dropper, waxed paper, and colored water to study water drops and how they roll to form larger drops, and how large drops roll faster on the waxed paper.

Going further

Neil Ardely, in his book, *The Science Book of Weather*, suggests letting children spray a fine water mist from an atomizer bottle on to a cookie sheet to see how rain is formed. Children will be able to observe that, "When a drop of water is large and heavy enough, it runs down the cookie sheet, gathering more drops as it goes." (pg. 22.)

4. Saturation

Materials

A basin, a sponge, water, newspaper to absorb possible mess.

Procedure

1 Tell children to:
  a Pour some water into a pan.
  b Place the sponge into the pan.

What will the sponge do to the water? (The sponge will absorb some of the water from the pan.) *Note*: The amount of water absorbed will vary with the size of the sponge in relation to the amount of water. If a lot of water is in the pan, the sponge will only be able to absorb a certain amount of the water. When the sponge reaches its capacity for absorbing the water, it will not be able to hold any more water.

2 Ask the children the following kinds of questions:

How will you know when the sponge has reached its limit? (If they lift the sponge out of the basin, it will drop water.)

How will you know the sponge has not reached its limit? (If they lift the sponge out of the water, it will hold all of the water it has absorbed without dripping water.)

When does the sponge stop soaking up or absorbing water? (When it is full.)

3 *Explain*: When the sponge reaches its holding peak, it is saturated. When it is saturated, it cannot hold another drop. A sponge that is filled beyond its capacity drips water.

How is an overly saturated sponge like the air in an overly saturated cloud? (They will both drip water. When water drops fall from a cloud or clouds, it is called precipitation. Precipitation can be in the form of drizzle, rain, snow, hail, or freezing rain.)

Note: Freezing rain is rain that falls on a cold enough surface so that the water freezes immediately after hitting the ground. Hail is the result of ice pieces being blown up through a cloud and falling again, perhaps repeated many times, catching more ice on its surface until it finally falls to the ground as a large chunk of ice. Snow is formed by going from water vapor directly to ice crystals.

4 Discuss air's ability to hold water.

5 Ask the following kinds of questions:

What kind of air holds more water, warm air or cool air? (Warm air.)

What happens when warm air cools off? (It cannot hold as much water as it did and condensation occurs.)

What does a professional weather person on TV mean when he/she refers to the "relative humidity?" (Humidity refers to the amount of water in the air. When it is raining, there is 100 percent relative humidity. On a hot, muggy day, the humidity is very high. On a dry, non-muggy day, the humidity is low.) *Note*: Water vapor is always present in the air of our atmosphere.

5. Types of clouds

Materials

An encyclopedia (under "Clouds") or pictures of clouds cut from magazines that illustrate various kinds of clouds: stratus, nimbostratus, cumulus, cumulonimbus, cirrus, fog, dew, and frost.

Procedure

1 Ask the following kinds of questions:

What do clouds look like? (Listen to their responses.)

Do clouds always look alike? (No.)

What color are clouds? (Many colors at sunrise and sunset, but usually white, or shades of gray.)

Are some clouds higher in the sky than other clouds? (Yes.)

Can clouds ever be touched? (Yes, fog can be touched.)

On a cloudy day, where is the sun? (Behind the clouds.)

When you fly in an airplane, can an airplane go above the clouds? (Yes.)

When you stare at a cloud, does it stay still or does it move? (It moves, and sometimes appears to form interesting and imaginative shapes.)

What are clouds made up of? (Water droplets and ice particles.)

2 Show the children the various pictures of clouds from magazines. Discuss the pictures, and discuss the kinds of weather that usually result with the appearance of the different kinds of

clouds. You might want to give the following type of explanation to the children as you show them the various cloud pictures:

There are three basic kinds of clouds: stratus, cumulus, cirrus. Stratus clouds are layered, flat, blanket-like and spread out. They usually mean rain will come soon. Sometimes they make the sky look overcast or "white." When stratus clouds become heavy with moisture and turn "grayish," they are then called nimbostratus clouds. "Nimbo" refers to rain. Rain, snow, and/or sleet fall from nimbostratus clouds. Fog and haze are very low stratus-type clouds that can be touched. Fog feels cool and moist. It has a high relative humidity. Dew and frost are special kinds of condensation. Dew and frost occur when water vapor condenses before it rises high in the air to become a cloud. Dew appears frequently in the morning or evening after a warm, sunny day. The air is heated during the day. After the sun goes down, the air cools off quickly. The fast change in temperature from warm to cool causes much of the water vapor in the air to condense. When the water vapor condenses, it is called dew. In the morning when the sun comes up, the air is heated and the dew evaporates and becomes water vapor again. When the temperature outside drops to freezing or below, frost occurs. Frost forms like dew, but when the water vapor condenses, it freezes directly into ice crystals.

Cumulus clouds are usually rounded, puffy, and white. They look like heaps of cotton, and usually mean sunny weather. When a lot of cumulus clouds blow or connect together they can form a large, tall cloud mass. If the large, tall cloud mass is surrounded by cooler air, condensation occurs in the cloud. The cloud grows darker and the cumulus cloud becomes a cumulonimbus cloud. Nimbus refers to rain. Cumulonimbus clouds carry a lot of water. The water falls out of them as heavy rain or hail. Thunder and lightning are often heard and seen during a heavy rain from cumulonimbus clouds.

Cirrus clouds look like feathery curls very high up in the atmosphere. They appear in dry weather and usually are a warning that the weather will be changing soon. They often indicate that a storm is coming.

Going further

- Ask older children to observe the clouds in the sky. Discuss what kinds of clouds they are.
- Have them observe clouds for several weeks, so that different kinds of weather conditions are experienced.
- Ask them to try to predict the weather based on their observations of the clouds. They will need to record their observations and predictions in their science journals as well as what the weather actually was, so that they will have a record of their thoughts and observations.
- At the end of several weeks, compare what the weather was like to what the predictions were that they made.

How often were they right at predicting the weather?

Why is it difficult to predict weather more than an hour in advance?

6. Making models of clouds

Materials

For each child or group of children: blue construction paper, white chalk, cotton balls, black chalk, glue.

Procedure

1 Show the children the materials.
2 Ask them how they could make a model of what a cumulus cloud looks like.
3 Listen to their responses.
4 Demonstrate how to make a cumulus cloud and other cloud types from the materials. (See Fig. 4-21.)

V. Weather formation and measurement

1. Air masses

Materials

A physical relief globe, a teacher-made diagram or commercial store-bought diagram illustrating the various climate zones on the earth. (See Fig. 4-22.)

Procedure

1 Show the children the globe, a model of the earth.
2 *Explain*: The globe is a model of the earth. Discuss how the colors on the globe represent where land and water areas are located and what these land and water forms look like. Discuss how

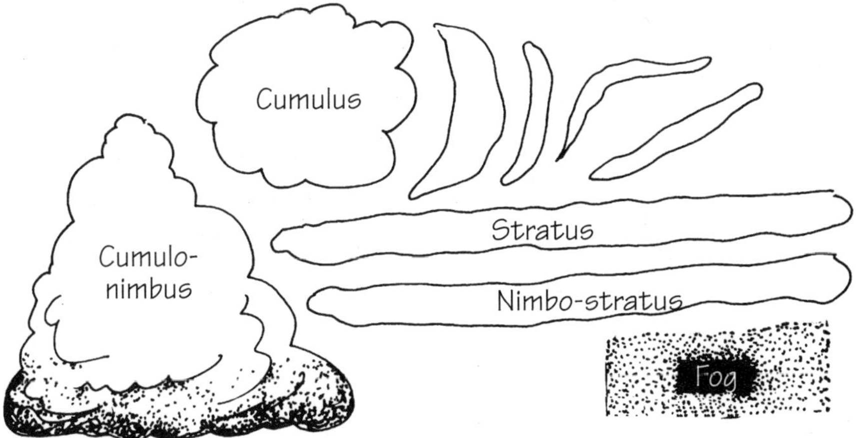

4-21 *Types of clouds.*

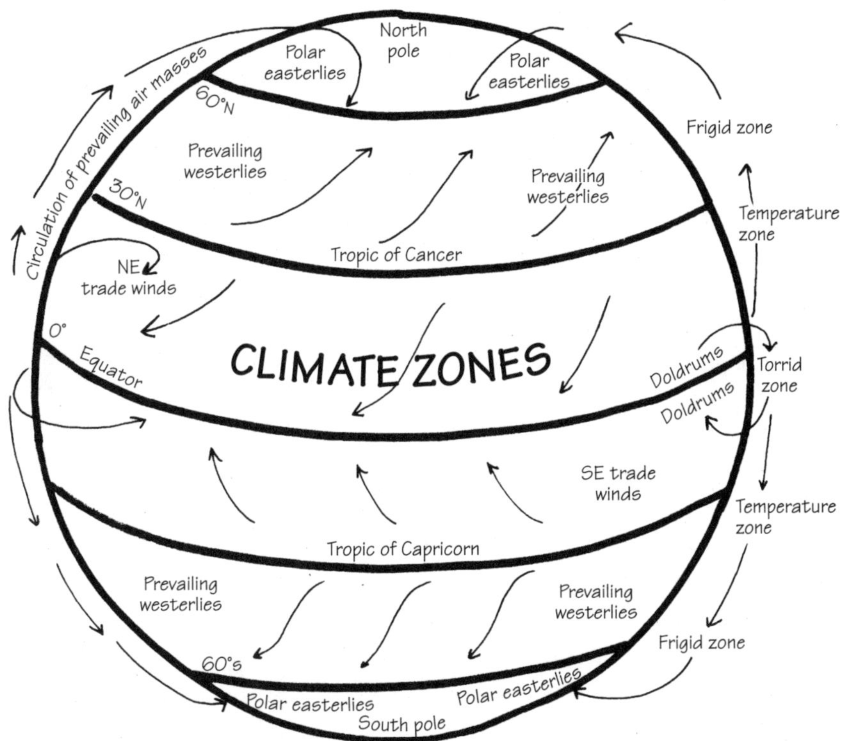

4-22 *Climate zones and circulation of prevailing air masses.*

usually the blue colors represent water areas. Different shades of blue usually mean different depths of water. Browns, greens, and yellows usually represent land areas. Greens usually represent tropical and warm areas. Yellows usually represent dry desert areas, and white usually represents cold and icy areas.

3 Study the globe with the children and help them make observations about what the climate or weather might be like at different locations on the globe. Then show them the climate zone chart and discuss how the earth's land and water areas shown on the globe can affect climate. *Note*: You might also review with the children the experience with direct and indirect rays from the sun (or from the flashlight on the globe) which was described in Activity II, Procedure 8 of this chapter. (See again Fig. 4-13.)

4 Ask the children the following kinds of questions:

When a large body of air is over the ocean and another large body of air is over the land,

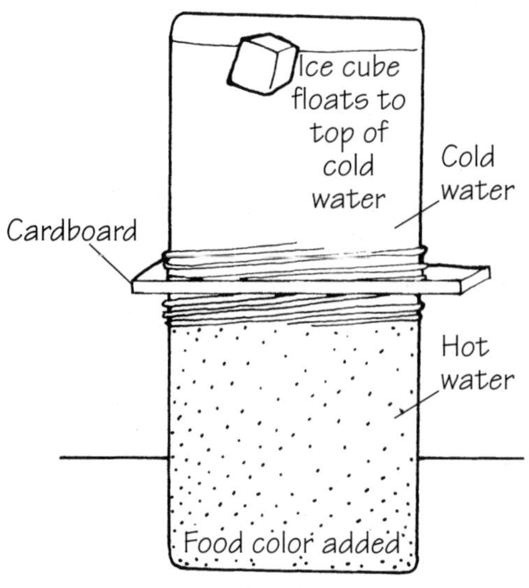

4-23 *Observe air masses meeting.*

which would be cooler during the day? (The air over the ocean.)

Which air would be warmer during the day? (The air over the land.)

Which air would feel more moist, the air over the land or the air over the water? (The air over the water would feel more moist.)

Which air would feel drier? (The air over the land or the continents would feel drier.)

Which air is warmer, the air above the poles or the air above the equator? (The air above the equator is warmer.)

Where does cooler air form? (Above the poles or ice caps.)

5 *Explain*: Air masses form over the land or the water. An air mass formed over the land or water can be very cold if it is near the poles, and very warm if it is formed near the equator. Air masses formed at the poles are called polar air masses; those that are formed near the equator are called tropical air masses. If the air mass is formed over land, it is called continental. If it is formed over water, it is called maritime. In general, air masses that form over land are dry, those that form over water are moist, those that form near the poles are cold, and those that form near the equator are warm. Winds are created when air masses with different temperatures meet. These winds blow the different air masses around the globe. Weather changes come about because of shifting or moving air masses. Air masses can be warm or cool, moist, or dry. *Note*: The different combinations of air, its temperature, and humidity bring about changes in weather, especially when two different air masses meet.

2. Air masses meet

Materials

Two small glass jars with wide mouths; food color; a piece of cardboard; hot water; cold water; an ice cube; a large basin; newspaper to absorb possible mess from water.

Procedure

1 Tell the children you are going to demonstrate for them what happens when two air masses with different temperatures meet.

2 *Explain*: Because air is difficult to see, I am going to do this demonstration with colored water.

3 Fill one of the small jars to capacity with hot water. Fill the other small jar to capacity with cold water. Add an ice cube to the jar filled with cold water. Add food color to the jar filled with hot water.

How can you tell if the air surrounding the water is hot or cold? (By feeling it.)

What do you think will happen to the hot water if you place the jar of cold water on top of it upside-down? (Listen to their responses.)

4 Place the jar filled with hot water in a basin. Take a piece of cardboard and place it on top of the lip of the jar filled with cold water. As you turn the jar upside-down, push down on the cardboard so that the water does not spill out of the jar. Gently place the two jar lips together with the piece of cardboard placed between them. Slowly remove the cardboard by sliding it out from between the lips of the two jars. (See Fig. 4-23.)

5 Discuss the results with the children. The hot, colored water will move up into the cold water in a swirling pattern. They will be able to see the hot water moving up because it will have had food color added to it. If they look closely at the water near the ice cube, they will notice that a current is floating down from the ice cube as the cube melts. Eventually, the cold water is the same color as the colored hot water. It all happens in less than a minute.

6 *Explain*: All of this motion that happens so quickly is called wind or turbulence. It is a fast, violent action. Wind or turbulence happens to large air masses when they meet, if they have different air temperatures. Storms grow out of turbulence. Storms are winds that move extremely fast. The stronger the wind blows, the more force it has.

Going further

Audrey Brainard suggested placing a small vial with colored hot water covered with clear plastic wrap at the bottom of a deep, clear basin or bowl filled with cold water. Pierce the plastic wrap with a toothpick after it is placed in the container with cold water. Observe what happens to the hot water in the small vial.

What will happen if you freeze water colored with food color in an ice cube tray and let these colored ice cubes melt in a container filled with room-temperature water?

Will the color in the melting ice cubes float up or sink to the bottom?

3. Beaufort wind scale

Materials

A chart illustrating the symbols that represent the Beaufort Wind Scale (can be homemade). (See NOAA Hurricane Warning by Branley and Kessler, stock #03-018-00075-0, 35¢ each, U.S. Government Printing Office.)

Procedure

1 *Explain*: In 1805, Sir Francis Beaufort invented a way to record wind speed or force of the wind. He described the wind as happening at a force between 0 and 12. A force of 1 means a calm, gentle breeze. A force of 12 is a strong, powerful, and destructive wind called a hurricane. He suggested that you could tell how fast the wind was blowing by looking at what the wind did to other things.

What does the force of wind tell us? (How fast a weather change might occur and the kind of weather it might bring.)

2 Show the children the chart and discuss the different kinds of wind they have experienced. A wind can be described as light, gentle, moderate, or strong. It can be called a breeze, a gale, or a storm.

What kind of wind is blowing outside of our window now?

4. Anemometer

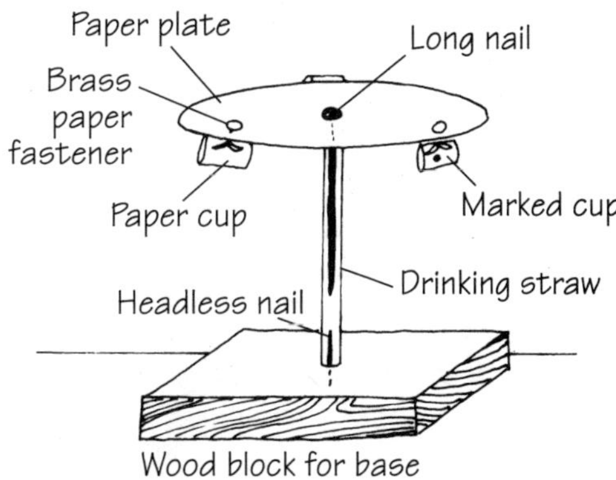

4-24 *Model anemometer.*

Materials

For each child or group of children to make a model of an anemometer: a paper plate, three paper fasteners, three paper cups, a headless nail, half of a drinking straw, a small block of wood, and a marking pen.

Procedure

1 Another way that we can find out how fast the wind is blowing is by using an anemometer. An anemometer is a special instrument that weather people use to measure how fast the wind is blowing. Demonstrate how the model of an anemometer works.

2 *Explain*: The little black mark has to be counted each time the anemometer turns so that you know how many times it turned during a certain amount of time, like a minute. The wind speed can be figured out by counting the number of times the anemometer spins per unit of time.

3 Have children make their own model of an anemometer.

5. Weather vane

Materials

For each child or group of children to make a model of a weather vane: an arrow that can spin, tagboard, glue, a headless nail, half of a drinking straw, a small block of wood, a marking pen. (See Fig. 4-25.)

Procedure

1 *Explain*: Another weather instrument that weather people use to help them record weather is a weather vane. Show the children the model of a

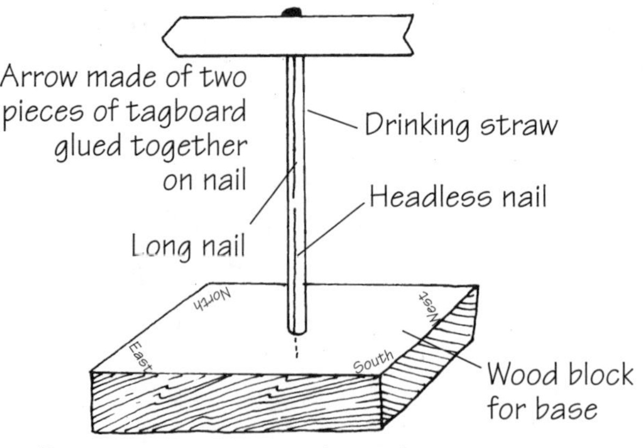

4-25 *Model weather vane.*

weather vane. Have the children blow on it. It will spin. The weather vane shows us which direction wind is blowing from. When the arrow points, it points toward the direction from which the wind is blowing. If the arrow points north, that means the wind is coming from the north.

2 Have the children make their own model of a weather vane.

6. Thermometer

Materials

Two basins, hot water, cold water, two weather thermometers, newspaper to absorb possible mess, front page of morning newspaper for weather report.

Procedure

1 Show the children the thermometer. Ask them if they know what it is.

What is a thermometer used for? (It measures the amount of heat in the air.)

2 Ask the following kinds of questions:

How can you tell what the weather and temperature are like outside without going outside to find out? (By reading an outside thermometer through an indoor window, by listening to the radio or television weather report, or by looking at the front page of the morning newspaper. Have children look at the front page of the paper to see the weather summary located in the top left- or right-hand corner of the front page. A full weather report is also listed in the index at the bottom of the page.)

What is inside a thermometer? (A liquid that is very sensitive to changes in air temperature. The liquid is usually a metal called mercury. It expands and contracts with changing temperature.)

Will the liquid inside a thermometer go up or down when it is cold? (Down.)

3 Show the children the two thermometers. Pour hot water into one of the basins and cold water into the other basin. Place a thermometer into each basin. Look for the results on the thermometer.

(Hot will register high, cold will register low.)

7. A bottle thermometer

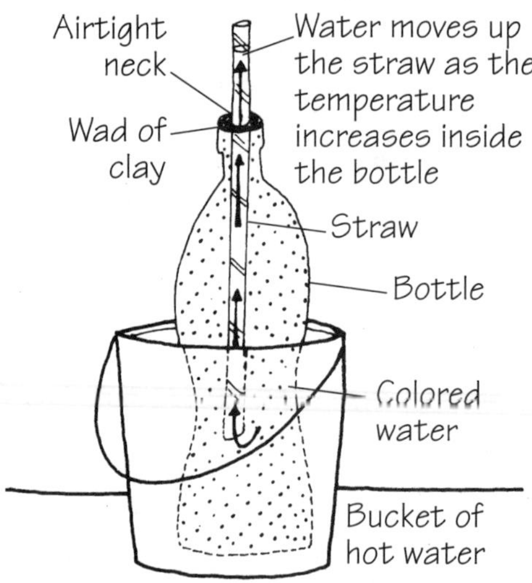

4-26 *As temperature increases, the water will move up the straw.*

Materials

A small, empty soda bottle; water; a drinking straw; plasticine or clay; a bucket of ice water; a bucket of hot water; an index card; Scotch tape; food color; newspaper to absorb possible mess.

Procedure

1 Fill the empty soda bottle with colored water. Place a wad of clay around the

perimeter of a drinking straw. Put the drinking straw with clay wrapped around it on top of the soda bottle so that half of the straw is in the bottle and half of the straw is sticking out of the bottle. Be sure the clay is squeezed in between the straw and the neck of the soda bottle so that it is airtight. (See Fig. 4-26.)

2 Put the bottle in the bucket of hot water. Observe what happens to the colored liquid in the bottle. (It will start to rise. It might even go out the top of the straw.

3 Put the bottle thermometer in the bucket of ice water. Observe what happens to the liquid in the straw. (It will go down, just like a real thermometer.)

Why does the liquid go up and down inside the straw? (The liquid moves up and down in the straw because it is affected by temperature. Warm things expand and take up more space; cool things contract and take up less space.) *Note*: You can use the index card as a marker. Tape it to the straw. Take a reading on the bottle thermometer when it is hot and mark it on the card with a line. Take another reading when it is cool and mark it on the card. Take another reading that is at room temperature. Compare the readings to that of the mercury thermometer. You can put degree numbers on the line marks on the index card by taking another measurement with a mercury thermometer at the same time.

The bottle expands from the heat too, when it is heated, but it does not expand as much as the water does. Different materials have different rates of expansion.

4 After your demonstration, allow older children to make their own bottle thermometers.

Glass bottles are probably too dangerous for younger children to play with unless they are closely supervised one-on-one by a responsible adult.

8. Weather fronts

Materials

Teacher- or parent-made models of sun, rain, and clouds to represent a warm front and a cold front made from: tagboard, crayons, and marking pen.

Procedure

1 *Explain*: Air masses can be warm or cold. When the air masses meet, they form a front. A front is the line that forms between two air masses before the "battle" occurs. When the "battle" occurs, weather changes.

2 Show the children the models of the rain, the sun, and the clouds that represent a warm front and a cold front. Code the clouds with different colors like red for warm and blue for

4-27 *Weather front demonstrated by children. When air masses meet they form a front. The weather changes. Warm air rises up and cool air settles down. The air masses "battle" and wind and turbulence are seen and felt. Circular movements occur both up and down and sideways.*

cold, or with symbols: + for warm, and – for cool. Let the children decide.

3 Tell the children that you will be using these models of the rain, the sun, and the warm and cold air masses to demonstrate how weather fronts move and how they "battle" each other. Use the cloud models as you explain about fronts. You might want to explain fronts in the following way:
   - A warm front contains a mass of warm air. Warm air has low pressure. It is light in weight. It spreads out and rises.
   - A cold front contains a mass of cool air. Cool air has high pressure. It is heavy and sinks.
   - A stationary front is a stalemate on the "battle" line between two masses of air that do not move. A stationary front can change quickly or can stay around a while. If the stationary front moves on quickly so that the two air masses slide past each other, the weather does not change much. If the stationary front stays for a few days, the weather will gradually change. First, it will rain for a few days, and then the sky will clear.

9. Barometer

Materials

A real aneroid barometer (with a dial) or a mercury barometer (with a long glass tube); a model of a barometer made from: tagboard, paper fastener, marking pen, crayons. See Fig. 4-28.

Procedure

1 Show the children the barometer and the model of a barometer.

2 *Explain*: A barometer is a special weather instrument that measures the amount of pressure in the air. Barometers help us to predict the weather. Move the pointer on the model barometer. Tell the children that when the pointer moves, it tells us about the weather and when the barometer does not change; it also tells us about the weather.

3 Move the pointer on the dial as you give the following kind of explanation: If the pointer on the dial moves down to a low number, it means that the pressure is low. When the pressure is low, it means that a warm front is approaching and that rainy days might be arriving soon. If the pointer on the

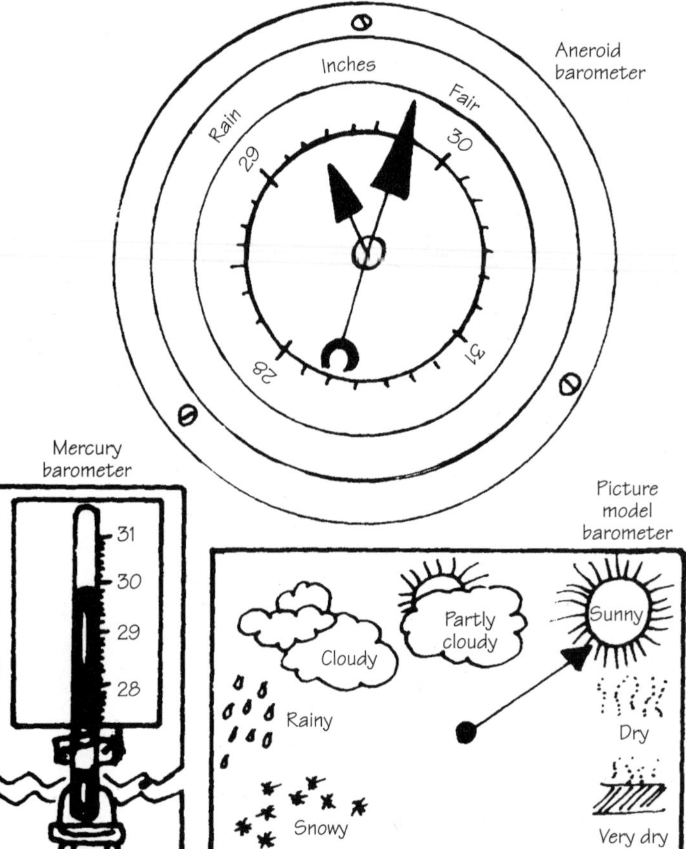

4-28 *Kinds of barometers.*

dial stays still or steady, it means that the weather is not changing or is stationary. A stationary front means that two air masses have met, but they are not moving. If a stationary front moves on or only stays for a short time, the weather does not change much. If the stationary front stays put for a while and does not move, then the weather does change. The change is gradual and slow. It will rain or snow for a few days and then the sky will look clear again.

If the pointer on the dial moves up to a high number, it means that the pressure is high. When the pressure is high, it means that a cold front is approaching. A quick rainstorm or snowstorm that will last only a few hours will occur, and then the sky will clear and sunny days will follow.

4 Have children make their own model of a barometer.

10. Rain gauge

Materials

For each child or group of children to make a model rain gauge: an empty tin can, a funnel, a ruler, a sprinkling can filled with water, newspaper to absorb possible mess from water.

Procedure

1 Tell the children that when it rains, weather people like to record how much rain fell. They keep records of rainfall. They measure the rainfall by collecting the rain when it falls. Demonstrate how to use the model rain gauge. Explain that because it cannot rain indoors, you are using a sprinkling can filled with water to represent a cloud that is dropping rain. Let the "rain" fall into the funnel on top of the can. See Fig. 4-29.

2 Let it "rain" for a minute or less. Then use the ruler to measure how much

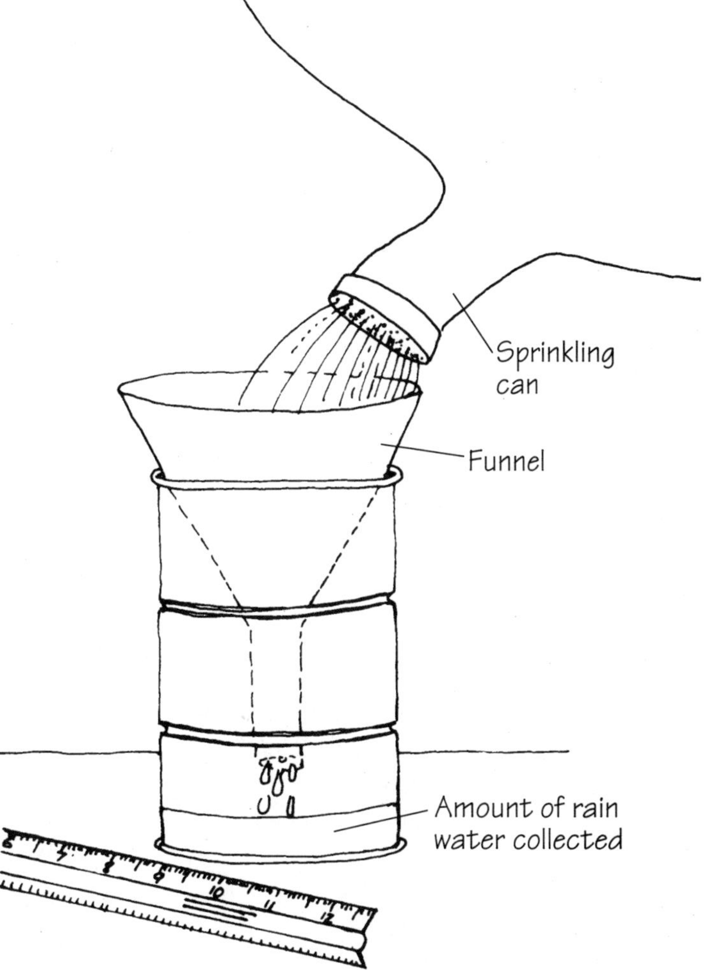

4-29 *To measure the amount of "rain" that falls, stick the ruler into the can when the "rain" stops.*

"rain" fell. Stick the ruler in the water and take a reading. Explain that a real rain gauge is much larger than the model, but that a real rain gauge measures rain water in the same way.

3 Have children make their own model of a rain gauge.

II. Record keeping

Materials

Tagboard calendar for a weather-keeping chart; ruler; crayons and marking pens; cut paper symbols of the sun, clouds, rain, and snow.

Procedure

1 Tell the children that the chart represents a month. It is like a calendar. Weather people record their day-to-day measurements. The measurements are called data. Ask the children the following kinds of questions:

What kinds of data do weather people collect? (Temperature, air pressure, rainfall, humidity, wind speed and wind direction, cloud formation, sunrise and sunset, high tide, and low tide.)

What are the names of some of the weather instruments that weather people use? (Thermometer, wind vane, anemometer, barometer, rain gauge, satellite pictures of clouds.)

What kinds of things could you collect data on during a month? (Temperature, rainfall, the kind of day it was, i.e., sunny, cloudy, rainy, snowy. The other data would depend on the weather instruments available to you.

2 Suggest that children make and keep their own records of weather for a month. Supply them with materials to make their own charts.

Further resources

Selected books for children

The Dewey Decimal Classification number for weather is: 551.5, 536 (hot and cold.)

Ardley, Neil. *The Science Book of Weather*. New York: Gulliver Books (HBJ, 1992. (Beautiful color photographs of weather experiments.)

Ardley, Neil. *The Science Book of Hot and Cold*. New York: Gulliver Books (HBJ, 1992. (Beautiful color photographs of experiments with hot and cold temperatures.)

Bains, Rae. *Water*. Mahwah, NJ: Troll, 1985. (Explains the water cycle.)

Branley, Franklyn M. *It's Raining Cats and Dogs*. New York: Houghton-Mifflin, 1987. (Grades 2–4.)

Branley, Franklyn M. *Flash, Crash, Rumble and Roll: Let's Read and Find Out*. New York: Thomas Y. Crowell, rev. ed., 1985. (Describes and illustrates how and why electrical storms occur.)

Branley, Franklyn M. *Rain and Hail: Let's Read and Find Out*. New York: Thomas Y. Crowell, rev. ed., 1983. (Picture book for young children and older children with large illustrations explaining the process of precipitation and the water cycle.)

Branley, Franklyn. *Hurricane Watch: A Let's Read to Find Out Book*. New York: Crowell Jr. Books, 1985. (Appropriate for children from K–3.)

Carlisle, Madelyn Wood. *Sparkling, Silent Snow*. Hauppauge, N.Y.: Barron's Educational, 1992. (snow/experiments.)

Dorros, Arthur. *Feel the Wind: A Let's-Read-and-Find-Out Book*. New York: Thomas Y. Crowell, 1989. (The book explains what causes wind and how it affects our environment. Includes instructions for making a weather vane.)

Ganeri, Anita. *The Usborne Book of Weather Facts*. London: Usborne, 1987. (For children who can read.)

Gans, Roma. *Water for Dinosaurs and You: Let's Read and Find Out*. New York: Thomas Y. Crowell, 1973. (Picture book appropriate for young children. It describes the water cycle.)

Gibbons, Gail. *Weather Words and What They Mean*. New York: Holiday, 1990.

Gibbons, Gail. *Weather Forecasting*. New York: Holiday, 1990.

Jennings, Terry. *Weather*. New York: Gloucester Press, 1990.

Lerner, Carol. *A Forest Year*. New York: Morrow, 1987.

Selected resource books for adults and older children

Berger, Melvin. *Seasons*. New York: Doubleday, 1990.

Branley, Franklyn M., and Leonard Kessler. *Hurricane Warning*. Washington, D.C.: U.S. Dept. of Commerce, National Oceanic and Atmospheric Administration, and National Weather Service, Stock No. 003-018-00075-0, U.S. Government Printing Office. 35¢ each.

Lind, Karen K. *Water, Stones, 7 Fossil Bones: A CESI Sourcebook*. Washington, D.C.: Council for Elementary Science International, 1991.

Mandell, Muriel. *Simple Weather Experiments with Everyday Materials*. New York: Sterling, 1991.

Minnesota Environmental Sciences Foundation, Inc. *Snow and Ice: An Environmental Investigation*. Washington, D.C.: National Wildlife Federation, 1971. (Interesting investigative experiments.)

Pearce, Q.L. *Lightning and Other Wonders of the Sky; The Amazing Science Series*. Morristown, NJ: Silver Burdett, 1989. (Introduces wonders of the earth's atmosphere, including auroras, mirages, trade winds, dust storms, acid rain, and meteor showers.)

Ramsey, Dan. *Weather Forecasting: A Young Meteorologist's Guide*. TAB Books, 1990. (For older children who know how to read.)

Sabin, Louis. *Weather*. Mahwah, NJ: 1985. (Contains information about weather forecasting.)

Santrey, Laurence. *What Makes the Wind?* Mahwah, NJ: Troll, 1982. (Has beautiful watercolor pictures.)

Usborne Book of Weather Facts. London: Usborne, 1987.

Wellnitz, William R. *Science in Your Backyard*. TAB Books, 1992. (See Part III—Earth Science Experiments. For children who know how to read.)

Whitfield, Dr. Philip and Pope, Joyce. *Why Do Seasons Change?* New York: Viking, 1987.

Wood, Robert W. *Science for Kids: 39 Easy Meteorology Experiments*. TAB Books, 1991. (For children who know how to read and want to do more investigations about weather.)

Wyatt, Valerie. *Weatherwatch*. Reading, Mass: Addison-Wesley, 1990.

Selected Literature Connections for Younger Children

Barrett, Judi. *Cloudy with a Chance of Meatballs*. New York: Aladdin, 1978. (A humorous story about a tiny town where food falls from the sky. A place where it really rains cats and dogs.)

Ets, Marie Hall. *Gilberto and the Wind*. New York: Viking Press, 1963. (A story about a little boy who plays with the wind.

Gibbons, Gail. *Sun Up, Sun Down*. New York: HBJ, 1983. (A story about the sun and the water cycle for young children.)

Hutchins, Pat. *The Wind Blew*. New York: Scholastic, 1993. (A humorous story about the wind "stealing" objects from people.)

Martin Jr., Bill and John Archambault. New York: Holt, 1988. *Listen to the Rain*. (Story about the sounds of rain. Has rich vocabulary and beautiful pictures.

Pollaco, Patricia. *Thunder Cake*. New York: Philomel, 1990. (A story about a grandmother who comforts her granddaughter during a thunder storm.)

Shaw, Charles G. *It looked Like Spilt Milk*. New York: Harper, 1947. (A mystery story with white pictures on a blue background. About cloud shapes.)

General community enrichment activities

Visit a weather station A weather station can be found at an airport, college, or high school. Observe the profesional equipment used to measure and find out about weather. Observe the weather logs and the record keeping that takes place. Talk to the meteorologist on duty. Find out what kind of training he/she had, what he/she likes to rely on the most for predicting weather. How accurate are their forecasts?

Visit a meteorologist at a television station Observe a weather report being broadcast. Notice how the electronic equipment creates the weather report. Observe how the weather person needs to look at a monitor to see what he/she is pointing at. (The screen behind the weather person that we see at home is usually a blank blue wall for the weather person!) Observe how the weather person gathers information to report. Where does the information come from?

5

Volcanoes, rocks, and erosion

Objectives

For children to develop an understanding of the following:

- What volcanoes are.
- Why an eruption occurs.
- What a cross-section model represents.
- What seismic waves are.
- The differences between the interior layers of the earth and the outside layer of crust on the earth.
- That islands do not float in the ocean but are really tall, mountainous elevations that stick up above the water line.
- That different types of rocks have different physical properties or attributes that help us to distinguish rocks from one another.
- The various properties of rocks and the terms used to describe those properties.
- That rocks can be classified or grouped by the way they were formed.
- Erosion and how it can occur by mechanical action or through chemical action.
- How sediments can be loosened, moved, and built up.
- How mountains can form from pressure.

General background information for parents and teachers

Volcano An opening in the earth's crust. Magma, gases, rock fragments, lava, and ash are expelled from the opening or vent. It is often shaped like a mountain.

Shield volcanoes Shield volcanoes are basically flat-looking in their appearance. Magma can erupt from several vents at the same time. Lava flows very fast and is very fluid.

Cinder volcanoes Cinder volcanoes are shaped like flat-topped mountains. The lava from this kind of volcano flows slower and is sticky. It tends to have more rock fragments, ash, and dust than does the more fluid liquid lava that erupts from a shield volcano.

Composite volcanoes Composite volcanoes are shaped like high-peaked mountains. They are formed from both sticky and highly liquid lava in alternate layers.

Volcanic eruption A volcanic activity that allows magma, gases, ash, and rocks to move up and emerge from the interior of a volcano. Eruptions are often sudden and violent.

Volcanic activity Volcanoes can be active, inactive, or extinct. Active volcanoes still have eruptions. Inactive volcanoes have infrequent eruptions. Extinct volcanoes no longer have eruptions.

Volcanologist A scientist who studies volcanoes.

Magma Hot liquid rock. Igneous rocks are formed from magma.

Lava Magma that emerges from a volcano's interior.

Crater Opening or vent on top of a volcano.

Cone Shape of some volcanoes.

Magma pipe Located in the interior of the volcano. It is a vertical space or tunnel shape that is formed from the pressure of magma pushing up.

Magma chamber Located deep within the earth, under the volcanic area. It contains a large mass of magma.

Caldera A very large vent or crater opening caused by the collapse of a volcano's top.

Seismologist A scientist who studies the vibrations caused by earthquakes. The discoveries and findings of seismologists have helped us create theories and gain knowledge about the earth's interior and about the movements of the earth. Seismologists make predictions about sites and approximate times for future earthquakes and volcanic eruptions based on their knowledge gained from previous movements they have observed.

Seismic waves Waves or earth tremors that can be measured by a seismograph machine. There are three kinds of seismic waves: Primary waves are often called P waves. They are the first set of waves that are sent out from an earthquake. They travel the fastest and penetrate deeply. They create a ricocheting pattern of pushes and pulls. Secondary waves are often called S waves. They travel slower than the primary waves. S waves arrive after the P waves. S waves travel in an up-and-down or side-to-side pattern like an S. Surface waves or L waves arrive last but do the most damage. They travel the slowest of the seismic waves. They travel along the crust or surface of the earth and cause much destruction.

Seismograph A machine that measures and records vibrations on the earth's surface or crust.

Seismogram A picture of wavelengths made by a seismograph machine. The actual recording on paper by the machine.

Richter Scale A scale ranging in numerical value from 1 to 10. It indicates how violent or calm an earthquake's seismogram reading was. A numerical value of 1 indicates that the quake had the least amount of energy. A numerical value of 10 would indicate that an enormous amount of energy was expended.

Gas A state of matter. Gases have the ability to expand and contract greatly depending on the relative changes in the amount of temperature and pressure. Gases also have the ability to spread out easily and uniformly.

Cross-section A diagram that depicts an internal slice of something that has dimensions.

Globe A model of the earth.

Earth's crust The relatively thin outer layer of the earth that we live on. It consists of the land and the water we see. It is the outside layer of the earth, and is believed to be about 25 miles thick. Under the ocean, the crust is about 3 miles thick.

Bedrock Layer of solid rock that lies underneath the soil.

Earth's mantle The interior layer of the earth beneath the crust. It is believed to be about 1,800 miles thick and is thought to be made up of solid rock.

Core The innermost part of the earth. The core consists of an inner and an outer core. The inner core is thought to be a solid area made up of iron and nickel. The outer core is thought to be a nonsolid area that is molten (hot liquid).

Fault A broken section of the earth's crust along which movement occurs.

Fault line An extended fault. A weak section of the earth's crust where earthquakes and volcanoes have occurred.

Volcano or earthquake zones There are three principal areas where volcanic and earthquake activity frequently occur.

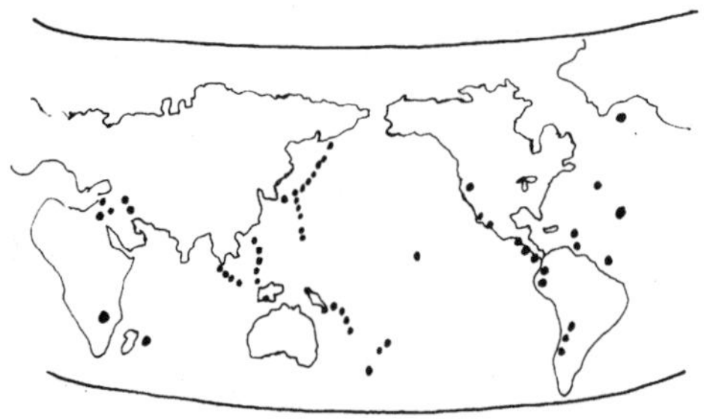

5-2 *Dots represent volcanic activity and eruptions.*

They are:

- The Ring of Fire—A circular line that runs along and near the edges or coastlines of the continents that border the Pacific Ocean.
- The Mid-Atlantic Ridge—A line that runs from Iceland to the South Pole under the midline of the Atlantic Ocean.
- The Mediterranean Region—A perpendicular extension line branching off the Mid-Atlantic Ridge. It runs under the Mediterranean Sea past Asia and India and connects to the Ring of Fire between Australia and New Zealand.

Earthquake When the earth's crust breaks apart suddenly and slides in two different directions, creating a disturbance of existing natural and human-made structures on the crust.

Rock A combination of two or more minerals.

Mineral A mineral is something that is found in nature that was never alive. No matter where it is found, it always has a nearly uniform chemical composition. Also, the atoms of a mineral are arranged in a regular pattern that forms a unique crystal structure. Minerals have fairly constant physical properties. Their physical properties are described in terms of: hardness, crystal formation, color, streak, luster, weight, and cleavage. Many minerals end with the suffix "ite." There are about 2,000 kinds of minerals. Only about one hundred of them are common.

Element A substance made up of molecules that consist of only one kind of atom.

Crystal formation A crystal is a pure mineral. The atoms of a crystal are arranged in a unique pattern. Every mineral has its own special crystal structure and formation or pattern.

Chemical bond A bond that holds the atoms together in a crystal.

Cleavage Refers to the way a rock breaks. Weak chemical bonds along an atomic structure or crystal formation form cleavage or breaking points where crystals or rocks break apart.

Luster Refers to the shine and sparkle of some rocks. Luster can be metallic, nonmetallic, pearly, dull, brilliant, glossy, etc.

Hardness Rocks vary in their degree of hardness and softness. Hard rocks can scratch softer rocks.

Moh's Hardness Scale A scale that is numbered 1 through 10, placing a numerical value on the relative hardness or softness of rocks in relation to other rocks. The softest is #1. The hardest is #10. The complete scale is: #1 talc, #2 gypsum, #3 calcite, #4 fluorite, #5 apatite, #6 feldspar, #7 quartz, #8 topaz, #9 corundum, #10 diamond. #1 and #2 can be scratched by a fingernail. #3 can be scratched by a copper coin. #4 and #5 can be scratched by a knife, scissor blade, or window glass. #6, #7, and #8 can scratch a knife, scissor blade, or window glass. #10 scratches most other materials.

Color Rocks with different kinds of minerals have different colors.

Streak A line of luster that runs through some rocks. Also the line of color that is left on an unglazed ceramic tile when certain rocks are rubbed on to the tile.

Weight or density Refers to the solidity of a rock. The more solid the density, the heavier the rock. A difference in density gives two rocks that are the same size a different weight.

Igneous rocks Rocks made from fire, formed by the cooling of hot liquid magma. The magma solidifies and forms igneous rocks. The original magma for igneous rocks comes from the inner depths of the earth. Lava, granite, and quartz are examples or forms of igneous rocks.

Metamorphic Refers to change. It means a change takes place.

Metamorphic rocks Rocks that began as another kind of rock and have undergone a change. Rocks undergo metamorphosis or change when they are subjected to extreme amounts of pressure and/or heat. Metamorphic rocks were originally igneous or sedimentary rocks. For example, marble is formed from limestone; slate is formed from shale.

Gemstone A precious or semiprecious stone that can be used as a jewel after it has been cut and polished. Most gemstones are forms of metamorphic rocks.

Lapidary A person who specializes in cutting, polishing, and engraving gemstones.

Sedimentary rocks Rocks that were formed over a period of time in layers. Often formed in low areas or under water from sediments of mud and silt that have been deposited by rivers and streams. The sediments become cemented together over time to form layers of sedimentary rock. Clay and limestone are examples of sedimentary rock.

Organic Materials that are organic contain molecules of carbon. Materials that were once alive and therefore are combustible and can be burned are organic. Fossil fuels like coal are organic.

Sediment Small pieces of dust and soil that have broken away from larger pieces of land and rock and all the shells of small sea animals. Sediment has usually been carried and dropped by water, wind, or glaciers.

Glacier A glacier is formed when water freezes inside of a valley. Glaciers are very high piles of ice. Pressure from heavy, newly fallen snow that has been compacted creates even higher piles of ice. The ice that is piled high above the bottommost layer of ice is under a lot of pressure. This immense pressure causes the bottom layer of ice to flow or move (but not melt). When a glacier flows or moves, it carries rocks with it. When the pressure is released through the movement of the glacier, the water created from friction of movement refreezes.

The refreezing of the glacier is similar to what happens to ice when you go ice-skating. The ice directly under the blade of an ice skate is under a lot of pressure. The ice under the blade melts for an instant and acts as a lubricant for the blade. When the blade moves, the ice refreezes.

Erosion A natural process that wears away rock and earth. Erosion can take place from weathering, from wind, from glacial action, from corrosion, from grinding action, and from movement of earth and rocks from one place to another.

Fold An area on the earth's crust that has been bent due to enormous internal pressure from gas or magma deep inside the earth. It can be an upward, downward, or lateral movement of the crust. Some mountains are formed due to folding. Some folds take 1,000 years or more to form. Some folds form quickly. Some folds are small; others are enormous.

Note: As you do these activities with your children, try to encourage them to keep a science journal of their observations and their thoughts.

Activities and procedures

I. Volcanoes

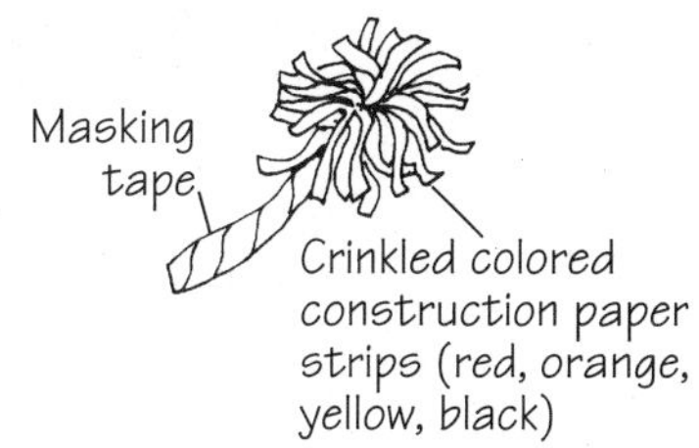

5-3A *Pom-pom for inside of volcano model.*

1. Three-dimensional cardboard model* of a volcano

Materials

For each child or group of children: piece of cardboard; paper rolled into a tube shape; pieces of yellow, red, black, and orange construction paper cut into strips ¼-inch wide by 8 inches long; corner of a cardboard box; masking tape; marking pens in assorted colors.

Preparation

1 Roll masking tape around the wad of colored construction paper strips. (Crinkle the strips up. It should look like a mini-pom-pom. See Fig. 5-3A.)
2 Mount the corner of a cardboard box onto the piece of cardboard.
3 Cut a hole at the top of the corner and through the piece of cardboard.
4 Stuff the piece of paper rolled into a tube shape through the two holes. (See Fig. 5-3B.)

* A model is a representation of the "real" thing. See chapter 1 for further explanation.

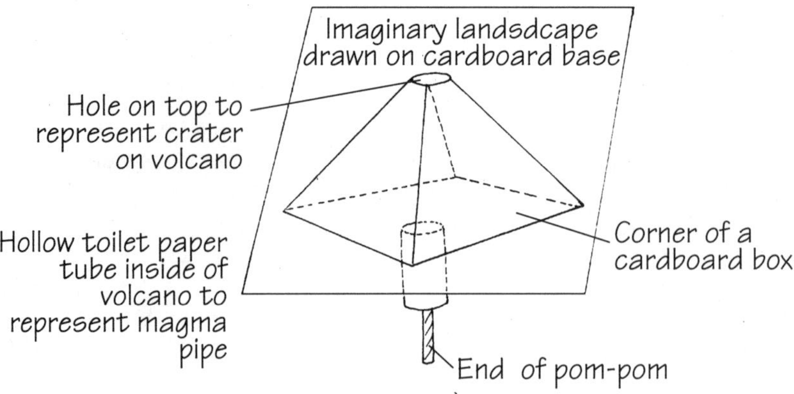

5-3B *Volcano model.*

5 Use colored marking pens to create an imaginary landscape on the piece of cardboard and on the cone-shaped cardboard corner.

Procedure

1 Show the children the three-dimensional cardboard model after it is constructed.

2 *Explain*: This is a model of a volcano. Ask the children to identify the parts of the model volcano. Encourage children to use the following terms to describe the parts of a volcano:
   - a Crater for the hole on the top of the cone.
   - b Cone for the cardboard corner.
   - c Magma pipe for the paper tube.
   - d Crust for the piece of flat cardboard.
   - e Magma for the pom-pom that is pushed up the paper tube. Push the pom-pom up the paper tube to demonstrate how the magma travels up the magma pipe.
   - f Magma chamber for the area directly underneath the magma pipe.

3 As you push the model magma up the magma pipe, explain:
   - a The magma rises up the pipe because of pressure that builds up inside of the earth from gases that have warmed up and expanded.
   - b The magma is hot liquid rock.
   - c Magma is made up of rocks that become so hot that they melt. The hot liquid rock causes gases to build up and expand.
   - d The pressure from the hot gases becomes so great and powerful that the gas cannot be contained. It has to escape.
   - e When these hot gases escape above the ground, an eruption occurs. It is called a volcanic eruption. The eruption continues until the built-up, hot gases escape through the open crater holes in the volcano.
   - f When the gases have finished escaping, the volcano stops erupting.
   - g Volcanoes that do not erupt any more are called extinct. Those that have a lot of eruptions are called active, and those that stay asleep or dormant for many years are called inactive.
   - h When magma comes to the surface, it is called lava. The lava is pushed out and continues to flow as long as the hot gases from deep inside are pushing up and escaping. Some of the lava forms into a fine volcanic dust that floats up with the escaping gas and forms large, black, smoky clouds.

4 Hold the flat cardboard (which represents the earth's crust) on your forehead so that your eyes are underneath the volcano.

5 *Explain*: This is where the magma chamber is located. It is deep underneath the ground. Magma is made up of hot liquid rock and gases. It expands and pressure builds up and pushes magma out. The force for the push comes from pressures inside the earth underneath the volcano.

6 After your demonstration, allow each child or group of children to make their own three-dimensional model of an erupting volcano with a magma pipe.

2. Breath

Materials

None.

Procedure

1 Tell the children to take a deep breath.
2 Explain: The air we breathe in and out is gas.
3 Tell the children to feel their breath with their hands as they breathe out. Ask them the following kinds of questions:

How does the air feel that comes out of your mouth, warm or cool? (Warm.)

How does the air feel before it enters your mouth? (Cooler.)

What is the gas called that we breathe in? (Oxygen—O_2, nitrogen, and small quantities of other gases: water vapor, carbon dioxide, etc.)

What is the gas called that we breathe out? (Carbon Dioxide—CO_2, the same as we breathe in except a little less oxygen and a little more carbon dioxide.)

4 *Explain*: When we breathe in oxygen, it goes into our lungs and body. It is a fuel that gets burned up. When the oxygen is used or burned up, it becomes carbon dioxide. The carbon dioxide becomes warm and expands. This causes us to feel "pressure" being built up in our lungs, forcing us to exhale.

INFORMATION It is not really due to "pressure," but to the medulla in our brain sensing a build-up of carbon dioxide that causes us to exhale. However, younger children will better understand the model of pressure building up in their lungs than a discussion about the sensors in their brain.

3. Holding a breath

Materials

None.

Procedure

1 Tell children to take a deep breath and to see how long they can hold their breath. (They will discover that it is impossible for them to hold their breath indefinitely because the medulla in the brain forces their bodies to let their breath out, thus allowing built-up warm gas to escape.
2 *Explain*: Our body is like an erupting volcano. When we hold our breath, gas builds up and our body forces us to open up or "erupt" and to take in a new breath of air. When our body "erupts," it forces the built-up hot gas to escape, and new gas to enter our body. When we hold our breath and "erupt," we cannot continue to erupt. Like a volcano, we stop erupting when our gas supply runs out. We are like an active volcano. We continue to erupt as long as we breathe. If we stay perfectly still and quiet, we are like an inactive volcano. Inactive volcanoes are still able to erupt. Scientists can detect rumblings inside thc magma chamber and magma pipe with seismographs and other special instruments. Sometimes these instruments can help them predict when an inactive volcano will erupt and be active. But most eruptions are difficult to predict.

Some of the instruments used by scientists to collect data on when a volcano will erupt are:

- Seismographs for detecting earthquakes in the suspected area.

Some seismographs are sensitive enough to detect earthquakes anywhere in the world (also nuclear explosions).

- Thermometers for detecting increases in temperature in the suspected area.
- Tiltmeters for detecting growth or expansion or change of a volcanic cone.
- Gas detectors for measuring increases in amounts of certain gases in the area.

4. Pictures

Materials

Assorted pictures from National Geographic magazine, Life magazine, or other pictorial source that depicts volcanic islands, volcanoes erupting, crater lakes, and/or inactive volcanoes.

Procedure

1 Show the children the pictures and discuss what volcanoes look like when they are erupting, inactive, and extinct.

What does extinct mean?

2 *Explain*: When something was, but is no longer. Dinosaurs were alive once, but they are extinct now. No one has ever seen a living dinosaur. Sometimes when a volcano becomes extinct, the

old crater fills up with water and the crater becomes a lake.

5. How a volcano grows

Materials

Flannel model of a volcanic mountain range; flannel pieces cut in assorted colors in various hues of brown to represent mountains and volcanic layers on the cone of the volcano; flannel in hues of red, gold, and orange to represent magma, magma pipe, and lava; a large flannel board about 18 inches by 24 inches.

Preparation

1 Create a mountain range out of flannel. Glue small pieces of brown flannel onto a larger piece (about 18 inches by 12 inches) to create a mountain range.

2 Create a separate magma chamber in bright red, orange, and yellow to create a feeling of intense heat.

3 Make a separate pipe-like shape that is able to slide up from the magma chamber underneath the flannel mountain range to the surface of the crust. Make the pipe about 24 inches long.

4 Cut out numerous curved strips in assorted hot colors and lengths to represent lava flowing from the volcano. Also cut out several brown cone shapes in sequential size to represent the hardened volcano after a volcanic eruption. With each eruption the volcano's cone grows in size or volume.

5 Hold the flannel board in a vertical position and place it upright. Place the pieces of flannel (which represent the magma chamber and magma pipe) underneath the mountain range, hidden from view on the flannel board. (See Figs. 5-4A and 5-4B.)

Procedure

1 Show children the flannel board. Ask them what the picture looks like on the flannel board. (A mountain range.)

2 *Explain*: A mountain range does not stay still. Change takes place gradually over a long period of time. Usually the change is so slight that we cannot see the change take place because it happens so slowly. Some mountains become smaller because weather conditions erode them away. Sometimes mountains grow very quickly, almost overnight. This happens when a lot of hot gases build up underneath them and need to escape. Sometimes the top blows off the mountain and hot lava flows out. When this happens, the mountain grows very suddenly and is called a volcano.

3 Pull up the piece of flannel that represents the magma pipe so that just a little bit of it can be seen. Ask the children the following kinds of questions:

What might be happening to the model of the mountain range? (A volcano is beginning to erupt.)

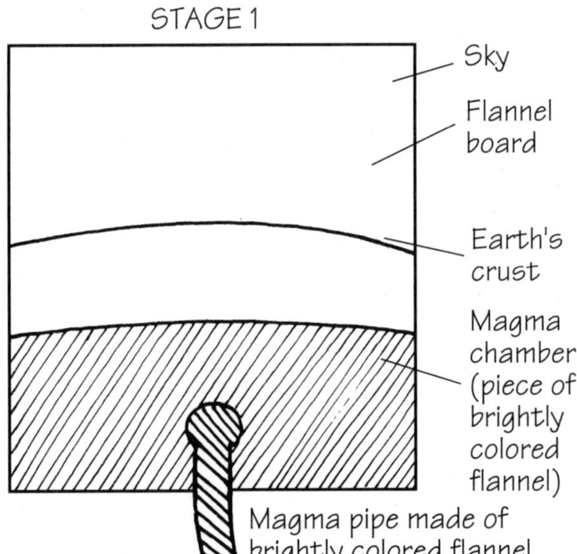

5-4A *A magma pipe begins deep inside of the earth's interior.*

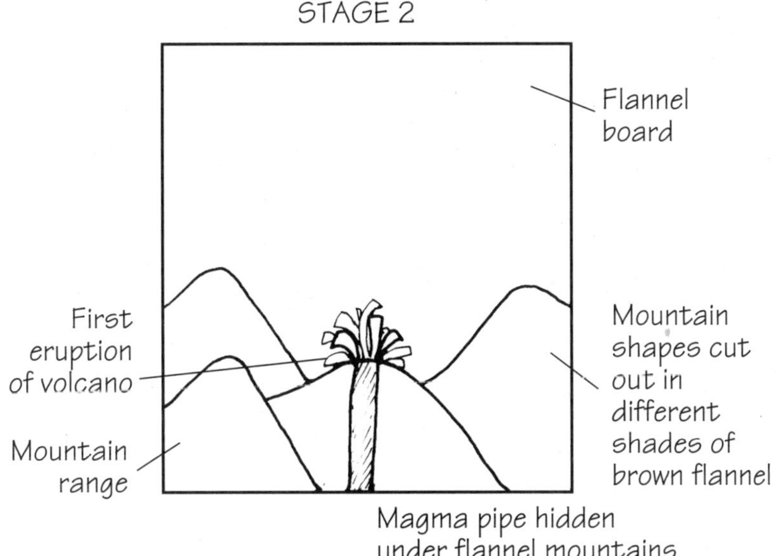

5-4B *A longer magma pipe just underneath the earth's crust, showing the first eruption.*

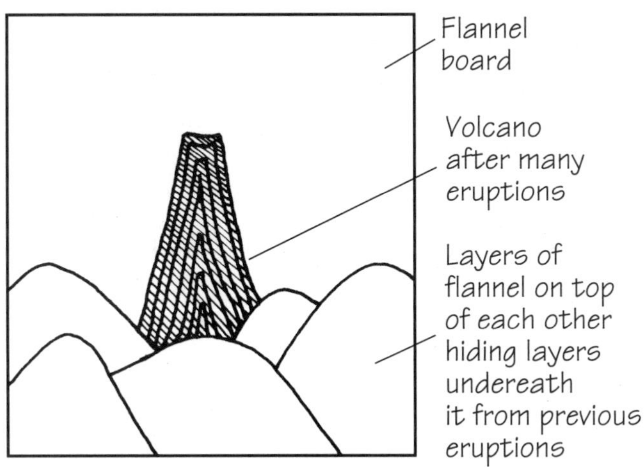

5-4C *Flannel board model after several eruptions.*

Where is the magma coming from? (From deep beneath the ground under the volcano.)

Can we normally see underneath the ground? (Normally, no.)

Is this a real volcano or a model of a volcano? (A model.)

Is it possible to look underneath the ground of a model? (Yes.)

If we lift up the mountain range and look underneath it, what might we be able to see? (The magma chamber, magma pipe, and magma.)

4 Lift off the mountain range by rolling up its right or left side.

5 Explain: The magma is coming from the magma chamber, rising through the magma pipe to the top of the volcanic cone called the crater.

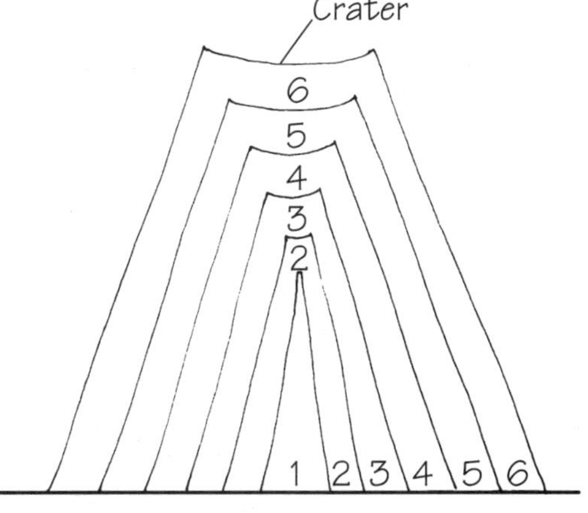

5-4D *This cross-section of a volcano indicates that it erupted six times.*

6 Place the mountain range in place again. Allow the volcano to erupt. Show the eruption by placing curved flannel strips on the flannel cone.

Then cover the cone with a larger flannel cone so that none of the lava or magma can be seen.

7 *Explain*: The volcano stays at rest or is inactive after it erupts. It stays that way until gas builds up again, and then it erupts again:
   a Pull the magma pipe up again.
   b Place lava strips on the cone again.
   c Cover the lava again with a larger sequential-sized cone.
   d Review what is happening each time by making the children describe what is happening using the appropriate vocabulary words.
   e Allow children to continue this four-step process for another three or four eruptions. (See Figs. 5-4C and 5-4D.)

8 *Explain*: Scientists are able to find out about volcanoes by taking soil samples from them and by using low-frequency sound waves that create X-ray-like pictures that give them information or data about the volcano, its age, the number of eruptions it had, and the kinds of eruptions it had.

9 When the volcano is finished erupting, call it an extinct volcano. Peel off the entire volcano so that the inside layers can be seen. Count the layers and find out how many eruptions occurred. Each sequential cone should be cut out in different shades of brown flannel.

10 Have children continue to use the flannel board model and simulate volcanic eruptions.

6. Building up layers

Materials

For each child or group of children: black, brown, and yellow construction paper; clear Contact paper; a picture of a crater lake.

Preparation

1 Cover the construction paper on both sides with clear Contact paper.

2 Cut the brown and black paper into sequential-sized V-like shapes with a flat top. Also cut out one small cone shape.

3 Cut out a yellow magma pipe and a yellow magma chamber.

Procedure

1 Show the children the construction paper shapes covered with clear Contact paper. Ask them what they look like. (Layers of a volcano.)

2 Show children how they can be arranged sequentially. Place the magma chamber down first. Slide the magma pipe underneath the magma chamber. Place the small cone on the magma pipe. Push the magma pipe up so that it sticks up above the cone. Add on a flat-topped V-shape over the cone to cover up the magma. Continue to push up the magma and to add new flat-topped V-shaped layers to the cone.

3 *Explain*: This kind of erupting volcano is called a composite volcano. It grows and expands by building up alternate

5-5 *Pieces of a paper puzzle showing volcanic eruptions.*

layers of thin and thick lava. Thin lava flows quickly, while thick lava flows more slowly. Volcanoes come in two basic shapes. They either have one crater and a cone-like shape that grows, or they are flat and have several craters or holes where hot lava shoots up and oozes out.

4 Show children the picture of a crater lake.

5 *Explain*: Sometimes when all of the gas from inside escapes, the magma chamber becomes empty. It becomes a large, empty hole. The hole collapses because of all of the weight from the earth on top of it. When this happens, the crater sinks inside of the extinct volcano and the crater's hole becomes quite large. The hole fills with water and becomes a natural lake.

7. Bottle model of an erupting volcano

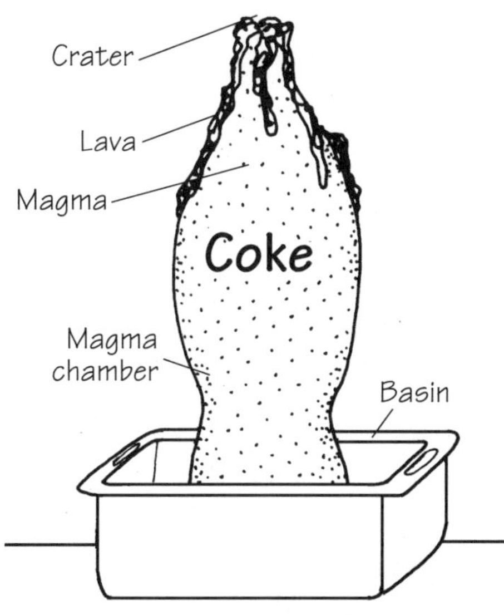

Pour water into bottle. Add liquid soap. Add baking soda. Add vinegar. Warm water brings about a faster reaction.

5-6 *Recipe for a CO_2 eruption inside a Coke bottle.*

Materials

For each child or group of children: a basin, an empty salad dressing bottle (Wishbone bottles are perfect), warm water, liquid soap, baking soda, vinegar, a teaspoon, a measuring cup.

Procedure

1 Place the bottle inside an empty basin.

2 Explain: The bottle is a model of the inside of a volcano. The inside of the bottle represents the magma chamber, the neck of the bottle represents the magma pipe, and the opening on top of the bottle represents the crater on top of the volcano where the lava flows out.

3 Have a child add about one cup of warm water to the bottle, and then have another child add a few drops of liquid detergent to the water.

4 *Explain*: The water and the soap represent hot, bubbly liquid magma inside of the magma chamber deep inside the earth.

5 Have a child add a teaspoon or two of baking soda to the warm water.

6 *Explain*: The baking soda added to warm water sets off a reaction. A gas called carbon dioxide is created when the baking soda dissolves in the warm water. The water inside the bottle is warm, and the gas expands. When air or gas expands, it tends to move up. (If a reaction does not occur, add a teaspoon or two of vinegar to the solution inside of the bottle.)

7 When the reaction occurs, suds will rise to the top of the bottle and overflow down the sides.

8 *Explain*: When magma comes to the surface of the earth and flows out of the volcano, it is called lava.

9 After your demonstration, allow the children to repeat the steps to this procedure several times. After each eruption, have the children empty the contents of the bottle into the basin, then have them fill the bottle with fresh ingredients.

10 *Explain*: The pool of liquid in the basin can represent lava before it solidifies into rock.

Fine points to discuss

Why does the model volcano stop flowing or erupting? (The gas has expanded, and the energy has been expended. It becomes inactive as it runs out of steam.)

When will the model erupt again? (When the gases build up again.)

What causes the eruption? (Gases that heat up and expand cause the eruption to occur. The eruption occurs because of internal pressure.)

8. Lava rock

Materials

A lava rock (can be purchased at a rock store, a natural history museum, or at a drugstore as a pumice stone); a non-lava rock about the same size as the lava rock; a basin of water.

Procedure

1 Show children the two rocks. Ask them if they can tell which one might weigh less by just looking at the two rocks. (The one that has lots of holes or bubbles on its surface will probably weigh less because it is not as solid-looking as the other rock.)

2 Have the children feel both rocks and notice which rock feels lighter. (The lava rock will feel lighter.)

3 Have the children smell each rock.

Do they smell alike dry? (Probably.)

4 Place the two rocks in the water and observe what happens to the lava rock. It will float. Smell the two rocks again and see if they have different odors when they are wet. (The lava rock will most likely smell like volcanic ash. It might have a very earthy and dusty odor.)

5 *Explain*: The lava rock is very light in weight because it is like a foam sponge that has hardened. It is full of air bubbles or holes like a sponge. It is not solid like other rocks, and it has a very rough texture.

9. Cross-section model of an erupting volcano

Materials

White construction paper, cross-section diagram of a volcano, colored pencils, a lift-off paper diagram of the outside of a volcanic cone, Contact paper word labels, mounting board or tagboard for finished model, clear Contact paper, masking tape. See preparation instructions below.

Preparation

1 Color in cross-section diagram of a volcano with colored pencils, mount on tagboard, label appropriate parts: crater, lava, magma, magma pipe, magma chamber, sedimentary rock, metamorphic rock, igneous rock, ash, volcanic cone. Make separate word labels for each part labeled on the diagram. Cover the diagram and word labels with clear Contact paper.

2 Cut out a volcanic cone shape that fits on top of the cross-section model of the volcano. Color in the cone shape with colored pencils and cover with clear Contact paper.

3 Mount the diagram of a cone on top of the cross-section diagram with a rolled piece of masking tape so that it acts like a hinge. The cone can then be lifted up to expose the cross-section diagram showing the interior of a volcano.

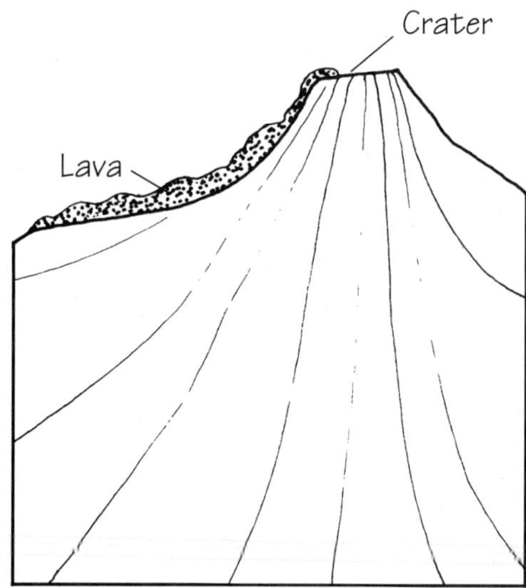

5-7A *Pictorial model of a lift-off cross-section of an erupting volcano.*

Procedure

1 Show children the finished model covered with clear Contact paper. Ask the children the following kinds of questions:

What is the picture a model of? (An erupting volcano.)

How can you tell it is an erupting volcano? (Ash and lava are coming out of the

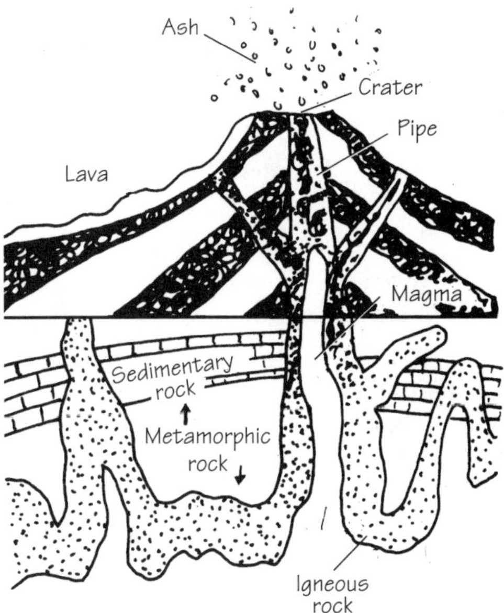

Erupting Volcano

5-7B *Interior of lift-off model.*

crater, the opening at the top of the volcano.)

What is inside an erupting volcano? (A magma pipe, with magma flowing up from a magma chamber.)

2 Lift up the cone and let the children look inside to see the cross-section of the volcano. Point to various parts inside of the volcano and ask them to name the part you are pointing to.

3 *Explain*: This is the way the volcano would look in the inside if we were able to slice the volcano open and look at a cross-section.

4 Hold up the word labels and name them. See if the children can find the appropriate spot or place on the chart as you name it and if they can place the word on top of the same word on the chart.

5 After your demonstration, allow children to make up their own cross-section model of a volcano with labeled parts.

10. Seismic waves

Materials

A globe or world map, a Slinky, 10 feet of rope, 2 wooden blocks, a ping-pong ball, a golf ball, a wooden table, a basin of water, newspaper to absorb possible mess from the water.

Procedure

1 *Explain*: More than one million earthquakes occur every year on the earth. Some of them are very destructive, while others are hardly even felt. Most of them occur along a belt called a fault line. A fault line is an area of the earth's crust that is known to break apart and slip or slide. There are three major fault lines or tremor areas on the earth where earthquakes and volcanoes are known to occur most frequently.

2 Show children the globe or a map of the world. Point out to them where the three major fault lines or belts of unrest occur on the earth's surface. (Refer to the information at the beginning of this chapter.)

3 *Explain*: Earthquake tremors usually start within the earth under the surface and travel to the surface. These tremors are called seismic waves. Seismic waves can be measured by a seismograph machine. Scientists called seismologists study seismograph readings and the movements or vibrations caused by earthquakes. They interpret their findings and attempt to make predictions about when and where earthquakes will happen and when and where volcanoes will erupt.

4 *Explain*: There are three types of seismic waves. With your help, I will demonstrate for you how seismic waves travel through the interior of the earth and on the surface of the earth:

5 Demonstrate a primary wave using a Slinky spring as a model. Hand one end of a Slinky to a child to hold. Stretch the other end out and then let go of about 20 coils of the spring. Ask the children to observe the ricocheting or back-and-forth pushing and pulling motion that takes place in the Slinky.

6 *Explain*: This kind of wave motion is like a primary seismic wave. It bounces back and forth, pushing and pulling as it penetrates through the crust of the earth.

7 Demonstrate a secondary wave by using a moving rope as a model. Give one end of a rope to a child to hold. Move the rope up and down or from side to side.

8 *Explain*: This kind of wave motion is like a secondary seismic wave. It moves

back and forth in a zig-zag pattern and arrives after a primary seismic wave.

9 Demonstrate a surface wave using two wooden blocks as a model. Press the two wooden blocks together in your hands. Slide the wooden blocks up and down or from one side to another.

10 *Explain*: This kind of sideways sliding motion takes place on the surface or crust of the earth. This kind of motion causes the most damage on the surface during an earthquake. It makes buildings fall over.

11 Demonstrate primary and secondary waves by using a ball as a model in liquid. Choose a child to hold a golf ball and a ping-pong ball about one foot above a basin filled with water. Tell the child to drop the golf ball into the water.

12 Observe what happens. (It sinks.)

13 Drop the ping-pong ball into the water.

14 Observe what happens. (It floats.)

15 *Explain*: The golf ball penetrates through the water like a primary seismic wave. The ping-pong ball acts like a secondary seismic wave. It does not penetrate through the liquid. The ping-pong ball comes to a halt on top of the water.

16 Demonstrate primary and secondary waves by using balls as models on solids. Choose a child to drop a ping-pong ball and a golf ball onto a wooden desk.

17 Observe the way the two balls bounce.

How many times does each ball bounce?

18 *Explain*: The golf ball acts like a primary seismic wave. It penetrates deeply and loses a lot of energy through the wood. The children can feel the wooden desk vibrate when the golf ball bounces on it. Like a secondary seismic wave, the ping-pong ball will penetrate less deeply and bounce up and down more frequently than the golf ball did.

II. Crust and interior of earth

1. A globe of the earth

Materials

A physical relief globe on an axis.

Procedure

1 Show children the globe.

2 *Explain*: This globe is a model of the earth.

3 Ask the following kinds of questions:

What do the colors of blue and brown and green represent? (Blue represents water; brown represents mountains and land area; green represents low areas of land.)

Where are the areas of land? (Have a child identify them.)

Where are the areas with water? (Have a child find the oceans and the large inland lakes and seas.)

What is underneath the oceans and all of the water on the earth? (Land.)

What are the highest areas of the earth called? (Mountains.)

What are the large low areas of the earth that are covered with water called? (Oceans, seas, and lakes.)

What is underneath the land? (Hot molten rocks.)

What is inside the earth? (Matter that is composed of many layers of solids, liquids, and gases.)

What is inside the globe? (Air. It is hollow inside. The globe is only a model of the outside or skin of the earth's surface. It's the part we can see with our eyes and from an airplane.)

2. Diagram of an island and a volcanic island

Materials

White paper; colored pencils; clear Contact paper; a sketch of an island, without water surrounding it.

Preparation

1 Sketch a diagram of an island. Show it as a mountain with a flat top, or a mountain with several peaks and plateaus. Draw in the water line to show where it would hit the mountain. Part of the island would be under the water, connected to the land under the water. The island would be grounded, not floating.

2 On a separate piece of paper, create a width that is as deep as the water in the island picture. Color in this sheet of paper the color of the water.

3 Color in the island picture with colored pencils so that it appears to be partially under water.

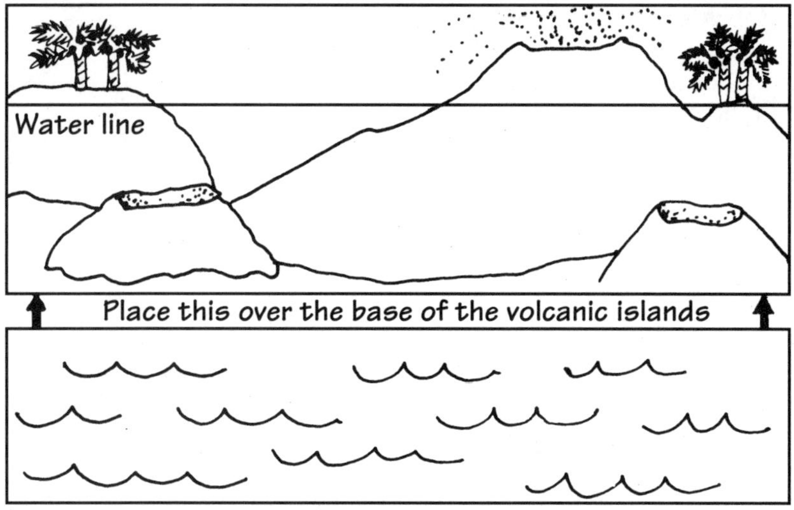

5-8 *Model of a volcanic island.*

4 Cover both papers with clear Contact paper. Attach the water picture to the larger picture so that the water can be lifted off the larger picture as if one could look underneath the water. (See Fig. 5-8.)

Procedure

1 Show children the picture of the island and the volcano.

2 Ask the following kinds of questions:

What is underneath the water at the beach? (Sand and land.)

What is a small area of land that is surrounded by water called? (An island.)

Does the island float in the water? (No, it is attached to the land underneath the water.)

If there were no water, what would the island look like? (A tall mountain or a tall flat mountain.)

3 Lift off the water and look at what is underneath the water. Have the children comment about the underwater landscape, and about the connection to the earth. Discuss how only the peak is above the water, and that the water usually occurs at the lowest altitudes of the earth's crust. The crust is the outer surface of the earth that we can see.

4 After your demonstration, allow children to design their own lift-off model of the ocean floor surrounding a volcanic island.

3. Apple as a model of the earth

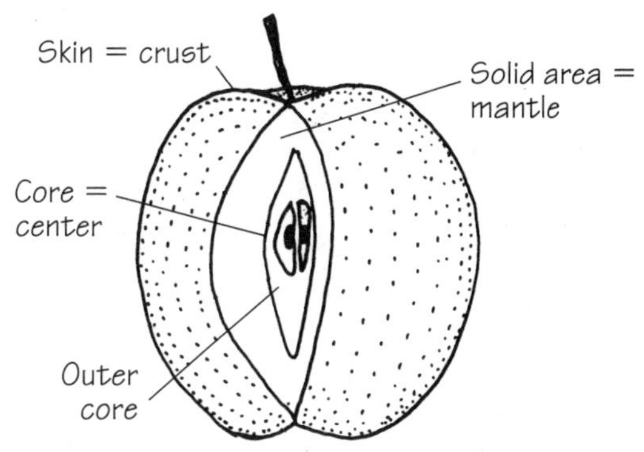

5-9 *Like the earth, the apple is solid—not hollow.*

Materials

Three apples, a sharp knife (for adult use only), a cutting board, paper towels.

Procedure

1 Ask the children the following question:

What is inside of the earth? (Listen to their responses. Discuss what they think is underneath the water and the land.)

2 Hold up an apple. Ask the children the following kinds of questions:

What is inside an apple? (A solid area.)

What is on the outside of the apple? (A skin.)

Are there any layers inside the solid area? (Yes, the core.)

What is the core surrounded by? (The fruit we eat.)

3 Cut the apple in half vertically, and cut another apple in half horizontally. Ask the following kinds of questions about the apples:

How are the apples like the earth? (They are round, surrounded by a skin or crust, and solid in the center.)

Can the apples be a model of the earth? (Yes.)

Is the skin on the model very thick? (No, it is a very thin layer.)

Is the meat or fruit area very thick? (Yes.)

What is in the center? (A core.)

4 *Explain*: Scientists have never seen the inside of the earth, but they believe that it is composed of many layers. They call the center of the earth the core, and the area surrounding the core the mantle. The part that we live on is called the crust. It is very thin in relation to the mantle, just as the apple skin is thin in relation to the apple's meat. The apple's skin represents the earth's crust. The meat of the apple represents the earth's mantle layer.

5 Cut a one-quarter section out of one of the uncut apples.

6 Discuss the different appearance of the apple's inside when it is cut in half vertically, cut in half horizontally, and cut with a quarter removed.

7 *Explain*: The same thing can look different when seen from different angles or from different points.

Going further

1 Give each child an M&M peanut. Tell them to bite into it with their front incisor teeth.

What do you see?

How could the interior cross-section of the M&M peanut be used as a miniature model of the earth?

2 Have children explain what each part could be. (crust is shell; white area is mantle; chocolate is outer core; peanut is inner core). (Brainard)

4. An Orange

Materials

An orange, a knife (for adult use only), a cutting board, paper towels.

Procedure

1 Cut the orange into quarters or into smaller sections. Have the children

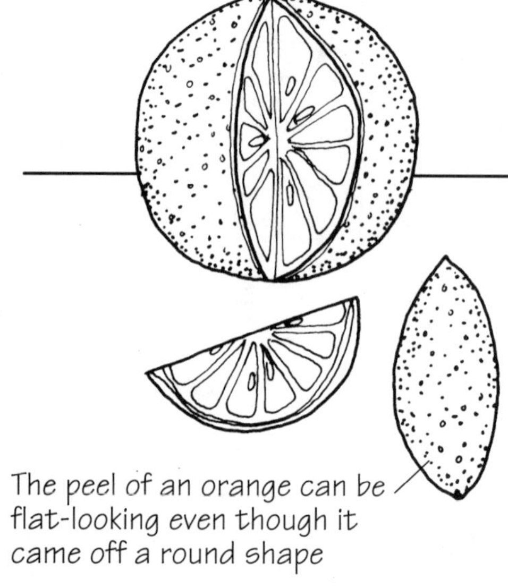

The peel of an orange can be flat-looking even though it came off a round shape

5-10 *Up close, round things can look flat.*

look at the surface of the cut sections. Peel the fruit away from the orange peel. Discuss the flatness of the section. It does not appear to be as round when it is a part of the whole. Small parts of an orange's peel appear flat rather than round.

2 Ask the following kinds of questions:

If we pretend that the orange is a model of the earth, what part would the peel of the orange be called? (The crust.)

What would the white on the inside of the peel be called? (The inner crust.)

What would the orange part of the peel be called? (The outer crust.)

Does the orange have a core? (It is not as well defined as the apple's core, but is a hollow area in the center.)

Which fruit is a better model of the earth, the orange or the apple? (The apple is a better model of the earth because it has a solid core in its center.)

Why does the earth appear to be flat rather than curved where we live? (We live on a small section of the earth and we cannot see it in its entirety. We are too close to the ground to appreciate its roundness.)

Where do we have to be to observe that the earth is round? (High up in space in a space capsule or at the beach or desert we can see the roundness of the horizon line. It has a very slight curve.)

INFORMATION

In olden days when large clipper ships with sails sailed the oceans, one could see the top of the ship's sails first, and then later more and more of the ship as it approached land.

5. Model of the interior layers of the earth

Materials

White, dark blue, yellow, red, orange, and brown construction paper; a compass; a pencil; colored pencils; scissors; clear Contact paper; tagboard.

Preparation

1 Cut out a series of graduated circles. Make two of each of the following circles: two small yellow circles, two red larger circles, two larger orange circles, and two brown circles (the brown circles should be the largest). Cut out one large white circle that is the same size as the large brown circles.

2 On the large, white circle, draw in shapes to represent the continents and the oceans. Color in the shapes with the colored pencils so that they look like land and water areas.

3 Glue one set of the graduated colored circles onto a piece of dark blue construction paper mounted on tagboard. (See Figs. 5-11 and 5-12.)

4 Cover the circles that are glued to the blue tagboard with clear Contact paper, and cover the individual circles with clear Contact paper.

Procedure

1 Show the children the model of the interior layers of the earth. Have the set of loose, colored circles on top of the matching graduated circles that have been glued to the blue paper. The white circle that represents the earth's outer crust should be the top circle and should be hiding or covering up the other circles.

2 Ask the following kinds of questions:

What is this a model of? (The earth or a globe of the earth.)

What is inside the earth? (Many layers.)

What surrounds the earth? (Outer space.)

If we were able to lift the crust off the earth and look inside, what would be the first layer we would see underneath the water and the land underneath the water? (The inner crust. Lift off the white land and water layer to see it.)

What is the next interior layer called? (The mantle. Lift off the brown layer to see it.)

3 Continue with the red outer core and the yellow inner core.

4 After your demonstration, allow children to make their own labeled model of the interior layers of the earth.

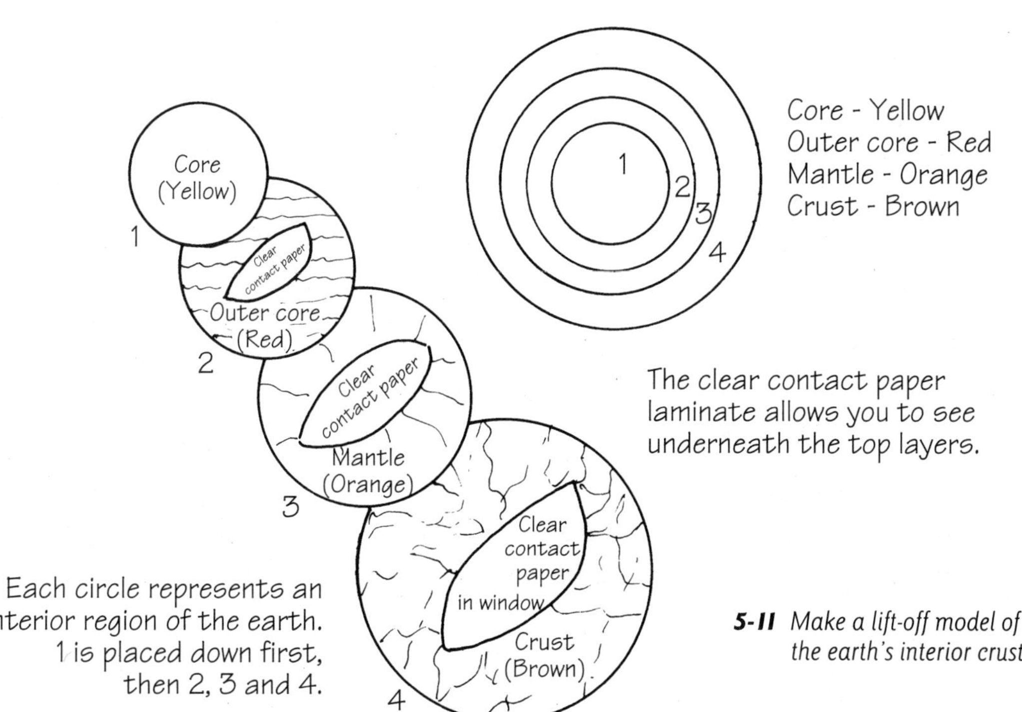

5-11 *Make a lift-off model of the earth's interior crust.*

5-12 Lift-off model of earth's interior—cross-section of earth, undercrust

6. Lift-up landscape model of interior of earth

Materials

Paper, colored pencils, clear Contact paper, scissors, tagboard, masking tape.

Preparation

1. Sketch a landscape drawing of a park or golf course, mostly flat rolling hills covered with grass and a few trees. Color in the sketch with colored pencils.
2. Sketch the same scene again, but in the middle of the paper draw in the interior layers of the earth so that it will appear as a cross-section of the land with a slice in it. Color in the sketch with colored pencils. (See Fig. 5-12.)
3. Mount the cross-section sketch on tagboard, and cover the two sketches with clear Contact paper. Hinge the full landscape sketch on top of the cross-section sketch with a curled piece of masking tape.

Procedure

1. Show the children the landscape with the lift-off land that reveals a cross-section underneath the land.
2. Ask the following kinds of questions:

What is underneath the park under the grass? (Layers of soil, then layers of bedrock. Then the mantle layer, then the core.)

3. Listen to their responses, then lift up the landscape to see the layers.

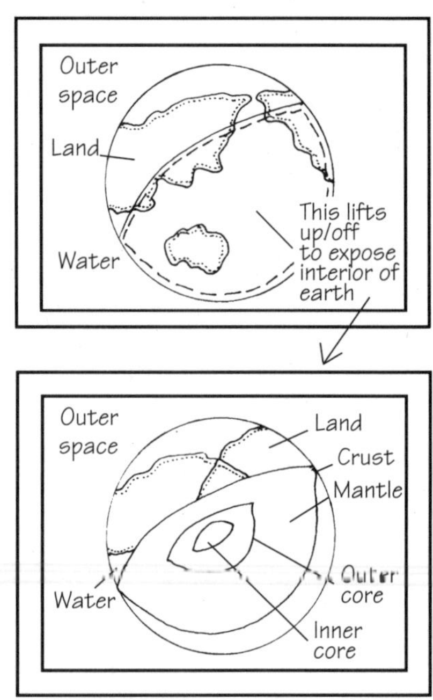

5-13 Lift-off model of earth's interior crust.

What is underneath all landscapes on the crust of the earth? (The same kinds of layers.)

Do volcanoes erupt in all parts of the earth? (No, there are certain areas of the earth where volcanoes erupt more frequently. Scientists are aware of these belts or sections of the earth where volcanoes are most likely to occur. These belts are called fault lines.)

What is a fault line? (A fault line is a weak section of the earth's crust where an earthquake or a volcano has occurred in the past and might occur again. Sometimes the movements inside the earth cause movements to occur on the crust, the crust breaks apart and slides in two different directions. When this occurs, it is called an earthquake.)

4 After your demonstration, allow children to create their own lift-up model of the layers of the earth underneath their house or the school.

III. Distinguishing rocks from one another

1. Matching and naming rocks that look alike

Materials

Two identical sets of store-bought rocks from a museum shop or lapidary store.

Preparation

1 Mount each rock on a separate piece of cardboard about 2 inches by 2 inches.
2 Label each rock in the set with a word label.

Procedure

1 Show the children one complete set of mounted individual rocks.
2 Discuss the properties of each rock and what the name of each rock is.
3 Describe a rock and see if the children can find the rock you are describing; name the rock for them if they cannot.
4 Show children the second set of identical matching rocks. Tell them that each rock has a matching pair and ask them to find the rock that matches each rock. The children can play a game with the rocks with one of their classmates by picking up one of the rocks and having their classmate find the matching rock, or guessing which rock is missing.

2. Cleavage

Materials

A variety of broken rocks; two pieces or more from: a broken bar of soap, a split piece of wood, a broken rock.

Procedure

1 Show the children the piece of soap. Hold it so that the crack does not show, so that it appears to be unbroken. Then split it open so that the children can see the crack. Do the same thing with the piece of wood and with the rock.

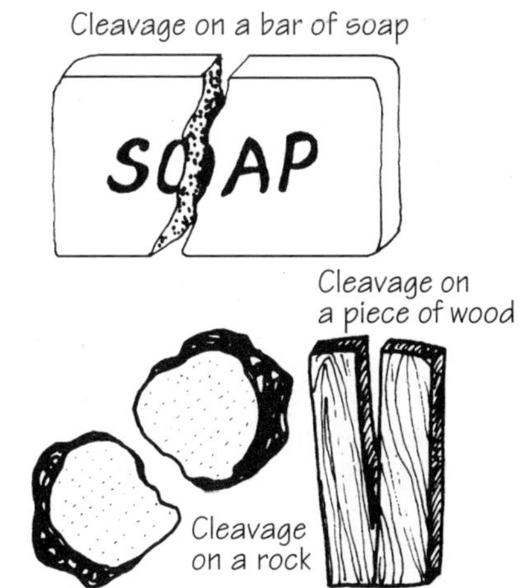

5-14 *Different materials break differently.*

2 *Explain*: When materials break, they break differently. Some break in a jagged line like the soap, some break in layers like the wood, and some break in a smooth line like the rock. Not all rocks break in a smooth line, but some do. Cleavage is a word that refers to the way something breaks. A cleavage line can be rough, smooth, jagged, layered, etc. Many rocks and minerals have a cleavage pattern that is constant no matter how small the pieces are broken.
3 Look at various rock samples and discuss the texture of the cleavage lines with the children.
4 Give children a small (hotel courtesy type) bar of soap or a thin wood scrap to break or a piece of paper to rip. Encourage them to examine the texture of the cleavage line and fit the two pieces together along the cleavage line.

3. Luster

Materials

A variety of rocks with and without luster mounted on 2-inch-by-2-inch cardboard squares. (You might need to buy rocks or samples from a museum or a rock and mineral supply store.)

Procedure

1 Show the children the rocks.
2 Have the children describe what the individual rocks look like.
3 *Explain*: The shine and sparkle of some of the rocks is called luster. Some rocks have luster; some do not. When a rock has the property of luster, the quality of the luster is used to describe the rock's

appearance. (Luster can be pearly, dull, brilliant, glassy, metallic, etc.)

4. Hardness

Materials

A variety of labeled rocks with varying degrees of hardness and softness that have been mounted on 2-inch-by-2-inch cardboard squares (i.e., talc, quartz, slate, sandstone, marble, sulfur, anthracite, limestone, calcite); a penny; a nail; a piece of glass; talc powder.

Procedure

1 Show the children the variety of rocks.
2 *Explain*: Rocks have different degrees of hardness. A very hard rock cannot be scratched by another rock. The hardest rock of all is a diamond. The softest rock of all is talc. Talc rubs off on any surface that rubs against it.
3 Demonstrate with a talc rock how soft talc is. Let the children touch the talc to feel how soft the piece of talc feels.

Do you know where talc powder comes from? (Talc powder is ground-up talc rock with scents of perfume added.)

4 Sprinkle talc powder out for children to see and smell.
5 *Explain*: A man named Moh set up a testing scale for measuring the hardness of rocks. He discovered that materials such as fingernails, glass, other rocks, nails, pennies, knives, etc., could be used to test the hardness of rocks. He rated the hardness of rocks with a number. The lower the number, the softer the rock. The numbers range in a scale of one to ten. Number one is talc and number ten is a diamond.
6 Tell children the numbers. Write them on a blackboard or prepare a chart ahead of time. (See Table 5-1.)

Table 5-1 Moh's hardness scale

1 — **Talc** (can be scratched by a fingernail)
2 — **Gypsum** (can be scratched by a fingernail)
3 — **Calcite** (can be scratched by a penny)
4 — **Fluorite** (can be scratched by a knife)
5 — **Apatite** (can almost be scratched by a knife and will scratch any other rock which has a lower number than itself)
6 — **Feldspar** (will scratch a knife blade)
7 — **Quartz** (will scratch a piece of glass)
8 — **Topaz** (will scratch the quartz)
9 — **Corundum** (will scratch the topaz and any other rock with a lower number than itself
10 — **Diamond** (will scratch any rocks that are softer than itself

- Allow children to experiment to find out which rock scratches what, and to arrange the rocks in an order from softest to hardest.

5. Streak

Materials

Assorted labeled rocks from a rock or mineral supply store that have been mounted on 2-inch-by-2-inch cardboard squares and that either have streaks of color running through them or leave a colored streak when rubbed on a piece of unglazed ceramic tile; a wet sponge. (Suggested rocks to use for streaking on a ceramic tile are: magnetite, graphite, anthracite, shale, galena, olivine, hematite, talc, slate, obsidian, calcite.)

Procedure

1 Show children the assorted rocks.
2 *Explain*: Some of the rocks will leave a streak of color when they are rubbed against a piece of unglazed ceramic tile. Demonstrate the streaking of the rocks on the tile. Compare the different textures and intensity of color that rubs off onto the tile from the different rocks. Not all rocks rub off a color; only some rocks do.
3 Allow children to experiment making streaks of color by rubbing the rocks on a piece of tile.
4 Discuss the streaks that run through some of the rocks and minerals.
5 *Explain*: A streak is a line of color or luster that runs through a rock.

6. Density

Materials

A piece of lava rock, a piece of granite rock about the same size as the lava rock.

Procedure

1 Show children the two rocks.

2 Ask the following kinds of questions:

Can we tell by just looking which rock weighs more? (No, but one rock has more holes in it than the other one does. The one with holes looks less dense.)

What kinds of rocks have a lot of holes in them? (Lava rocks. See Activity 1, Procedure 8, from this chapter.)

What kinds of rocks can float in water? (Lava rocks.)

Which rock will weigh more? (The non-lava rock will weigh more because it is more dense.) Let the children feel each of the rocks to experience the difference in their weights.

3 Pass around the two rocks so the children can feel the difference between them.

4 *Explain*: Rocks have different densities. Density refers to the solidness of a rock. The more closely packed the minerals are within the rock, the more solid or dense the rock is. More solid rocks weigh more than less solid rocks. "Bigness" does not mean that a rock is heavier. Many rocks could be the same size and each rock could weigh a different amount.

7. Weight

Materials

A simple balance scale with two pans; a set of plastic metric gram weights or paper clips, marbles, coins or washers to use as weights; various assorted labeled rocks mounted on 2-inch-by-2-inch cardboard squares.

Procedure

1 Show children the scale. Discuss what the scale is used for and how it works. When one side is high and the other side is low, it means that the scale is not balanced. The scale can be balanced by adding weights such as paper clips to the pan until both sides are even. When the scale is balanced, items can be weighed in the pans.

2 Ask the children the following kinds of questions as they weigh the rocks:

If I place a rock in the pan, what will happen to the pan? (The pan will go down on the side the rock went into, and up on the other side.)

How can the scale be balanced if a rock is in the pan? (By adding metric gram weights until the scale is balanced.)

If weights are added to the other pan and the scale is balanced, what information will we find out? (The number of weights we added to balance the scale will tell us how much the rock weighed.)

How many rocks can be weighed at the same time if we are trying to find out how many grams each rock weighs? (One rock at a time.)

3 Allow children to determine the amount of weight that each rock has in grams.

4 After children determine the approximate weight of each rock, encourage them to arrange the rocks in a sequential order, either heaviest to lightest or lightest to heaviest.

8. Magnetic test

Materials

Assorted black and gray rocks, including a piece of magnetite; a magnet; a paper clip.

Procedure

1 Place all of the black and gray rocks including magnetite on the floor or on a table near each other.

2 Show the children the magnet.

Do you think the magnet can pick up any of the rocks?

3 Hold the magnet out over the assorted rocks and have the children observe

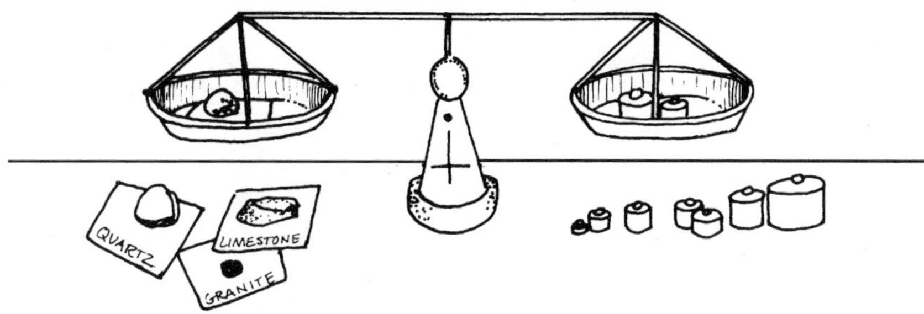

5-15 *Each rock sample should be weighed separately on a balanced scale.*

whether any of the rocks are affected by the magnet.

4 When the piece of magnetite is observed and singled out, pick up the magnetite and see if the magnetite will pick up a paper clip.
5 *Explain*: Magnetite is a natural magnet found in nature. (Refer to Chapter 4, which deals with magnetism.)
6 After your demonstration, allow children to experiment with the magnet to find the magnetite with a different mixture of rocks, and to pick up paper clips with the magnetite.

9. Test for limestone

Materials

For each child or group of children: lemon juice or vinegar; limestone; marble; rock; chalk (natural); calcite; chalk board chalk; a toothpick.

Procedure

1 Show the children the rocks. Tell them the names of each if they do not know what they are. Children will probably find it strange that chalk is a rock.
2 *Explain*: The chalk we use in the classroom is chalk that has been pressed and molded into a solid cylindrical shape. It is helpful to compare natural chalk with human-made chalk.
3 Have the children dip a toothpick into vinegar and drop a drop of vinegar onto each of the rocks. (The limestone, marble, calcite, and chalk will form little bubbles or fizz when the vinegar touches their surface. The other white rocks will most likely not have a bubbly or fizzy reaction unless they too contain traces of limestone, which the acid test is able to find out.)
4 *Explain*: The bubbles are caused by carbon dioxide (CO_2) gas that forms when limestone is touched by vinegar or lemon juice, which are acids.

IV. Three classes of rocks

1. Igneous rocks

Materials

Assorted igneous rocks (for example, obsidian, pumice, granite, quartz, feldspar, biotite, scoria, basalt); a wet sponge; human-made cellulose; a dry sponge; wet, soft clay; a magnifying glass; a pocket microscope.

Procedure

1 *Explain*: When rocks form due to volcanic eruptions or from magma, they are called igneous rocks or fire rocks. Rocks that form because of heat or fire all form from magma. Magma is hot liquid rock. It is made up of minerals and gases from deep inside the earth.
2 *Explain*: When magma flows, it is hot; as it begins to cool, it hardens. If it cools quickly, it looks different from when it cools slowly. If it cools quickly it looks glassy like obsidian, or full of holes like pumice. Show children a sample of obsidian and pumice. If the magma cools more slowly, it forms granite. Show children a sample of granite. Granite is made up of small crystals of quartz, feldspar, and biotite. Show children samples of quartz, feldspar, and biotite. Ask them if they

5-16 *Bubbles will appear if lime is present in the rock.*

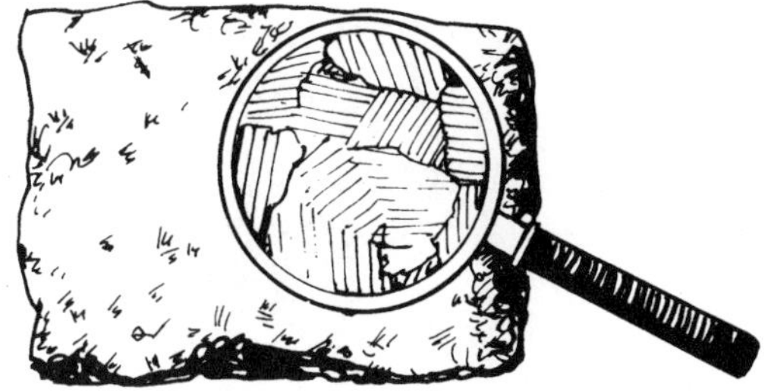

5-17 *Texture of igneous rocks.*

can find small flecks of the rock samples in the granite rock.

3 Show children the wet sponge and the wet soft clay.

4 *Explain*: The sponge and the clay are both models of igneous rocks that are still in a liquid form. They are not hot like liquid magma, but they are soft and malleable. The sponge can be squeezed, and the clay can be shaped into forms. Ask the following kinds of questions:

When a sponge dries, what happens? (It becomes very stiff and the shape remains the same. It cannot be squeezed easily, and the holes allow it to dry quickly.)

What happens to the clay when it dries out? (It becomes very hard and brittle. It takes longer to dry than the sponge.)

5 *Explain*: The sponge is like pumice. It dries quickly. The clay is like granite. It dries slowly. Like magma, both the sponge and the clay become hard when they no longer contain a liquid and are not in a liquid form.

6 Tell children to observe the igneous rock samples with a magnifying glass and a pocket microscope. Discuss what they see. (They should see particles meshed tightly together.)

2. Metamorphic rocks

Materials

A candle; a match; a piece of waxed paper; samples of metamorphic rocks (for example, marble, slate, schist, gneiss, quartzite); the cross-section model of an erupting volcano (Activity 1, Procedure 9 from this chapter); a magnifying glass; a pocket microscope.

Procedure

1 Show the children the cross-section model of an erupting volcano from Activity 1, Procedure 9 from this chapter. Have them notice that the area surrounding the magma under the ground continually heats and cools. The area near the magma is often surrounded by metamorphic rock.

2 *Explain*: Metamorphic rock is rock that changes. It changes due to extreme changes in heat or pressure. Metamorphic rocks are also called changing rocks. A rock that starts off as an igneous rock can become a metamorphic rock if it changes due to

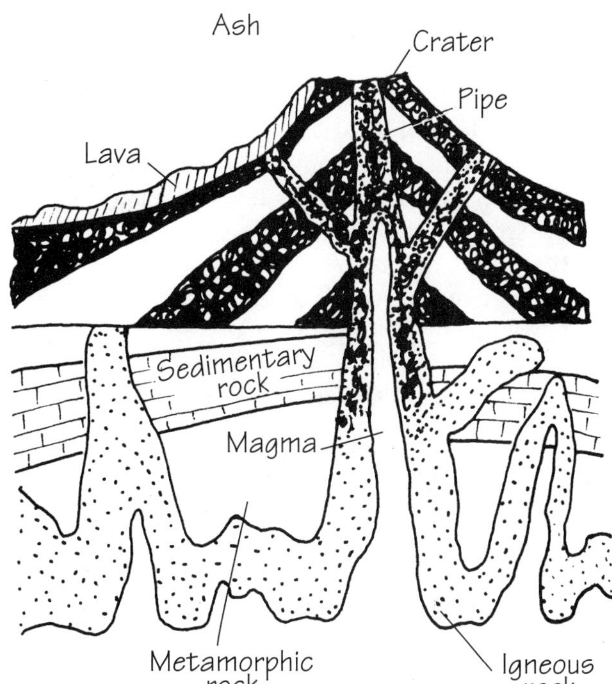

5-18 *Origin of igneous and metamorphic rocks.*

pressure or due to a temperature change.

This next activity requires adult supervision. (Lighting matches and fire are dangerous for young children.)

3 Light a candle with a match. Allow the drippings to fall onto a piece of waxed paper. Have the children observe how the candle becomes a liquid and drips, and that the drips become hard again.

4 Ask the following kinds of questions:

Can the drips ever be made into a candle again? (No, not unless they are all collected and molded into a candle again.)

Will the candle ever be the same again once it starts to drip? (No, its shape will remain changed. The shape of the drips will also remain changed.)

How is the candle like a rock that has gone through metamorphosis and changed? (The candle has a new shape. It can never be the way it was before.)

Can adults ever become small children again? (No, once they grow up, they will remain adults.)

Can you stay the age you are for your entire life? (No, we continually go through aging and changes while we are alive.)

How are metamorphic rocks like us? (Once a change occurs, the change cannot be reversed. Like Toyland, "Once you pass its borders, you can never return again.")

Note: Pottery can be shown as an example of a human-made metamorphic rock. Pottery is made from soft clay. It is shaped into a form by pressure from hands. When it is dried and then heated inside a kiln, it undergoes a change from one form of clay to another. It cannot be made soft again once it is heated.

5 Tell children to observe the metamorphic rock samples with a magnifying glass and a pocket microscope. Discuss what they see. (They should be able to see a striped texture. See Fig. 5-19.)

3. Opening up rocks

Materials

Assorted rocks picked up from outside on the playground or from the backyard; newspaper; a large paper bag; a hammer; an empty egg carton; potato or orange sack mesh or kitchen strainer.

5-19 *Texture of metamorphic rocks.*

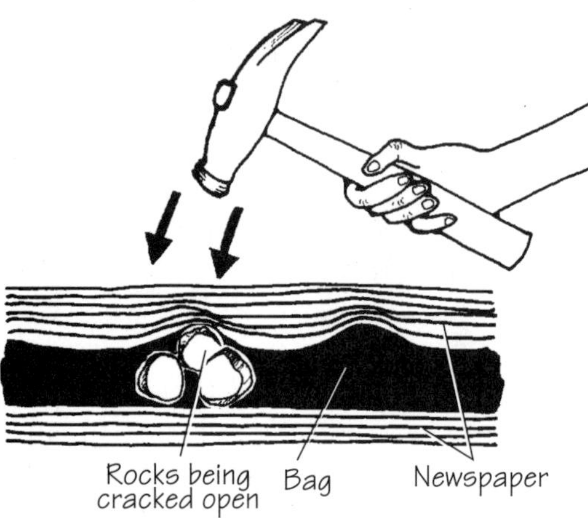

5-20 *Open up rocks.*

Procedure

1 Show the children the rocks. Place one of the rocks inside a paper bag. Choose a child to place newspaper on top of the paper bag and on the bottom of the paper bag. Tell the children that you are going to strike the paper bag with a hammer.

When I hit the bag with the hammer, what do you think will happen to the rock?

2 Have a child strike the paper bag with the hammer and then have the children observe what happens to the rock. (The children will observe that the rock has broken into several smaller pieces of rock. The inside of the rock might look slightly different from the outside of the rock. The inside might have brighter colors or might have a jagged cleavage line. The outside might be smooth and weathered compared to the inside, which might be brighter and rougher, or there might be no difference.)

3 Continue to let the children break the rocks with a hammer and to observe whether some rocks are harder to break

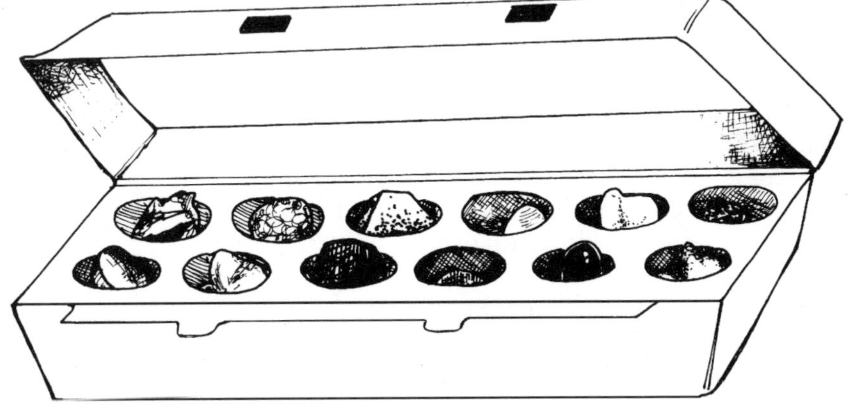

5-21 *Sort or grade the broken rocks or sediments by size or color.*

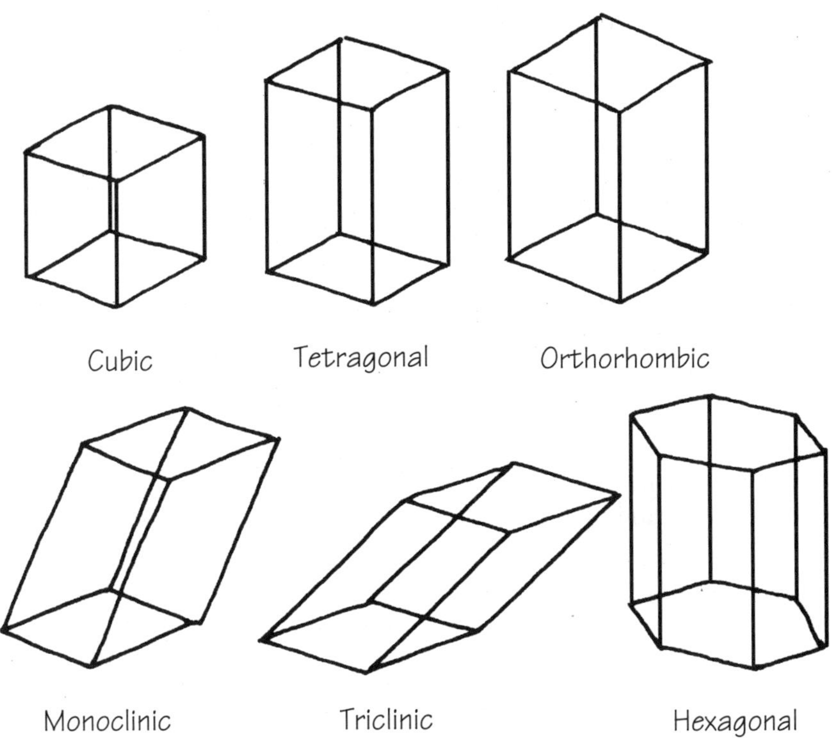

5-22 *Crystal shapes.*

than others and whether some rocks form smaller pieces when struck.

Can the small rocks be made even smaller?

Can the rocks be turned into sand or dust?

4 Have children use a kitchen strainer or mesh from a potato or orange sack to grade the small rocks and pieces of rock into piles. Have them pour their sorted and graded piles of different sized rocks into an egg carton or other sorting container.

4. Crystals

Materials

A variety of geodes* that have been cut open; rock crystals purchased from a rock supply store or from a museum shop; pictures of gemstones and crystals.

Procedure

1 Show the children the geodes. First show them the complete geode by holding the two halves together so that it looks like one unopened rock.

* A geode is a hollow rock with a crystal lining. A geode can be purchased at gift shops, and from science supply houses.

What do you think the inside of the rock will look like? (Listen to their responses, then open the rock (geode) so they can see the interior.)

2 *Explain*: The inside has not been polished. When some rocks are polished, they become very beautiful to look at. Harder rocks are easier to polish. When they are polished and sanded down to be smooth, they look beautiful. Inside of the geode are naturally made crystals that look like they had been polished.

Note: Sometimes gift shops sell geodes that have been polished on the flat outer area surrounding the hollow core that is filled with natural crystals.

3 Show children pictures of gemstones and crystals.

4 *Explain*: Some stones are cut into gemstones and polished by people called lapidaries. Jewelers then mount stones with precious metals like gold and silver. Minerals in rocks form crystals. Every mineral has its own unique crystal form. Some crystals are prettier than others and are treasured for their beauty and made into jewelry or displayed at museums.

Going further

Suggest that children visit the local natural history museum to see the rock and mineral collection, and to observe shapes and forms of crystallized minerals.

5. Growing sugar crystals

Materials

Clear or colored rock candy samples, boiling water, granulated sugar, food color, string, pencils, a teaspoon, clear plastic drinking glasses, salt.

Procedure

1 Pass around the rock candy. Tell the children that even though the crystals look like rock crystals, they are really candy. Break off pieces of the rock candy for the children to taste.

2 *Explain*: Rock candy is made from sugar. Rocks are made up of minerals. Sugar is not made up of minerals, but we can get sugar to crystallize.*

* Sugar is made from carbon and hydrogen, with some oxygen also. Sugar is organic, which means that it was once alive or once had life. Sugar is generated in many plants, but we can also make it chemically. Plants do not form crystalline sugar. However, we can get sugar to crystallize. (Ralph Brainard).

When minerals are exposed to moisture and then extreme temperature changes, crystals will frequently form or grow. Minerals are not alive; they grow larger from the outside by forming new layers on top of old layers. Materials that are alive (like plants and animals) grow from the inside out and all over, not just in layers on the outside.

3 *Explain*: We can make sugar into crystals.

4 Boil some water.

This activity requires adult supervision. (Boiling water can be dangerous to young children.)

5 Pour the water into a clear plastic drinking glass.

6 Choose a child to add some sugar to the hot water.

7 Stir the sugar until it dissolves.

8 Continue to add sugar to the glass until the water becomes "syrupy" or supersaturated. (It will be supersaturated when the water can no longer hold all of the sugar. Some of the sugar will sink to the bottom of the glass and will not dissolve in the water.)

Note: You will need to use approximately two cups of sugar for every cup of water to create this "sugar syrup."

9 Choose a child to add food color for interest.

10 Choose another child to place a pencil across the top of the glass and tie a piece of string to the pencil so that the string is submerged in the sugar water. (See Fig. 5-23.)

11 Place the sugar water with the pencil and string in it on top of a high shelf.

12 Let it sit undisturbed for a few days or a week. (Crystals will start to form and grow on the string. Eventually, all of the water will evaporate. If the water evaporates very slowly, the crystals will be large. If the water evaporates fast, the crystals will be smaller.)

13 *Explain*: The same process takes place in minerals that form rocks. Crystals form when moisture is trapped inside and evaporates slowly.

14 When salt water is boiled, it will form crystals too. Let the children experiment to see how different salt crystals look from sugar crystals.

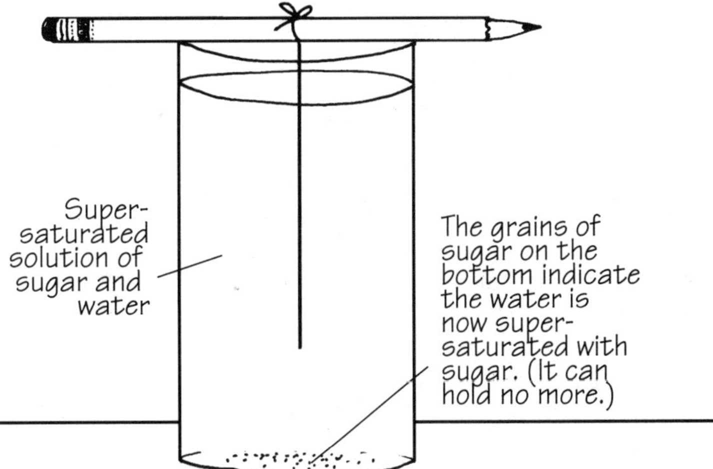
Super-
saturated
solution of
sugar and
water
The grains of
sugar on the
bottom indicate
the water is
now super-
saturated with
sugar. (It can
hold no more.)

5-23 *Crystals take time to form.*

Going further

1 Encourage children to grow a salt crystal. After several weeks, have the children compare and contrast the growth of the two kinds of crystals: salt; sugar.

2 Pass out magnifying glasses or pocket microscopes to the children so that they can examine salt and sugar with a magnifying device to see how different each kind of crystal looks.

3 Have them compare and contrast the appearance of one salt and one sugar crystal.

Does the single crystal of salt or sugar look similar to the larger crystal formation growing on the string hanging from a pencil?

Note: Crystal can also be grown on charcoal. To do this:

a Combine: 5 Tbsp. salt, 6 Tbsp. water, 1 Tbsp. ammonia and 6 Tbsp. liquid bluing in a jar.

CAUTION

Both liquid bluing and ammonia are dangerous for children. Adult supervision is needed. (Liquid bluing can be purchased from: IDEA FACTORY, Inc., 10710 Dixon Drive, Riverview, FL.)

b Mix thoroughly until the salt is dissolved.

c Pour the solution over 4 or 5 charcoal briquettes in a shallow dish. (For more colorful crystals, add drops of food color to the wet charcoal.)

d Let the shallow dish sit at room temperature undisturbed and wait for changes to occur.

6. Sedimentary rocks

Materials

Samples of sedimentary rocks with visible layers, plus store-bought samples of sandstone, shale, limestone, and clay conglomerates (rocks composed of small pebbles that have been cemented together by mud that has become rock); a magnifying glass, and/or a pocket microscope.

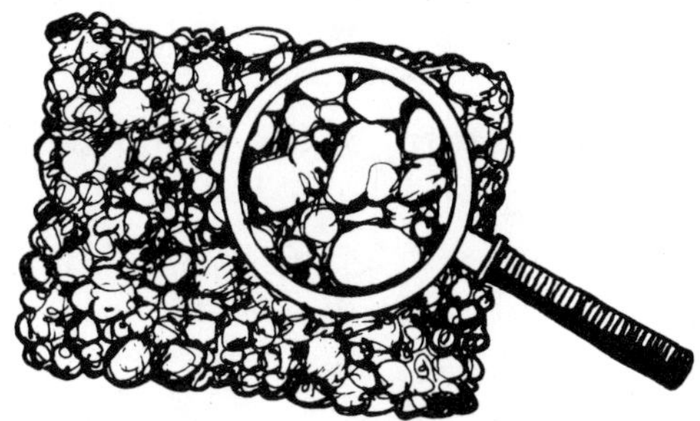

5-24A *Texture of a sedimentary rock.*

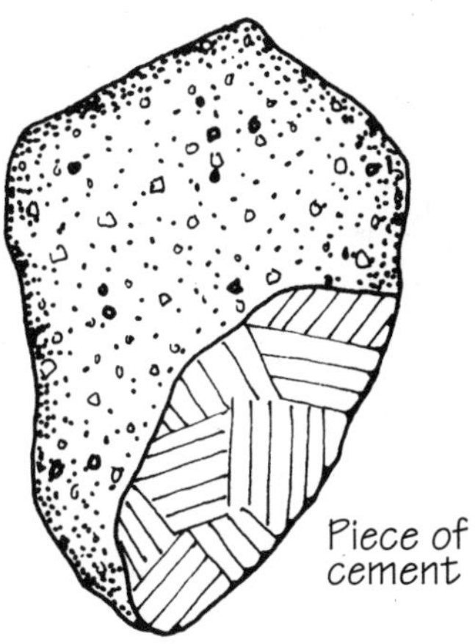
Piece of
cement

5-24B *Texture of a conglomerate rock.*

Procedure

1 Pass around the sedimentary rocks.

2 Observe the layers that have formed. (Lines or stripes of colors can be seen in the rocks.)

3 Pass around the store-bought rock samples.

4 Observe the granular look of the limestone and the sandstone.
5 Observe the way the conglomerate sticks together to form a large rock. Use a magnifying glass or a pocket microscope to take a closer look. Compare the way the sedimentary rocks look compared to the way the igneous and metamorphic rock samples looked under a magnifying glass or a pocket microscope.
6 *Explain*: Concrete is a conglomerate. It is held together by cement. The little pebbles and stones in the sedimentary conglomerate are cemented together by hardened mud. Sedimentary rock is usually of a softer variety than igneous and metamorphic rocks.

7. Pictures of the Grand Canyon

Materials

Pictures can be obtained from nature magazines or from the library.

Procedure

1 Pass around the pictures of the Grand Canyon or other similar pictures of sedimentary rock that have been built up over the centuries.
2 Discuss the visible layers that can be seen in the rock along the canyon walls.
3 Discuss how the water from the river keeps making the canyon deeper.

8. Uses of rocks

Materials

Samples of slate, coal, limestone, clay, gravel, granite, marble.

Procedure

1 Show the children the samples of rocks.
2 Discuss where the various rocks might be used. For example: Slate is used outside for walkways, on roofs, and for blackboards. Coal is used for heat.

INFORMATION (Coal burns because it is organic, which means it once had life. It is not made from minerals.) Limestone is used in buildings and is mixed with cement. It is also ground up and used to put lines on soccer and football fields. Limestone is formed from shells of small sea animals.

(Lime is also put on lawn and gardens to counteract excess acidity in the soil.) Clay is used to make bricks, in pottery and ceramics. Gravel is used to build roads, paths, and driveways. Granite and marble are used in buildings, and are often used by artists to carve out statues or monuments.

3 Have children look for rocks in buildings and on bridges, roads, and sidewalks.

V. Erosion and formation of rocks

1. Grinding rocks and erosion

Materials

For each child or group of children: an empty can with a plastic cover; several small rocks.

Procedure

1 Show children the rocks.
2 Place them in the empty can.
3 Place a plastic cover over the end of the can.

What do you think will happen to the rocks if they are shaken vigorously inside the can?

4 Have children shake the covered can vigorously and observe what happens to the rocks as a result of the motion and shaking. (The rocks will hit against each other and break into smaller rocks and particles of rocks. Dust and sand will be present in the can.)

Note: A program in the "3,2,1, Contact" television series suggested playing rock and roll music on a tape recorder or a record player for children to keep a beat to while they shake their rocks in the capped container. Children take turns shaking their cans to the music until the music stops, then they pass it on to the next child to shake.

5 *Explain*: Erosion of rocks has taken place inside the can. Erosion means that rocks are breaking apart. Erosion takes place because of a mechanical action such as being shaken up, rubbed, or hit, or from a chemical action such as might occur when a volcano erupts.
6 Ask the children the following kinds of questions:

What happens to rocks when they hit against each other? (They break apart and become smaller and jagged; eventually they become smooth.)

What happens to rocks that travel in a river or are carried in a stream? (The water erodes them. The water pushes the rocks around and the rocks are bounced around and off each other.)

7 *Explain*: Sedimentary rock is made up of small fragments, or sediments. Sediments are tiny pieces of soil or particles that are often carried by water. When a lot of sediments collect together, they form a layer of soil or a layer of rock.

2. Observing sand samples

Materials

For each child or group of children: empty film canisters, index cards, paper-hole puncher, transparent tape, pocket microscope or magnifying glass. Optional: fine mesh material (panty hose), a magnet inside a clear zip-lock plastic bag, paper towels, science journal.

Procedure

1 Ask the following kinds of questions:

What is sand?

Is sand the same color and size?

Where does sand come from?

2 Distribute empty* film canisters to children and tell them to bring in sand samples. Have them bring in sand samples from different places: the beach, their back yard, a nearby stream, the playground at school, sand from along a roadside, a lake shore, or from a vacation in a distant place.

3 Instruct them to:

- a Collect a sample of sand in the empty film canister.
- b Label the sand so they will know where it came from.
- c Make a microscope slide for each sand sample by using a paper hole punch to make a hole in a 3-inch-by-5-inch index card and affixing transparent tape to the hole. Place a few grains of sand onto the tape and cover the sand with another piece of clear transparent tape. Label the sand sample.
- d Observe the sand through a pocket microscope or with a magnifying glass.
- e Record their observations in their science journals.
- f Discuss the similarities and differences in the sand samples, and why these similarities and differences exist.

* Empty film canisters can be obtained easily by the bagful from your local film developer.

Going further

1 Sift each sand sample through a fine mesh material (an old pair of panty hose will do fine) to sort out larger sand particles from the smaller particles.

How do the larger particles look?

Are they the same color and texture as the smaller particles?

2 Let children use a magnet* to find iron particles in each of the sand samples stored in the film canisters. (Use a paper towel to collect each set of iron particles from the different sand samples. Label each paper towel so that you will remember which sand sample the iron particles came from.)

Do some samples of sand have more iron particles than other samples do?

Where did the iron come from?

Why would some sand have more iron particles than other sand does?

3. Sorting sediments

Materials

For each child or group of children: sand, gravel, pebbles, mud, a clear plastic glass, water, a teaspoon.

Procedure

1 Tell children to:

- a Fill a clear plastic glass with water.
- b Drop in a teaspoon of sand, a teaspoon of gravel, a teaspoon of pebbles, and a teaspoon of mud.
- c Stir all of the ingredients vigorously together in the glass.
- d Observe the color of the water. (It will be brownish and hard to see through.)

2 Ask children the following kinds of questions:

What is another name for all of the dirt that is floating around in the water? (Sediments.)

*Be sure to place your magnet inside of a zip-lock baggie first, so that the iron particles can easily be removed from the exterior of the bag after the magnet is removed. Otherwise, it will be difficult to remove the loose iron particles from the magnet. (Audrey Brainard).

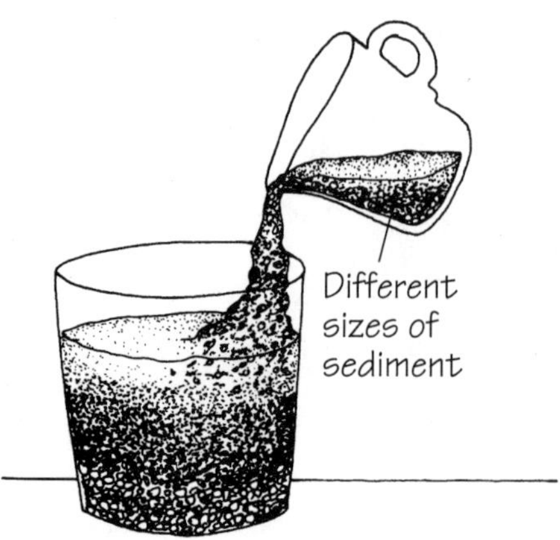

5-25 *Different sizes of sediments will sink differently.*

Will the water remain muddy-looking? (No, the sediments will settle to the bottom of the glass.)

Will the water ever become clear again? (Yes, the water will become clearer, but it will most likely not become as clear as it originally was unless it is filtered.)

If the sediments settle out and sink to the bottom, how will they settle out? (The sediments will sink differently. The heaviest particles will settle to the bottom first. Layers will form. Sorting will take place as the sediments settle.)

3 Let the muddy water sit for several hours or overnight and have the children observe what happens to it.

4. Separating salt from sand

5-26 *Sand sinks; salt floats.*

Materials

For each child or group of children: sand, salt, a clear plastic container, a teaspoon, water, clear plastic glasses.

Procedure

1 Show the children the sand and the salt.

2 Tell the children to mix the sand in a glass of water and observe what happens.

3 Then tell them to mix the salt into the water and observe what happens. (The sand will sink to the bottom. The salt will mix in with the water and float.)

4 Tell the children to mix the dry sand and salt together.

Can you think of a way to separate the salt from the sand? (See if they suggest adding water to the dry sand and salt.)

What do you think will happen to the salt when the water is added to the dry mixture of sand and salt? (The salt will separate itself from the heavier pieces of sand. The sand will sink. The salt will float.) *Note*: If the water with salt is poured into another glass, the salt will be separated from the sand. When the water evaporates, the salt will remain.

5 *Explain*: When some things are dissolved and others are not, it is called chemical erosion. Sometimes erosion is mechanical because rocks bounce against each other and break apart. When salt dissolves, it is a chemical reaction that causes erosion.

6 Allow children to continue to mix and separate the sand and salt. Also encourage them to tumble rocks together in a closed container so that they can see and experience the difference between chemical erosion and mechanical erosion.

5. Soil erosion due to water

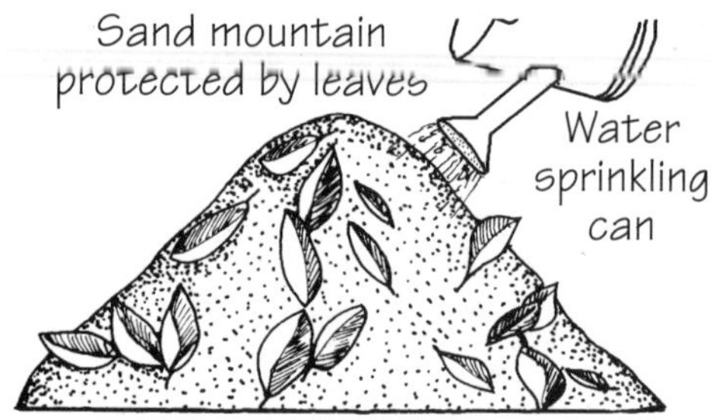

5-27A *Fallen leaves and roots help prevent erosion.*

Materials

A rectangular pan, sand, a block of wood, a water-sprinkling can, water, dead leaves, Popsicle sticks, an eye dropper.

Procedure

1 Create a miniature wet sand mountain inside one end of a rectangular pan. Place a wooden block underneath the

side of the pan that has the sand mountain so that the pan will be slightly elevated and tilted.

2 *Explain*: This wet sand mountain is a model of a mountain without any trees or grass.

What do you think will happen to the soil on the mountain when rain falls on it?

3 Choose a child to pour "rain" out of the sprinkling can.

4 Observe what happens to the mountain as the water hits the sand mountain.

Where does most of the erosion take place? (At the top of the mountain).

Where does the eroded soil go to? (It will tend to flow down and be carried by the water.)

5 Have the children rebuild the sand mountain.

6 Place some dead leaves on the sand mountain.

What do you think will happen when it rains if there are leaves covering the soil?

7 Choose a child to pour "rain" from the sprinkling can again and see if the dead leaves make a difference in the amount of soil that erodes away when it rains. (The leaves will control some of the erosion.)

8 Have children build up the sand mountain again. This time add Popsicle sticks to the sand mountain. (See Fig. 5-27B.)

5-27B *Roots help prevent erosion.*

9 *Explain*: The Popsicle sticks are like trees.

How do you think trees might affect the way water flows down the sand mountain?

10 Choose a child to pour the "rain" from the sprinkling can and observe the results. (The children might notice the formation of streams, dams, fan formations of water flowing, and delta formations being formed from the flow of water down the mountain.)

11 Have the children build up the sand mountain again.

12 Choose a child to use an eye dropper to drop water on the mountain.

13 Observe the erosion caused by a drop of water on the sand.

Will the height the drop of water falls from affect how much erosion occurs? (Yes, the higher the drop, the more force it will carry when it hits the sand surface.

14 Allow children to drop water drops very close to the sand surface and very far away from the sand surface.

15 Observe whether a drop causes more erosion when it falls at a slant or when it falls straight. Most importantly, be sure they observe where the soil goes when it erodes away. (It flows downhill with the water and is deposited there until it is moved again.)

6. Soil erosion due to wind

Materials

For each child or group of children: a pile of dry sand, a basin, some dead leaves, a drinking straw for each child, pictures cut from magazines showing wind erosion in the desert and on the plains.

Procedure

1 Tell the children you are going to blow on the sand with the drinking straw.

What do you think will happen to the sand when I blow on it? (Listen to their responses.)

2 Blow through the straw.

3 Let children observe the holes the wind is able to create in the mountain.

4 Observe the pictures of wind erosion cut from magazines. Discuss how the wind changed the landscape and blew sediments away causing erosion to take place.

5 Give children their own straw to experiment with to see the effects of wind erosion on the sand.

7. After a heavy rain

Materials

Access to puddles on a blacktopped area, to a flower bed, and to a run-off or stream caused by the rain.

Procedure

1 Observe puddles after a rain.

2 Ask the children the following question:

Where are puddles found? (Puddles are usually found where the soil is very hard, or where there is a low spot. Puddles are not usually found in flower beds, or in high places. Puddles are frequently found on sidewalks, on outdoor tennis courts, and on playgrounds. Note: Water cannot be absorbed into the soil when the soil is very hard or when it is cemented over or blacktopped.)

Going further

1 Draw a chalk mark around the perimeter of a puddle. After a few hours observe the puddle to see if it has changed. If it has, draw another chalk line around the new perimeter of the puddle. Continue to observe the puddle every few hours and to draw a chalk line around the new perimeter of the puddle as the puddle changes in size.

Which part of a deep puddle evaporates last? (The deepest part.)

Which part disappears first? (The outer edge, where water is more shallow.)

2 Discuss what makes a puddle go away: filling in the low spot with an absorbent material like sawdust or woodchips, sweeping the puddle with a broom, or waiting for the air to evaporate the puddle.

3 Observe any streams that might have formed due to the rain and any sediments that are being carried by the run-off of water from the land to the street.

8. Erosion due to freezing

Materials

A plastic container with a lid, water, access to a freezer or freezing outside temperature.

Procedure

1 Fill the container to the top with water. Cap the top with a lid. Tell the children you are going to place the filled container in the freezer.

What will happen to the water in the container when it is placed in the freezer? (They will probably respond that the water will freeze.)

2 Place the container in the freezer.

3 Allow the children to observe the container the next day after the water has frozen. The cap will be off or the container might be split open.

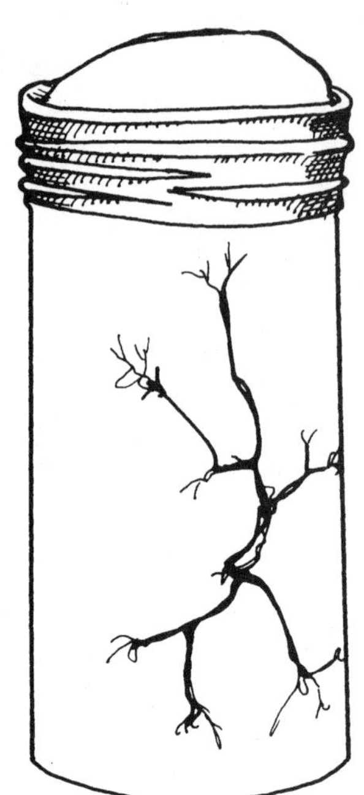

Water expands
when frozen
and cracks
plastic jar

5-28A *A closed jar filled with water will crack if the water inside freezes.*

A road contracts when it cools off
and expands when it heats up.
If it freezes, it also expands.

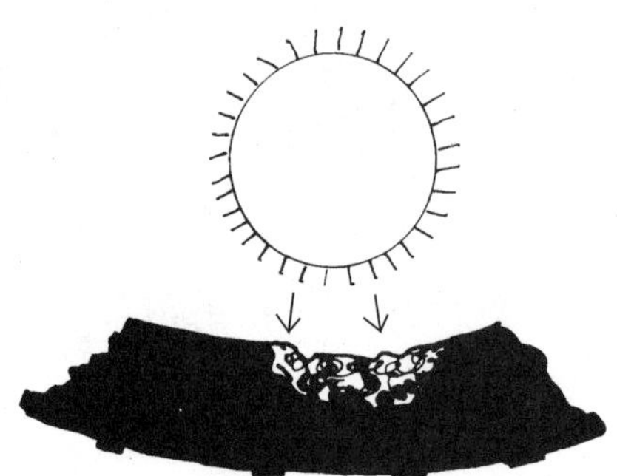

Eventually, the ground becomes
loose and a pothole occurs

5-28B *The formation of potholes in roads.*

Why did this container split open or why has the cap popped off? (You might have to explain to the children that when water freezes, it takes up more space. It expands, and when it does, things around it might break.)

Fine points to discuss

Why do potholes form in roads? (In the heat of day, the road expands; when it gets cold, the road contracts. But when the road freezes, it expands. The abrupt expansion and contraction of the roadway with uneven temperatures causes the road to break apart and potholes to form. (See Fig. 5-28B.)

Why do pipes burst when they freeze? (Pipes burst when the water in them freezes and expands. The frozen water pops the pipe. If water is running, the water leaks out of the frozen pipe and much water damage can take place.)

Why do sidewalks have cracks between joints, and why do bridges have expansion joints? (Cracks at joints in sidewalks and expansion joints in bridges help prevent possible damage due to expansion and contraction from changing temperatures and uneven temperature in the cement or steel.)

Why do railroad tracks have space between their joints and between railroad ties? (For the same reason that sidewalks and bridges have space—to allow for expansion and contraction with the least amount of damage from freezing temperatures.)

9. Erosion due to glaciers

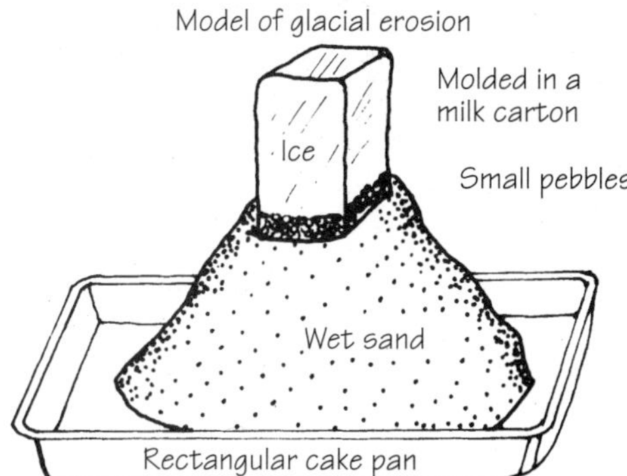

5-29 *Erosion from an ice-cube glacier.*

Materials

Wet sand, a rectangular pan, sand and small rocks frozen in water at the bottom of a cut-open quart milk container.

Procedure

1 *Explain*: In the far North and in the far South, the temperatures are very cold. In fact, the poles of the earth are surrounded by ice, and there are ice caps on both poles of the earth. Glaciers also form in high mountains at lower altitudes. When water freezes inside of a valley, a glacier is formed. As a glacier flows, or moves, it carries rocks and sediments with it. When the dinosaurs died out, there was a very cold time on the earth known as the Ice Age. During the Ice Age, there were a lot of glaciers on the earth. As the glaciers moved, they dug out pieces of land and formed lakes and valleys.

2 Have the children build a small, wet sand mountain in the rectangular pan. Place the frozen water with small rocks in it shaped like a small rectangle on top of the sand mountain.

3 *Explain*: The small block of ice with rocks frozen in it is a miniature model of a glacier. Glaciers often had rocks or boulders frozen in them. As the glacier moved, the rocks and boulders that were carried by them broke off or became loose.

4 Ask the following kinds of questions:

What will happen to the rocks in the frozen ice as the ice melts? (They will come loose.)

Where will the rocks move to? (It is not clear, but they will most likely fall off or roll down the sand mountain.)

What will happen to the sand mountain as the model glacier (ice cube) moves? (The mountain might have a change in its appearance due to the action of the model glacier. The rocks that the ice carries scrapes the rocks that are underneath the glacier and wears the rocks and surface of the earth's crust away.)

Going further

1 Let children slide an ice cube around on a smooth piece of tinfoil. Have them observe how easily it glides along.

2 Then have them place the model glacier (block of ice with small pebbles in its base) on the same piece of tinfoil and slide it around on the foil.

As you slide the glacier, what do you see, hear, and feel? Can the model glacier be slid around the foil without damaging it?

What does the glacier leave behind?

3 Place a meat tray under the tin foil so that one end of the meat tray creates

an elevation for the glacier to move down. (See Fig. 5-29.)

What do you observe as the glacier moves? (As the glacier moves, the smaller particles of sand will be carried down from the elevated area with the water that has melted off the top surface of the glacier that is next to the warm air. Most of the larger particles (rocks) will stay on top of the elevated area. *Note*: Heavier particles will tend to stay higher up. They usually fall out of the liquid right away, whereas smaller particles like sand and silt will be carried farther down with the melting stream.)

4 *Explain*: A glacial moraine occurs from particles—large and small—being carried or washed down a stream from a glacier's run-off of ice at the top surface, which has been melted by warm air. Sometimes, when you see large boulders in the middle of a park like those in Central Park in New York City, it is evidence of a terminal moraine. A glacier reached its southernmost point, dropped off particles of debris, and receded.

10. Falling sediment chart

Materials

For each child or group of children: white paper; colored pencils; clear Contact paper; a sketch of horizontal lines showing different depths of the ocean and the ocean floor; a strip of paper covered with spots; masking tape.

Preparation

1 Sketch a picture of the sky, the ocean, and the ocean floor—a sketch with a lot of straight horizontal lines. Another piece of paper should be colored all blue to represent the top of the ocean. (See Fig. 5-30.)

2 Color in the sketch with blues to represent the sky and the ocean, and browns to represent the ocean floor. Write labels for the sky, the ocean, and the ocean floor. Attach the labels to the sketch at appropriate places.

3 Cover the blue piece of paper and the sketch of the sky, ocean, and ocean floor with Contact paper. Cover the strip of paper covered with spots with Contact paper too. Label the sediments before covering it with Contact paper.

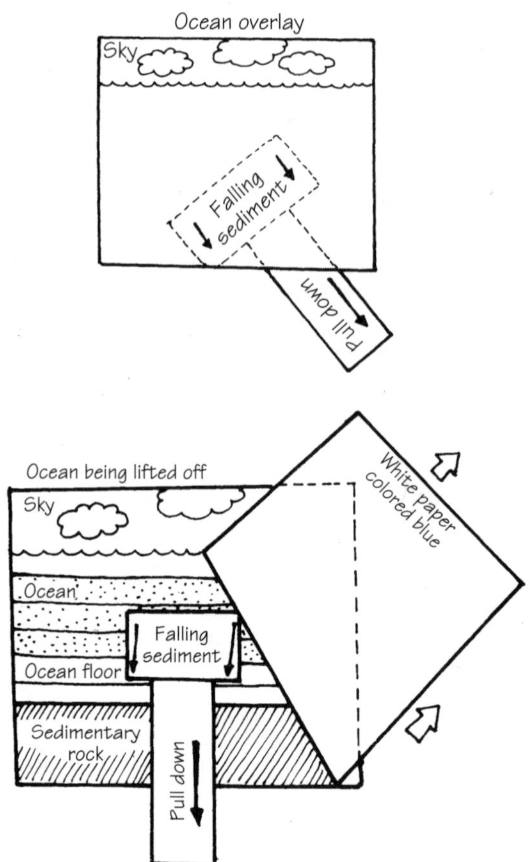

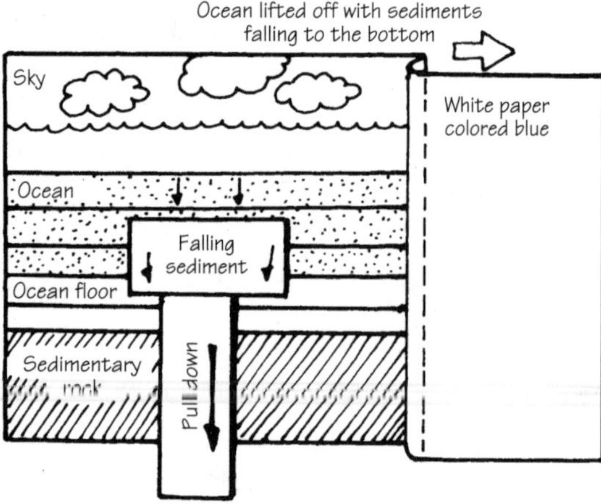

5-30 *Moving pictorial model that shows how sedimentary rock is formed.*

4 Use masking tape to form a hinge for the top of the ocean to connect to the sketch.

Procedure

1 Show the children the model of the ocean and the ocean floor. Lift off the top of the ocean to expose the layers of water inside of the ocean at the different depths and the ocean floor.

2 *Explain*: When it rains, water runs into streams and rivers, and eventually, much of the water that falls runs into

the ocean. The water that flows into the ocean is loaded with sediment. Show the sediment falling through the water. It eventually settles on the ocean floor. When a new layer of sediment falls, a new layer of soil is created and the bottom layer of soil gets pushed down and forms a new layer of sedimentary rock.

3 After your demonstration, allow children to make their own model of the ocean floor with falling sediment. (See Fig. 5-30).

11. Model of sedimentary rock formation

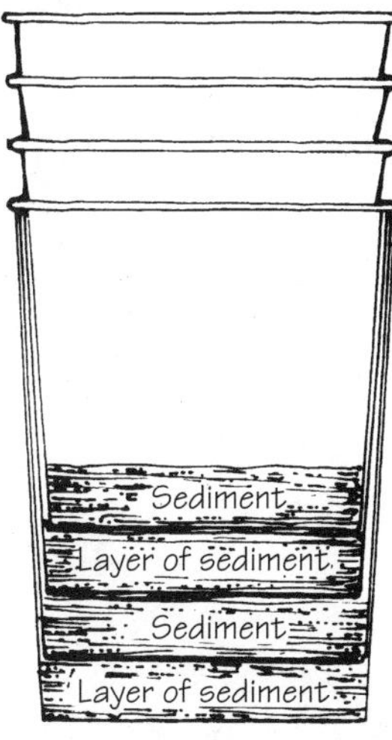

A series of plastic glasses on top of one another. Each glass contains some soil or sand and represents a layer of sediment.

5-31 *Model of sedimentary rock formation.*

Materials

For each child or group of children: several clear plastic glasses, sand.

Procedure

1 Fill several clear plastic glasses with a quarter of an inch of sand. Place one glass inside another. Several layers of sand will be seen through the clear plastic glasses.

2 *Explain*: The sand in the glasses is like a layer of sediment that settles out. Each glass of sand is like another layer of sediment that settles out. The layers fall on top of one another. Each glass holds a different layer of sediment. All of the layers are pressed together and form a piece of sedimentary rock. Sedimentary rock is made up of small particles or fragments that once belonged to another rock before it began to erode.

3 Allow children to make their own model showing layers of sedimentary rock.

12. Folds and faults on the earth's crust

Materials

Three towels in three different colors; three colors of clay; a butter knife.

Procedure

1 Fold the towels in strips, lengthwise. Place the three towels on top of each other. Press in on the sides so that the towels slide toward the center and form folds. (See Fig. 5-32.)

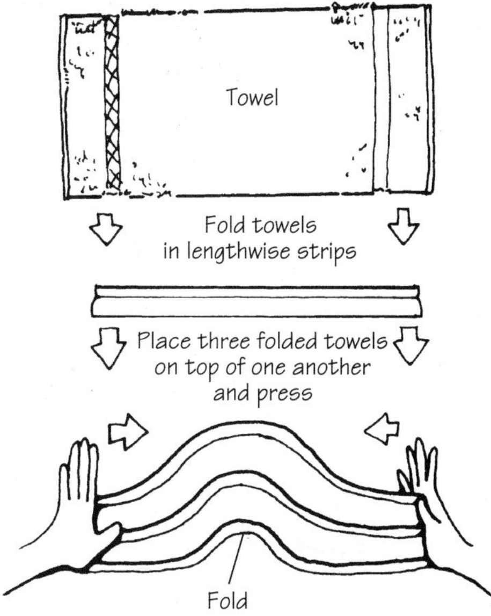

5-32 *Model of a fold.*

2 *Explain*: The layers of sedimentary rock and the layers of rock on the earth's crust form layers, just as the towels do. Pressures from inside or outside of the crust force the layers to fold up. When the layers fold up or to the side, different land forms are made. When the folds go up and down, mountains are formed. Mountains can be folded or can look like blocks if they were formed by breaks or faults.

3 Repeat the same procedure with the clay. Place the three different colors on top of each other in flat strips. Press in on each of the sides so that the clay folds up due to the external pressure.

4 Observe the folds and the formation of the layers.

5 *Explain*: The layers of the rocks get all mixed up when the folds occur. Parts

that were on top can be buried beneath in a fold. Parts that were on the bottom can come up to the top surface after a fold occurs.

6 Slice the clay with a bread knife to separate it. The clay will break. Place the two pieces of clay near each other, but do not align them evenly. This is what a fault looks like. A fault occurs when a break occurs in the earth's crust and the land shifts up or down along the crack or sideways along the crack. This occurs during an earthquake. (See Fig. 5-33.)

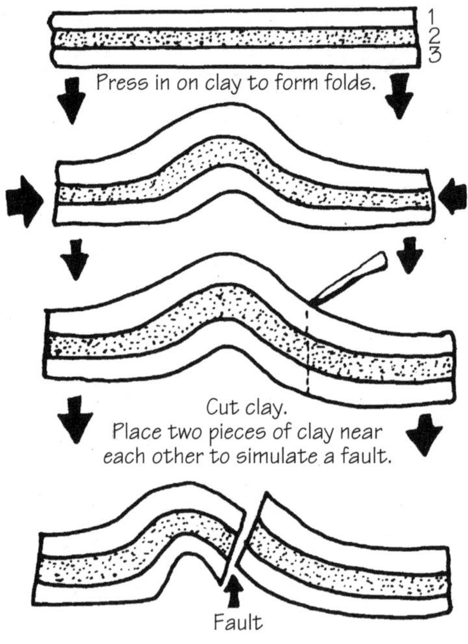
1
2
3
Press in on clay to form folds.
Cut clay.
Place two pieces of clay near each other to simulate a fault.
Fault

5-33 *Model of a fault with three colors of clay.*

7 Allow children to create a "fold" with a towel and with clay.

Further resources

Selected books for children and adults

Dewey Decimal Classification Number for rocks is 550, for volcanoes, 551.

Aliki. *Fossils Tell of Long Ago*. New York: Harper, 1990.

Barton, Byron. *Bones, Bones, Dinosaur Bones*. New York: Thomas Y. Crowell, 1990.

Bender, Lionel. *Mountain*. New York: Watts, 1989.

Boltin, Lee, and T. S. White. *Color Under Ground: The Mineral Picture Book*. New York: Charles Scribners Sons, 1971.

Borgeois, Paulette. *The Amazing Dirt Book*. Reading, Mass: Addison-Wesley. 1990.

Bramwell, Martyn. *Understanding and Collecting Rocks and Fossils*. Usborne, 1983.

Bramwell, Martyn. *Volcanoes and Earthquakes*. New York: Watts, 1986.

Branley, Franklyn M. *Earthquakes*. New York: Harper and Row, 1990. (Discusses why earthquakes happen, and their sometimes devastating effects.)

Branley, Franklyn M. *Volcanoes*. New York: Thomas Y. Crowell, 1985.

Challand, Helen. *A New True Book: Volcanoes*. Chicago: Children's Press, 1983.

Coldin, Augusta. *Salt*. New York: Thomas Y. Crowell, 1965. (Tells where salt comes from and how it is used, and how to grow a salt crystal.)

Cole, Joanna. *Evolution: The Story of How Life Developed on Earth*. New York: Harper & Row, 1987.

Cole, Joanna. *The Magic Schoolbus: Inside the Earth*. New York: Scholastic, 1987.

Gans, Roma. *Rock Collecting*. New York: Harper and Row, 1985.

Heavilin, Jay. *Rocks and Gems*. New York: Macmillan, 1964. (Large picture book.)

Hanif, M. *As the Earth Quakes, What Happens?* Science and Children, January 1990.

Hardy, G.R., and M.N. Tolman. *Cakequake! An Earthshaking Experience*. Science and Children, September, 1991. (A great article for adults and a wonderful picture to show children.)

Lasky, Kathryn. *Dinosaur Dig*. New York: Wm. Morrow, 1990.

Lasky, Kathyrn and photographs by Christopher Knight. *Surtsey: The Newest Place on Earth*. New York: Hyperion Books for Children, 1992. (Describes formation, naming and colonization of the 27-year-old volcanic island Surtsey, and how the first animals and plants became established there. This book has beautiful color photographs that show the birth of a volcanic island over a 30-year period.)

Lauber, Patricia. *The Eruption and Healing of Mount St. Helen's*. New York: Bradbury, 1986.

Lauber, Patricia. *How We Learned the Earth is Round.* New York: Thomas Y. Crowell, 1990.

Marcus, Elizabeth. *Rocks and Minerals.* Mahwah, NJ: Troll, 1983. (Book contains information on how to identify rocks.)

McGowen, Tom. *Album of Rocks and Minerals.* New York: Random House, 1982.

NSTA. *Earthquakes.* The National Science Teachers Association, Washington, DC.

Pearce, Q.L. *Quicksand and Other Earthly Wonders.* New York: Julian Messner, 1989. (From the Amazing Science Series, Grades 3–6.)

Peters, David. *Gallery of Dinosaurs and Other Early Reptiles.* New York: Knopf, 1989.

Podendorf, Illa. *The True Book of Pebbles and Shells.* Chicago: Children's Press, 1972. (K–4)

Podendorf, Illa. *Rocks & Minerals.* Chicago: Children's Press, 1982. (Appropriate for children in grades K–4.)

Pringle, Lawrence. *The Golden Book of Volcanoes, Earthquakes, and Powerful Storms.* Racine, WI: Western Publishers, 1992.

Simon, Seymour. *Earthquakes.* New York: Wm. Morrow, 1991. (Examines the phenomenon of earthquakes, describes how and where they occur, and how they can be predicted.)

Selsam, Millicent E. and Hunt, Joyce. *A First Look at Rocks.* Walker. 1984.

Van Rose, Susan. *Eyewitness Books: Volcanoe and Earthquake.* New York: Knopf, 1992. (Contains beautiful color photographs.)

Wyler, Rose. *Science Fun with Mud and Dirt.* New York: Simon & Schuster, 1986. (Contains "projects" that can be made with mud, as well as information about insects that use mud to build their homes. For children who can read.)

Selected resource books for more ideas

Lind, Karen K. *Water, Stones & Fossil Bones: A CESI Sourcebook.* Washington, D.C.: NSTA and CESI, 1991. (Contains a variety of earth science activities. Activities were contributed by individual teachers.)

Ortleb, Edward and Richard Cadice. *Geology—Rocks and Minerals* Saint Louis: Milliken Publishing Co, 1986.

Raymo, Chet. *The Crust of the Earth: An Armchair Traveler's Guide to the New Geology.* Englewood Cliffs, New Jersey: Prentice-Hall, 1983.

Van Cleave, Janice. *Earth Science of Every Kind.* John Wiley and Sons, 1991. (For children who can read. Grades 2–5.)

Weiner Esther. *Dirt Cheap Science: Activity Based Units, Games, Experiments and Reproducibles.* New York: Scholastic, 1992.

Wood, Robert W. *Science for Kids: 39 Easy Geology Experiments.* TAB Books, 1991. (Contains earth science activities for children who are able to read. Grades 3–6.)

Zim, Herbert, and Paul Shaffer. *Rocks and Minerals.* New York: Golden Books, 1989. (Guide book for identifying rocks and minerals.)

Zero Population Growth, ZPG. *The Earth As An Apple.* Kui Tatk Newsletter, Vol.1, No.1, Spring, 1984. Native American Science Education Association.

Selected literature connections for younger children

Baylor, Byrd. *Everybody Needs a Rock.* New York: Macmillan, 1985. (Story about finding and making a rock "special" by knowing what its special attributes are. K–3.)

Hoban, Tana. *More Than One.* (Beautiful photographs of collections of things. Good book for introducing the idea of starting a rock collection or nature collection. K–3.)

McNulty, Faith. *How to Dig a Hole to the Other Side of the World.* New York: Harper, 1979. (A story about a child who takes an imaginary 8,000-mile journey through the earth and discovers what's inside. K–3).

Peters, Lisa Westberg. *The Sun, the Wind, and the Rain.* New York: Holt, 1988. (Presents side-by-side narration of a mountain being formed, its shape being affected by the sun, wind, and rain, and a child's efforts at the beach to make a tall sand mountain that is also affected by nature's elements.)

General community enrichment activities

Visit a natural history museum Observe their collection of rocks and minerals.

Visit a rock and mineral show Observe the unfinished "natural" minerals and what they can be shaped into after they have been sliced, or cut and polished.

Visit a jewlery store or lapidary shop Observe how gem stones are cut, and the special equipment the lapidarist uses.

Visit a rock quarry Observe layers of rock and how it is quarried.

Visit a local potter or art class Observe an art teacher or potter shaping clay into bowls and/or other objects. Buy some clay to make your own creations.

6 Animals

Objectives

The objectives of this chapter are for children to develop an awareness of the following:

- That the world is made up of living and nonliving things.
- That most living things are either plants or animals.
- That animals live in many places.
- That all animals need food and water.
- That each animal needs its own kind of food.
- That animals are mobile.
- That animals can move in different ways (crawl, jump, slither, walk, run, etc.).
- That most animals move, eat, and grow.*

* Most animals do move, but exceptions are animals like sponges that do not move at all (except to grow), certain coelenterates (such as sea anemones, which seldom move about) and barnacles (which, as adults, stay anchored on their rocks)

- That animals adapt to their environment in different ways to aid their survival.
- That animals kept in captivity need to be taken care of.
- That life and living things should be respected.
- How to group or classify animals with similar characteristics or attributes.
- The meaning of the following terms: skeleton, exoskeleton, segmented, backbone, vertebrate, invertebrate, characteristic, group, classify.

General background information for parents and teachers

This chapter contains a lot of enrichment vocabulary for children as well as for you, the teacher. As adults, please use your discretion as to how much vocabulary a younger child is ready for. It is more important for younger children to become aware of a big concept. For example: Some animals eat meat, some animals eat plants, some animals eat both. Don't expect them to remember such words as carnivore, herbivore, and omnivore. It is good for children to be introduced to appropriate words, but please do not expect them to memorize the vocabulary.

Use of magnifying glass A good way for young children to use a magnifying glass is to place the magnifying glass next to the eye the way a jeweler does. Then move the object closer or nearer to the eye. This helps reduce the field of vision and eases the focusing problem young children might encounter. *Note*: If you hold the magnifying glass too far away from the eye, everything will look upside-down.

Observe To actually see, feel, smell, taste, or hear something.

Inference An interpretation of an observation we have made by using our senses.

Vertebrates Animals with backbones.

Invertebrates (small creatures) Animals without backbones.

Zoo A place where animals are cared for in captivity.

Camouflage Protective coloration to aid an animal to survive in its environment.

Metamorphosis Change in the structure and habits of an animal during normal growth, usually in the post-embryonic stage, prior to adulthood. Metamorphosis is common in the life cycle of insects and amphibians.

Adult insect All adult insects have six legs and three body regions (the head, thorax, and abdomen). All six legs and the wings are connected to an insect's thorax, which is in the middle of its body. Not all insects have wings. [Caterpillars are not adult insects.]

Regeneration When an animal is able to grow a new body part, it is called regeneration. Regeneration enables some animals to grow back a lost body part. (See III. 4. Growing new parts.)

Environment The natural world that surrounds an animal and influences its growth and development.

Domestic animal An animal that is raised and cared for by people.

Wild animal An animal that lives in the wild on its own and fends for itself.

Classify To arrange or organize according to a general or specific class or category.

Dichotomous classification To divide into two parts or classifications on the basis of one characteristic by only allowing two choices. Branching occurs through successive forking of two approximately equal divisions. For example: This animal has a backbone, or this animal has no backbone; this animal has six legs, or this animal has more than six legs; this animal has a segmented body, or this animal does not have a segmented body.

Classification scheme An orderly plan for classifying.

Method of classification Move from general to specific.

Scientific scheme for classification of animals Moves from a broad, general division to a more specific division that narrows the field of animals to one animal species. (See Table 6-1.)

- In studying animals with children, emphasis should be placed on gathering experiences and on developing a child's understanding of likenesses and differences between animals. It is a wonderful opportunity to help children become familiar with descriptive words to describe these

Table 6-1 Scientific names

		Human Being	Dog	Squirrel	Monarch Butterfly
General	Kingdom:	Animal	Animal	Animal	Animal
↓	Phylum:	Chordate (or vertebrate)	Chordate (or vertebrate)	Chordate (or vertebrate)	Arthropod
	Class:	Mammal	Mammal	Mammal	Insect
	Order:	Primate	Carnivore	Rodent	Lepidoptera
	Family:	Huminidae	Canidae	Sciurus	
	Genus:	Homo	Canis	Tamiasciurus	Danaus
Specific	Species:	Sapiens	Familiaris (or domestic)	Carolenis	Plexippus

likenesses and differences, and to develop the ability to make inferences about these observations.

- It is also a great opportunity to help children develop their ability to skillfully sort and group animals, and to work out a dichotomous classification scheme.
- Actually observing live animals gives children an opportunity to use their senses and to learn from the sensory input. Use live specimens or pictures of animals. Avoid doing mental activity without any materials. Telling does not work as well as real experiences with tangible materials. Encourage children to do something with the materials. Also avoid having children memorize trivia and vocabulary for the sake of enriching their vocabulary.
- Ask as many questions as possible to arouse children to become even more astute as observers. Help children find answers to your questions, listen to their responses and questions, and continue to ask more questions.
- Remember that the world is new to children. Help guide them to see things that are evident to us as adults, but not evident to them.
- When experimenting with animals, five criteria for good investigations are:
  1 The animals should be respected and not harmed.
  2 In order to know if the animal is doing something different when it approaches an obstacle or is disturbed, we first must know what its usual behavior is.
  3 An animal must be given a choice if it is going to show a preference for doing one thing instead of another.
  4 Before reaching a conclusion, the same experiment should be done more than once.
  5 The animal should be returned to its natural environment when the experiment or investigation is finished.
- When studying and observing animals, try to start with living things. Then, after careful observation, have the children try to build models of the animals. If live specimens are not available, then use high-quality color photographs. These kinds of animal photographs are abundant in publications like *National Wildlife*, *Ranger Rick Magazine*, and *World Magazine*. There are also many recently published books with good quality color pictures at the library.

Note: As you do these activities with your children, try to encourage them to keep a science journal of their observations and their thoughts.

Activities and procedures

I. Introduction to animals

6-2 *Sort the living things and non-living things.*

What is an animal?

Materials

For each child or group of children: assorted living and nonliving things, such as: various house plants; small pets like a goldfish, canary, kitten, puppy, hamster, guinea pig, rabbit, turtle; smaller animals such as insects (grasshopper, beetle, cricket, ant), millipede, spider, snail; rocks, sea shells, etc.

Procedure

1 Introduce the children to the assorted living and nonliving things. Have them observe at least two or three animals that are alive. Ask them to compare the animals to one another by asking the following kinds of questions:

How are the animals different? (They have different features such as: different skin coverings and colors, and different sizes and shapes. They make different kinds of sounds or none at all. They move differently from one another. Some move faster or slower than the others, etc.)

How are they alike? (They are all alive. They each have a way to eat and a way to move.)

How are animals different from plants? (Plants cannot walk or move from where they are planted unless someone moves them. Animals are mobile.)

What makes plants and animals alike? (They are both living things.)

Are we living things? (Yes.)

Are we plants or animals? (Animals.)

What kind of animal are we? (Human beings.)

What do human beings have in common with cats, dogs and mice? (We have legs, eyes, ears, tongues, noses, hair on our bodies, hearts, lungs, bones, etc.)

What is the largest animal you can think of? (The blue whale is the largest animal alive today, but whatever answer your children give is the largest they can think of.)

What is the smallest animal you can think of? (One-celled animals like the amoeba are the smallest animals; however, these animals are probably not in a young child's experience, so whatever animal a child names as the smallest is the smallest for that child to think of.)

2 Instruct children to:
  a Find or make pictures of living things and nonliving things.
  b Sort the pictures into piles of living and nonliving things.
  c Further sort the pictures of living things into plants and animals.

2. Where do animals live?

Materials

Assorted pictures of various terrains and environments; assorted pictures of animals, at the zoo or in their natural environment.

Procedure

1 Show the children the pictures. Discuss where the various animals live.
2 Ask the following kinds of questions:

Can polar bears live in warm climates? Why not? (No. Their heavy fur would make them too hot.)

Can seals live on land away from water? Why not? (No. They need to be able to catch fish so they will not starve.)

Can turtles live in the Antarctic? Why not? (No. They cannot control their body temperature.)

Can tropical birds from warm areas live outdoors during the winter if it snows? Why not? (No. Tropical birds are not adapted to cold weather. Also, their bright colors would not provide them with good camouflage in the snow.)

Where do earthworms live? (Under the ground in moist soil.)

Do earthworms live in deserts? (Not usually; it is too dry for them.*

Is there any place animals do not live on the earth? (Animals live almost every place on the earth, unless the conditions are too extreme for them to live.)

When animals are alive at the zoo, do they all have the same kinds of surroundings? (No. Zookeepers make the homes and environments of the animals they care for as much as possible like the environment the animals are accustomed to in their natural environment.)

Are all animals at the zoo fed the same thing? (Probably not. This can be found out by visiting the zoo at feeding time.)

Is your backyard a natural environment? (Yes.)

Where can you find animals in your backyard? (In the soil, under logs and rocks, in trees, on flowers, in the grass, in puddles, under lawn furniture.)

Are the animals you would find in your backyard larger or smaller than you are? (Most of the animals would be smaller than you are.)

II. Small creatures

1. Looking for small creatures

Materials

For each child or group of children: a magnifying glass, flashlight, shovel, hand trowel, strainer.

Procedure

1 Take the children outside and look for small creatures with them. Have them gently turn over large rocks, roll logs over, look under dead leaves, examine tree bark, and inspect different parts of plants for small creatures. If there is a

* "Earthworms live in most lands of the world, including oceanic islands and subaractic regions. They are scarce in poor, acid, sandy, or dry situations." (Storer, T. I., General Zoology, pp. 517-18. See Bibliography.)

6-3 Lift a rock or log to find small creatures.

pond in your vicinity, go to it and look for small creatures along the edge of the pond, on the banks, and in the long grasses.

2 Use the flashlight to see better under rocks and logs. Small creatures are often the same color as the soil and are hard to see. Once you find them, look at them through the magnifying glass. To find small creatures, you might have to turn the soil over with a shovel or a small hand trowel and sift loose soil with a strainer.

3 Help children come to the understanding that the soil, plants, and ponds are filled with animal life. Have children notice:
- The colors of these small animals.
- How they move.
- Where they live.
- What they appear to be doing.
- What they appear to be eating.

4 Have the children observe the small creatures in their natural environment.

How many different kinds of small creatures are on one plant?

How many of the same kind of small creatures are on the plant or under one rock?

How many flying insects visit one flower?

How many bees visit the same flower?

5 Help children observe the physical surroundings where the animal lives.

Does the animal appear to like light or dark places?

Does it appear to like moist or dry places?

Going further

Additional trips outdoors would be useful for observing where small creatures can be found on a sunny day, and where they can be found on a rainy day. Also, to observe whether the time of day or season of the year makes a difference as to where animals are found, and as to whether or not the animals are found at all.

2. Creating a zoo for small creatures

Materials

For each child or group of children: nature guidebook about invertebrates, a large number of clear plastic shoe boxes or empty one-quart jars with wide mouths (peanut butter and mayonnaise jars are excellent), aquarium tanks, soil, compost, dried food, cut-up fresh fruits and vegetables, dead leaves, cotton balls, black construction paper, cheesecloth or nylon mesh from old pantyhose, rubber bands, cardboard boxes, marking pens, index cards, Scotch tape.

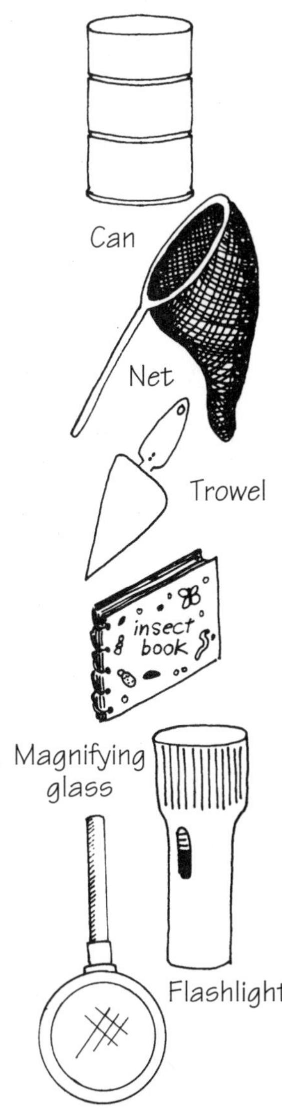

6-4 Materials for starting a small-creature zoo.

Procedure

1 *Explain:* It is possible to collect a large variety of small creatures and create a zoo of small creatures.

2 Ask the children the following kinds of questions:

What is a zoo? (A place where animals live.)

What do zoos have? (Animals, zookeepers, cages or houses for animals, benches, trash cans, trees and grass and flowers, food stands for visitors.)

How does a zoo keep animals? (By taking care of the animals that are living there, by providing the animals with the kind of environment and foods that keep them healthy.)

How do zookeepers know how to take care of the animals in the zoo? (By observing them in their natural environment before they are captured, and by observing the way the animal acts in captivity.)

Why do people enjoy visiting zoos? (Probably because they enjoy observing animals and enjoy watching the way the various animals move and eat and play. Also because they want to learn about other animals.)

What could we find out if we created a zoo for small creatures? (We could compare the small creatures. We could observe the ways they move and eat. We could observe the way they live.)

What would we have to do to run a small creature zoo? (Keep the animals safe, well fed, and comfortable.)

3 Show the children the various materials and ask them to suggest how these materials could be used to create cages or houses for the animals or labels or instructions about caring for the animals.

3. Collecting small creatures for a classroom or home small-creature zoo

Materials

For each child or group of children: assorted empty jars with lids, a sturdy butterfly net (can be used in a pond as well as in the air), flashlight, a magnifying glass, hand trowel, rectangular plastic basin or cardboard box to carry everything in and to keep the jars safe, masking tape, marking pen, nature guidebook about invertebrates.

Procedure

1 Follow the same procedure as in Activity II, Procedure 1, but this time, when you find the small creatures try to catch them. *Note*: Catching small creatures is not always easy. Some of them move very fast. It is their ability to move quickly that often saves their lives.

2 After capturing a small creature:
a Place it in a jar and close the lid.
b Observe what it looks like.

3 Have the children thumb through the nature guidebook until they find an animal that looks like the one you just captured. Read about it. Find out what kind of food it likes to eat. If there is no mention of the food the animal eats, then place a sample of soil or leaves in the jar with the animal from where it was found so that it will not starve. Place a piece of masking tape on the jar and use a marking pen to write the identity of the kind of creature that is in the jar.

6-5A Catch a small creature.

6-5B Identify the creature's picture in a nature field guide book.

Note: Do not worry about putting holes in the jar lid. There is enough air in the jar for the animal to live for several hours. If you open the jar lids every few hours for a few seconds, the small creatures will have enough air. If you poke holes in the metal lids, the sharp points on the lids could injure the small animals inside the jars and/or the animals might be able to escape out of the holes.

4 Emphasize to the children that they should leave the places they have looked for small creatures as undisturbed as possible. They should replace rocks and logs that they have lifted. Remind them that it is necessary to capture only a few of the small creatures they have seen, not everything that moves. Stress the care of living things and a respect for life. Animals should not just be collected. Children should understand that the animals are being collected so they can be observed. The animals should be provided with a suitable place to live for a few days while they are being observed. After they are observed they should be returned to natural surroundings outside. Children can watch them return to the soil when they are brought back outside.

4. Suitable temporary housing for small creatures

Note: The small creatures are listed in alphabetical order. Most of them require similar housing with slight variations. Read on for specifics.

CAUTION An adult needs to supervise the capturing of small creatures and also needs to carry any glass container. Glass containers could be hazardous for a small child to carry.

Ants

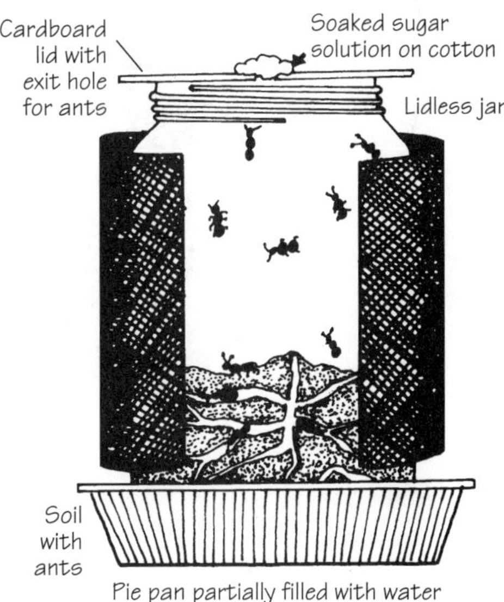

6-6 *Ant home.*

Materials

An empty one-quart jar, a pie pan filled with water, a piece of black construction paper, a rubber band, a small piece of cardboard with a hole in the center to rest on top of the jar, soil containing ants, a hand trowel, a piece of cotton soaked with sugar water.

Procedure

Have a child place the soil containing the ants in the jar with the hand trowel. Then have him or her place the jar in the pie pan filled with water. (The water will prevent the ants from escaping.) Have a child place a piece of cotton soaked in sugar water on top of a piece of cardboard with a hole in the center. (The ants will come to the surface to feed. You might want to add a piece of dark-colored construction paper to the outside of the jar since the ants will feel more at home in a dark environment. Then you can lift off the paper to see the activity along the sides of the jar.) (See Fig. 6-6.)

Caterpillars

6-7 *Caterpillar home.*

Materials

An empty one-quart jar or clear plastic shoe box, a small container for water, a small twig from the tree or plant where the caterpillar was found, some moist soil, a piece of bark, nylon mesh, a rubber band to secure the mesh as a lid.

Procedure

Have a child place the soil on the bottom of the jar and a piece of bark at a slant against the jar. Place the twig in the water on top of the soil so that the leaves will stay alive longer. Place the caterpillar on the twigs. Caterpillars are very fussy about what they munch. They have very specific kinds of leaves they enjoy eating. So be sure you take a twig with you that the caterpillar was crawling on when you caught it. See Fig. 6-7.

Note: The soil and the bark are in the cage in case the caterpillar decides to pupate while it is in captivity. Different species pupate in different kinds of places, so allow for all possibilities.

Crickets

Materials

An empty one-quart jar or clear plastic shoe box, soil, clumps of grass or dead leaves, a medium-size rock to hide under, raisins, dry cereal, bread or cake crumbs, lettuce, a few drops of water shaken from your hands.

Procedure

Have a child fill the bottom of the container with soil and add a layer of leaves or grass clumps to the top of the soil. Have another child place a rock on top of the soil so the cricket can hide under it. Then have another child place some food for the cricket to eat on top of a large leaf, and add the cricket or crickets to the container. Remember to have the children sprinkle a few drops of water into the container every day.

Earthworms

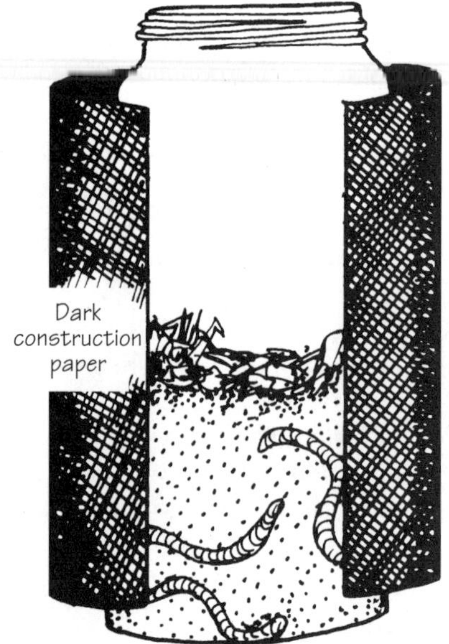

6-8 *Earthworm home.*

Materials

An empty jar or clear plastic shoe box, moist soil taken from where the earthworms were found, pieces of grass or dead leaves, dark construction paper, a rubber band or Scotch tape, dry oatmeal, coffee grounds or cornmeal.

Procedure

Have a child fill the jar about three-quarters full with moist soil. Have another child sprinkle some dry food and grass or dead leaves on top of the soil. Choose another child to mix the soil lightly so that the food matter is in the soil. Then have children add the worms to the jar. Cover the sides of the jar with dark construction paper. Secure the paper with Scotch tape or a rubber band. Be sure to have the children sprinkle the soil with water every day so that it stays moist. Remind the children not to make the soil too moist or the worms will drown.

Fireflies

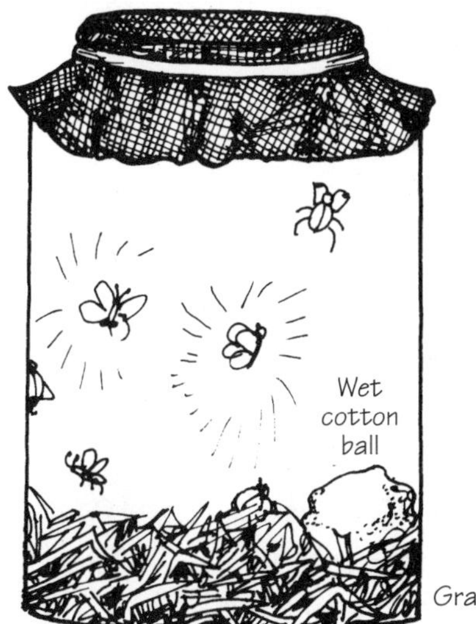

6-9 *Firefly home.*

Materials

An empty jar with a lid, nylon mesh, a rubber band, a wet cotton ball, pieces of grass to cover the bottom of the jar.

Procedure

Have a child place some pieces of grass at the bottom of a jar. Take the children outside at twilight in spring or summer. Instruct the children to use a butterfly net or their two hands to catch some fireflies. Place the fireflies inside the jar. Quickly place the lid on top so that they will not fly away. Put a wet piece of cotton in the jar so that they will have some water. Replace the metal lid with a mesh lid and a rubber band so that they can receive air. Keep them in captivity only a day or less. They do not eat much. They live only to mate. Both the male and the female light their light to attract each other.

Note: It is not respectful to the firefly to keep it in captivity. Captivity prevents fireflies from finding a mate and from allowing the female to lay her eggs.

Flies

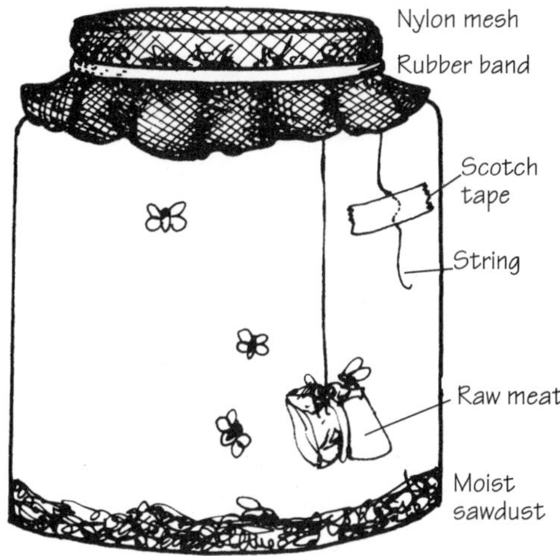

6-10 *Housefly home.*

Materials

An empty one-quart jar; cheesecloth or nylon mesh obtained from an old pair of cut-up pantyhose; a rubber band; a piece of string with a small piece of raw meat tied to one end, or a cotton ball soaked in sugar water or honey; moist sawdust.

Procedure

Have a child place moist sawdust at the bottom of the jar. Have another child place a string with meat or a cotton ball soaked with honey or sugar water so that it dangles inside the jar. Place the fly or flies in the jar. Cover the jar with the cheesecloth or nylon mesh. Secure the mesh to the top of the jar. (The transfer will be easier if it is possible to place the fly in a freezer for a few seconds to slow it down.) (See Fig. 6-10.)

Grasshoppers

Materials

An empty clear plastic shoe box or other clear container, sand or soil, nylon mesh, a rubber band or a piece of string, wheat, raw corn cob, grasses, a wet cotton ball.

Procedure

Have a child make the container ready for the grasshopper by placing sand or soil on the bottom of the container and a layer of grasses on top of the soil. Have another child sprinkle wheat grasses or part of a corn cob in the container. Choose another child to add a wet cotton ball. Then add the grasshopper or grasshoppers. Cover the top with a mesh lid secured with a rubber band or a piece of string tied together.

Ladybugs

Materials

An empty one-quart jar, a piece of cheesecloth or nylon mesh, a rubber band, a cotton ball soaked in water to create dampness inside the jar, a piece of a rose plant containing live aphids.

Note: Aphids are insect pests. They often live on rose plants. Aphids attack the young shoots and buds of the plant.

Procedure

Have a child place a wet cotton ball inside a jar. Add a piece of rose plant infested with live aphids and add the ladybugs to the jar. Secure the piece of cheesecloth or nylon mesh over the opening of the jar with the rubber band.

Mealworms

Materials

An empty clear plastic shoe box, oatmeal or a bran cereal box, a piece of cut-up apple or a moist cotton ball, a small bottle cap.

Procedure

You do not need to place a lid on top of the mealworms. They cannot climb out of the container. Have a child fill the bottom of the container with oatmeal. Have another child place a piece of cut-up apple inside the container for moisture, or add a moist cotton ball to a small bottle cap. Mealworms are the larva form of a beetle. They can be purchased at a pet store. Pet stores usually sell mealworms as food for other animals like lizards and fish.

Millipedes

Materials

Damp earth; soft green leaves or small pieces of cut-up apple, banana or orange; an empty one-quart jar with a mesh lid secured by a rubber band.

Procedure

Have a child place a layer of moist soil on the bottom of the jar. Then choose another child to place a layer of soft green leaves and a layer of small cut-up fruit pieces inside the jar. Then place the millipedes inside and cover the jar with nylon mesh secured with a rubber band.

Slugs

Materials

A small cardboard carton; an empty one-quart jar; moist compost soil; a cut-up carrot, apple, potato, or pear; nylon mesh and a rubber band.

Procedure

Have a child fill the bottom of the jar with moist soil and dead leaves. Have another child place a cut-up fruit or vegetable on top of the soil. Have the children put slugs into the jar and cover the lid of the jar with nylon mesh and a rubber band. Put the jar into a cardboard box so that it will seem dark to the slugs. They prefer a dark, damp environment.

Land snails

Materials

An empty one-quart jar; moist soil; dead leaves; a small dish sunk into the moist soil and filled with food, which should consist of raw vegetables or oats.

Procedure

Set up an aquarium filled with moist soil for the snails.

Pond snails

Materials

An empty one-quart jar, some sand, a water plant from an aquarium supply store, water. Pond snails can also be bought at the aquarium supply store if you cannot find your own.

Procedure

Set up an aquarium filled with water for the snails.

Sow bugs

Materials

An empty one-quart jar or shoe box, damp soil, a thick piece of bark, moist dead leaves, mesh netting, a rubber band.

Procedure

Have a child fill the bottom of the jar with the damp soil. Have another child place a

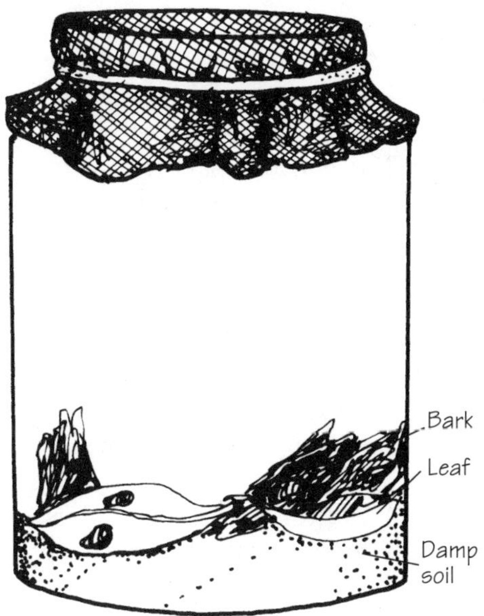

6-11 Sowbug home.

layer of moist dead leaves on top of the soil. Choose another child to place a piece of bark on top of the leaves as a shelter for the sow bug. Add the sow bug, cover the jar with mesh, and secure it with a rubber band.

Spiders

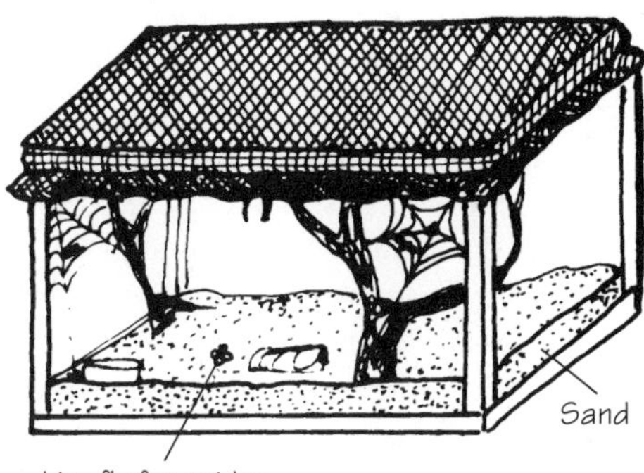

6-12 Spider home.

Materials

An empty aquarium, sand, twigs planted in the sand to supply supports for a possible web that might be spun, a dish of water, a toilet paper tube (for spider to hide in), a nylon mesh covering, a string to secure nylon mesh covering as a lid, flies to eat. (See Fig. 6-12.)

Procedure

Obtain a spider from your house or from the garden outside. After the jar has been made ready for it, place the spider inside the jar. Do not worry about catching flies for it right away. Spiders can live several days without food.

Of the four kinds of widow spiders, only the female widow spiders are dangerous. They are usually found in low, dark places, under logs, in wood piles, in barns, in sheds and in basements. When concerned, a widow will bite in self defense. It also rushes out to attack if its web is triggered. The black widow has a shiny black body with a red or yellow spot shaped like an hourglass on the underside of its abdomen. There are very few around, but children should be warned about them. The brown recluse is another poisonous species of spider.

5. Creating general guidelines with children for observing and investigating small creatures in captivity

Materials

None.

Procedure

1 Discuss with the children how to observe and handle the small creatures. "Observe" means to use our senses—our noses, ears, and eyes. Explain that taste is not used unless we know it is safe to taste. Touch is not used unless we know we are not hurting the small creature. Explain that it is necessary to be gentle with our touch when we feel a small creature because we can hurt it.

2 Discuss the things that children can be looking for when they make observations. The following is a partial list of the kinds of things children can be looking for and thinking about when they observe the small creatures in the small-creature zoo.

How does it use its body to move?

How does it use its body to eat?

How does it find its food?

Does it have legs? How many?

Does it have wings? How many?

Does its color help camouflage it? How?

How steep a slope can the small creature climb?

How does the small creature react to water?

How does it react to obstacles in its path?

How does it react when it meets another small creature?

What does it do when it is disturbed?

Can it be made to back up?

What does it have in common with other small creatures?

Which of all the small creatures seems to move the slowest?

Which small creatures appear to like well-lit places? Why?

Which small creatures appear to like dark places? Why?

Which animals prefer dry places?

Which prefer moist places? Why?

Which animals appear to be helpful to us? Why?

Which animals appear to be pests to us? Why?

Does the creature prefer to be on top of things or hidden underneath?

Which of all the small creatures seems to be able to move the fastest?

6. Materials for observing and investigating small creatures in captivity

Materials

For each child or group of children: a magnifying glass, eye dropper, water, a clear plastic container, a plastic lid, toothpick, a twig, a ruler, a piece of black construction paper and a piece of white construction paper taped together so that they lie side by side with a common border, a moist paper towel, a cellulose sponge.

Procedure

1 Show the children the materials. Discuss how each of the items can be used to observe and find out more about each of the animals in captivity.

Fine points: Encourage older children to record their observations and investigations of the small creatures in their science journals.

2 A magnifying glass can be used for observing the small creature's body, its parts, its color and texture, and for taking a closer look at how the animal moves or eats.

3 An eye dropper can be used for lifting and dropping water in the small creature's path, and for creating a small puddle of water. Also used for touching and lifting the small creature.

4 A clear plastic container can be used for observing the small creature in a small space.

5 A plastic lid can be used as an obstacle in the small creature's path, or for a closer look at the way the small creature behaves in a small space.

6 A toothpick or a twig can be used as an obstacle or as a touching and lifting tool, and as a tool for making the small creature back up or climb.

7 A ruler can be used for measuring the length of small creature. It can also be used as an incline to see how steep an incline the animal can climb up or down.

8 Black-and-white construction paper taped together can be used for finding out whether an animal prefers to be on light or dark surfaces, or under light or dark surfaces.

9 A moist paper towel can be used to find out if the creature prefers to be on top of or underneath moist surfaces.

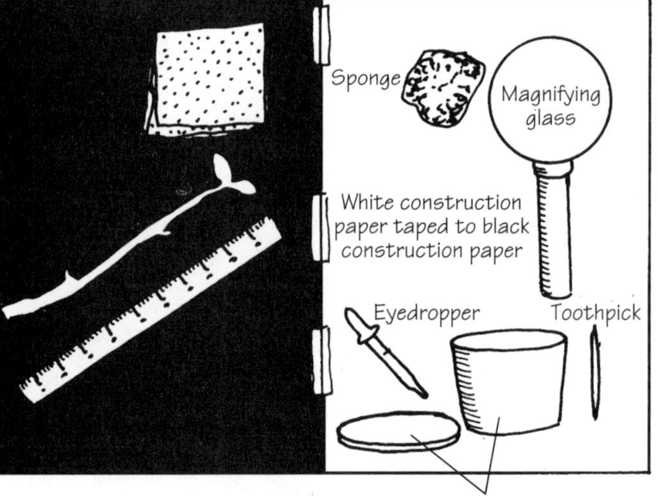

6-13 *Materials needed for observing interactions of small creatures.*

10 A moist cellulose sponge can be used as an obstacle in a small creature's path and as an item for a small creature to crawl under.

7. Investigations and observations of specific small creatures while in captivity

Note: The small creatures are listed in alphabetical order. Activities are suggested for each animal. The choice should be up to the individual child as to whether or not the child wishes to participate. Some children and adults are squeamish around crawly, small creatures. If, as an adult, you do not feel comfortable, your attitude will be felt by the children. If you do feel uncomfortable, try to get over it by dealing with your fears. Discuss your fears and the fears the children have with them. Remember that the animals are much smaller than you are and that they have more to fear than you do. They do not inflict death if they bite you. If they do bite you, it will feel like a slight pinch. Unless there is an extremely allergic reaction, the bite would be no worse than a mosquito's bite. If you use a twig, toothpick, or eye dropper to gently handle the small creature, there is less chance of being bitten and/or damaging the small creature's body.

Ants

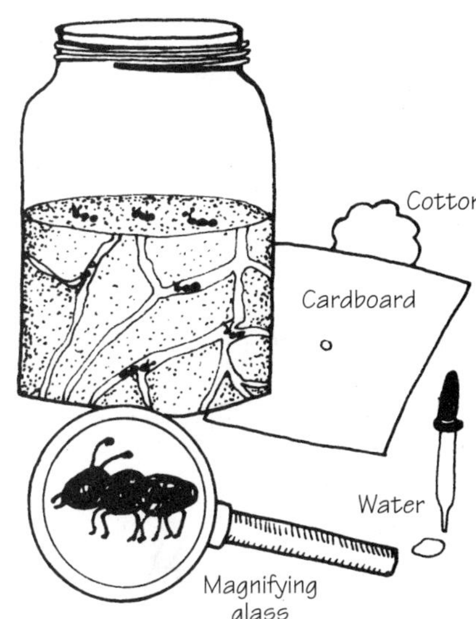

6-14 *Observing ants.*

Materials

For each child or group of children: a magnifying glass, a small plastic container, cookie or cake crumbs, ants in a jar filled with soil and covered on the outside with dark construction paper, water, eye dropper.

Procedure

1 Have a child remove the dark paper from the outside of the jar.

Are there any visible tunnels?

Are ants in the tunnels?

How many ants come to the surface of the lid at one time to eat the sugar water in the cotton ball?

How do the ants move in the light and in the dark?

What do two ants do when they meet each other?

How do ants use their feelers or antennae on top of their heads?

2 After you have observed the ants, cover the jar with the dark paper again. Next time you look, see if there are more tunnels.

3 Suggest that older children record their observations in their science journals.

4 Remove a few ants that are feeding on the cotton soaked with sugar water from the lid of the jar.

5 Place the ants in a small container. (If you place the container in the refrigerator with a cover, it will slow the ants down a little so that it will be easier to observe them.)

6 Observe the ants through a magnifying glass.

How many legs do they have? (Six.)

How many sections do their bodies have? (Three.)

How many antennae do they have? (Two.)

What colors are they? (Brown, red, or black.)

7 Place a few drops of water in the container.

What do ants do when they feel water?

8 Drop a few food crumbs into the container.

What do the ants do?

9 Place the ants back in the jar with the other ants or put them back outside when you finish with them.

Caterpillars

Materials

For each child or group of children: a magnifying glass, jar of caterpillars with the

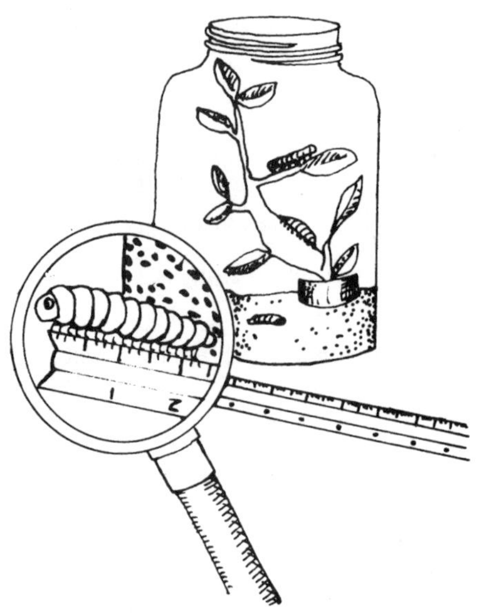

6-15 *Observing caterpillars.*

food they like to eat, a piece of paper, a ruler, eye dropper, water.

Procedure

1 Have the children observe the caterpillars in the jar.

What are they doing?

Where are they located?

How much have they eaten?

What do the leaves that they have been on look like?

Has the caterpillar built a cocoon?

2 Have the children remove a caterpillar or two from the jar. Place them on a piece of paper. Place a ruler next to one. Try to measure how long it is. Look at it through the magnifying glass.

How many segments does it have?

How many legs does it have?

Does every segment have legs?

How does it move?

Does it slide or hump along?

3 Hold the paper at a slant.

Can the caterpillar crawl up a steep slope?

How steep?

What happens when the caterpillar comes to water?

What do two caterpillars do when they meet?

Note: Caterpillars are the larval form of moths and butterflies. Most of them are considered pests because they eat a lot.

Crickets

Materials

For each child or group of children: crickets in a plastic container with soil, bark, and dead leaves; a magnifying glass.

Procedure

1 Have the children observe the crickets in captivity.

What do they do?

Where do they go to?

What do they do when they meet?

Do they all chirp?

Where does the noise come from?

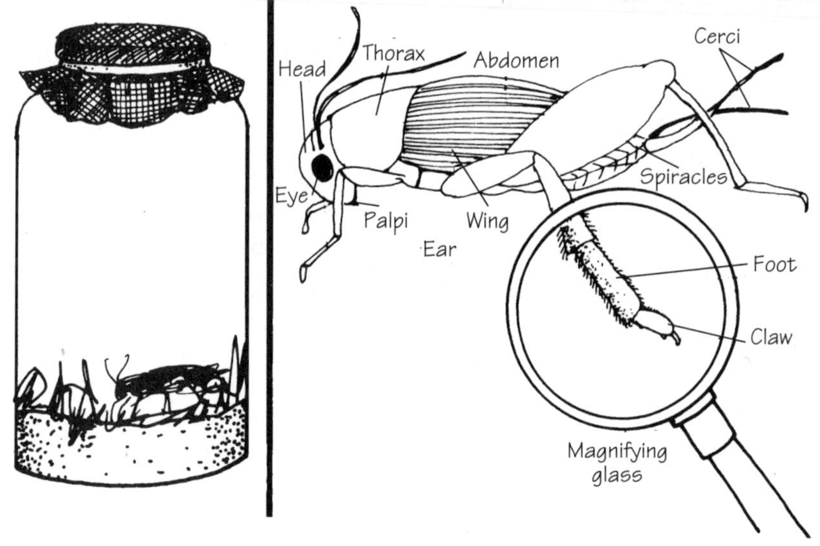

6-16 *Observing a cricket close up.*

How many legs do they have?

Why do they make noise?

Do all of the crickets look alike?

Note: Only male crickets make noise or chirp. They chirp to attract a female mate. The noise is made when the male cricket lifts its wings and rubs them together. Male crickets can be easily distinguished from female crickets; female crickets have a long-looking spike at the end of their abdomen. The spike is called an ovipositor. An ovipositor is used to store eggs and to bury eggs under the ground. (Young children will enjoy hearing you read Eric Carle's *The Very Quiet Cricket*. The book has a noise making device contained within the book that makes a cricket's chirping sound.)

2 Have the children find a female and a male cricket. Place the male cricket in one jar and the female cricket in another jar.

When the male chirps, what does the female do?

3 Move the jar a little farther away from the female.

What does the female do?

If you move the male cricket into another room so that the female can no longer see the male cricket, what does the female do when the male chirps?

How can you tell if the female can hear the male? (When the female hears the male, she turns toward the male, or she hops in his direction.)

4 Place a cricket in a small box. Have the children examine the cricket with a magnifying glass. See if children can locate the following parts: head, thorax, abdomen, four wings, eyes, antennae, palpi, feet, ears (located on each of its front legs under the knees), cerci (the two short spikes), spiracles (along the abdomen, for breathing). See Fig. 6-16.

5 Locate the abdomen on the cricket. Watch the abdomen move in and out as the cricket breathes.

Who breathes faster, you or the cricket?

Earthworms

Materials

For each child or group of children: a magnifying glass, container with worms in soil, black or brown construction paper, white construction paper, an eye dropper, water, moist paper towel, plastic lid, cellulose sponge, a toothpick.

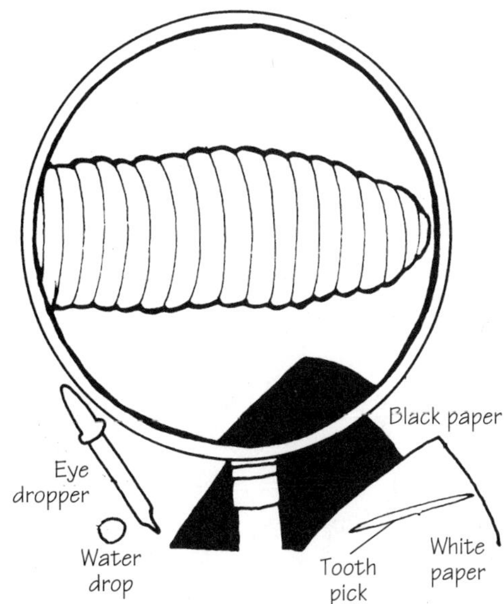

6-17 *Observing earthworms.*

Procedure

1 Have a child lift the cardboard box off the container. Have the children observe the tunnels that the worms might have made in the soil.

What do they appear to be doing in the soil?

Do they stay still or move?

2 Have a child place a worm on top of the soil.

What does it do? How does it move?

How long does it take to bury itself in the soil?

3 Have a child place a worm on a table. Put a piece of black paper and a piece of white paper alongside each other on the table. Place the worm on the two pieces of paper so that its body is touching both pieces of paper.

Does the worm prefer to be on the black or the white piece of paper? (Try it several times and see if there is a preference.)

Note: Worms usually prefer to be on lighter colors. Worms cannot see, but their bodies can sense the warmth from darker colors. Darker colors absorb more heat. They need to keep their bodies cool and moist. If worms become too hot and dry, they die. They stay alive by burrowing deeper into the soil when it becomes too hot or too cold.

4 Have a child place an earthworm on a moist paper towel on a table. Have the children look at its body through a magnifying glass.

Which end of its body is its head and which end is its tail?

How can you tell which is which?

Does it have a top and a bottom?

5 Roll the worm over and see what it does.

What does its skin feel like?

Does it have any legs or feet?

6 Gently have a child touch the worm's tail or head with a toothpick.

How does it respond?

7 Drop water on the worm with an eye dropper so that its skin does not dry out. Drop a small drop of water near its head.

How does the worm respond to the drop of water?

8 Have a child place a wet sponge next to the worm.

What does it do when it feels the sponge?

9 Have another child place the worm on a plastic lid. Put a small amount of water in the lid.

How does the worm react to water?

10 Place the worm next to the lid.

Does the worm try to go under the lid?

11 Place the worm on top of a rolled piece of paper so that it is elevated.

How does the worm move from one height to another?

What do worms do when they meet?

Can you hear a worm move on a piece of paper?

Does the worm appear to prefer moving forward or backward?

Can it move as well in both directions?

As the worm moves like a Slinky, stretching and shrinking as it moves, can you see the intestinal tract inside the worm?

12 Be sure to have children place the worm back with the other worms when they are through investigating its reactions and movements. The worm will need to rest after so much excitement and activity.

Fireflies

Materials

For each child or group of children: a magnifying glass; fireflies in a clear, closed container.

Procedure

1 Have children observe the fireflies in the jar.

Are their lights always on?

What do fireflies look like? Are they really flies? (No, they have four wings, not two.)

How are their two sets of wings different from one another? (The outside wings are hard, the inner wings are hidden and transparent.)

What colors are fireflies?

Do they all look alike?

Do they blink their lights or do they stay lit for awhile?

Are the colors of the lights the same?

If one firefly blinks, do others blink in response?

How many legs does it have?

2 Have the children use a magnifying glass to take a better look at the body of the firefly, and at the light when it goes on.

Flies

Materials

For each child or group of children: a magnifying glass, container with a fly or flies.

Procedure

1 Have the children observe the fly in captivity.

What does it do?

Does it buzz?

When does it buzz?

Does it stay on its food or prefer another place to rest?

Does the fly clean itself?

Does the fly stay still or move around a lot?

What do the fly's legs look like?

Can the fly's legs bend?

How many wings does a fly have?

What color is the fly?

What color are the fly's eyes?

Why can the fly walk on a ceiling or along the side of a jar?

Do flies have claws or suction cups on their feet?

2 Have the children observe the fly with a magnifying glass while it is at rest on the side of the glass jar. Look at its eyes and its feet.

Can they see hair on the legs?

Can they see the parts in the surface of the compound eye?

Can you see the veins running through its transparent wings? How many legs does it have? (Six.)

How does it eat? (Look for its proboscis [sucking tongue].)

Note: A fly is an insect that has two wings. Other insects that fly and are not flies have four wings. Dragonflies and butterflies have four wings and are not flies.

Grasshoppers

Materials

For each child or group of children: a magnifying glass, a container with one or more grasshoppers.

Procedure

1 Have the children observe the grasshoppers in the container.

How do they eat?

Can they fly in the container?

How many wings do they have?

Are they easy to see in the grass?

How does their color help protect them?

How does the grasshopper move?

Does it walk, hop, or jump?

Why can the grasshopper jump high?

Are all of its legs the same length?

How many legs does the grasshopper have?

Can the grasshopper's legs bend?

How many joints does each leg have?

What section of the body do the wings grow from? (The middle part called the thorax.)

2 Have the children use the magnifying glass to find the simple eye, the ear, the spiracles on the abdomen, the palpi near the mouth, and the claws on the feet for gripping. (See Fig. 6-18 to find the parts listed.)

3 Have the children compare the grasshopper to the cricket.

How are they alike and how are they different?

How do the colors of each of their bodies help protect them?

Where do each of them live?

Ladybugs

Materials

For each child or group of children: a magnifying glass, a closed container with ladybugs and aphids, an eye dropper, water.

Procedure

1 Have the children observe the ladybugs in the container.

What are they doing?

Do all ladybugs look alike?

Are they all the same color?

Do they all have the same number of spots on their back?

How do the ladybugs move?

Do they fly?

Can you see them eating aphids?

2 Have a child take a ladybug out of the container and then watch it walk on a table.

Does it walk in a straight line, or zig-zag?

If you hold the ladybug between your thumb and your index finger and then smell your finger, does it have an odor?

3 Use a magnifying glass to look at the ladybug's body.

How many legs does it have?

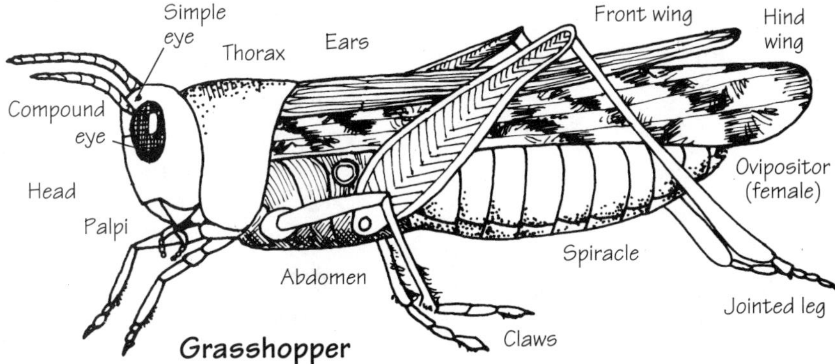

6-18 *Observing grasshoppers.*

Do the legs have joints?

Are the legs different sizes?

What does it do when it is flipped over on its back?

How many wings does it have?

Which wings are hard?

Which wings are transparent?

4 Drop a drop of water in the ladybug's path.

How does it react to the water?

Note: Ladybugs are helpful insects because they eat aphids and other insect pests.

Mealworms

Materials

For each child or group of children: a container with mealworms; dried cereal and a piece of cut-up apple; plus all of the materials listed for earthworms.

Procedure

1 Have the children observe the mealworms in the cereal inside the container.

How do the mealworms move?

How do they know where to go?

Where do they walk most of the time?

What does a mealworm do when you put something in its way?

2 Have the children experiment with a mealworm on a table.

What does a mealworm do when you put something in its way?

How can you make it back up?

How does the mealworm move?

How many legs does it have?

Which end is its mouth on?

3 Have children do all of the activities they did for earthworms.

4 Ask children to compare the responses of the mealworms to those of the earthworms.

Do they respond the same or differently?

How are mealworms like earthworms?

How are they different from earthworms?

Note: Mealworms are insect pests that live in ground grain, which is called meal. Mealworms are the larval form of beetles. They are called mealworms because they live in meal.

Millipedes

Materials

For each child or group of children: a container with a millipede; a magnifying glass; a toothpick; an eye dropper; some water.

Procedure

1 Have children observe the millipede.

Does it like light or dark places?

2 Have a child place the millipede out on a table.

How does it move?

How many legs does it have? (Two on each segment of its body.)

What does it do when it is disturbed? (Roll up.)

How does it react to a drop of water in its path?

How can you make it back up?

3 Observe the millipede's body through a magnifying glass.

Can you find its head?

Does it make any noise when it moves?

How does it react to noise?

4 Compare the millipede to the earthworm and the mealworm.

How are these animals alike?

How are they different?

Which of these animals moves the fastest?

Which moves the slowest?

Which animal has a dry body?

Which animal has a moist body?

Which animal has no legs?

Which animal has the most legs?

5 Compare the colors of their bodies and discuss their individual environments and how their colors protect them.

Which animal can climb along the sides of a container the best?

Slugs

Materials

For each child or group of children: a clear, covered container with slugs covered with a cardboard box; a magnifying glass; a toothpick; sand; an eye dropper; water.

Procedure

1 Have children observe the slugs when the container is uncovered (by lifting the cardboard box).

What do the slugs do?

Do they like to be in dark or light places?

How do they move?

2 Have a child remove a slug from the container and place it on a table.

Can the children tell by looking where it has crawled? (Yes, slugs leave a slimy trail wherever they move.)

How does the slug react to a drop of water in its path?

How does the slug react to a small puddle of water?

How does a slug react to the end of a toothpick?

What color is the slug?

How does it feel when you touch it?

3 Place sand in its path.

Does the sand stick to the slug's body as the slug moves over it?

4 Have the children look at the slug through a magnifying glass.

What does it have on its head?

What does its skin look like?

What does the slug do when it is flipped over?

Can you make the slug back up?

Snails

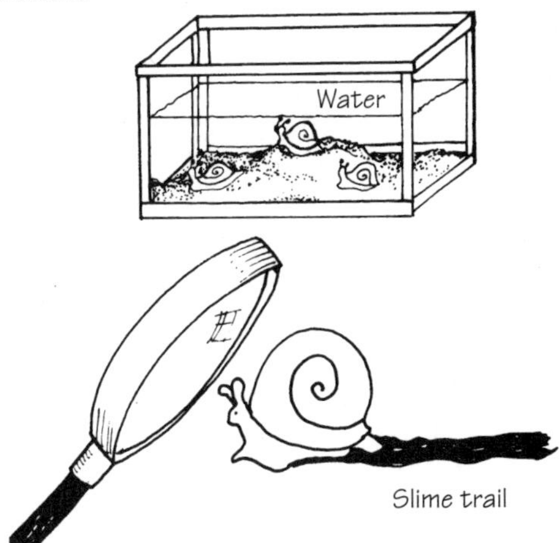

6-19 *Observing snails.*

Materials

For each child or group of children: a clear container with land snails; an aquarium with pond snails; a magnifying glass; a toothpick.

Procedure

1 Have the children observe the two kinds of snails.

How are they different from each other?

How are they the same?

How do they move?

What does the land snail leave behind as it moves?

Which moves faster, the pond snail or the land snail?

When does the snail go into its shell?

When does it come out of its shell?

Can the children make it back up?

What happens to the green algae along the sides of the aquarium as the pond snail moves over it?

2 Have the children look at the snails through a magnifying glass.

What do their heads look like?

3 Compare the way a snail's head looks to the way a slug's head looks.

How are they alike?

How are they different?

Sow bugs

Materials

For each child or group of children: a container with sow bugs; a magnifying glass; a toothpick; an eye dropper; some water; dry sand and wet sand; dark paper and white paper.

Procedure

1 Have a child observe the sow bugs in the container.

Are they easy to find? Are they underneath something?

What are they doing?

2 Have a child take a sow bug out of the container and place it on a table.

What does it do when you pick it up?

What does it do when it feels the table?

What does it do when it is flipped over?

How many feet does it have?

3 Have another child drop a drop of water in its path.

How does it respond to a drop of water?

How does it respond to a small puddle?

Does it prefer light or dark places?

Does it prefer dry or moist places?

Can it climb up the side of a jar?

What does it do when a toothpick touches it?

4 Have children observe the sow bug through a magnifying glass.

How many scales does it have?

Does it have any antennae?

What else can they see about the sow bug through the magnifying glass?

Spiders

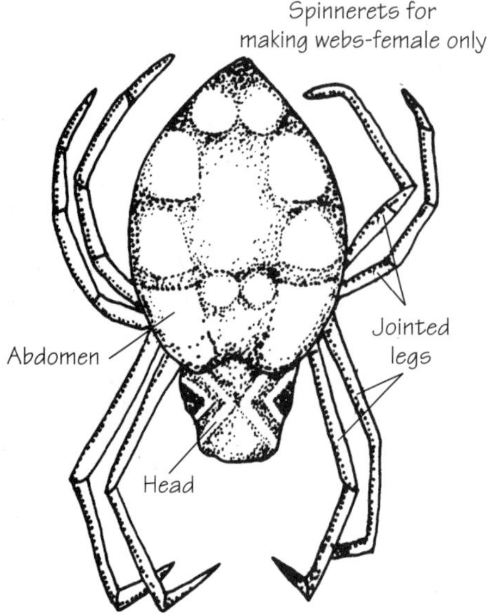

6-20 *A spider has eight jointed legs.*

Materials

For each child or group of children: a clear, plastic-covered container with a spider; a magnifying glass; a toothpick.

Procedure

1 Have the children observe the spider in the container.

Where does the spider spend its time?

Is the spider active?

Has it made a web?

Why does a spider spin a web?

Can the spider jump?

What does it do when it is disturbed?

2 If the spider has spun a web, ask a child to touch the web with a toothpick.

What happens to the web?

Is the web sticky?

What kinds of creatures do spiders catch in their webs?

What do they do to creatures they catch?

What does a spider do to its legs when it spins silk for its web?

3 Have the children look at the spider through a magnifying glass.

How many sections does it have on its body?

How many legs?

Does it have eyes?

Are its legs jointed?

What color is its body?

How does it move?

Do all of its legs move at the same time?

Can you find the spinnerets on the underside of the abdomen?*

III. Observing how small creatures develop and grow

1. Small creatures zoo

Materials

For each child or group of children: small creatures in captivity.

Procedure

If you are lucky, the animals that are in captivity will cooperate and supply you with eggs, larvae, and pupae so that the children can see the four stages of a complete metamorphosis take place. If not, purchase mealworms.

2. Mealworm colony

Materials

For each child or group of children: mealworms; a shoebox with a lid; bran cereal; apple slice or carrot; chart paper and a marking pen.

Procedure

1 Mealworms can be purchased at a pet store. They are used as food for fish and lizards. Once a day, have the children look in the box to count the number of larvae, pupae, and adults. At first, only larvae will be seen. Keep a simple chart with the children of what is seen. Record results. Encourage older children to record their observations and measurements in their science journals.

2 After several weeks, there should be some obvious changes. The larvae begin to turn a darker color before they are ready to pupate. Pupae will look dead.

3 *Explain:* The mealworms are growing while they appear to be resting. Eventually, they will emerge as adult beetles. When an animal changes its form (the way the larva does to

* Spinnerets are used in web making. Only females have them. See Fig. 6-20 to identify the spider's body parts.

become an adult beetle) metamorphosis takes place. *Note*: Not all insects have a complete metamorphosis like the beetle. Some just have a gradual change or an incomplete metamorphosis.

Do our bodies grow gradually, or do we have a metamorphic change? (We grow gradually.)

3. Create a fruitfly culture

Materials

For each child or group of children: an empty jar, a funnel with spout down, an over-ripe banana, cotton, wool, a magnifying glass.

Procedure

1 A fruitfly culture can be created by attracting fruitflies to a jar. Place a piece of over-ripened banana into a jar to attract them. Place a funnel on top of the jar so that they can fly in but will have trouble flying out.

2 After several fruitflies have been captured, stuff the top of the jar with cotton so that air can still come in but the fruitflies cannot come out. If the weather is warm, the container can be placed outside.

3 With luck, eggs will be deposited. The eggs will hatch into hungry larvae. The larvae will grow, pupate, and complete their metamorphosis. Eventually, they will emerge as adult fruitflies. Fruitflies are very small. Their larvae are harder to see than the mealworms. Children will need a magnifying glass.

4. Growing new parts

Materials

A living or dead crab or crayfish with two different-sized claws, a starfish (alive or dead) with one short foot, an earthworm that is alive.

Procedure

1 Show the children the animals. If the animals listed cannot be found, then a picture or diagram can be substituted.

How can an animal like the crayfish or crab have one large claw and one small claw?

2 Discuss how this could happen.

3 *Explain:* Some animals can grow new parts when their body parts are broken off. It takes time for the part to grow back, and that is why they look unbalanced for a while. When the new claw grows back, it will remain slightly smaller than the old claw. If we lose a finger, an arm, or a leg, we cannot grow a new one. If a starfish is cut into several pieces, each piece can become a new starfish.

Note: A lobster, crayfish, or crab can grow a new claw, but if a lobster, crayfish, or crab is cut into pieces, it will die. Only very primitive animals can be cut into pieces and continue to live and grow. When an animal is able to grow a new body part, regeneration has taken place. Regeneration helps an animal grow back a lost part.

4 Show the children the earthworm that is alive.

5 *Explain:* If the earthworm is cut into two different pieces at certain places, both parts will continue to live. But only one part will have a mouth. So, one part will live longer than the other part and grow a new tail.

Why is a mouth important to the animal?

If we could not eat, what would happen to us?

(We would starve to death if we could not eat.)

Note to the adult reading this book: It is advisable not to cut the worm in half, as it might upset the children.

Why do animals need to be able to eat? (So they can have energy to grow and move. Food gives animals energy.)

IV. Learning to classify small creatures

1. Distinguishing small creatures from one another

Materials

Small-creature zoo, nature guidebooks on invertebrates with large photographs of animals in color.

Procedure

1 Discuss with children how we can tell one animal from another. What makes each animal in the small-creature zoo unique or special?

2 Ask the following kinds of questions:

Do some of the animals look alike? Which ones?

What do they have in common?

Which animals have no legs?

Which animals have one foot and a hard shell?

Which animals have six legs?

Which animals have eight legs?

Which animals have many legs?

Which animals have antennae?

Which animals have segmented bodies?

Which animals have a head, a thorax, and an abdomen?

Which animals have a head and an abdomen?

Which animals have soft bodies?

Which animals have wings?

Are the wings hard, soft, or transparent?

Which animals have hard outer coverings or exoskeleton made up of several shell-like pieces?

What makes an animal an insect? (Three body parts, six legs, exoskeleton.)

What makes an animal a spider? (Two body parts, eight legs.)

What makes an animal a snail? (Soft, unsegmented body with a shell.)

What makes an animal an earthworm? (Soft, segmented, round body.)

*What makes an animal a larva?** (Usually a soft, segmented, round body with a few sets of legs, but not a pair of legs on every segment.)

What makes an animal a millipede? (A soft, segmented, round body with a pair of legs on each segment.)

2. Distinguishing insects from one another

Materials

A variety of live insects from the small-creature zoo to observe, and/or nature books about insects with large, color photographs of insects (for example, *A Golden Guide to Insects*, and/or *The How and Why Wonder Book of Insects*).

Procedure

1 Observe the live insects and browse through the insect nature books.

2 Ask the following kinds of questions:

Which of the animals in the small-creature zoo are insects?

How can you tell?

Can you find their picture in the insect guidebook?

How many insect groups are there in the insect guidebook? (About sixteen.)

What are the major groups? (Grasshoppers and their relatives; dragonflies; termites, earwigs, and lice; true bugs; beetles; moths and butterflies; flies; ants, bees, and wasps.)

Going further

- Use your insect guidebook's classification scheme to determine which category the insects from the small-creature zoo fit into (fly, beetle, true bug, lepidoptera [moths and butterflies], etc.)
- Have the children take a closer look at their insects, or at the pictures of the insects in nature guidebooks. Ask them the following kinds of questions:

What kinds of wings do beetles have? (An outer set of hard wings, and an inner set of transparent, soft wings.)

What are the differences between moths and butterflies? (The antennae of moths are usually full and feathery, and their abdomens are thicker. Also, the colors of moths tend to be drabber, whereas butterflies usually have brighter colors, thinner abdomens, and knobs at the ends of their antennae. Butterflies rest with their wings held vertically and moths tend to rest with their wings held horizontally.)

Which insects are true bugs? (Insects that have a beak on their mouth with joints for sucking.)

How are ants, bees, and wasps alike? (They each have transparent wings [when they have wings] and "wasp waists.")

How are flies different from other flying insects? (Flies have two wings. Other kinds of flying insects have four wings.)

Which insects undergo an incomplete metamorphosis (a gradual change) when they grow? (Grasshoppers, dragonflies, termites, earwigs, lice, and true bugs.)

Which insects go through a complete metamorphosis when they grow? (Most flies, beetles, butterflies, moths, ants, bees, and wasps.)

* A larva is the young of an insect that undergoes a complete metamorphosis. Larvae do not always have soft bodies, and some have no legs at all. (Also, young frogs and toads are called larvae.)

What is a difference between a larva and an adult insect? (Insect larvae cannot lay eggs, but usually eat a lot.)*

3. Creating models of insects, spiders, and worms

6-21 *Build a model of your favorite creature from the small-creature zoo.*

Materials

For each child or group of children: pipe cleaners, scissors, construction paper, crayons, glue, cellophane, tissue paper, large sequins, Play-Doh or modeling clay, colored pencils, marking pens.

Procedure

1. Show the children the materials.
2. Tell them to use the materials to design a model of an insect, spider, or worm. They can use the materials for any part of the animals they create.
3. Discuss with the children what parts each of the animals would need to have in order to be a worm, an insect, or a spider. For example, if an insect model were being made, it would need to have six jointed legs, three body parts (head, thorax, abdomen), two antennae, possibly wings.
4. Have the children notice where the legs and wings are attached to the body of an insect (on the thorax), where the legs are connected on a spider's body (between the abdomen and head), and where the legs are on a larva's body. Remind them to design their model with these proper body connections in mind.
5. Have children use cellophane for transparent wings, sequins for compound eyes, tissue paper for opaque wings, pipe cleaners cut at different lengths for legs and antennae. Remind children that sometimes we cannot see all the body parts on an insect because the parts are hidden by the wings, but ask them to put in all the parts even if they cannot be seen. For example, a beetle model can be designed so that the wings can be lifted off to expose the hidden abdomen and the hidden transparent wings.

* A larva is a young insect that does not resemble the adult. From a human point of view, some insect larvae cause damage, but not all larvae cause damage. Bee larvae do no damage. Some larvae are even helpful, such as the larval flies of maggots, which eat decaying material.

4. Mounting dead insects

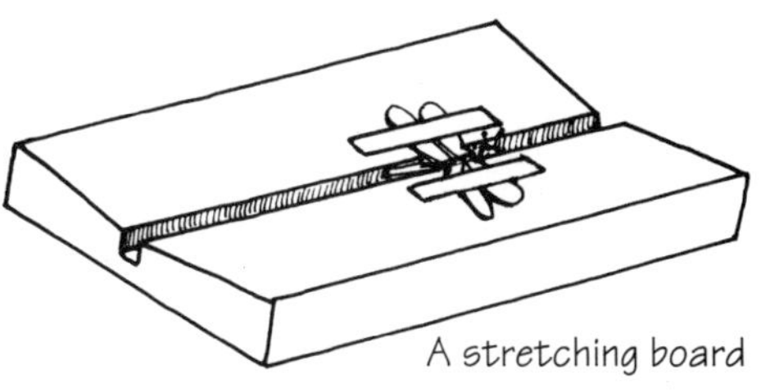

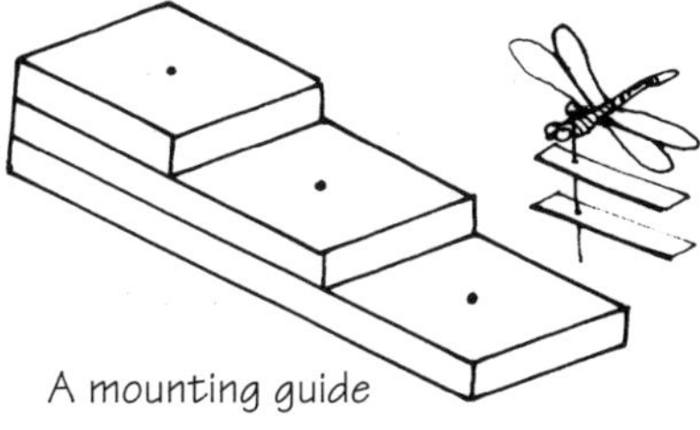

6-22 *Dead insects can be observed better when they are "pinned" and "stretched"*

Materials

Straight pins, cardboard, marking pen, plastic wrap, cotton balls, jar lids.

Procedure

If an insect dies and the children find it, the insect can be mounted. There are two easy ways to mount a dead insect. One way is to place the dead insect on a cotton ball inside of a jar lid and cover it with plastic wrap. The other way is to stick a straight pin through its thorax and mount the pin on a piece of cardboard.

INFORMATION When insects die, their bodies tend to dry out quickly. They become brittle. It is hard to stretch their legs and their wings out without breaking them. Usually, their legs are all bent up. If the insect is frozen to death, it can be mounted more easily for observation. The legs can be straightened out and the wings can be opened without being broken.

INFORMATION To the adult reading this book, if you want to make a professional-looking insect mounting, it is advisable to freeze an insect while it is alive by placing it in the freezer in a closed jar. It will freeze to death. Then the insect can be thawed out quickly. The body will still be moist and soft. It will be easier to stick a straight pin through its thorax, and to mount it for stretching. The wings of the insect can be opened to a flying position by placing pins in the opened wings. The legs can also be stretched out and positioned as you want them to be. They will also need to have additional pins placed around them to hold them in position. When it dries out, the insect will remain in the position it is pinned and stretched to. The pins can be removed.

Note: Show the children the mounted insects after they have been pinned and stretched. Do not ask young children to freeze, thaw, stretch, and pin insects for mounting. Their muscular coordination is not developed enough and it does not engender a respect for life. Mounted insects are easier for children to study and observe. If a magnifying glass is used, a butterfly's proboscis can be seen, veins on a wing can be looked at, hairs on legs can be seen, compound eyes can be looked at up-close, and other features can be observed. Obviously, it is easier to keep a still object in focus than a moving one. When animals are alive and moving, it is harder to observe their parts. A lot can be gained by studying the insects that have died, and by creating mounts on 2-inch-by-2-inch cardboard squares of insects that have been frozen and stretched.

V. The animal kingdom

1. Classifying animals

Materials

A picture or a rubber model of a human skeleton; a cleaned crab or lobster exoskeleton left over from dinner; snail and clam shells.

Procedure

1 *Explain:* There are many kinds of animals. Scientists called zoologists study animals. Zoologists have created classification groupings to understand and study animals. Animals can be grouped into two large groups—those that have a backbone and those that do not. Animals with backbones are called vertebrates. Those without backbones are called invertebrates.

2 Ask the children what kind of animal they think they are, one with or without a backbone. Have them feel their backbone or another child's backbone. Have them feel their ribs and follow their rib bones around to their backbone. Show the children a picture or a model of a human skeleton. Ask the following kinds of questions:

Is this a real skeleton? (No, it is a model of a skeleton.)

Do the bones in our bodies connect to each other? (Yes, they are all connected to our skeleton.)

Can we see our bones? (No, not unless they are photographed by an X-ray machine, but we can feel them under our skin.)

What do our bones do for our body? (They provide a frame for our body to rest on, and they protect our lungs and our heart. Our skull protects our brain.)

What would your body look like without bones? (Probably, it would look like a deflated balloon.)

- *Explain:* Some animals do not have backbones. They have hard shells or they have exoskeletons made up of many thin shell-like pieces to protect their bodies. Animals with exoskeleton or hard outer shells do not have bones inside their bodies.

3 Show children the crab and lobster exoskeleton, snail and clam shells.

4 *Explain:* Animals that have shells or exoskeleton belong to the group of animals without backbones called invertebrates. Invertebrates are animals that do not have a backbone. Ask the following kinds of questions:

Are the exoskeleton and hard shells real or are they models? (They are real. They came from animals.)

Can we feel the exoskeleton and hard shell on these animals? (Yes, they are an outer covering on the animal's body.)

How does an exoskeleton or hard shell protect an animal? (An exoskeleton protects the soft parts of an animal. The soft parts are in an armor-like coat. The hard shells on mollusks protect the animals' soft parts when the animals withdraw inside their shells.)*

5 Show the children the assorted pictures of animals. See if they can create two piles with the pictures—one pile to contain pictures of vertebrates, the other pile to contain pictures of invertebrates.

2. Dividing vertebrate animals into smaller groups

Materials

For each child or group of children: pictures and small rubber models of assorted vertebrates. (See Fig. 6-23.)

Procedure

1 Have the children study the pictures and/or models of assorted vertebrates. Ask them what makes each of the animals look different from the others. Ask the following kinds of questions:

Do any of the animals have hair or fur?

Do any of the animals have feathers?

Do all of the animals have feet?

Do any of the animals have rough, scaly skin?

Do any of the animals appear to have a smooth, moist skin?

2 Suggest to the children that the pictures and models of animals can be further divided by the kind of skin the animals appear to have.

3 *Explain:* Zoologists have divided the animals that have backbones into five large groups or classes of animals. Ask the children if they can guess what the five groups or classes of animals with backbones might be. Listen to their ideas and then tell them the five classes. (See Table 6-2.)

Table 6-2 The five classes of animals with backbones

(Listed in order from the group of animals that have more complicated organ systems to the group of animals that have less complicated systems.)

1 <u>Mammals</u> All animals with backbones that have fur or hair are mammals.

Note: A main characteristic of mammals is that female mammals have mammary glands to feed milk to their babies. Mention should be made of this fact. However, it is easier for young children to see fur or hair in pictures and in models than it is for them to see teats, nipples, or breasts giving milk.

2 <u>Birds</u> All animals with backbones that have feathers are birds.

3 <u>Reptiles</u> All animals with backbones that have rough, scaly skin and breathe through lungs are reptiles.

4 <u>Amphibians</u> All animals with backbones that have smooth, moist skins and breathe through lungs as adults but breathe through gills when young are amphibians.

Note: The most important feature about amphibians, as their name suggests, is that they have "two lives" (larval and adult). Tadpoles are the larval stage of frogs and toads. Frogs and toads go through a metamorphosis.

5 <u>Fish</u> All animals with backbones that have fins and scales, live in water, and breathe through gills are fish.

Note: Fish Group includes three subclasses (boney; boneless fish with cartilage like sharks; and eel like aquatic animals).

4 Ask the children to sort the pictures and models of vertebrates into piles of mammals, birds, reptiles, amphibians, and fish.

3. Dividing invertebrate animals into smaller groups

Materials

For each child or group of children: pictures and rubber models of assorted invertebrates, and animals from the small-creature zoo.

* Arthropods have exoskeleton; mollusks have one or two hard shells.

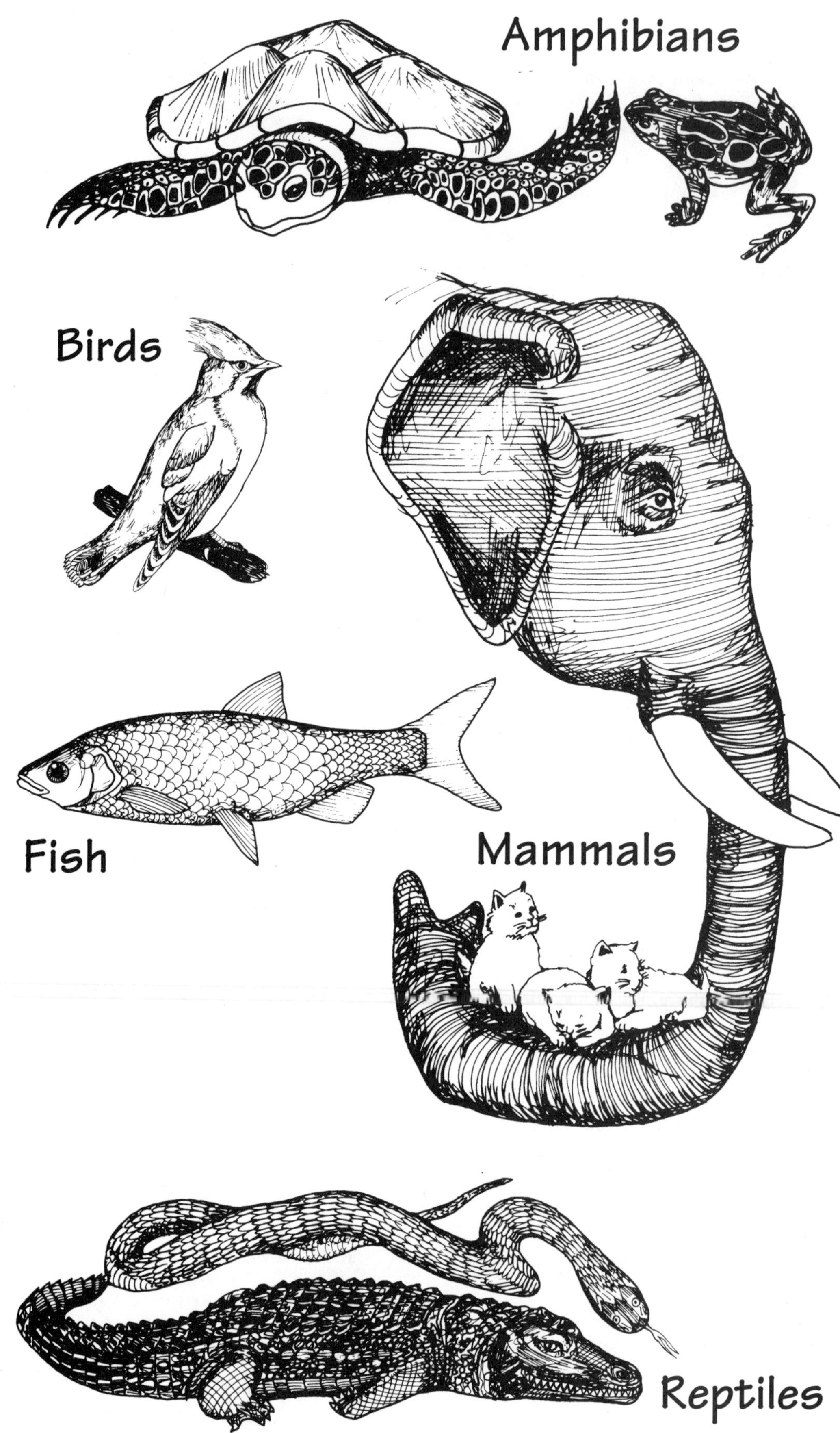

6-23 *Models of animals with backbones can be sorted into groups.*

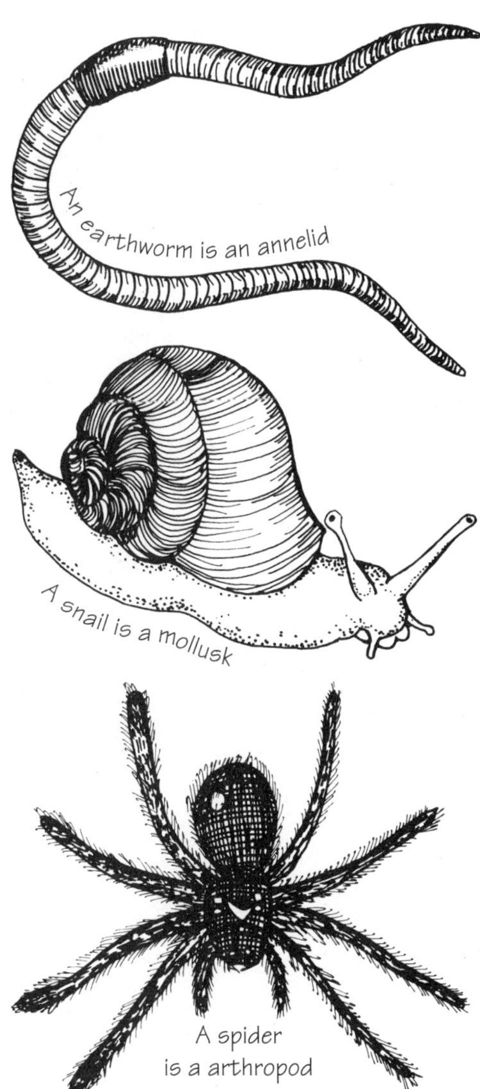
An earthworm is an annelid
A snail is a mollusk
A spider
is a arthropod

6-24 *Models of animals without backbones can be sorted into groups.*

Procedure

1 Have children look at the pictures, models, and the animals from the small-creature zoo.

How can the small creatures be grouped into smaller groups?

2 Discuss what the characteristics are that make each of the animals alike or different.

3 Allow children to come up with ways to group the animals. For example, the animals in the small-creature zoo could be divided into animals with shells and animals without shells. They could be further divided into animals with segmented bodies and animals without segmented bodies. Or they could be divided into animals with many legs, eight legs, six legs, or no legs.

Can you guess what some of the animal groupings are that zoologists have come up with for animals without backbones? (Listen to their ideas and then help them see the differences that zoologists have used or found for grouping the animals they have collected in their small-creature zoo.)

4 *Explain:* The animals in the small-creature zoo belong to different zoological groups. Earthworms belong to a zoological group known as annelids. Annelids have segmented bodies. Slugs and snails are members of the mollusk family. "Mollusk" means soft bodies. Mollusks have bodies that are not segmented. Most mollusks have well-developed heads with eyes, tentacles, and a muscular foot. Spiders, millipedes, sow bugs, and insects are all arthropods. All arthropods have jointed feet, and most except the spider have a segmented abdomen, an exoskeleton, and antennae.

4. Subdividing invertebrates into smaller groups

Materials

For each child or group of children: assorted models and living or nonliving specimens, pictures of arthropods from the five classes of arthropods.

Note: There are five classes of arthropods. The five classes are: crustaceans, like lobsters and crabs; centipedes; millipedes; spiders;* and insects. *Note*: Zoologists do not always agree on the ways to classify animals into groups.

Procedure

1 *Explain:* Each of the large zoological groups of animals can be further divided into smaller groups, and each

* Spiders are another group or class of arthropods. Mites, ticks, horseshoe crabs, and scorpions are grouped with spiders. They are called arachnids. Arachnids have eight legs, no antennae, and two body regions. The largest group of arthropods, and the largest group of animals in the animal kingdom, are the insects. Insects can be further subdivided into about 16 or more major groups. All insects have six legs, three body regions, and two antennae (see Section IV, Activity 2, in this chapter). There are more than 800,000 known insect species that are unique.

of those groups can also be further subdivided into even smaller groups of animals with specific characteristics.

2 Show children the assorted models, pictures, and living and nonliving specimens of arthropods.

3 Have children observe them closely.

What are ways you can think of to group these creatures into smaller groups? (Allow the children to come up with ways to divide the arthropods into groups.)

4 Ask the children to sort out the pictures of arthropods and models of arthropods, and arthropod specimens into groups of animals the way a zoologist might divide them.

5. Subdividing mammals into groups

Materials

Mammals to observe (like a dog, cat, rabbit, guinea pig, hamster); or a field trip to a pet store that stocks mammals; or a trip to a farm or zoo.

Procedure

1 Have children observe mammals that are alive. If it is possible, encourage the children to touch or pet the mammals gently, and to use their five senses to observe the mammals.

2 Ask the following kinds of questions as the children observe each mammal:

What kind of animal is this?

Does it have a backbone?

Can you feel the backbone?

How is this animal different from the invertebrates that were observed?

Does the animal feel warm or cold when you hold it?

Does your own body feel warm when you touch it?

How does the animal move?

Does the animal make noise?

Does the animal have toenails or fingernails?

What covers the animal's body? (Hair or fur.)

What are some of the body parts the animal has that you have on your body? (Eyes, ears, nose, mouth, legs, hair, teeth, tongue, nails, etc.)

How does the animal eat?

What kind of food do you think this animal eats?

How can you tell?

Does the animal have teeth?

Do the animal's teeth look like your teeth?

What kind of food do you think an animal with sharp, jagged teeth eats?

What kind of food do you think an animal with straight, nonjagged teeth eats?

3 *Explain:* Mammals can be divided into three large groups based on what they eat. If they eat only plants, they are called herbivores. If they eat only other animals, they are called carnivores. If they eat both plants and animals, they are called omnivores. Usually you can tell what kind of diet a mammal has by the way its teeth look. If the teeth are sharp and jagged-looking like those of a dog or wolf, then it is obvious that it uses its teeth to rip apart other animals. If the teeth are mostly large and flat and the front incisor teeth are sharp, with a large space between them and the molars with no canine teeth, it means that the mammal eats plants. If the teeth look like our teeth with incisors, canines called cuspids, and molars, then the animal can eat both plants and animals.

6. Subdividing mammals into smaller groups

A mammal (like a cat, dog, rabbit, guinea pig or hamster) to observe; assorted small rubber models and/or pictures of mammals.

Procedure

1 Show children the assorted models and pictures of mammals.

2 *Explain:* When animals have mammary glands to feed milk to their babies, have fur or hair, and feel warm to touch, they are called mammals. Mammals can be grouped by the way they look.

Can you think of ways to sort the pictures and models of mammals into smaller groups? (Allow the children to come up with ways to group the mammals, and to sort the pictures and models of mammals into groups by the way the mammals look: by their color, size, body covering, or other characteristics or attributes.)

A bat is a flying mammal
A koala is a marsupial
A porpoise is a marine mammal
An armadillo is a toothless mammal
A platypus is an egg-laying mammal
A shrew is an insect eating mammal
A rabbit is a rodent
A seal is a carnivore
A horse is a hoofed mammal
Elephant

***6-25** Mammals can be subdivided into smaller groups.*

3 After the children have grouped the pictures and models of mammals, explain the characteristics that zoologists have used to sort or separate mammals from one another. As you describe the various groupings, show the children an example (a model or a picture) of each of the major orders or groupings of mammals listed. The zoological groupings that include most mammals are:

- Egg-laying mammals. They are almost extinct. They are the only mammals that lay eggs. Examples are the platypus and the spiny anteater.
- Marsupials. Marsupials are mammals that have pouches. The females have pouches that they carry their babies in. Examples are the kangaroo, opossum, and koala bear.
- Toothless mammals. These are mammals that either lack teeth or have no front teeth. They are protected with an armor. They burrow in the ground. Examples are the anteater, armadillo, and aardvark.
- Insect-eating mammals. These are mammals that eat insects. They are usually animals that live underground, sleep during the day, and roam around at night. Examples are shrews, moles, and hedgehogs.
- Marine mammals. These are mammals that live in the water and breathe with lungs. They have two front limbs that look like paddles, and no back limbs. Examples are whales, dolphins, and porpoises. *Note*: Unlike fish, the babies of marine mammals are born alive. They do not have scales, and they do have some hair on their bodies.
- Carnivores. These are mammals that eat other animals. They have strong jaws, sharp canine teeth, and sharp claws for ripping the flesh of other animals. Examples of water or aquatic carnivores are sea lions, seals, and walruses. Examples of carnivores that live on the land are bears, cats, dogs, raccoons, and minks. Land carnivores have keen senses for hearing, seeing, and smelling.

  Note: Some carnivores like bears and raccoons also eat plants.
- Rodents. These are mammals that gnaw their food with their two front incisor teeth. Their two front incisors continue to grow throughout the animal's life. They continually wear down from gnawing at things. Rodents eat only plants. Examples are beavers, rabbits, squirrels, mice, rats, and porcupines.
- Hoofed mammals. These are mammals with hooves on their feet. They are all plant eaters. They use their teeth for grinding grasses. Hoofed mammals can be further divided into mammals with single toes, those with an odd number of toes on their feet, and those with split hooves. Examples of hoofed mammals are horses, sheep, cattle, hogs, pigs, camels, deer, and hippopotamuses.
- Elephants. These are mammals that have long incisor teeth that have been modified to form tusks, large flat teeth for grinding plants, and a long, modified nose or proboscis that is used for grasping. *Note*: Butterflies and moths have a proboscis also, but obviously it is a more delicate one.
- Flying mammals. These are mammals that can fly. They have a web of skin between their fingers and limbs for flying. They eat insects. Examples are bats.
- Monkeys, apes, and humans. These are mammals with flexible fingers, opposable thumbs, and long toes used for grasping. They can walk erect or semierect, and they have brains that are well developed. *Note:* People are grouped with the primates along with monkeys and apes. Humans belong to the family of Homo Sapiens. They walk erect, have well-developed brains, and are the most intelligent form of life in the animal kingdom. They can eat both plants and animals.

VI. Vertebrates—animals with backbones

Comparing backboned pets

Materials

Live horse, cat, dog, rabbit, bird, fish, turtle, guinea pig, hamster, or other available animal with a backbone. *Note:* It might be necessary to visit a farm, zoo, pet store, or aquarium with the children.

Procedure

1 As the children observe the animals, help them to compare two animals to each other.

2 Ask the following kinds of questions:

How are they alike?

How are they different?

Where do they usually live?

How does their color help protect them?

How does the texture of their skin help protect them?

Do the animals leave a footprint when they walk?

Do the footprints of the two animals look alike?

How can you tell which footprint belongs to which animal?

Do the animals feel warm or cold to touch?

Do these two animals prefer living on the land or in the water?

What kinds of noises do these two animals make?

If they make noise, when do they make the noise?

If these two animals have front legs, how do they use them?

How do these two animals keep clean?

How active are these two animals—do they move around a lot or rest a lot?

Where are the mammary glands located?

What kind of teeth do they have?

Can you tell by looking at their teeth what kind of food each animal might eat?

Where are each animal's eyes located, on the front of its face or on the sides of its face?

Note: Horses and many fish have their eyes located on the sides of their face. This allows them to see on each side of their head at the same time. They can look in two different directions at once.

Going further

- What can you guess about an animal's eating habits by observing the location of its eyes and the kind of teeth it has? (Davis)
- *Explain:* In general, most meat-eating birds and mammals have their eyes positioned frontally on their faces. This allows both of their eyes to focus with depth perception on their prey for an attack. In general, most grazing animals have their eyes located further apart on the sides of their faces. This allows their eyes to pick up movement in two directions at the same time.
- Observe real animals or look closely at animal pictures to observe the location of the eyes. Read about the eating habits of the animals you look at. Take notes in your science journals.

Is there a relationship between location of eyes and the food that is eaten?

Is there a relationship between eye location and feeding habits in: fish, reptiles, amphibians and insects too?

What does your pet do to get attention?

Can you tell how your pet feels?

How does it talk to you?

Further resources

Dewey Decimal Classification Number for animals is: 590 to 595.

Selected resource books about mammals for children and adults

Arnosky, Jim. *Watching Foxes*. New York: Lothrop, 1985.

Baker, Lucy. *Polar Bears*. New York: Puffin books, 1990.

Caduto and Bruchac. *Keepers of the Animals and Wildlife Activities for Children*. Golden, CO: Fulcrum, 1991.

Cole, Joanna. *A Dog's Body*. New York: Morrow, 1986.

Cole, Joanna. *A Horse's Body*. New York: Morrow, 1981.

Cole, Joanna. *My Puppy Is Born*. New York: Morrow Junior Books, 1991.

Gibbons, Gail. *Whales*. New York: Holiday, 1991. (Illustrations show ten different physical characteristics of various species of whales.)

Isenbart, Hans-Heinrich. *Birth of a Foal*. Minneapolis: Carolrhoda, 1986.

Lewin, Ted. *Inside the Whale and Other Animals*. New York: Doubleday, 1992. (Has excellent illustrations depicting animals inside and outside in the same diagram, which gives the illustrations a 3-D perspective.)

McMillan, Bruce. *Going on a Whale Watch*. New York: Scholastic, 1992. (A photo essay.)

Miller, Margaret. *My Puppy Is Born*. New York: Morrow, 1991.

Patent, Dorothy Hinshaw. *Humpback Whales*. New York: Holiday, 1989. (A photo essay.)

Patent, Dorothy Hinshaw. *The Way of the Grizzly*. New York: Clarion, 1987.

Pope, Joyce. *Taking Care of Your Guinea Pig*. New York: Watts, 1986.

Simon, Seymour. *Big Cats*. New York: Harper, 1991.

Storer, Tracy I., et al. *General Zoology, 5th edition*. New York: McGraw-Hill, 1972.

Watts, Barrie. *Hamster*. Morristown, NJ: Silver Burdett, 1986.

Zim, Herbert. *Mammals, a Golden Guide*. New York: Golden Press, 1976.

Selected resource books for children and adults about: Birds, fish, reptiles and amphibians

Bernhard, Emery. *Ladybug*. New York: Holiday House, 1992.

Golden, Augusta. *Ducks Don't Get Wet*. New York: Harper Child, 1989.

Griffin, Margaret, and Deborah Seed. *The Amazing Egg Book*. Reading, Mass.: Addison-Wesley, 1990. (Discusses: where eggs come from, what function they serve, and how they can be used for food and decoration.)

Heller, Ruth. *Chickens Aren't the Only Ones*. New York: Grosset and Dunlap, 1981. (A picture book about the variety of animals that hatch from eggs.)

Hewett, Richard. *Snakes*. New York: Morrow, 1991.

Grant, Lesley. *Discover Bones: Explore the Science of Skeletons*. Reading, Mass.: Addison-Wesley, 1991. (After-school enrichment activities for children 7–12. (Discusses: bones, structure function, growth, archaeology, and fortune telling, with related activities.)

Koss, Amy Goldman. *Where Fish Go in Winter and Answers to Other Great Mysteries*. Los Angeles: Price, Stern, Sloan, 1987. (Non-fiction, poetry.)

Schwart, David M. *The Hidden Life of the Pond*. New York: Crown, 1988.

Lauber, Patricia. *What's Hatching Out of That Egg*. New York: Crown, 1979.

Lavies, Bianca. *The Secretive Timber Rattlesnakes*. New York: Dutton, 1990.

Malnig, Anita. *Where the Waves Break: Life at the Edge of the Sea*. Minneapolis: Carolrhoda, 1985.

McLure, John. The Senses of Fish. An article in *Science Activities*, the September/October 1986 issue, pp. 18-21.

McLure, John. Investigating Fish Behavior, Inside the Classroom and Out. An article in *Science Activities*, November/December 1986 issue, pp. 6–9.

Pallotta, Jerry. *The Bird Alphabet Book*. Watertown, Mass.: Charlesbridge Publishing, 1990.

Parker, Nancy Winslow and Wright, Joan Richards. *Frogs, Toads, Lizards, and Salamanders*. New York: Greenwillow, 1990.

Parsons, Alexandra. *Amazing Birds*. New York: Knopf, 1990. (Has beautiful color photographs.)

Pearce, Q.L. *Why Is a Frog Not a Toad? Discovering the Differences Between Animal Look-Alikes*. Los Angeles: Lowell House, 1992.

Rowan, Peter. *Can You Get Warts from Touchings Toads? Ask Dr. Pete*. New York: Messner, 1986.

Robinson, Howard F., ed. *Amazing Creatures of the Sea*. Washington, D.C.: The National Wildlife Federation, 1987.

Sabin, Louis. *Reptiles and Amphibians*. Mahwah, NJ: 1985.

Schlein, Miriam. *Pigeons*. New York: Thomas Y. Crowell, 1989.

Scholastic. *The Egg: A First Discovery Book*. New York: Scholastic, 1992.

Simon, Seymour. *Snakes*. New York: Harper, 1993. (K–3.)

Waters, John. *A Jellyfish Is Not a Fish*. New York: Thomas Y. Crowell, 1979. (All about jellyfish.)

Watts, Barrie. *Tadpole and Frog*. Morristown, NJ: Silver, Burdett, 1986.

Webster, David. *Frog and Toad Watching*. New York: Messner, 1986.

Wexo, John Bonnett. *Alligators and Crocodiles*. Washington, D.C.: Wildlife, 1984.

Selected resource books for children and adults about small invertebrate creatures

Brandt, Keith. *Insects*. Mahwah, NJ: Troll, 1985.

Burnett, Robin. *The Pillbug Project: A Guide to Investigation*. Washington, D.C.: National Science Teachers Association, 1992.

Craig, Janet. *The Amazing World of Spiders*. Mahwah, NJ: Troll, 1990.

Dashefsky, Steven H. *Insect Biology: 49 Science Fair Projects*. TAB Books, 1992. (Projects for children who know how to read.)

Greenberg, David. *Slugs*. New York: Little, Brown, and Co., 1989.

Hopf, Alice L. *Spiders*. New York: Cobblehill Books, Dutton, 1990.

Goor, Ron and Nancy. *Insect Metamorphosis: From Egg to Adult*. New York: Atheneum, 1990.

Jourdans, Eveline. *Butterflies and Moths Around the World*. Minneapolis: Lerner, 1981.

Kerby, Mona. *Cockroaches*. New York: Watts, 1989.

Kneidel, Sally Stenhouse. *Creepy Crawlies and the Scientific Method*. Golden, CO: Fulcrum, 1993. (Emphasis on scientific method and recording data.)

Lavies, Bianca. *Monarch Butterflies: Mysterious Travelers*. New York: Dutton, 1992.

McLaughlin, Molly. *Earthworms, Dirt, and Rotten Leaves*. New York: Macmillan, 1986.

Norsgaard, E. Jaediker. *How to Raise Butterflies*. New York: Putnam, 1988.

Olesen, Jens. *Snail*. Morristown, NJ: Silver Burdett, 1986.

Parker, Nancy Winslow, and Joan Richards Wright. *Bugs*. New York: Greenwillow, 1987.

Parsons, Alexandra. *Eyewitness Juniors: Amazing Spiders*. New York: Knopf, 1990. (Has beautiful color photographs.)

Pringle, Lawrence. *Insects and Spiders*. Racine, WI: Western Publishing, 1990.

Scholastic. *The Ladybug and Other Insects: A First Discovery Book*. New York: Scholastic, 1991.

Selsam, Millicent E. *Backyard Insects*. New York: Scholastic, 1988.

Simon, Seymour. *Pets in a Jar: Caring for Small Wild Animals*. New York: Penguin, 1979.

Still, John. *Eyewitness Juniors: Amazing Butterflies & Moths*. New York: Knopf, 1991. (Has beautiful color photographs.)

Watts, Barrie. *Ladybug*. Morristown, NJ: Silver Burdett, 1987.

Whallcy, Paul. *Butterfly and Moth*. New York: Knopf, 1988.

Whitcombe, Bobbie. *Insects*. New York: Checkerboard Press, 1990.

Wood, Robert W. *Science for Kids: 39 Easy Animal Biology Experiments*. TAB Books, 1991. (Experiments for children who know how to read.)

Brown, Vinson. *How to Make a Miniature Zoo*. New York: Dodd, Mead, 1987. (Adult reading level.)

Wellnitz, William R. *Science in Your Backyard*. TAB Books, 1992. (See Part l—for children who know how to read and who want to do more activities with animals.)

Zim, Herbert. *Insects: a Golden Guide*. New York: Golden Press, 1976.

Selected resource books for adults and children about the human body

Cole, Joanna. *Cuts, Breaks, Bruises, and Burns*. New York: Thomas Y. Crowell, 1985.

Cole, Joanna. *Inside the Human Body*. New York: Scholastic, 1989.

Cole, Joanna. *The Magic School Bus: Inside the Human Body*. New York: Scholastic, 1989.

Ingoglia, Gina. *Look Inside Your Body*. New York: Grosset & Dunlap, 1987.

Markle, Sandra. *Outside and Inside You*. New York: Bradbury, 1991.

Peppe, Rodney. *Thumbprint Circus*. New York: Dell, 1988.

Settel, Joanne, and Nancy Baggett. *Why Does My Nose Run? and Other Questions Kids Ask about Their Bodies*. New York: Atheneum, 1985.

Suzuki, Dr. David and Hehner, Barbara. *Looking At the Body*. New York: Wiley. 1991.

Western, Joan, Ronald Wilson. *The Human Body*. Mahwah NJ: Troll, 1991.

Selected general resource books for adults and older children about animals

Ford, B. G. *Do You Know?* New York: Random House, 1979.

Halow, Rosie, and Gareth Morgan. *175 Amazing Nature Experiments*. New York: Random House, 1992.

Heller, Ruth. *How to Hide an Octopus*. New York: Grosset, 1985.

Kuhn, Dwight. My *First Book of Nature: How Living Things Grow*. New York: Scholastic: 1993. (Has beautiful color photographs.)

Messner, Julian. *The Living World*. Morristown, NJ: Silver Burdett, 1990.

National Wildlife Federation. *Amazing Mammals*, Part 1, Vol.2, No.3 and Part 2, Vol.2., No.4. Ranger Rick's Nature Scope, 1986. Washington, D.C.: National Wildlife Federation.

Prochnow, Dave and Kathy. *How? More Experiments for the Young Scientist*. (See Part 5—The Young Biologist. For children who know how to read.)

Sisson, Edith. *Nature with Children of All Ages*. Englewood Cliffs, NJ: Prentice-Hall, rev. ed., 1990.

Selsam, Millicent. *Hidden Animals*. New York: Harper and Row, 1969. (Camouflage.)

Selsam, Millicent. *How to Be a Nature Detective*. New York: Harper and Row, 1966. (Appropriate for children in grades 1–5.)

Stokes, Donald and Lillian. *The Bird Feeder Book: An Easy Guide to Attracting, Identifying, and Understanding Your Feeder Birds*. Boston: Little, Brown, 1987.

Selected literature connections for younger children

Arnosky, Jim. *Otters Under Water*. New York: Putnam, 1992. (About two otters that interact with each other in a fresh-water pond.)

Dr. Seuss. *The Foot Book*. New York: Random, 1968.

Carle, Eric. *The Very Busy Spider*. New York: Dutton, 1969.

Carle, Eric. *A House for a Hermit Crab*. Saxonville, Mass: Picture Book Studio, 1987.

Carle, Eric. *The Very Hungry Caterpillar*. New York: Dutton, 1990.

Carle, Eric. *The Very Quiet Cricket*. New York: Philomel Books. 1990.

Eastman, P.D. *Are You My Mother?*. New York: Random House, 1960.

Ets, Marie Hall. *Play With Me*. New York: Viking Press, 1955.

Flemming, Denise. *In the Tall, Tall Grass*. New York: Scholastic, 1991.

Hoberman, Mary Ann. *A House is a House for Me*. New York: Penguin, 1978.

James, Simon. *Dear Mr. Blueberry*. New York: Macmillan, 1991.

Lewison, Wendy Cheyette. *Going to Sleep on the Farm*. New York: Dial, 1992.

Lionni, Leo. *The Biggest House in the World*. New York: Knopf, 1968.

Zion, Gene. *No Roses for Harry*. New York: Scholastic, 1971.

General community enrichment activities

When you observe animals, notice how they interact, what they eat, how they defend themselves, how they are cared for, how they care for their young, how they play, how they interact with people, what seems to frighten them, how much space they seem to need to feel happy, etc.

Each community has different resources available to it. The following are the kinds of places in your community that would have animals available for your child to observe.

- Pet store.
- Zoo.
- Aquarium.
- Farm with animals.
- Dairy farm.
- Veterinarian.
- Circus.
- Humane Society.
- Fish hatchery
- Chicken hatchery.

7

All about seed-bearing plants

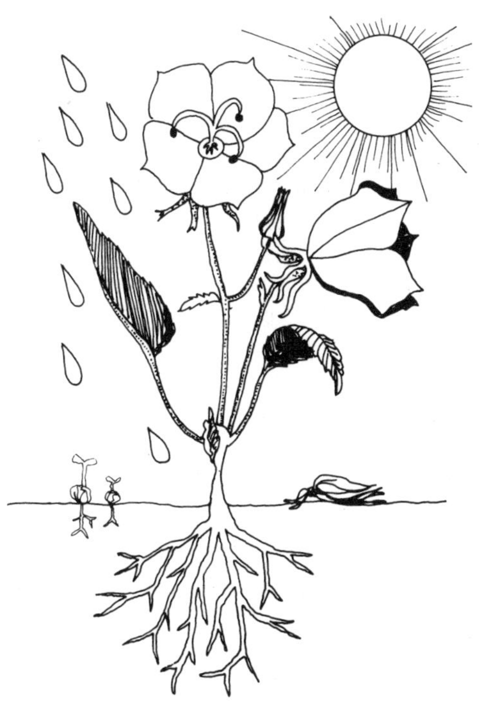

Objectives

The objectives of this chapter are for children to:

- Be able to distinguish living from nonliving things.
- Become aware that seeds house dormant baby plants.
- Understand that each plant has its own unique seed that can only grow into the kind of plant that produced it—for example, tomato seeds can only grow into tomato plants.
- Understand that if seeds are planted in soil and are kept moist and receive sunlight, they have the potential to become mature plants.
- Become aware that gravity, moisture, and sunlight affect plant growth.
- Become aware that roots, stems, and leaves have tubes or veins running through them that carry liquids to and from the leaves and to and from the roots.
- Be able to distinguish a simple leaf from a compound leaf, a monocot leaf from a dicot leaf, a pinnate midrib from a palmate midrib, and a deciduous leaf from an evergreen leaf.
- Develop an awareness that the fruit of a plant is where the seeds for the plant are produced and found.
- Become aware that dead flowers left on plants grow into fruits that will eventually contain seeds.

General background information for parents and teachers

This chapter contains a lot of enrichment vocabulary for children as well as for teachers. As adults, please use your discretion as to how much vocabulary a younger child is ready for. It is more important for younger children to become aware of a big concept. For example, children can learn that leaves have different vein patterns and can be sorted by what their vein pattern looks like; you should not expect younger children to remember such words as pinnate, palmate, compound, monocot, or dicot. It is good for children to be introduced to appropriate words, but please do not expect them to memorize the vocabulary.

Plants

Plant Everything that grows in the ground is a plant.

Botany The biological science of plants.

Botanist A scientist who specializes in the study of plants.

Classification of Major Plant Groups

- *Simple plants*. Plants lacking roots, stems, and leaves.
- *Seedless complex plants*. Plants with tubes that run through stems to and from leaves and to and from roots (ferns, horsetails, and club-mosses).
- *Complex plants with seeds*. Plants that are divided into two categories: those that have cones such as pine, fir, and spruce, and those that have flowers. Flowering plants are divided into two main categories: those that belong to the monocotyledon and those that belong to the dicotyledon family of plants.

Cotyledon Part of the embryo of a seed. Plants with seeds have either one cotyledon or two cotyledons.

Monocotyledons Monocotyledons are called monocots for short. They have one cotyledon. Monocot seeds grow into plants that have a fibrous root system and leaves with parallel vein patterns, and they bear flowers that grow their parts in threes. Examples are: tulips, irises, lilies, and orchids. All of the grasses—including corn, rye, wheat, and trees such as the palms and bamboos—are monocots.

Dicotyledons Dicotyledons are called dicots for short. They have two cotyledons. Dicot seeds grow into plants that have a taproot system, a webbed vein pattern, and that bear flowers that grow their parts in fours and fives. Examples are: roses, pear trees, geraniums, beans. Most of the flowering trees, herbs, and shrubs, as well as the composite flowers, are dicots.

Composite flower Flowers that appear to be one flower but actually consist of many tiny flowers. Examples are: a daisy, a sunflower, and a dandelion.

Vegetable Roots, stems, leaves, and flowers that are grown to be eaten are usually called vegetables. However, a vegetable in the botanical sense is any organism that is classified as a plant. All plants are members of the vegetable kingdom.

Fruit The ripened ovary or ovaries of a seed-bearing plant. Examples are: tomatoes, eggplant, squash, apples, and bananas.

Weed A plant that is considered undesirable or troublesome. It grows where it is not wanted.

Coniferous trees Nonflowering evergreen trees that produce cones that have seeds. Examples are: pine, spruce, hemlock, and redwood.

Evergreen plants Plants that do not lose their leaves all at once, but lose them gradually all year. Most coniferous trees are evergreens. Examples are: ivy, holly, boxwood, yew, rhododendron.

Deciduous plants Plants that lose all of their leaves in the fall and stay dormant during the winter. The leaves of many deciduous plants change colors in the fall. The green color in leaves comes from chlorophyll, a pigment in the chloroplast cells. The green hides or covers up the other colors that are there. When the leaf begins to die in early fall because the days are shorter and the temperature is cooler, the other colors that were hidden but "there" begin to show. In addition, new colors are formed.

Seasonal color change in leaves This change is caused by pigments (colorations) that are in the leaf. During the growing season, leaves appear to be different shades of green due to the different amounts of colored pigment present underneath the chlorophyll pigment.

- Green comes from chlorophyll pigments.
- Yellow, brown, and orange come from carotenoid pigments.
- Red and purple come from anthocyanin pigments.
- Anthocyanin pigments occur in the sap of cells and are not present during the growing season of the leaves as are the chlorophyll and carotenoid pigments.

Perennial plants Perennial plants that bloom year after year. They have a set time to bloom, then they lose their leaves and lie dormant the rest of the year.

7-2 A seasonal color change in leaves is caused by pigments.

Annual plants Annual plants from seeds each year. They only live and grow for one year or season.

Flowers

Flower A flower is the reproductive structure of a seed-bearing plant. Flowers usually have specialized male and female organs. The stamen is the male part and the pistil is the female part of the flower. Usually, the pistil and stamen are in the center of the flower and are surrounded by colorful petals and sepals. (See Fig. 7-3.)

Stamen The specialized male organ on a flower. It is the part of the flower that produces pollen. It usually consists of a filament and an anther. The pollen grows on the anther.

Pistil The specialized female organ on the flower. It is the part that produces the seeds for a plant. It includes a stigma, style, and ovary. The stigma is a hollow, sticky opening at the top of the style tube that connects to the ovary at the base of the style tube. The pistil is usually in the center of the flower inside the petals and sepals.

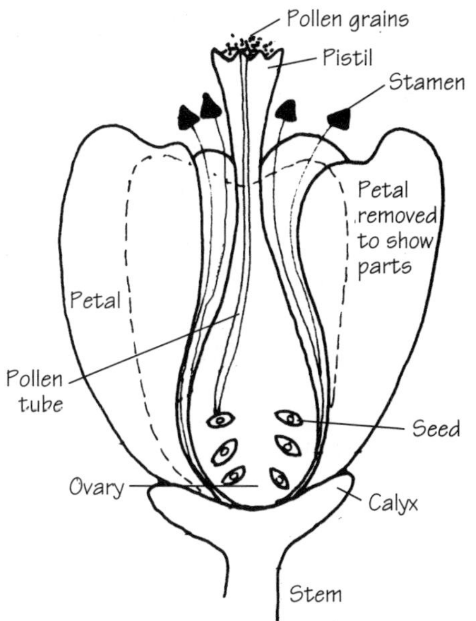

7-3 Parts of a flower.

Pollination Pollination occurs when the pollen from a flower's stamen comes in contact with the pistil of the flower.

Cross-pollination Cross-pollination occurs when the pollen from one flower comes in contact with the pistil of another flower of the same species. Bees, other insects, and the wind are responsible for pollination and cross-pollination.

Fertilization When the pollen comes in contact with the pistil, a tube begins to grow down the style to the ovary. When the pollen attaches itself to an ovule in the ovary, the ovule begins to develop into a seed. The seeds in the ovary are not capable of growing into new plants unless fertilization occurs. Flowers often have eye-catching colors or aromas. The colors and aromas help attract insects. The insects help fertilization occur by pollinating flowers.

Seeds

Seed The fertilized and ripened small body produced by a flowering plant. It contains an embryo capable of germinating to produce a new plant. Seeds remain dormant until conditions are right for them to sprout.

Embryo The minute rudimentary plant contained within a seed.

Germinate To begin to grow. When a seed sprouts, it has germinated.

Seedling A seed that has germinated and become a young plant. The cotyledons are still attached to a seedling.

Sapling A very young tree that has lost its cotyledons.

Roots

Roots The portion of a plant that is usually underground. Roots serve to support, to draw food and water from the surrounding soil, and to store food. Rhizomes, corms, and tubers are often classified as roots because they grow under the ground, but they are really special kinds of stems.

Fibrous root system Found on monocot plants. It is a system of roots that consists of many branching roots. The branching roots grow from the bottom of the stem. (See Fig. 7-4.)

Grass plant

Fiberous roots

Monocot roots

7-4 *Monocot plants have fibrous roots.*

Taproot system Found on dicot plants and coniferous trees. It is a system of roots that consists of a main or taproot growing straight downward with other roots branching from it. (See Fig. 7-5.)

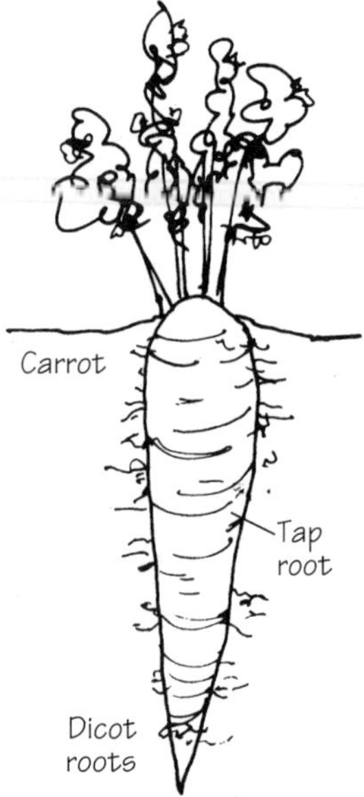

7-5 *Dicot plants have tap roots.*

Stems

Stem The part of a plant that has leaves and buds. The function of the stem is to supply a support system for the production of leaves and flowers, to store food, and to conduct liquids up and down the stem to different parts of the plant. Most stems grow above the ground, but some specialized stems grow under the ground.

Specialized stems that grow under the ground Rhizomes, tubers, bulbs, and corms.

Rhizomes Horizontal stems that grow under the ground. They are perennial plants and grow new shoots year after year.

Tubers Tubers store a lot of food. Potatoes are tubers. The "eyes" on the potato are buds. The "eyes" or buds are capable of growing into stems that grow above the ground. A new potato plant can be started with a piece of a tuber that has one or more eyes.

Bulb A bulb is a perennial bud that has a small stem and many overlapping leaves. Tulips and onions are bulbs. A bulb is mainly leaves.

Corm A corm is a perennial stem with thin, papery leaves. A corm is mainly stem.

Specialized aerial stems Runners, storage stems, tendrils, and thorns.

Runners Runners grow from the main plant and produce new plants. Strawberries, spider plants, and other plants that grow close to the ground have runners.

Storage stems Storage stems store food and water. Cactus plants are a familiar example.

Tendrils Tendrils help a plant climb and cling to other objects. Grape plants and other plants with vines often have tendrils.

Thorns Thorns help protect the plant.

INFORMATION **Vascular bundles** Vascular bundles are bundles of tubes that run up and down the plant from the root system to the leaves. In the leaves, they form a network of veins.

INFORMATION **Xylem** The xylem is the part of the vascular system that moves liquids from the roots to all parts of the plant, including the leaves. Xylem tubes move liquids to the sides and up.

INFORMATION **Phloem** The phloem is the part of the vascular system that moves liquids from the leaves to all parts of the plant including the roots. Phloem tubes move liquids to the sides and down.

Leaves

Green leaves make food for plants, and oxygen is released into the atmosphere as a by-product. (This process is called photosynthesis.)

- Leaves are an excellent and inexpensive tool for sharpening observation skills and for learning to group like items into sets (and for learning rudimentary classification skills).
- Every kind of plant with leaves has its own distinct and unique leaf. Plants can be identified by their leaves.
- Leaves come in a great variety of shapes and patterns. They can be studied, identified, and sorted into groups by their edge, their vein pattern, their shape, the length of their leafstalks or stems, and their color.
- Edges or margins of broadleaf plants can be smooth, serrated, lobed, serrated and lobed, wavy, fine-toothed, double-toothed, dissected, or they can have a combination of several edge types.

Vein patterns Vein patterns can be parallel or webbed. (See Fig. 7-6A.) Most leaves can be divided into three large groups: broad leaves, needle leaves, and narrow leaves.

Veins of a leaf The veins of a leaf have two kinds of tissue flowing through them: xylem and phloem tissue. Xylem tissue carries water up to the leaves from the roots. This water is called sap. Phloem tissue carries food (sugar that is converted to

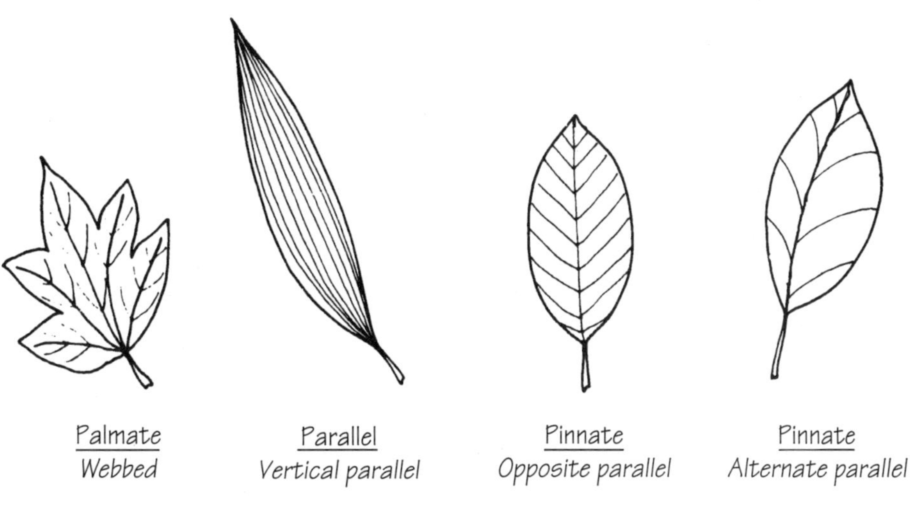

7-6A *Vein patterns on leaves.*

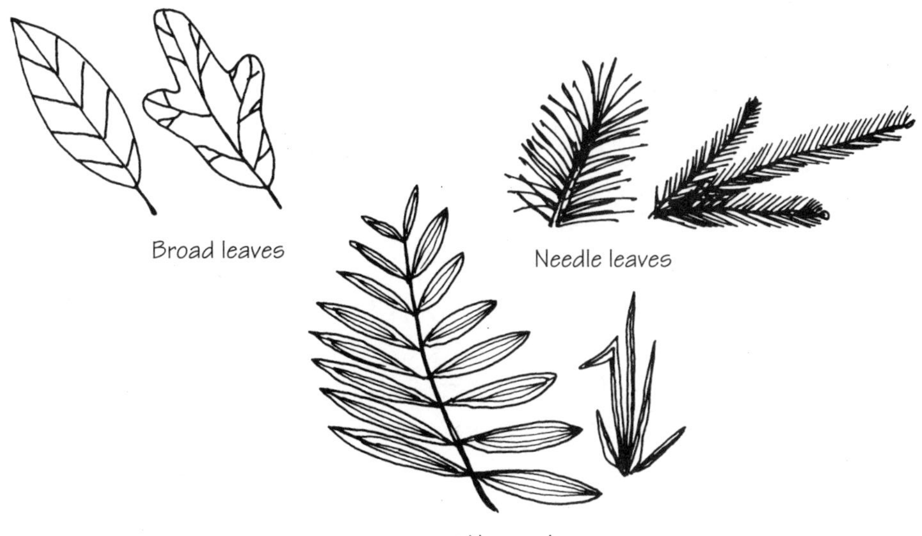

7-6B *Kinds of leaves.*

starch) away from the leaves toward the roots. It also carries food up to flowers and fruits.

Leaves have many parts Each leaf part serves a purpose for the leaf's health and well-being (as does each of our own body parts). The important concept for children to become aware of is that many parts make up a whole; all parts are needed to make a "whole."

Leaves from deciduous trees can be grouped according to their growth patterns. Some leaves are simple, some are compound, and some are double compound.

A simple leaf A simple leaf is composed of one leaf blade and a leafstalk, which connects directly to a woody twig. There is often a bud on the twig at the base of the leafstalk.

Compound leaf A compound leaf is composed of many leaflets on a stem. The leaflets connect to a nonwoody leafstalk that connects to a woody twig. There is often a bud on the twig at the base of the leafstalk. (See Fig. 7-7C.)

Opposite and alternate Leaves can grow on the woody twig of a tree in an opposite or in an alternate pattern. (See Fig. 7-8.)

INFORMATION

Photosynthesis Photosynthesis is the process by which sunlight is turned into energy for the plant by the leaf. The leaves are food factories for the plant. The chlorophyll in the chloroplast cells allows

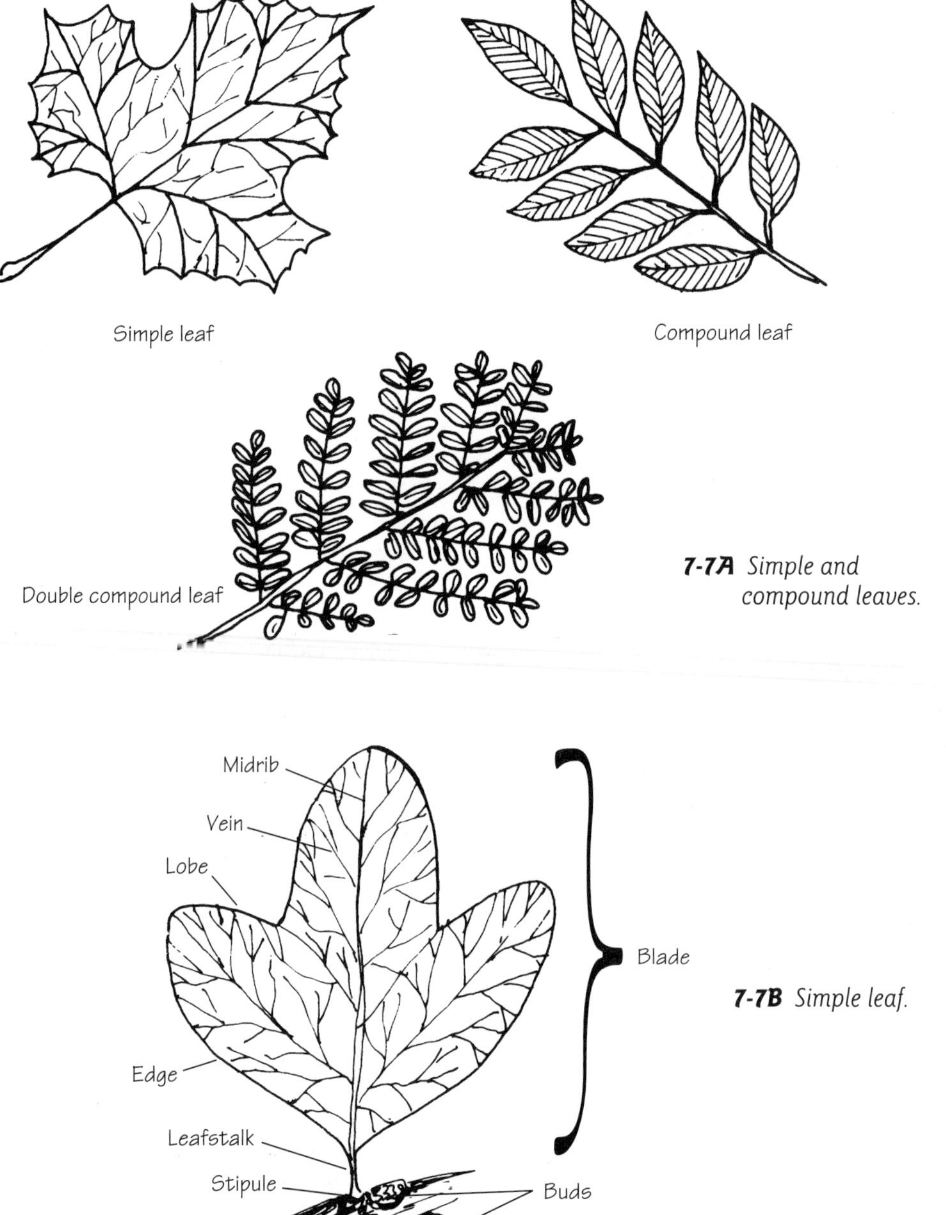

7-7A *Simple and compound leaves.*

7-7B *Simple leaf.*

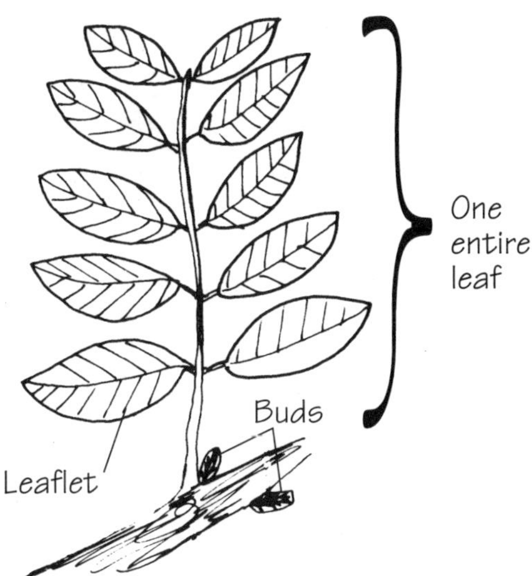

7-7C *Compound leaf.*

water and carbon dioxide from the stomata cells to combine to form a molecule of sugar. Energy is stored in the sugar molecule for the plant.

- Oxygen is a by-product of the photosynthesis process and is released into the atmosphere. (The energy from the sunlight splits the water molecule into hydrogen and oxygen atoms. The hydrogen atoms combine with carbon dioxide, which forms a sugar, thereby leaving oxygen atoms over as a by-product.)
- Chloroplasts are the green cells in the green leaves. Chloroplast cells contain chlorophyll. These cells are usually located on the top surface of leaves and are exposed to sunlight. The chlorophyll stores and holds the energy from the sunlight.
- Stomata cells. Most of the stomata cells are located on the underside of a leaf, the side not facing the sun. Stomata cells regulate evaporation. Air and water vapor come in and out of the leaf cells through the stomata cells.

Note: The concept that a leaf needs to breathe can be demonstrated by covering the surface of a leaf with Vaseline. The leaf will not be able to breathe and will become limp.

Transpiration Transpiration is the loss of water vapor from plants. Most of the loss occurs through the stomata cells.

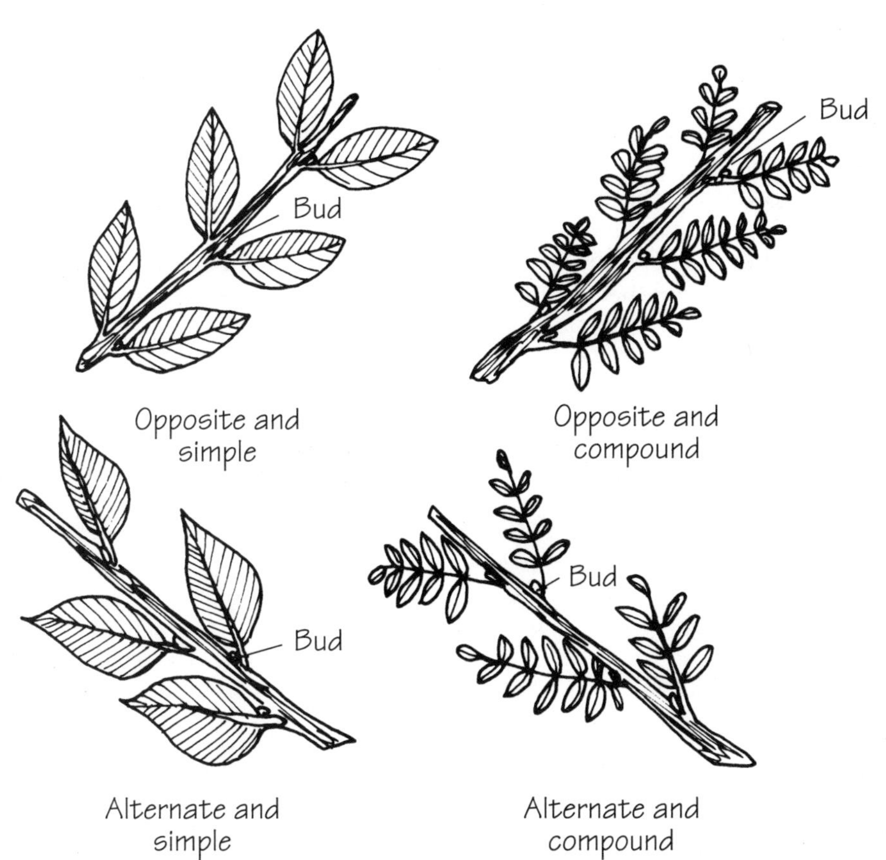

7-8 *Opposite and alternate leaf growth on a twig.*

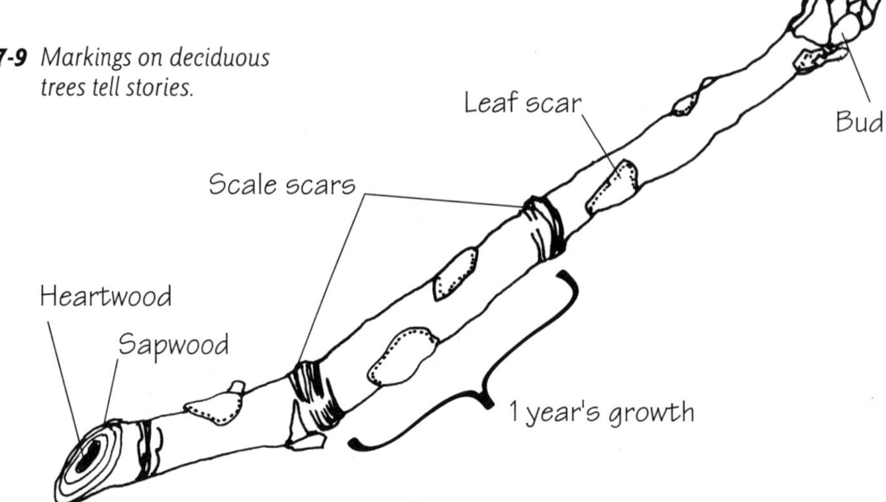

7-9 *Markings on deciduous trees tell stories.*

Twigs

Twigs tell stories if you can read their markings. Leaves leave a scar when they fall off. Also, for each year of growth, a new scale scar grows on the bark. It is possible to tell the age of a twig by counting the scale scars on its bark. It is also possible, if the twig has been cut, to count the rings on the inside. Each ring indicates a year of growth. The darker ring in the center is the heart wood. The lighter circles are the sap wood. The outer layer is the bark. Twigs are smaller versions of tree trunks.

Twigs should be examined closely. They are easy to find, are often overlooked, and they are a good way to begin a study about trees. Twigs are miniature trees; they lack roots, but otherwise have all the parts of a tree. It is easy to bring them inside. Some twigs can even grow roots if they are allowed to soak in water. It is interesting to experiment with them.

Leaf growth patterns Leaf growth patterns can be identified by observing leaf scars on twigs. It can be ascertained whether a leaf grows in an opposite or in an alternate pattern. Most common trees have an alternate growth pattern. Most shrubs have an opposite growth pattern.

According to A *Field Guide To Trees and Shrubs*, by George A. Petrides (Houghton Mifflin, 1958), there are only four common trees with opposite leaves and twigs. They are maple, ash, dogwood, and horse chestnut.

Buds on deciduous trees When deciduous trees lose their leaves in the fall, they leave a bud behind. The winter buds are usually larger than the spring and summer

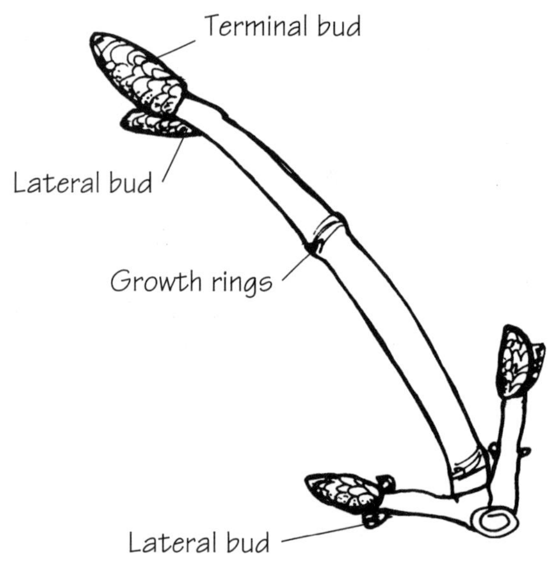

7-10 *Kinds of buds on a deciduous tree.*

buds. Winter buds have an extra layer of scales to protect them from the cold of winter.

They also enclose embryonic leaves and flowers for the spring. Winter buds contain not only leaves and flowers, but also beginnings of new twigs. These twigs eventually become new branches.

There are two kinds of buds on a twig: the terminal ones at the end of the twig, and the lateral ones that grow from the sides of the twig. The terminal buds are the ones that grow the most. Lateral buds act like terminal buds when terminal buds are damaged or pruned. Every year in the fall, when the growing season ends, the plant produces new terminal and lateral buds.

Note: Many of the plant activities are demonstrations. Be sure to involve children in your demonstrations by: asking them to make predictions as you go along; writing experience charts about predictions and observations; having children record their observations by either drawing pictures or writing about their predictions and observations in their own science journals. (Try to encourage them to keep a science journal of their observations and their thoughts.)

Activities and procedures

I. Seeds

1. Identifying things that are alive

Materials

A large color photograph of an outdoor scene.

Procedure

1 Show the children the picture.
2 Ask them to name all the things in the picture that are alive, and to explain how they know that the things they name are alive.
3 Ask the following questions:

Are the plants in the picture alive?

How can you tell that the plants are alive? (They look healthy and full of color.)

How are plants and animals alike? (They each grow and change and adapt to their surroundings, and they are able to reproduce their own kind.)

How are plants different from animals? (Plants are not mobile. They are anchored to the ground where they grow, unless they are transported and moved by something or someone. Animals have to find food to eat or be fed. Plants are able to make their own food.)

Are there any things in the picture that are not alive? (The sky, rocks, soil, water, roads, sidewalks, buildings, machines, the clothes people are wearing, etc.)

How are the plants in the picture alike? (They have leaves.) *Note*: Not all plants have leaves.

How are the plants in the picture different? (The plants come in lots of different shapes and sizes. Trees are big plants; grasses and flowers are small plants. The colors of the plants are different.)

2. Seeds and pebbles

Materials

For each child or group of children: lima beans, small pebbles the size of lima beans, water, two equal-size plastic containers.

Procedure

1 Show the children the lima beans and the small pebbles.

Which of these two things are alive and which are not?

2 Tell children to:
   - **a** Sort out the lima beans from the pebbles.
   - **b** Count out ten lima beans and ten pebbles.
   - **c** Place ten pebbles in a plastic container, and place ten lima beans in another plastic container.
   - **d** Fill each container with water.
   - **e** Leave the pebbles and lima beans in water overnight.

Do you think any change will occur to the pebbles or the beans overnight?

3 After the pebbles and beans have soaked in water overnight, have the children observe the change. (The beans will be larger. They will have absorbed water. Their skins might have popped, and they will feel soft. The pebbles will have remained the same.)

3. Looking inside a seed

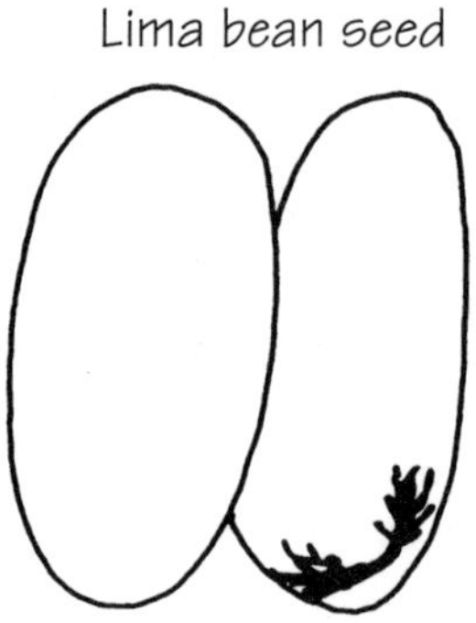

Lima bean seed

7-11 Each half of the open seed is called a cotyledon.

Materials

For each child: pebbles and lima beans soaked in water overnight, a toothpick or pin, a magnifying glass.

Procedure

1 Instruct children to:
 a Use a pin or a toothpick to peel the outer skin off the bean.
 b Open up a soft, water-soaked lima bean.
 c Examine the inside of the seed with a magnifying glass.
 d Discuss the difference between the pebbles and the hard and soft lima beans.

2 Ask the following kinds of questions:

What happened to the seed while it soaked in the water? (It absorbed water.)

How did the water get inside the seed? (It seeped in.)

Can you find a baby plant? (You might need a magnifying glass for this. Help the children find the tiny plant inside the bean.)

What does it look like? (A baby plant.)

3 *Explain:* The small plant inside the seed is called an embryo. The two halves of the seed are called the cotyledons and store food for the embryo.

4. Water enters seeds

Materials

A colored candle, a match, 20–40 lima beans with unchipped skins, a plastic container, water.

Procedure

1 Distribute the lima beans.

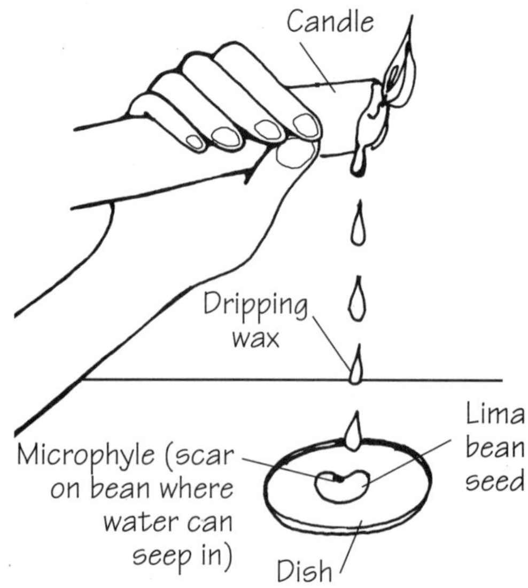

7-12 Sealing a seed's microphyl so water cannot enter.

2 Have children examine the lima beans to see if they can find any marks or cracks on them other than the scar mark on one side. The scar on the side will have one tiny spot on one of its ends.

An adult should light a candle and allow some wax to drip on the scar and the tiny spot on the scar. Do this to ten lima beans.

3 Have a child count out another ten lima beans that have unchipped skins. Instruct another child to put both sets of ten beans in a container filled with water. Let them soak overnight. Have the children examine the beans the next day.

4 Ask the following kinds of questions:

Do all of the beans look alike? (No, some are swollen, and some are unchanged.)

Which beans are swollen or have wrinkled skin? (The ones without the wax.)

How does water seep into the seed? (Water seeps into the seed through a little opening on the side of the seed where the scar is.)

Why didn't the seeds covered with wax drops swell? (The wax prevented the water from entering the opening.)

The opening on the seed is called the micropyle.

Going further

What do you suppose would happen if you used water colored with food color? Try it and find out.

5. Seeds absorb water

Materials

Assorted beans, dry peas, an empty plastic spice jar with a lid, water, a plastic bag, a rubber band.

Procedure

1 Fill the jar to the top with the beans and peas. Force as many seeds as you possibly can into the container by shaking it or tapping it to create more space. Then add as much water as the container will take and screw the top on tightly. Place the container inside a plastic bag, and close the plastic bag with a rubber band. Let the closed jar sit overnight.

2 Have the children observe the container the next day. (Usually, the container has burst open because, as the seeds absorb water, they swell and create pressure inside of the container.)

6. Sprouting lima beans

Materials

For each child: lima beans, paper towel, water, clear plastic bag.

Procedure

1 Moisten a paper towel. Fold it in half three times. Place several beans on the paper towel. Then place the paper towel with the beans on it inside a plastic bag so that the paper will stay moist.

2 Ask children to make a prediction about what they think will happen to the moist beans.

3 Let the seeds stay on the moist paper towel inside the plastic bag for a day or two. Then check to see if the seeds have changed. If they have not sprouted, continue to check until they do. *Note*: Do not make the paper towel too wet or the seeds will grow mildew and rot. To further avoid the possibility of mildew, create a water solution that consists of one tablespoon of household bleach to one gallon of water.

7. Seed hunt

Materials

A knife (for adult use only), a cutting board. For each child: assorted fresh fruits and vegetables (cucumber, tomato, orange, apple, cantaloupe, peas, green beans, etc.); paper plates; paper towels; a magnifying glass.

Procedure

1 Ask the following question:

Where do seeds come from? (Listen to their responses.)

2 Show children the assorted fruits and vegetables.

What is inside the fruits and vegetables?

3 An adult should cut up the fruits and vegetables. The children should remove the seeds.

4 Tell children to place the seeds from each kind of fruit or vegetable on a different paper plate. Allow the seeds to dry out. Have the children look at them through a magnifying glass.

5 Tell children to count and record how many seeds came from each fruit or vegetable.

6 Ask the following kinds of questions:

Which fruit or vegetable had the most seeds?

Which fruit or vegetable had the least number of seeds?

Which had the largest seeds?

Which had the smallest seeds?

Can these seeds grow into new plants? (Yes.)

How many plants could one tomato start? (It depends on the number of seeds.)

If an apple has ten seeds, how many new apple trees could be started from the seeds? (Ten.)

Which can produce more new plants from one piece of fruit? (The fruit or vegetable that produces the most seeds.)

Do all of the seeds grow into new plants? (No.)

Why not? (They are eaten by animals; only some of the seeds are used to produce new plants.)

7 Dry out some of the seeds for a week.

8 Observe and record how they change as they dry out. Then place them on a moist paper towel inside a clear plastic bag for a few days to see if they will sprout.

9 *Explain:* When a seed sprouts, "germination" occurs. To germinate means that the seed has begun to grow into a plant.

8. Sorting seeds

Materials

For each child or group of children: assorted seeds, an empty egg carton, a small plastic container.

Procedure

1 Place the assorted seeds inside the plastic container. Show the children the assorted seeds and the egg carton.

2 Ask children to sort the seeds into the egg cups in the egg carton.

Can you guess what plants the different seeds will grow into?

How could you find out?

9. Monocot and dicot seeds

Materials

For each child or group of children: corn kernels, lima beans, water, paper towel.

Procedure

1 Tell children to place the two kinds of seeds on a moist paper towel. (Let them sit overnight so that they will be soft and easy to open the next day.)

2 *Explain:* Both the corn kernels and the beans are seeds. They are very different from each other; not only do they look different, but they also grow quite differently.

3 The next day, tell children to:

a Open up their corn kernel and bean seed

b Observe how different the two kinds of seeds look from each other. (The bean seeds have two parts and split open easily. The corn kernels do not split open easily, and they have one part.)

4 *Explain:* Bean seeds belong to the dicot family of plants because they have two parts that become two cotyledons. The corn kernel belongs to the monocot family of plants because it has only one cotyledon. "Mono" means one; "di" means two. Monocot seeds grow into grasses, palm and bamboo trees, and flowers with three to six petals like daffodils, tulips, and lilies. Dicot seeds grow into flowering trees, shrubs, herbs, and flowers that have four or five petals or multiples of four and five; examples are roses or complex flowers that contain many tiny flowers inside a flower (such as a sunflower or a daisy).

10. How seeds spread

Materials

For each child or group of children: a dandelion puff; seed with burrs; a wool mitten or sock; maple seeds (which are shaped like helicopter propellers and twirl when they are thrown in the air); pine cone with seeds; an exploding seed in a pod; dried seeds found anywhere outside (acorns, catkins, or grass seeds).

Procedure

1 Show children the dandelion puff.

How do new dandelions get planted?

2 Take one of the seeds off the puff and let it fall. (If there is a rug on the floor, it will probably land straight up on the rug. The seed plants itself in the ground.)

3 Show children the burr.

How do the "stickers" on the seed help it move? (Discuss how seeds with burrs can travel from one place to another by sticking to animal fur as an animal goes by or by sticking to our clothes when we walk through a field.)

4 Have children put a wool mitten or sock on their hand and rub it next to the burr.

What happens? (The burr clings and attaches itself.)

5 Demonstrate how a maple seed hovers through the air like a helicopter. Hold the seed above your head, then let it go, and it will hover and spin until it lands on the ground. The design of the seed allows it to twirl and hover in flight.

6 Give each child a maple seed to experiment with so that he or she can become familiar with how maple seeds and other similarly shaped seeds travel.

7 Discuss how the other seeds on display are dispersed from the plants they grow on, and how animals such as squirrels and birds also help distribute seeds.

8 Allow children to continue to manipulate and experience the different kinds of seed designs.

II. The parts of green plants

1. The parts of a dandelion plant

Materials

A fresh dandelion flower, a hand trowel, a dandelion weed tool to dig up dandelion roots, newspaper.

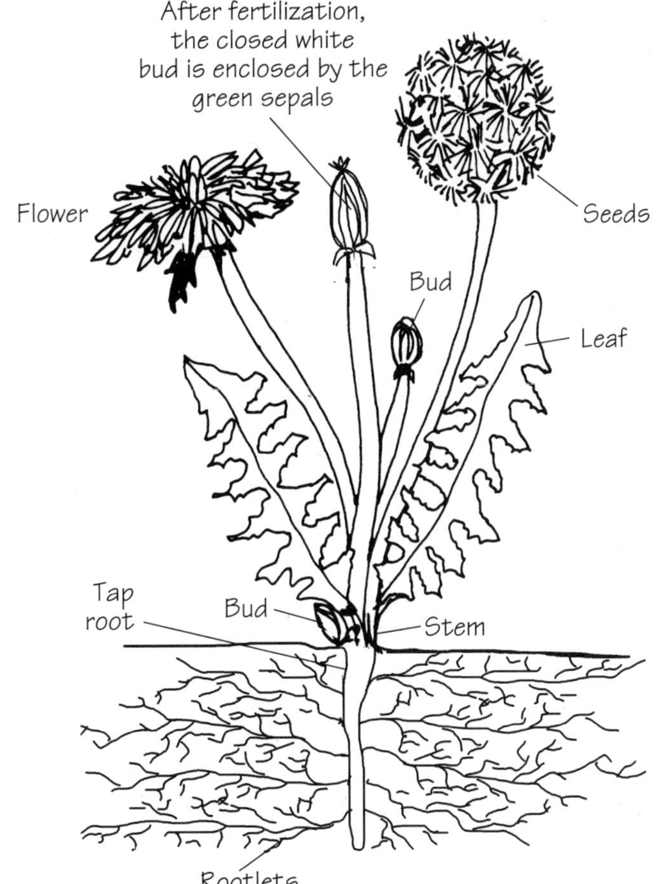

7-13 *A complete dandelion plant.*

Procedure

1 Take children outside to dig up a dandelion. Dandelions are easiest to dig up after a heavy rain. Show the children how to use the weeding tool. Ask the children why it is easier to dig up a plant after it rains. (The soil is easier to dig because it is diluted from the rain.)

2 Show children a dandelion flower.

3 *Explain:* The dandelion is a wild flower. It is also a weed. A weed is a plant that grows someplace where you do not want it to grow.

4 Find a dandelion plant in the grass. Have the children notice the way the dandelion grows in the grass. The leaves spread out flat and close to the ground.

5 *Explain:* A dandelion is a very sturdy plant. It can be stepped on directly and it will not die. The leaves grow in a circular pattern off a very short stem. They grow in a rosette pattern.

6 Have children look at the plant and ask children the following kinds of questions as they examine the dandelion plant growing in the ground:

Can you find the leaves? What do they look like? (They look like jagged teeth.)

Can you find the flower? How is the flower attached to the plant? (The flower is attached to the plant on a long hollow scope.)

7 Pick a dandelion flower and then remove the scope from the flower to see what the scope looks like. (It is hollow.)

Can you find a bud? What is inside of the bud? (A baby flower that is undeveloped.)

How many buds are there? How can you tell which buds are going to blossom soon? (The larger buds with the longer scopes are going to blossom the soonest.)

What happens to the flower after it blossoms? (It shrivels up and stays closed until it opens to become a seed puff.)

How can you tell which of the dead flowers is going to be a seed puff? (It has a white tip rather than a yellow tip.)

How many seeds are on each seed puff? Too many to count.)

What happens to the seeds on the seed puff when the wind blows on it? (The seeds come off and blow in the wind.)

What happens to the flower when the sun goes down? (The flower closes up. It reopens when the sun shines on it.)

8 Dig up a dandelion plant. Try to get the complete root.

9 Have the children observe how long the root is. (The main root has little rootlets on it. The main root is called a taproot. Soil clings to the roots and rootlets.)

10 Show children where the stem is located. The stem on the dandelion plant is very short because the leaves grow off it in a rosette pattern close to the ground. (See Fig. 7-13 for location of the stem.)

Going further

- Use the parts of a dandelion plant to draw a picture of a dandelion plant or other picture.
- Rub the flower on a white sheet of paper. The pollen grains and petals will color the paper yellow.
- Rub the leaves, and the chlorophyll in the leaves will color the paper green.
- Rub the root, and the soil that still clings to the root will color the paper brown.
- Experiment with other plants to find out if you can rub color out of their parts too.

2. Fruits and vegetables (the parts of a plant we eat)

Materials

CAUTION Fresh fruits and vegetables, a knife (for adult use only), a cutting board, a paper towel or paper plate.

Procedure

1 Show children the fresh fruits and vegetables.

2 *Explain:* When we eat fruits and vegetables, we are eating plants or parts of plants. All things that grow in the ground are plants and are members of the vegetable kingdom. Flowers and fruits, grasses and trees, bushes and ferns are all plants.

3 Introduce a few fruits or vegetables to the children each day.

4 Discuss with them what part of the plant they are looking at or about to eat.

5 See Fig. 7-14 for the parts of plants we eat.

6 *Explain:* When you taste roots, they sometimes taste sweet. Roots store food in the form of sugar and/or starch for

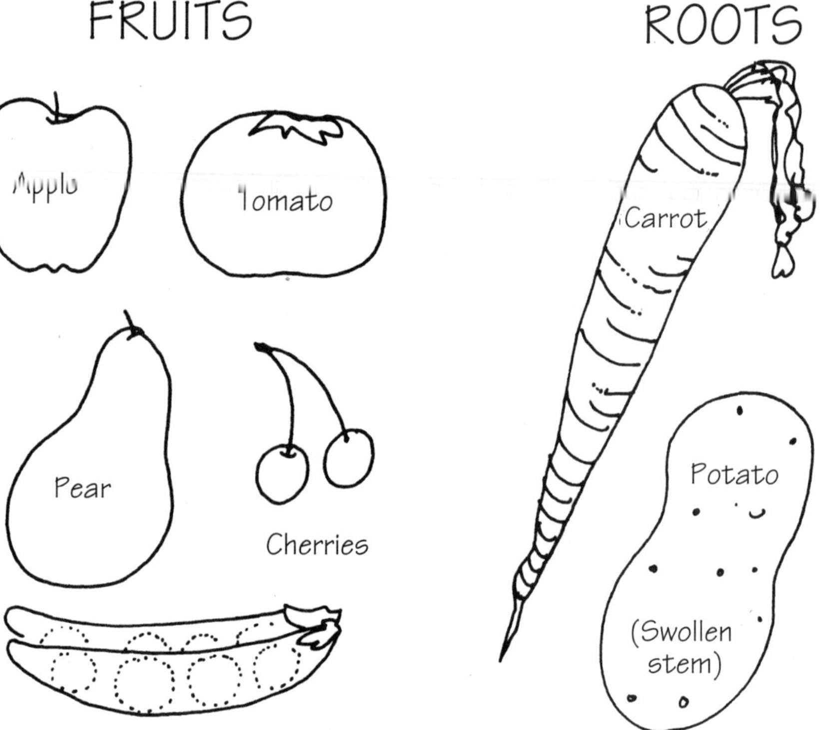

7-14 *The parts of plants we eat.*

the plant to use to grow more new leaves and flowers. Roots like carrots are pulled from the ground before more leaves and flowers are produced by the plant. When we eat the roots, we are eating the food that the plant has stored for itself.

7 *Explain:* Botanists are scientists who study plants. Botanists classify as fruits many of the fruits and vegetables we eat. A botanist classifies the part of a plant that contains its seeds as the plant's ovary or the fruit of the plant. So, things like tomatoes, eggplants, cucumbers, and squash are each classified as fruits. A plant's ovary or fruit is the place where seeds develop and are nourished by the plant. The fruit or ovary supplies food to the seeds until the seeds germinate and grow into new plants able to make their own food.

III. Leaves

1. A leaf-collecting walk

Materials

Newspaper. For each child: a small paper bag.

Procedure

1 Take the children out on a walk around the backyard or the schoolyard. Have them collect leaves.

2 Tell children to take only one sample of all of the leaves they find. (The children should look in the grass for a variety of growth there. They should also take a sample from the shrubs and the flowers and the trees.)

3 Instruct them to place all their leaves inside the paper bag.

4 Bring the paper bags filled with leaves back into your classroom and spread them out on a piece of newspaper. Have the children examine all the leaves together.

5 Ask the following kinds of questions:

Do any of these leaves look alike?

How are they alike? (Color, size, shape, edge, length of stem, vein pattern, texture of surface.)

Do any of the leaves look exactly alike? (Only if they come from the same plant will they look exactly alike, but even then, no two leaves are ever exactly identical. Every individual leaf is unique. Fingerprints on people's hands are also unique. Even though fingerprints fall into general patterns, each individual has a unique set of fingerprints.)

Can you find two matching leaves from the same plant?

Can you find a group of leaves that have a smooth edge?

Can you find a group of leaves that have a jagged edge?

Can you find a group of leaves that have a combination of smooth and jagged edges?

How many different ways can you think of to group the leaves that were collected?

6 Give each child a part of the leaf collection and ask each child to sort or

Table 7-1 Edible Plants

Roots	Stems	Bark	Leaves	Flowers	Ovaries or fruits with edible seeds	Ovaries or fruits without edible seeds	Seeds
Beets	Asparagus	Cinnamon	Basil	Artichokes	Allspice*	Apple	Caraway
Carrots	Celery		Bay leaf	Broccoli	Banana	Cherry	Corn kernels
Garlic	Rhubarb		Cabbage	Cauliflower	Black pepper*	Orange	Dill
Ginger			Kale	Cloves	Corn	Peach	Dried beans
Onions			Lettuce	Saffron†	Cucumber	Plum	Mustard
Potatoes			Oregano		Eggplant		Nutmeg
Radishes			Parsley		Green beans		Nuts
Turnips			Rosemary		Hot pepper		Peas
			Sage		Peas		Poppy seeds
			Spinach		Squash		Sesame Seeds
			Tarragon		Strawberry		
					Tomatoes		

Note: This chart is only a sample listing. It does not include all edible plants and parts of plants.

*Allspice and black pepper are dried-up berries.

†Saffron comes from the stamen of crocus blossoms.

group the leaves they have been given into two different piles based on a way that they can think of for separating the leaves. Then let each child share how they divided their leaves into piles and why.

2. Taking a closer look at the edges of leaves

7-15 *Leaf with a serrated edge.*

Materials

For each child or group of children: leaves from leaf-collecting walk, newspaper. For demonstration: a knife with a serrated edge, a knife with a smooth edge. (Knives are for adult use only.)

Procedure

1 Ask the children the following question:

Can you find a leaf with a smooth edge and one with a jagged edge? (Hold up both leaves after they are identified by the children.)

2 *Explain:* The edge that is jagged is called a serrated edge. When a leaf has an edge with many points, it is called a serrated edge. The edge looks like the edge of some kitchen knives. Some kitchen knives have a smooth edge and some have a serrated edge. As you show children both knives, explain that knives are hard and very sharp. They can cut you, but leaves that are soft cannot cut you.

3 Hold up a leaf with a lobed edge.

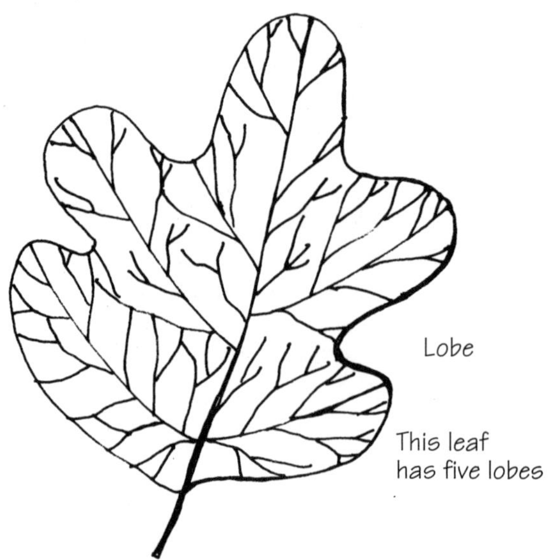

7-16 *Leaf with a lobed edge.*

4 *Explain:* When a leaf has an edge that looks as though a part of it was cut out, it is called a lobed edge; the leaf you are holding has a lobed edge.

5 Point to the lobes and count them. The number of lobes will vary on different leaves from different plants.

Can you find another leaf with a lobed edge from the collection of leaves?

6 Hold up another leaf that is both serrated and lobed, like that from a maple tree.

7 *Explain:* Leaves sometimes have a combination of edges. They can have an edge that is both smooth and serrated or serrated and lobed, or another combination.

Can you find other leaves from the collection of leaves that have a combination of two patterns for an edge?

8 Have children make a paper model of what a smooth-edged and serrated-edged leaf look like.

3. Find matching real leaves

Materials

For each child: leaves that came from the backyard or schoolyard.

Procedure

Show children the leaves and give each child a set of leaves. Have them find a matching pair for each of the leaves outside, or have each child find another child with a set of leaves that matches his/her set of leaves. Discuss the edge of each leaf when its pair is found.

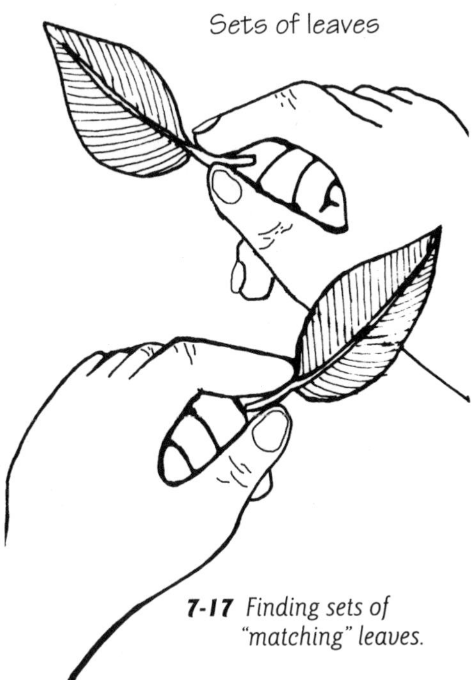

7-17 *Finding sets of "matching" leaves.*

7-18A *Cardboard leaf shapes made from real leaves.*

4. Monocot and dicot leaves

Materials

For each child or group of children: assorted leaves from monocot and dicot plants, a magnifying glass. (Most grasses have monocot leaves; most trees and shrubs have dicot leaves.)

Procedure

1 Have the children see the difference between the monocot vein pattern and the dicot vein pattern. Monocots have veins that run parallel to the midrib. Dicots have veins that form a webbed or branched pattern from the midrib. Have the children look through the magnifying glass at the vein patterns and sort the leaves into two piles, one with monocot leaves, the other with dicot leaves.

2 Have children make a model of a monocot leaf and a dicot leaf.

5. Taking a closer look at veins on leaves

Materials

For each child or group of children: cardboard shapes of leaves and real leaves with the same shapes (for example: oak, tulip, elm, willow); a pencil; paper.

Procedure

1 Show the children the cardboard leaf shapes and the real leaves that match the shapes. Have them find the cardboard leaves that match the real leaves.

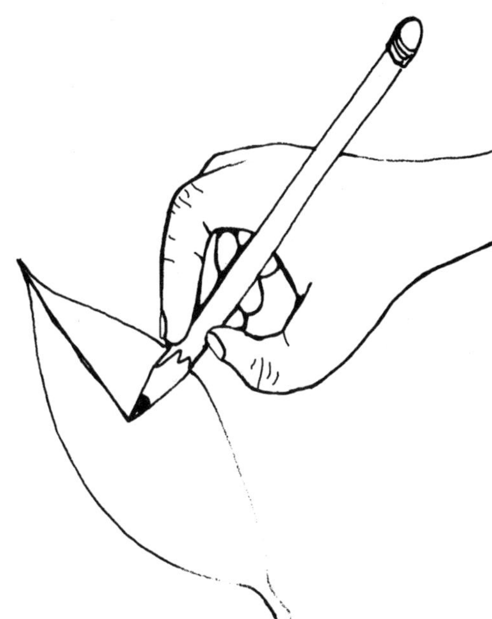

7-18B *Add a midrib and veins to cardboard.*

2 Have children use a pencil to trace around a cardboard leaf shape.

What is needed to make the leaf shape look more like a real leaf? (If they do not suggest adding the midrib and veins, then show them the midrib and veins on the real leaf, and then have them add these lines that represent midribs and veins to their leaf tracing.)

3 *Explain:* The line in the center of the leaf is called the midrib. It is the main vein. Smaller veins are connected to the midrib. Liquids flow through the

midrib and veins of the leaf. Veins help move food or energy from one part of the leaf to another. The midrib of a leaf connects to the leafstalk or stem and the leafstalk connects to a branch of the plant. (See Figs. 7-18A and 7-18B.)

4 Have the children trace around the remaining cardboard leaf shapes and add lines to the shapes to represent a midrib and the veins.

5 Ask the following kinds of questions:

What do the veins look like on the real leaf?

Are the veins straight and parallel to each other or wavy looking?

What does the midrib look like?

Does the midrib go straight up and down like a straight pin, or does it appear to have branches like the fingers branching off your palm?

Do the lines you have added to your leaf shape look like the kind of pattern that the veins have on the real leaf that matches the leaf shape?

6 *Explain*: The midrib of a leaf can be either pinnate or palmate. If it is pinnate, it will be straight like a pin. If it is palmate, it will appear to have several branches. The veins on a leaf can be webbed and wavy or very straight. The smallest and thinnest veins on a leaf are called capillaries. They are usually wavy looking.

7 *Explain:* Our bodies also have veins in them that carry liquid. Our veins also carry food or energy. The food is in the blood. Our tiniest veins are called capillaries, and our major veins are called arteries. Have the children locate a vein on their body.

How is your body like that of a leaf? (We each have veins to carry liquids in our body from one place to another.)

6. Parts of a simple leaf

Materials

A leaved twig from a shrub with a simple leaf.

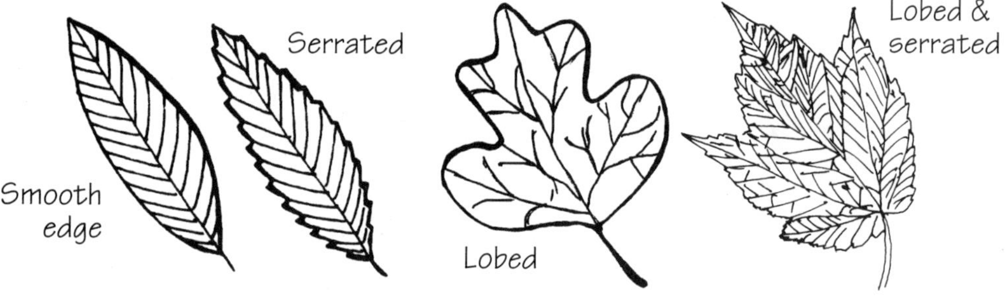

7-19 *Leaves with a pinnate midrib; leaves with a palmate midrib*

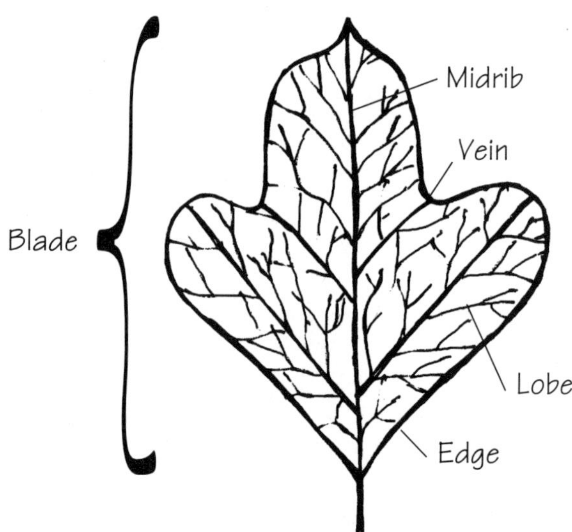

7-20 *Parts of a simple leaf.*

Procedure

1 Show the children the leaved twig. Take off a leaf from the twig and have the children notice the bud on the twig next to the leafstalk, and the scar that is left on the twig from where the leaf was pulled off.

2 *Explain:* When a leaf has one blade and a leafstalk that connects directly to a wood twig, it is called a simple leaf.

3 Give each child a leaf from the twig. As you rip off each leaf from the twig, have the children notice where the scar is from the leaf on the twig and where the new leaf bud is on the twig.

4 Instruct children to:
  a Touch the midrib on your leaf.
  b Hold your leaf by its leafstalk.
  c Place your index finger on the edge of your leaf.
  d Point to a vein on your leaf.

5 *Explain:* The leaf is called a blade. The bud of a leaf is often protected by a stipule. Sometimes stipules are hard to find because they often wither and dry up early in the season.

7. Parts of a compound leaf

Materials

Samples of real compound leaves on a twig, and of double compound leaves on a twig; a pencil; crayons; paper.

Procedure

1 Show children the samples of compound and double compound leaves. Show them how these leaves are quite different looking from the simple leaves. Remind the children that simple leaves often have a bud on the twig at the base of their leafstalk.

2 Show that the compound leaf also has a bud on the twig at the base of its leafstalk, but it appears to be more than one leaf.

3 *Explain:* The compound leaf is made up of several leaflets. All of the leaflets combined make up one leaf. There is only one bud on the twig at the base of the leafstalk; therefore, botanists classify it as a single leaf, even though it looks like several leaves.

4 Have children examine a compound leaf and a double compound leaf.

5 *Explain:* Simple leaves grow in an opposite or alternate pattern on a twig.

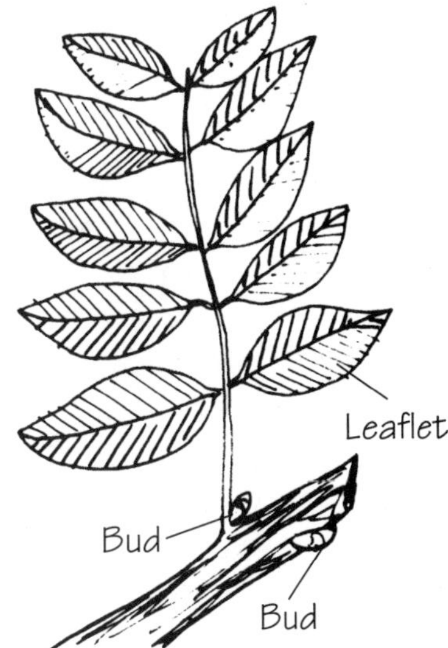

7-21 *Parts of a compound leaf.*

Leaflets on a compound leaf grow opposite each other on a leafstalk. Model with your fingers what opposite and alternate patterns look like and show children an opposite and an alternate growth pattern on a twig. (Have them model alternate and opposite with their fingers too.)

6 Ask children to draw a sketch of what a simple, a compound, and a double compound leaf look like. (See Fig. 7-7A.)

8. Finding out the names of plants that leaves grow on

Materials

A sample of a leaf from a tree, a nature guidebook about trees. For example, *Trees, A Golden Guide*, by Herbert Zim, or *Spotter's Guide to Trees of North America*, by Alan Mitchell.

Procedure

1 Show children the leaf. Explain that the leaf came from a tree. If we want to find out what kind of tree it came from and we do not know, then we can look up the kind of tree it came from by consulting a reference book. Every tree and plant has its own unique leaf. It is possible to identify the kind of tree the leaf came from by finding a picture of the leaf in the reference book.

2 Decide with the children whether the leaf is simple or compound. Also have the children decide whether the leaf is a broadleaf or a needle-like leaf from an evergreen.

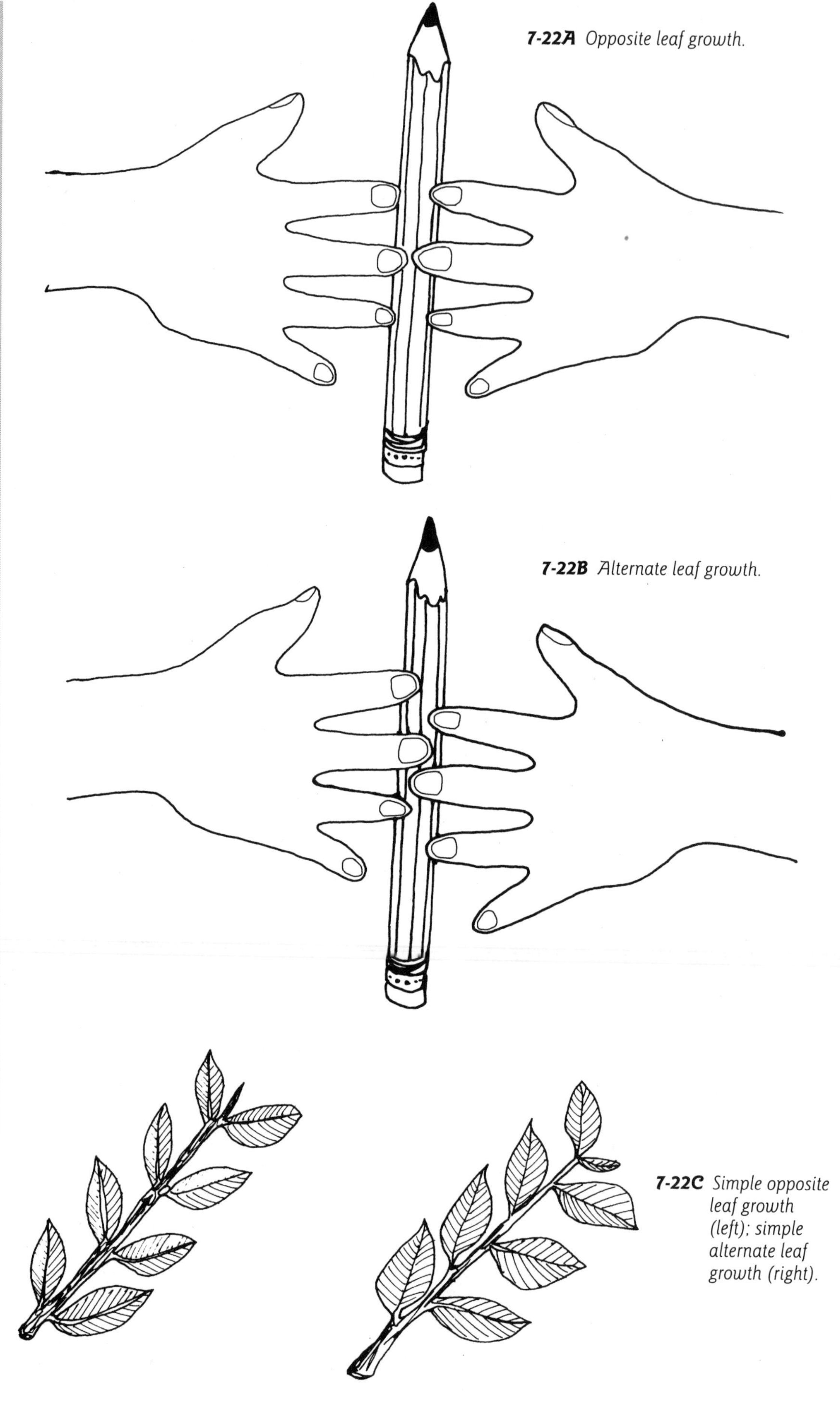

7-22A *Opposite leaf growth.*

7-22B *Alternate leaf growth.*

7-22C *Simple opposite leaf growth (left); simple alternate leaf growth (right).*

3 Show the children how the guidebook is divided into sections to make it easier to identify plants. (Refer to the nature books as reference books.)

4 Ask each child to find a leaf from a tree, and then consult a nature book to find out what kind of tree it grew on.

9. Deciduous and evergreen leaves

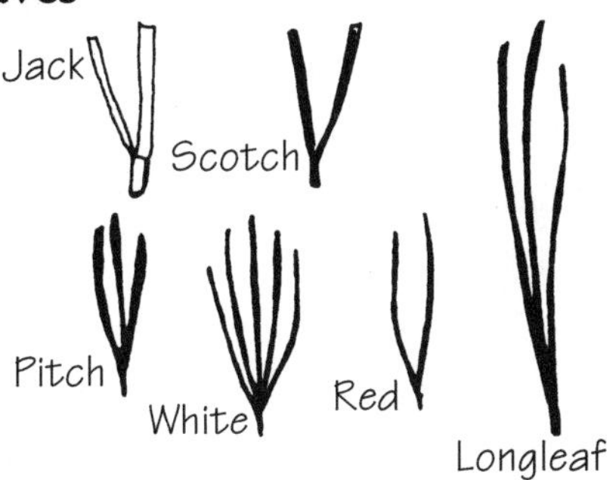

7-23A Evergreen pine needles.

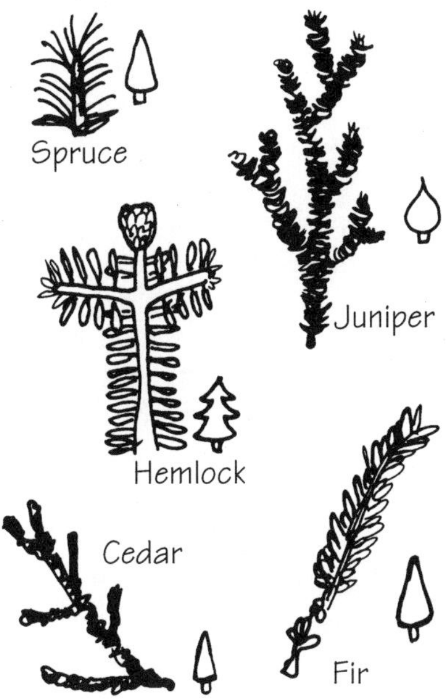

7-23B Evergreens.

Materials

Gather assorted twigs with leaves from evergreen trees and deciduous trees.

Procedure

1 Show the children the assorted twigs with leaves.

2 *Explain:* The leaves that look like needles are from evergreen trees. Each evergreen tree has its own distinct needle leaf. Trees can be identified by the way the needles grow on the twigs. Some of the needles grow in clumps of three or five, or in pairs; some have short, single, stubby needles; some have long needles; some have white stripes on them; and some feel prickly. Some evergreens have broad, leathery leaves. There is a great variety of evergreens and needle-leaf evergreens.

3 Have the children sort out which twigs with leaves came from evergreens and which twigs are not from evergreen trees. Then have them try to identify which twigs with leaves came from which evergreen.

4 Ask children to check a nature guidebook on trees to identify the needles they are looking at.

5 Help them understand the difference between a pine, a fir, a spruce tree, and a cedar tree. Show them the difference between the scales on a cedar leaf and the short, stiff needles on a spruce tree. *Note*: Show them the long, flexible needles that a pine tree has as opposed to the shorter needles on spruces and firs.

6 *Explain:* If a tree is an evergreen, that means it does not lose its leaves in the fall. It stays green all year. The leaves on evergreens are usually tough and waxy. Instead of losing all of their leaves at once in the fall, evergreen trees lose their leaves all year, a few at a time. Evergreens continually grow new leaves. A deciduous tree has leaves that fall off every fall. Evergreens and deciduous trees are perennial plants. A perennial plant is any plant that continues to live for many seasons (even though it might appear to be dead in the fall).

7 Tell children to check the vein pattern on a pine tree needle with a magnifying glass. A pine tree is not a flowering tree. It grows cones, but not flowers. The needle leaves have parallel veins like monocot plants. Plants with needle leaves that grow cones are called conifers or cone-bearing plants and are classified as gymnosperms, or plants without flowers.

IV. Roots and stems

1. A closer look at a carrot

Materials

Freshly picked carrots with green tops still on, a knife (for adult use only), a magnifying glass, paper and pencil.

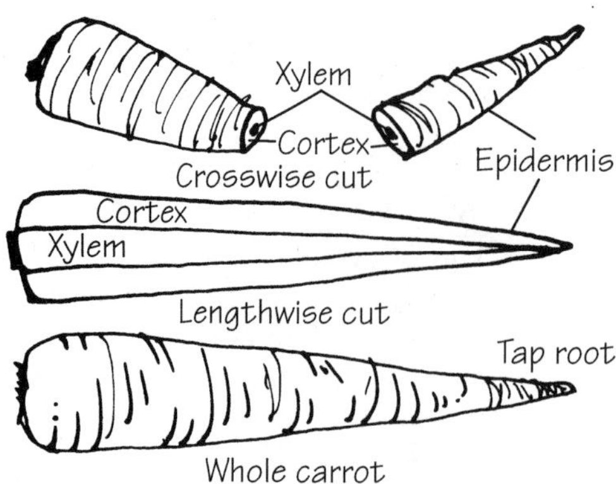

7-24 *Carrots have tap roots.*

Procedure

1 Show children a carrot.

What part of the plant is a carrot? (It is a root.)

2 Observe how long the greens are on top of the carrot.

3 If the carrot has been freshly picked, the children might be able to see the fine root hairs that are on each of the rootlets. Use a magnifying glass to look at the rootlets. (If the rootlets are not still attached, there will be small scars on the sides of the carrot root.)

4 *Explain:* The carrot itself is called a taproot. A taproot is a long, thick root that grows down deep and straight.

5 An adult should slice two carrots with a knife. Slice one carrot crosswise and the other one lengthwise.

6 Have children observe the inside of the carrot. (There are three parts on the inside of the root.)

7 *Explain:* There is an inner layer or circle of fibers in the middle of the carrot and another layer that surrounds that layer. The entire carrot is surrounded by a thin layer of skin. Each layer inside the root appears to be a different shade of orange. The lengthwise cut shows that the layers extend from the top of the root to the bottom of the root. They are long fibers. The fibers look like circles in the crosswise cut.

The outer skin on the carrot is called the epidermis. Our body is surrounded by an epidermis. We usually call our epidermis "skin." Inside the epidermis is the cortex. The cortex is the part of the carrot root where food is stored for the plant. The cortex of the root usually tastes sweet because it contains a lot of stored-up sugar for the plant made by the leaves. The very center of the carrot root is made up of tissues or tubes that transport food up and down the root. The food is absorbed from the soil in the form of moisture and minerals and travels to and from the leaves and to and from the roots in a circular path. The blood in our body also travels through tubes in a circular path.

8 Ask children to draw a model of a carrot slice and label the parts of the slice (in their science journals, or on a piece of drawing paper).

2. Looking at the roots of a tree sapling

Materials

An acorn, a dug-up oak tree seedling or oak tree sapling (or any other seedling of a tree) replanted in a large flower pot, a hand trowel.

Procedure

1 Show the children the acorn.

2 *Explain:* When an acorn sprouts, an oak tree begins to grow.

3 Show children the oak tree seedling or sapling in the flower pot.

4 *Explain:* This is a baby tree. *Note*: If the oak tree is a seedling, you will probably still be able to see the acorn attached to the tree roots. If it is a sapling, the acorn will have already broken off.

5 Dig the tree up out of the flower pot and have the children look at the roots.

6 Ask the following kinds of questions:

Is the acorn still attached?

Where are the roots?

How do the roots anchor the plant to the ground? (They spread out and down and grip the ground.)

Are there more roots or branches?

Which is longer, the roots or the branches?

How do the roots grow? (One root grows down; the rest grow off of the main or taproot.)

Do all the roots grow down? (Some grow to the side and are called lateral roots.)

What color are the roots?

Do the roots look different from the bark?

Will this tree be able to continue to grow? (Yes, if it is replanted and the roots do not dry out.)

7 Have the children replant the tree in the pot and transplant it to a place they choose outside.

8 *Explain:* The tree will grow to be a very large plant. Trees need a lot of space to grow. Have the children use a hand trowel to break up the soil and to dig a hole for the tree seedling or sapling.

3. Cross-section of a log

Materials

An unsplit firewood log or a tree stump; paper; pencil.

Procedure

1 Show the children an unsplit firewood log.

2 *Explain:* This used to be part of a living tree. The tree it was growing on either died or is still alive.

What part of the tree do you think this piece came from? (It could be from the tree's trunk or from a branch on the tree.)

3 Ask children to examine the bark on the outside and to look at the rings on the inside of the log.

4 *Explain:* The bark is the epidermis or skin that protects the tree. Bark helps keep moisture inside the tree and it protects the tree from insects and diseases. As the tree grows thicker each year, the bark splits or peels, and new bark forms underneath the old layer of bark. The center of the log has a darker color to it. This center wood is called heartwood. It is the oldest wood. It is also harder than the outer wood. In the spring, the tree grows new wood. The new wood is called sapwood. The sapwood is lighter in color than the heartwood. Heartwood is dead sapwood. It acts as a support for the tree. Heartwood does not transport any liquids. If you count the rings from the center out, you can find out how old the log was when it was cut from the tree. Each year the tree forms a new circle. Each circle represents a year's growth.

The trunk of a tree is connected to the roots. The trunk is really the stem of the plant. Trees are very large plants. They are the largest plants in the world. The trunk of a tree has branches that grow off it, and the branches have smaller branches that grow off them. All of the branches are connected to the stem and the root system through tubes that run up and down the tree. Food is transported from the leaves to other parts of the tree, and minerals and water are transported to the leaves

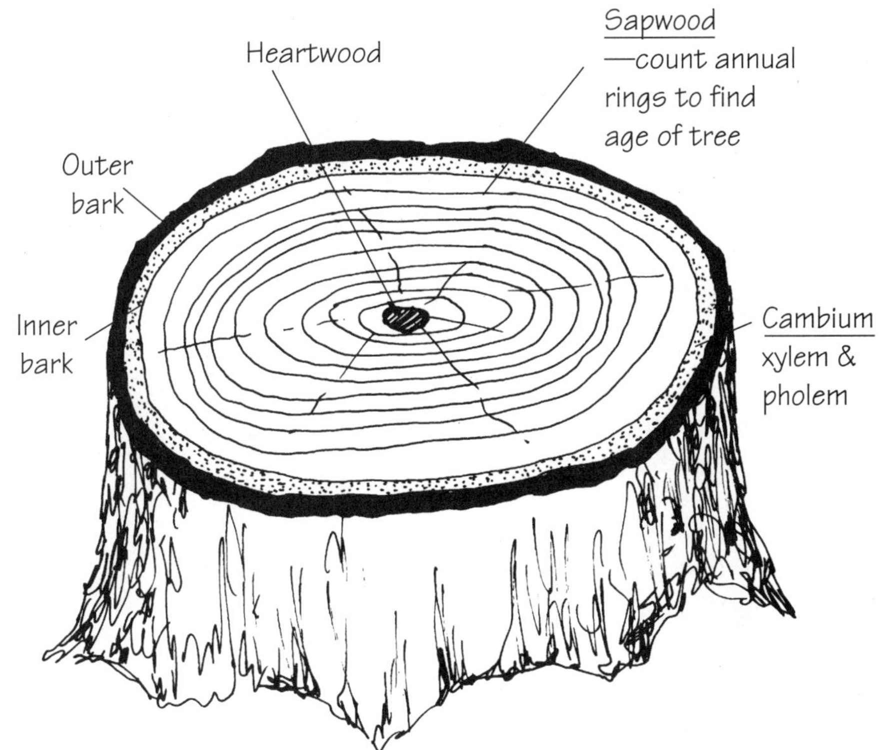

7-25 *Ten-year-old tree.*

from the roots. The tubes that move foods and liquids up the tree are called xylem tubes. The tubes that move liquids down the tree are called phloem tubes.

5 Have the children compare the carrot root's cross-section with the tree's cross-section.

6 *Explain:* The carrot root's xylem tubes were in the very center and were surrounded by phloem tubes. The xylem and phloem tubes in the carrot were surrounded by the cortex or stored food for the plant. In trees, the central part of the stem or trunk is dead. The heartwood merely supports the tree and keeps it from falling over. The xylem and phloem tubes in the tree are located near the bark layer and in the sapwood.

7 Have children draw a model of a cross-section of a log and label the parts of the cross-section.

4. How a twig grows

Materials

Fall or winter* twigs from a tree with buds, a magnifying glass.

Procedure

1 Show the children a twig from a tree.

2 *Explain:* This twig was once a branch on a tree. It cannot continue to grow because it was cut from the tree it grew on. Sometimes, twigs fall from trees when the wind blows hard. Sometimes, twigs fall from trees because they are old. And sometimes, twigs are picked off or cut off, as this twig was.

3 Have the children examine a twig from a tree.

4 Show them that you can count how old the twig is by looking at its cross-section and by counting its rings or by counting the circle scars along the twig that indicate a year's growth.

5 Help children find a growth ring.

6 Observe how much a twig can grow in one year.

Which appears to grow more in length each year, you or the tree?

7 Observe the buds on the twig.

8 *Explain:* The bud at the tip of the twig is called a terminal bud. The twig grows longer at the terminal bud. When the bud opens and the growth takes place, a new growth ring is left on the twig. The buds on the side are called lateral buds. Lateral buds or side buds grow new shoots or tiny branches off the main branch.

9 Pull a leaf off the twig. Have children notice: the scar or mark left on the twig when the leaf is taken off; the new bud that is next to the leafstalk that was pulled off; the protective covering that covers the new buds on the twig.

10 Tell children to pick a bud apart and see if they can find tiny leaves all folded up inside.

11 *Explain:* Twigs are like small tree trunks. Trunks of trees have heartwood, sapwood, and bark, just like twigs. But instead of leaf scars, tree trunks have scars or knots at places where twigs once grew.

12 In the spring, take children outside to find a tree full of large buds. Have children examine a twig from a tree and pick a bud apart to see if they can find tiny leaves all folded up inside.

* This activity is best done in the fall or the winter after the buds have had a chance to develop and be visible.

V. Flowers and fruits

1. A closer look at flowers

Materials

A variety of large, fresh, simple flowers like a tulip, lily, daffodil, poppy, buttercup, azalea blossom, apple or cherry blossom, pansy, etc.

Procedure

1 Have children observe the flowers.

2 Ask the following kinds of questions:

How are all the flowers alike?

How are all the flowers different?

Does each flower have an aroma?

Does the aroma of each flower smell the same?

Which flowers look flat? Which look like bells? Which look like cones?

Which flowers have more than one color on them?

What is underneath the flower? (A calyx made up of sepals that protected the flower when it was a bud.)

What is the flower attached to on the plant? (A long stalk or part of the stem.)

Why do plants grow flowers? (To produce seeds.)

What can you see inside the flowers? (Stamens and pistils.)

Do all the inside parts look alike? (No, they look different from each other.)

How does the tallest part in the center feel at its tip? (Sticky.)

2. Dissecting a simple flower

Materials

A large, simple flower like a lily or a tulip (or large azalea) blossom; pieces of paper; magnifying glasses; toothpicks.

Procedure

1 Give each child a flower and a piece of paper.

2 Tell children to:

a Locate the petals on the flower.

b Count the petals.

c Remove the petals.

Note: All the petals are attached to each other on an azalea blossom; on a tulip, the petals are attached separately.

3 *Explain:* All the petals together are called the corolla. Place the entire corolla on a piece of paper. After the petals are off, it is easier to see the insides of the flower. The insides consist of the pistil (which has a sticky end) and the stamens (which have pollen grains on their ends).

4 Tell children to feel the sticky end of the pistil.

5 *Explain:* This sticky end is called the stigma.

6 Tell children to:

a Take off a stamen.

b Look at the pollen grains with a magnifying glass.

c Rub a stamen on the pistil.

d Observe what happens to the pollen grains. (Some of the grains will stick to the pistil's stigma.)

e Place the stamen on their paper.

7 *Explain:* When the pollen from the stamen touches the stigma (sticky end) of the pistil, "pollination" occurs.

Note: Not all flowers are complete. Some flowers only have pistils. Some flowers only have stamens. Bees, other insects, and the wind help pollinate flowers. (See Fig. 7-26.)

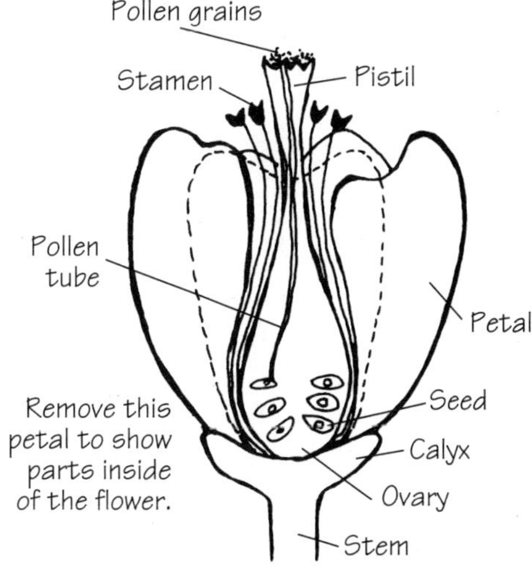

7-26 *Parts of a "model" of a complete simple flower.*

8 Show children a flower's ovary.

9 Have children locate the ovary* at the base of the pistil.

10 Ask children to split the ovary open with their fingernail or a toothpick and count the eggs inside of the flower's ovary. (The eggs are called ovules.)

11 *Explain:* After pollination takes place, fertilization follows. The pollen grains grow tubes down the pistil into the ovary and into an ovule. When this occurs, a seed begins to develop and grow. The pistil grows larger and the ovary grows and develops into a fruit. The mature fruit holds seeds for new plants.

Note: Not all flowers are simple. Some, like the sunflower or daisy, are called compound and are a composite of hundreds of little flowers. See Activity IX, Procedure 1 of this chapter for more information about compound flowers.

3. Making a model of a simple flower

Materials

For each child: colored construction paper, pipe cleaners, paper fasteners, scissors.

Procedure

1 Tell children that they are going to make a model of a flower out of

* Lily flowers have ovaries and ovules that children can easily see.

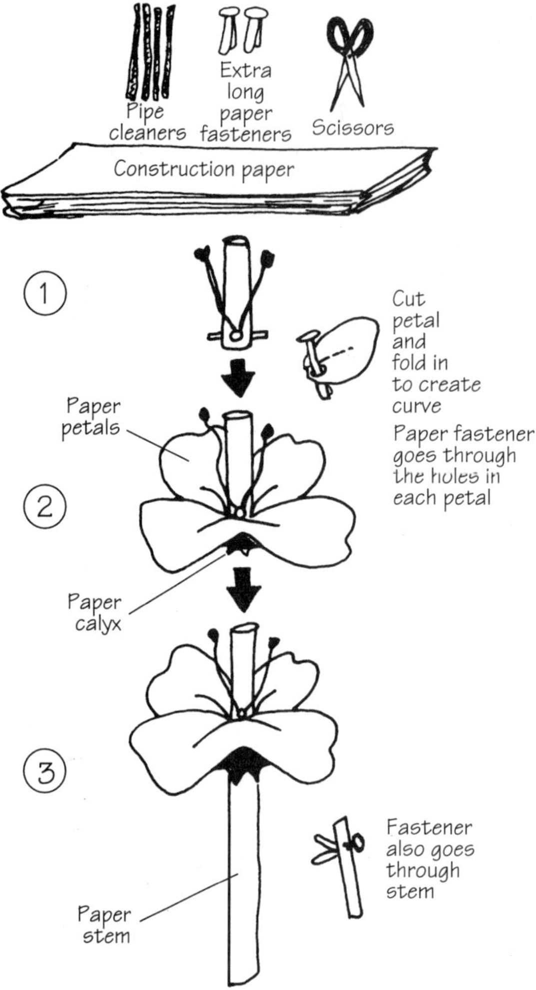

7-27 *Steps for making a take-apart flower model.*

colored paper, pipe cleaners, and a paper fastener.

What can the pipe cleaners represent?

What colors of paper will be best to represent the stem, calyx, and petals?

2 Tell children to:
  a Roll up a piece of green construction paper to represent the stem.
  b Cut out a green star shape to represent the calyx.
  c Choose a color of construction paper for the petals. (Fold a piece of paper in half twice so that when you cut out the petal shape, the petals will all be the same size and shape.)
  d Use pipe cleaners to represent the stamens.
  e Use a small piece of rolled-up yellow paper to represent the pistil.

How should you begin the construction of the model flower? (Suggest to them that it be constructed from the inside out.) Begin by:

  a Attaching the pistil (the hollow yellow paper tube) to the stamens (the two pipe cleaners) with a long paper fastener.
  b Push the paper fastener through the petals (the colored pieces of paper).
  c Push the paper fastener through the calyx (the green paper star).
  d Finally, attach the flower to the long green paper stem. (See Fig. 7-27.)

Fine point to discuss

If children are older,* just show them the materials and ask them to tell you how each of the materials could be used and what each of the materials could represent when the children make the model of a flower. Do this rather than telling and giving them so much information.

4. Dissecting a piece of fruit

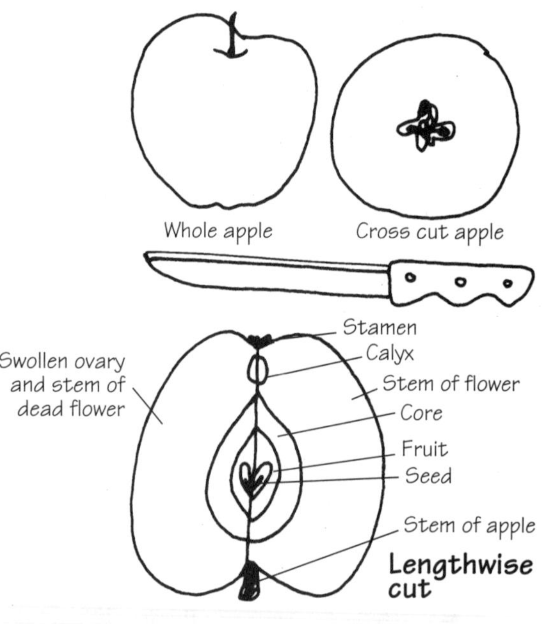

7-28 *Dissect an apple*

Materials

Two apples, a knife (for adult use only), a cutting board.

Procedure

1 Show the children the apples.
2 *Explain:* The apple is a fruit of a plant. It grows on an apple tree and it holds seeds inside for new apple trees.
3 Ask children to observe the outside of an apple and locate the stem.
4 *Explain:* The stem is where the apple was attached to the tree.

* "Older children" refers to children in third grade and up.

5 Have children observe the bottom of an apple.

What do you see? (There are lots of little leaves and dead parts.)

6 *Explain:* The bottom part of the apple is the old part of the flower blossom that died. The green is the old calyx, and the dead flower parts are the stamens of the dead apple blossom. The apple meat that we eat is the swollen old flower stem. Inside the apple meat is the core. The core contains the ovary that has ripened into a fruit with mature seeds.

7 An adult should slice both apples in half.

8 Slice one apple crosswise and the other apple lengthwise. Both cuts will produce different views of the inside of the apple. (The crosswise cut will look like a star exposing all the sections of the ovary. The lengthwise section will expose the new stem and the old calyx in relation to the fruit. See Fig. 7-28.)

9 *Explain:* When the apple first starts to grow on the tree, it grows up, and the stem is on the bottom of the apple. As the apple matures, it becomes heavier and the apple begins to hang as it grows. When the apple is mature, it becomes very heavy, and if it is not picked from the tree, it will fall off by itself. When the apple falls off and eventually rots, the seeds will be free to begin to grow into new apple trees. Most apples get eaten by other animals after they fall to the ground. But a few apples grow into new apple trees. Some apples are carried away and partially eaten, leaving seeds a distance from the parent tree to grow in the new location.

How many apple trees could grow from the seeds in one apple? (As many trees as there are seeds.)

VI. Experiments with seeds

1. Seeds have air in them

Materials

A bag of dried lima beans, warm water, a container.

Procedure

1 Pour some beans into the container. Pour warm water on top of the beans in the container.

2 Tell children to observe the small bubbles of air that come from the seeds and that stay on the seeds.

Where do most of the bubbles come from? (The tiny hole on the seed through which water will pass when the seed germinates.)

3 *Explain:* All living things need air, even seeds.

2. Germinating seeds

Materials

For each child or group of children: lima beans and other seeds (possibly birdseed), paper towels, water, an empty pie tin, zip lock bags, dark paper.

Procedure

1 Show children the seeds. Tell them they are going to germinate the seeds by placing them between moist paper towels.

2 *Explain:* When a seed germinates, it begins to grow.

What do you think the seeds will need to have in order to germinate?

3 Based on their responses, set up some experiments to find out what conditions are best for the seeds to germinate. (See Fig. 7-29.)

4 Possible things that children might want to test out when they conduct their experiments to germinate seeds are the effects of the following conditions or variables:
- Water—Do seeds germinate faster if the towel is damp or very soggy?
- Sunlight—Do seeds germinate faster in the sunlight or in the dark?
- Seeds—Do some seed varieties sprout faster than others?
- Temperature—Will a boiled seed germinate? Will a frozen seed germinate? Will seeds germinate in the refrigerator?
- Whole or broken seeds—Will incomplete or broken seeds germinate? (Broken or incomplete seeds might germinate, but they will most likely suffer stunted growth.)

Note: As children experiment with the seeds and the conditions for growing, they will notice that seeds without water or those kept in the refrigerator or some other cold place will usually not sprout and that warmth and moisture are necessary for germination.* Light or lack of

* Some seeds such as apple, pear, peach, plum, cherry, dogwood, barberry, holly, and others need a period of cold and will not germinate without it. These kinds of trees grow in places where cold winters occur.

7-29A Experiment to find out what conditions are needed for a seed to germinate.

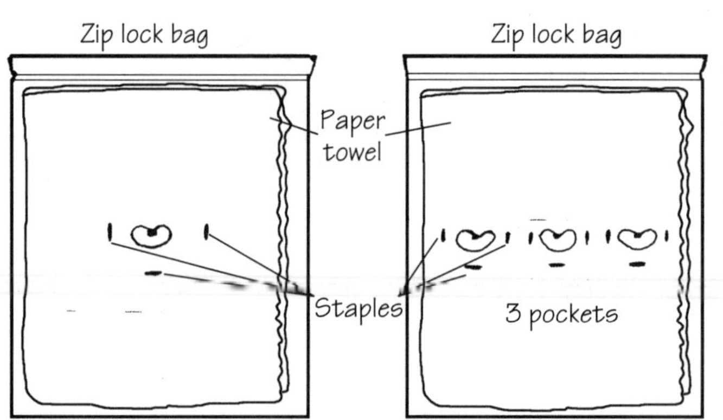

7-29B Germinating seeds in plastic bags.

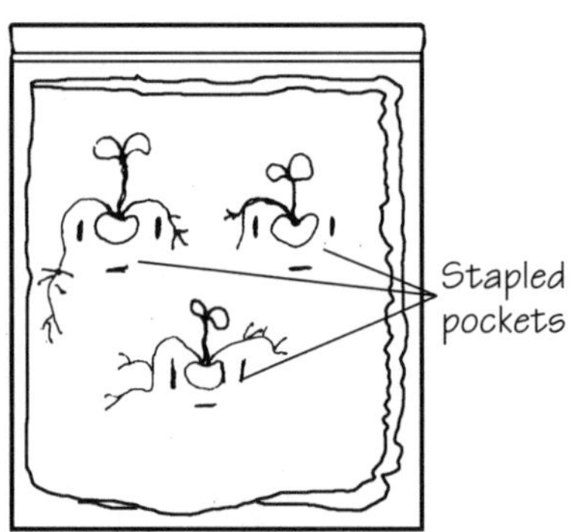

7-29C Observing germinated seeds grow inside of a plastic bag.

light does not affect whether germination occurs. As long as seeds are kept warm and moist, they will sprout whether there is light or not. However, seeds do germinate faster without light.

3. Germinate and grow a variety of seeds in a bag

Materials

Zip-lock bags (one-quart size), paper towels, staples, water/bleach solution.* For

* The water/bleach solution helps prevent mildew from growing.

each child: assorted seeds (lentil, lima beans, corn, radish, marigold, grass, navy beans, kidney beans, etc.).

Preparation

Create three pockets for six different kinds of seeds in a zip-lock bag. To do this:

1. Place a folded paper towel inside a zip-lock bag.
2. Use nine staples to create three pockets. (Each pocket is created with three staples. See Fig. 7-29.)

Procedure

1. Pass out the seeds. Tell children to sort the seeds and choose which seeds they would like to germinate. (They can take one of each kind or several of one kind.)
2. Show children the prepared bags.
3. Tell children to add one seed to each pocket. Place three seeds on one side of the pocket and three seeds on the other side of the pocket.
4. An adult should wet the folded paper towels inside each zip-lock bag with a solution made up of one tablespoon of household bleach to one gallon of water.

(Younger children might add too much water and might taste the solution.)

5 Remind children to observe and record growth daily.

4. Observe how germinated seeds grow

Materials

For each child or group of children: germinated seeds growing in a moist paper towel; an empty clear plastic glass, or zip-lock bag.

Procedure

1. Have children observe the germinated seeds. Ask the following kinds of questions:

Which part of the seed grows first? (The roots.)

What develops after the roots? (The leaves.)

In which direction do the roots grow? (Down.)

2. Tell children to place the seeds and the paper towel inside the clear plastic glass or zip-lock bag. Then have the children turn the seeds around in the glass or bag so that the roots are facing up. Have children observe the seeds the next day to see if the roots are still growing up or if they have bent to grow downward again. (Roots have a tendency to curve downward no matter what position they are in.)

Note: This effect is caused by gravity and is called geotropism. The main stem of a plant shows negative geotropism and grows upwards toward sunlight and away from the roots.

5. The conditions in which seedlings grow best

Materials

Some healthy germinated seeds, eight small containers (like empty milk car-

7-30 *Germinating seeds in different soils.*

tons), soil to transplant the germinated seeds to.

Procedure

1 Have children transplant four germinated seeds to each of the eight small containers and plant them in some soil.

What do you think a seedling or plant needs to live a healthy life?

2 To find out which conditions work best for the seedlings, set up some experimental conditions based on the the children's responses.

3 Possible conditions children could experiment with might be the effect of the following: water or lack of water on the seedling; light or lack of light on the seedling (cover the plant with a paper bag or place it in a closet); good soil, and no soil (coffee grounds instead).

Going further

1 *Explain:* In order to conduct a scientific experiment to find out what plants need, seedlings need to be planted so that it is clear what conditions are best for the seedlings to grow. The following eight labels need to be made up for the seedlings by the children, and the directions need to be followed by the children for a few days or until results occur:
- Water, sunlight, good soil.
- Water, sunlight, coffee grounds.
- Water, no sunlight, good soil.
- No water, sunlight, good soil.
- No water, no sunlight, coffee grounds.
- No water, no sunlight, good soil.
- Water, no sunlight, coffee grounds.
- No water, sunlight, coffee grounds.

2 Write up an experience chart with the children when the experiment with seedlings is finished. An experience chart might look like Fig. 7-31.

VII. Experiments with leaves and stems

1. Leaves give off water

Materials

A large leaf with a long leafstalk, four clear plastic glasses, a piece of cardboard, water, transparent tape, scissors.

Procedure

1 Ask the children the following questions:

Do leaves give off water?

How can we tell?

2 Choose one child to fill two of the plastic glasses half full with water. Choose a second child to cut a piece of cardboard into two pieces and cut a tiny hole in each piece of cardboard. Choose a third child to put the cardboard on top of each of the plastic glasses filled with water.

3 Add the leaf with a long leafstalk to one of the glasses and fit the leafstalk through the hole in the cardboard.

4 Place an empty plastic glass on top of each of the glasses with water in them. Place each of the double cups in the sun.

5 Seal with transparent tape.

6 *Explain:* This is an experiment to see if the leaf will give off water. The

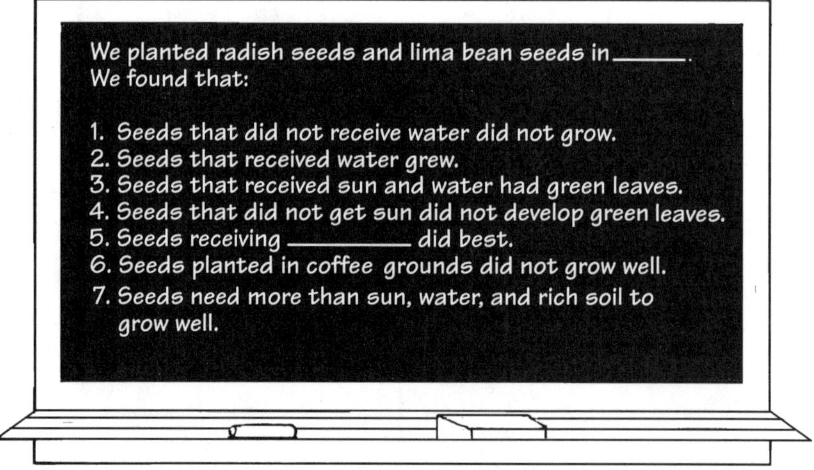

We planted radish seeds and lima bean seeds in ______.
We found that:
1. Seeds that did not receive water did not grow.
2. Seeds that received water grew.
3. Seeds that received sun and water had green leaves.
4. Seeds that did not get sun did not develop green leaves.
5. Seeds receiving ________ did best.
6. Seeds planted in coffee grounds did not grow well.
7. Seeds need more than sun, water, and rich soil to grow well.

7-31 *Write an experience chart about your observations.*

experiment has to sit in the sun as it is for several hours to see results.

What do you think might happen to the leaves if the leaves have water in them?

What might happen inside the glass?

7 Have the children check the experiment and observe the results. (The glass with the leaf in it will have water vapor or tiny water droplets formed on the inside of the glass.) This process of leaves giving off moisture is called transpiration. The glasses without a leaf will not have moisture inside the inverted glass.

8 *Explain:* Leaves have tiny holes on their surface. When leaves become warm, tiny water droplets escape from the tiny holes into the air as water vapor. That is why it feels cooler to sit under a shade tree on a warm, sunny day. Not only does the tree block the sun, it also adds moisture to the air.

2. Leaves need sunshine

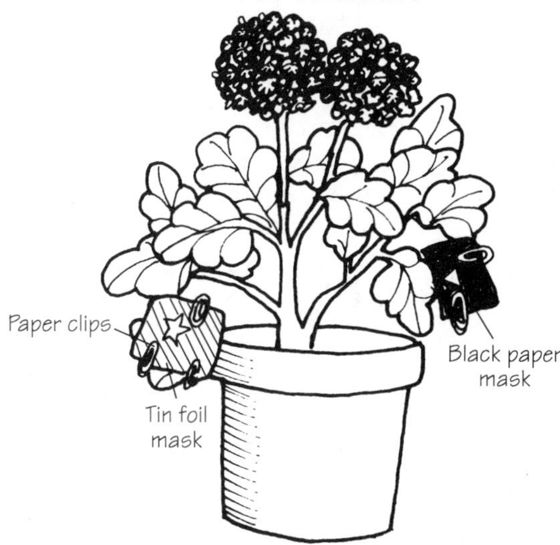

7-32 *Observe transpiration in a leaf.*

Materials

A small, leafy plant like a geranium in a flower pot, a piece of tinfoil, a piece of black paper, scissors, paper clips.

Procedure

1 Ask the children the following questions:

Do leaves need sunshine?

How can we find out?

2 Show children the plant. Tell them you are going to cover one of the leaves with a piece of tinfoil and another leaf on the plant with a piece of black paper. Cut a design in the black paper (like a diamond shape, a circle, and a triangle). Attach the tinfoil and black paper to the leaf with paper clips.

What do you think might happen to the leaves that are covered up with the tinfoil and the black paper mask? (See Fig. 7-32.)

3 Have the children check the covered leaves on the plant in a few days.

4 Remove the tinfoil and the black paper mask from the leaves.

5 Have the children observe what has happened to the covered leaves. (The covered parts of the leaf will turn a dull green.)

6 *Explain:* Leaves need sunshine. Without enough light, the leaves will die. Keep the plant out in the sun for a few days and have the children observe whether the leaves recover and turn bright green again or if permanent damage was done to the leaf.

3. Growing new plants from leaves

Materials

Leaves from a variety of plants like geranium, jade plant, coleus, begonia, African violet, impatiens, and wandering Jew; several paper cups; water; a spider plant with baby plants or shoots.

Procedure

1 Ask the children the following questions:

Can new plants grow from leaves?

How can we find out?

2 *Explain:* Some plants are capable of producing new plants if their leaves are placed in water. Roots start to form at the base of the leaf, and then a new plant can grow.

3 Have children place each of the leaves into a small paper cup filled with water. Leave the paper cups on a sunny window for several weeks and check on them once a week. (Eventually, small roots will be seen, and new leaves will begin to grow.)

4 Have children observe the spider plant. Help them notice the shoots and the baby plants that are growing on the ends of the shoot.

5 Have a child cut off one of the shoots and place it in water. (The buds for

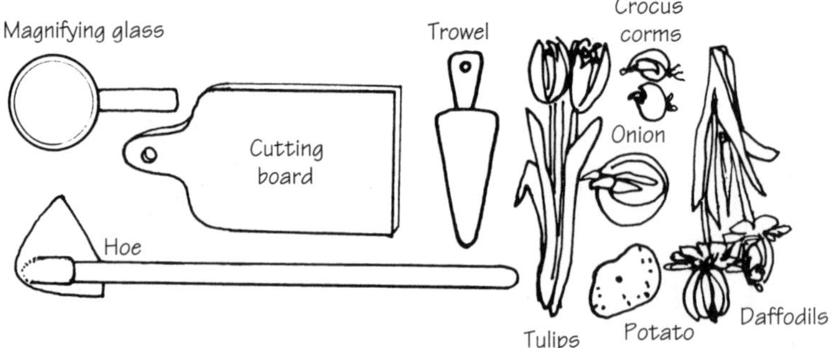

7-33 *Tulip bulb, crocus corm, potato tuber.*

roots are already on the baby plant. The water helps them grow longer.)

4. Bulbs and corms and tubers

Materials

Freshly picked tulips, daffodils, and/or crocus or pictures of them; onions; daffodil bulbs; tulip bulbs; potatoes; crocus corms; a magnifying glass; a knife (for adult use only); a cutting board; a hoe or trowel.

Procedure

1. Show children the fresh flowers (or pictures of the flowers) and then explain that they did not grow from seeds. They grew from bulbs or corms.
2. Show children the bulbs, corms, and tubers.
3. *Explain:* These are underground stems. The scales that make up a bulb or a corm are leaves that are tightly packed. A bulb is a dormant plant. It can be dug up, stored, and replanted. Bulbs are usually planted in the fall and bloom in the spring. Bulbs need to be planted in a soil that has been prepared for them. After the bulb blooms, a new set of stems, leaves, and a bud are formed again in the bulb underground for the following year's bloom.
4. An adult should slice a potato, an onion, and a crocus corm with a knife. Have children observe how different they look on the inside. Have children observe the center of each.

Note: There is a tiny plant inside the corm and the bulb. Bulbs are leaves that store food, and in their center is a flower bud. Tubers (like potatoes) are swollen stems. The eyes on the outside of the potato are where buds grow. If a potato is cut up and planted under the ground, each eye can produce a new potato plant.

5. Have children prepare the ground by loosening the soil with a hoe or trowel. If it is spring, plant some potato eyes outside. If it is fall, plant some flower bulbs and corms outside. *Note*: Preplan the planting so that the tall-stemmed flowers grow behind the shorter-stemmed flowers.

Going further

Have children measure the spring bulbs before they are planted. Later in the spring when the bulbs are blooming, have children dig them up and remeasure them. Then have children replant them and measure them again in a few weeks, after they bloom.

5. Liquids move through stems

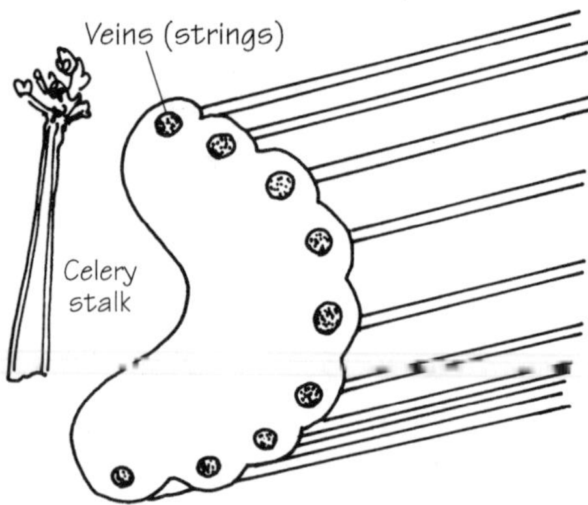

7-34 *Cross-section of a celery stalk.*

Materials

A freshly cut twig from a tree, celery stalks with leaves, a white carnation, a knife (for adult use only), a cutting board, cold water, food colors or colored inks, clear plastic glasses, a magnifying glass.

Procedure

1. Ask the chidren the following questions:

Does water travel through stems?

How can we find out?

2 Cut off the end of a celery stalk near the roots. Also cut off the end of a twig and the carnation stem.
3 Place the celery stalks, the carnation, and the twig in cold water to freshen up and stiffen the tubes in the stems.
4 Place each of the stems in a separate clear plastic glass or jar of water.
5 Have the children add different colors of food color or colored ink to the water of each stem specimen.
6 *Explain:* This is an experiment to find out how stems of plants act as pipelines when they transport liquids. The celery stalks, the carnation, and the twig each have their stems in the colored water.

What do you think might happen to the colored water if the stems are left in the colored water overnight or for a few days? (The water will travel up the stems to the leaves and the flowers. The leaves and the flowers will turn the color of the ink or food color. The color will be in the veins of the flower and the leaves.)

7 In a day or two, if the color has reached the flowers and the leaves, take the stems out of the colored water and slice them off at the bottom to see the color inside of the stem.
8 Have children use a magnifying glass to look at the celery stalk.
9 *Explain:* Each little colored dot is a vein that travels up and down the stalk.
10 Tell children to try to pull a vein out. A vein is like a string. Celery stalks are very stringy.
11 *Explain:* Each string is a tube that carries liquids up and down the stalk to and from the leaves and to and from the roots. (See Fig. 7-34.)

6. Growth toward light (phototropism)

Materials

A sprouting potato planted in a small container, a shoe box with a lid, a knife (for adult use only), two pieces of cardboard, masking tape.

Preparation

Place a sprouted potato at one end of the shoe box. Cut a hole at the opposite end of the shoe box. Place two cardboard dividers inside the box so that a maze is created inside the box. (See Fig. 7-35.)

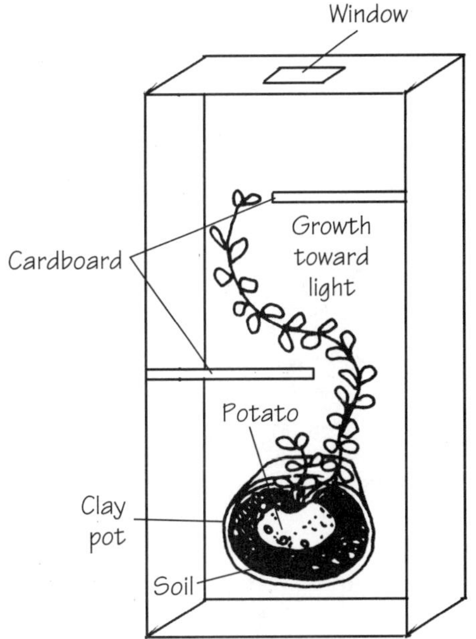

7-35 *Plants grow toward light.*

Procedure

1 Ask the children the following questions:

Do plants grow toward light?

How can we find out?

2 Show the children the maze box with the sprouted potato. Tell them that you are going to keep the box covered.
3 *Explain:* This is an experiment to find out whether stems and leaves of a plant grow toward sunlight.

What do you think might happen as the potato continues to grow and sprout?

4 Remember to have the children water the plant every day, and while the top is off the box, have the children observe how the potato plant's stems are growing.

7. The effect of gravity on stem growth (geotropism)

INFORMATION

Materials

Three bean seedlings planted in pots; water; string; cardboard; a wire coat hanger; labels: A, B, C.

Procedure

1 Ask the children the following questions:

Does gravity affect the growth of stems?

How can we find out?

2 Show children the three bean seedlings planted in pots.

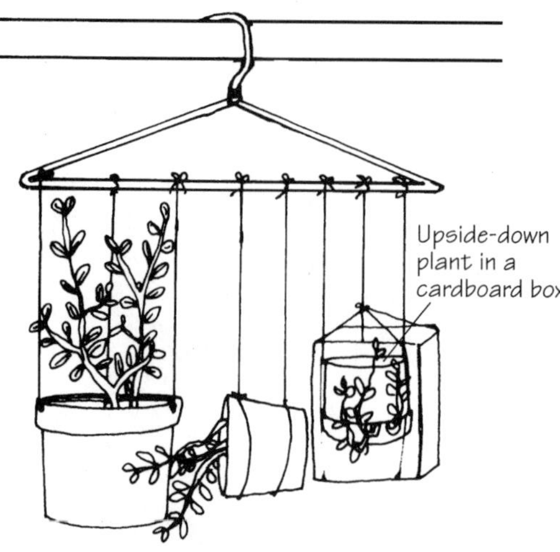

7-36 *Leaves and stems grow away from roots.*

3 Tell them that you are going to conduct an experiment to see how stems want to grow.

4 Place one plant on its side, labeled "A." Hang one plant upside-down, labeled "B." Leave one plant in a right-side-up position, labeled "C." Cover plant "B" (the one that hangs upside-down) with cardboard so the soil will not fall out. (See Fig. 7-36.)

What do you think might happen to the stems of plant: A, B, and C?

5 Remember to water plants A, B, and C daily.

6 Have the children observe what happens to the growth of the three plants. (The three plants will all grow upwards. Leaves and stems of plants grow away from roots. Roots grow toward gravity.)

8. Monocot and dicot stems

Materials

Assorted leafy stems from various plants such as corn, bamboo, grass, a small tree, rose, forsythia.

Procedure

1 Show children the assorted stems from the various plants.

2 Have children observe the cross-section of the stems.

Do they look alike?

Are they hollow or woody inside?

Do the leaves have a vein pattern that is parallel to the midrib or do the leaves have a netted vein pattern off the midrib?

3 Have the children observe:

a The solid yet scattered pattern of bundles of stringy tubes that run through the corn and the bamboo.

b The distinct circles inside the cross-section of the stems of the small tree, the rose, and forsythia plant.

4 Tell them to scrape the outside of each of the stems with their fingernail. (They will observe that the small tree and the rose and forsythia plants each have a bright green color underneath their epidermis or outer skin.)

5 *Explain:* This bright green layer is the cambium layer. The cambium layer is the layer that grows new xylem and phloem cells, which allows the plant's stem to increase in diameter. Monocots lack a cambium layer. Dicots can be either woody or hollow, but they all have a layer of cambium that can be seen if the outer layer on the stem is scraped off.

6 Ask children to classify the leafy stem samples as monocots or as woody or hollow dicots.

Further investigations

How much water should a plant receive?

How do salt or other household substances like sugar, vinegar, oil affect plant growth?

VIII. Roots

1. Roots take up moisture

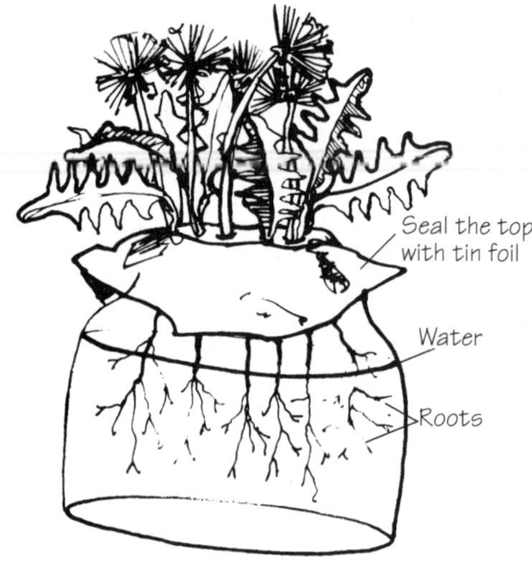

7-37 *Roots absorb water.*

Materials

Dug-up dandelions or other weeds from the grass with their roots connected, water, a small-necked jar, tinfoil.

Preparation

1 Place a large number of plants with their roots connected into a jar, so that the roots are in the water and the stems and leaves are out of the water.
2 Fill the jar up to the mouth with water.
3 Seal the top with a piece of tinfoil so that the water cannot evaporate.

Procedure

1 *Explain:* This is an experiment to see if water leaves the jar.
2 If the top of the jar is sealed, how might the water be able to leave the jar?
3 Have the children check the jar periodically over the next few days to see if the water level in the jar has gone down. (If it has, it means that the water was absorbed by the roots of the plants and travelled up to the leaves.

2. Dyeing a carrot to trace moisture absorption

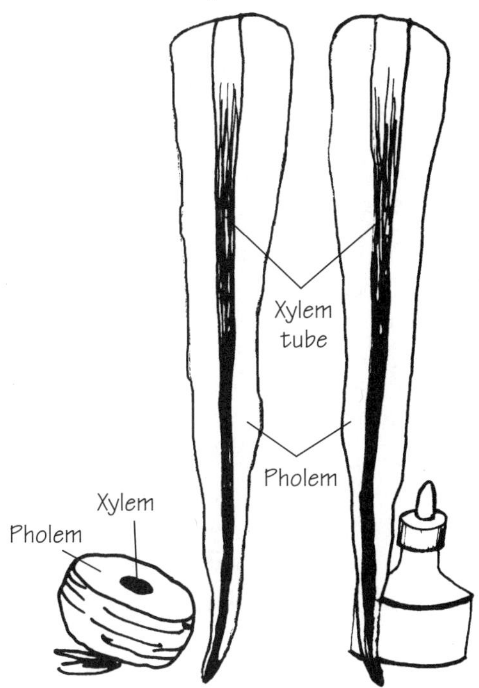

7-38 *Lengthwise cross-section of a carrot.*

Materials

A carrot, red food color or red ink, water, a clear plastic glass, a knife (for adult use only, a magnifying glass.

Procedure

1 Place the carrot in the colored water.
2 *Explain:* This is an experiment to find out where the water goes when it enters the carrot.

Do you know how you will be able to find out what happens to water when it enters the carrot? (The red water will make the inside of the carrot turn red. Wherever they can see the red, will mean that the water has passed through.)

3 Let it stay in the colored water overnight.
4 Wait a day, then slice the top off the carrot. Make another cut lengthwise to see where the colored water has gone.
5 Have children use a magnifying glass to follow the red trace lines. (The center of the carrot will be red. This red part is called xylem.)
6 *Explain:* Xylem tubes carry water up. The phloem carries food up and down. It carries food down for storage and up for the plant when it needs it. The phloem does not turn red. It remains light orange.

Why did coloring the water make it easier to see the xylem? (The colored water dyed or stained the inside of the carrot. Plain water just passes through and does not leave a trace mark.)

3. Growing a root garden

Materials

A beet, a carrot, a parsnip, a radish, a sweet potato, an onion, a potato containing eyes, sand or gravel, water, a deep bowl, a magnifying glass.

Procedure

1 Show children the roots. Discuss what each root is.
2 *Explain:* We are going to start a root garden.
3 Have a child pour the sand or gravel into the bowl. Place the various roots in the bowl with the gravel so that the root is in the gravel, but the top, where greens grow, is above the gravel.
4 Choose another child to pour some water into the bowl so that all of the roots touch the water. (See Fig. 7-39.)

What do you think might grow out of the top of the roots?

5 Keep the water level high enough for the roots to reach the water. (After several days green stems and leaves will sprout from the water.)

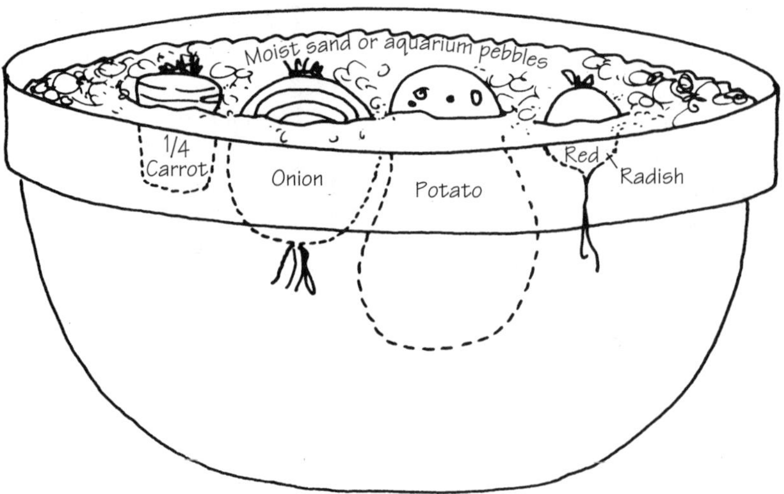

7-39 Grow a root garden.

6 When the roots begin to grow toward the water, pull them out of the sand and observe the roots and root hairs under a magnifying glass.

4. The effect of moisture on roots (hydrotropism)

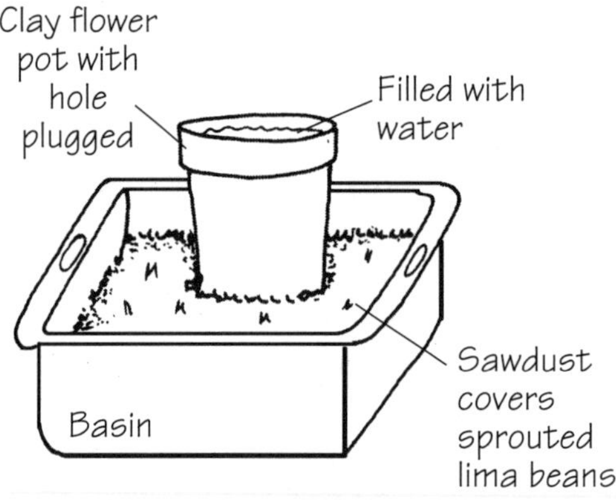

7-40 Roots grow towards moisture.

Materials

A basin, a clay flower pot, water, sprouted bean seeds, sawdust.

Procedure

1 Have children spread some sawdust in a basin and place sprouted bean seeds on the sawdust and cover them up with more sawdust.
2 Place a clay flowerpot filled with water in the center of the basin.
3 Tell the children this is an experiment to see if roots always grow down or if they can be made to grow sideways.

What do you think will happen to the roots?

4 In a few days, have a child dust away the sawdust from around the beans. (The roots will most likely show a tendency to be growing sideways toward the clay flower pot filled with water, rather than just down.) (See Fig. 7-40.)

IX. Investigating flowers and fruits

1. How flowers are different from each other

Materials

Assorted fresh flowers, like: rose, fuchsia, lily, columbine, dandelion, daffodil, crocus, daisy, violet, sunflower, aster, chrysanthemum, or whatever flower is in season; a magnifying glass.

Procedure

1 Have the children observe all the flowers. Review the parts of a flower with them and how flowers are alike. (They have the parts that make them flowers.)
2 Discuss how each of these flowers is different.
3 Ask the following kinds of questions:

Are any of the flowers the same color?

Do any of the flowers smell?

Do any of the flowers feel the same?

Are any of them the same size?

Do flowers have the same kinds of petals? (Some flowers, like violets, have petals that have two different sizes on the same flower. Some flowers have petals that are joined together.)

Do all the flowers have sepals?

Are the sepals green on all the flowers? (Fuchsia sometimes have brightly colored sepals. The daffodil sepals are the same color as the petals. There are three petals and three sepals. The sepals are on the outside of the petals.)

Do pistils always have one stigma? (No. Some flowers like the crocus have a pistil with many stigma on the end.)

4 Have the children tear a petal off a daisy or a dandelion. They will notice a tiny flower on the side of the petal.

5 *Explain:* The petal is actually a long petal on the tiny flower. A daisy and a dandelion are made up of hundreds of flowers. They give the appearance that they are only one large flower. But each flower is composed of many clusters of tiny flowers. The tiny flowers are easier to see if the flower is pulled apart. Often, there are two kinds of tiny flowers on the large flower. The flowers on the outside near the long petals are called ray flowers and are usually different from the flowers on the inside without the long petal.

6 Have the children look at the tiny flowers through the magnifying glass. Help them find: the sepal; the pistil with a split stigma; the ovary on the tiny flowers. (See Fig. 7-41.)

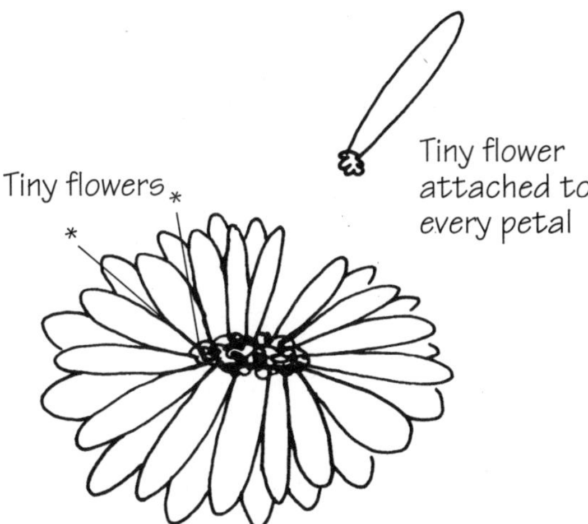

7-41 *A daisy is a composite flower made up of many tiny flowers.*

7 *Explain:* Flowers that are composed of many flowers are called compound or composite flowers, and flowers with only a single complete flower are called simple flowers.

8 Have children sort out the flowers according to whether they are simple or compound.

9 See if they can tell by looking at the leaves attached to the stem on the flowers whether the flowers are from monocot or dicot plants.

Note: The daffodil and lily are monocots. The rose, columbine, and violet are dicots. The sunflower, aster, chrysanthemum, dandelion, and daisy are composite flowers.

10 *Explain:* Monocot flowers usually have parts that grow in three and multiples of three. Like the daffodil (which has three sepals and three petals and six stamens), monocots usually have three or six stamens, and leaves with veins that run parallel to each other.

Dicots have a netted vein pattern. The dicot flowers usually have parts that grow in fours and fives. Often, the leaves of dicots have four or five lobes (look at a maple or sycamore leaf). Palm trees, lilies, and grasses are monocots. Otherwise, most flowering trees, shrubs, herbs, and composite flowers are dicots.

2. Pollen from different flowers

Materials

For each child or group of children: a variety of several fresh flowers, a magnifying glass, black paper.

Procedure

1 Ask children to shake each of the flowers onto a different part of the black paper. If pollen does not shake loose, then have them pull off the stamen from the inside of the individual flowers and rub the stamen on the black paper so that pollen grains can be seen.

2 Tell children to look at the pollen grains through the magnifying glass to see if all the pollen grains look alike or if each flower has a different-looking kind of pollen.

3. Observing the development of fruit from a blossom

Materials

A fruit tree growing outside (apple or pear trees are ideal), pruning clipper, a knife (for adult use only).

From Blossom to Fruit

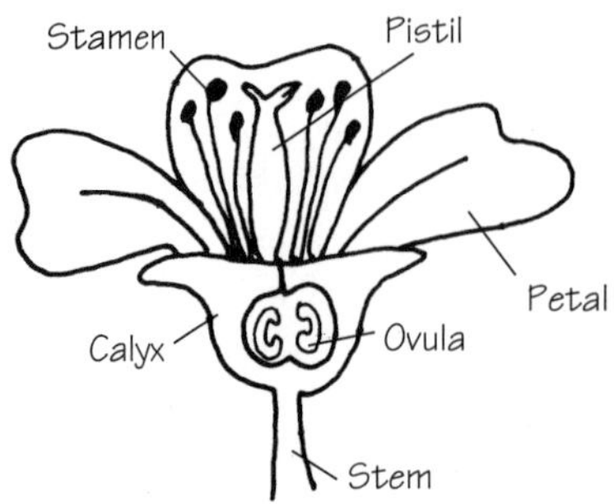

Fertilized flower

Fertilized flower with fallen petals

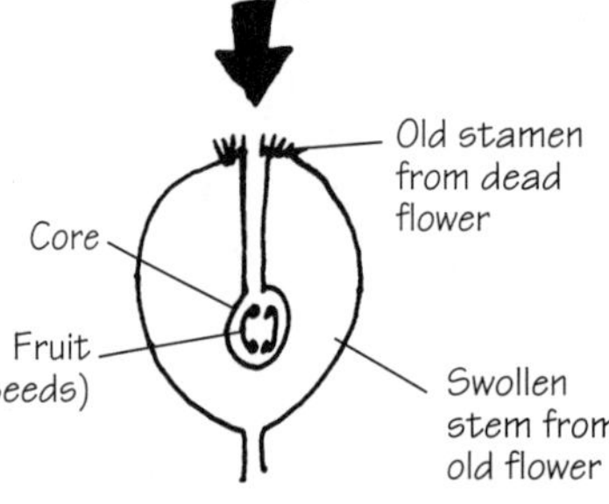

Early fruit development

7-42 *Flowers grow into fruit (if not cut from plant).*

Procedure

1 In the spring when a fruit tree is in bloom, bring the children outside to observe the fruit tree growing. Have them check the tree once a week thereafter to see how the ovaries of the flowers are swelling into fruit.

2 Take a few of the old flowers that are swelling into fruit off the tree. An adult should cut a swollen ovary open with a knife.

3 Have children observe the different stages of growth, from freshly opened flowers to almost dead flowers to dead flowers to flowers with swollen fruits on them that are beginning to look like baby fruit. (See Fig. 7-42.) *Note*: If a fruit tree is not available, then observe spring bulbs like daffodils or tulips that have died on their stems.

Further investigations

Material

Science journals and flowering plants in your yard or the park to observe daily.

How many days does it take for a flower bud to unfold into a flower?

Does the size of a flower make a difference?

Do large magnolia blossoms take longer to develop into flowers than do azalea blossoms?

Does the temperature or the amount of rainfall affect the time it takes for flowers to develop from bud to blossom?

Do all of the buds from the same plant unfold to become fully bloomed flowers in the same number of days?

How long do the flowers stay in bloom before they start to show signs of decay? What seems to be the deciding factors in how long a flower stays fresh? (Wind, rain, temperature. Usually a flower starts to show signs of decay after it is pollinated. If the flower's pistil has pollen grains on it, the flower will usually decay faster than a flower that does not have pollen grains on its pistil.)

Do cut flowers live as long as the ones that are left to grow naturally on their plants?

What conditions will keep a cut flower looking fresh longer?

Further resources

Suggested books for children

Dewey Decimal Classification numbers: leaves-581, A seeds-581.46; flowers-582.13; trees-582.16.

Aliki. *The Story of Johnny Appleseed*. Englewood Cliffs, New Jersey: Prentice-Hall, rev. ed., 1987.

Althea. *Trees and Leaves*. Mahwah, NJ: Troll, 1990.

Back, Christine. *Bean and Plant*. Morristown, NJ: Silver Burdett, 1986.

Bourgeois, Paulette. *The Amazing Apple Book*. Reading, Mass.: Addison-Wesley, 1991. (Great after-school enrichment activities to do with apples or for special school projects done at home to share with classmates. (Ages 6-11).

Brandt, Keith. *Discovering Trees*. Mahwah, NJ: Troll, 1982.

Brown, Bob. *Science For You: 112 Illustrated Experiments*. TAB Books, 1988. (See chapter 5, Experiments with Seeds and Plants. For children who are able to read.)

Burns, Joe and Joan. Classroom gardening. *Dimensions of Early Childhood.* Vol. 22, No. 1, Fall, 1993. (This article gives very practical tips.)

Busch, Phyllis. *Cactus in the Desert.* New York: Thomas Y. Crowell, 1979.

Burnie, David. *Eyewitness Books: Tree.* New York: Alfred A. Knopf, 1988. (Has beautiful color photographs.)

Coldrey, Jennifer. *Discovering Flowering Plants.* New York: Watts, 1987.

Harlow, Rosie, and Morgan, Gareth. *175 Amazing Nature Experiments.* Random House: New York, 1992.

Heller, Ruth. *Plants That Never Bloom.* New York: Grosset and Dunlap, 1984.

Heller, Ruth. *The Reason for a Flower.* New York: Scholastic, 1983.

Hogan, Paula. *Dandelion.* Milwaukee, Wisconsin: Raintree, rev. ed., 1984. (Appropriate for children in grades K–4.)

Hogan, Paula. *Oak Tree.* Milwaukee, Wisconsin: Raintree, rev. ed., 1984. (Appropriate for children in grades K–4.)

Jennings, Terry. *Seeds.* New York: Gloucester Press, 1988.

Jennings, Terry. *Trees.* New York: Glouster Press, 1990.

Jordan, Helene J. *How a Seed Grows.* New York: Harper Child Books, rev. ed., 1992.

Jordan, Helene J. *Seed by Wind and Water.* New York: Thomas Y. Crowell, 1962.

Kelly, M.A. *A Child's Book of Wildflowers.* New York: Four Winds (Macmillan), 1992.

Kenda, Margaret and Phyllis S. Williams. *Science Wizardry for Kids.* Barron's Educational Service: Hauppauge, N.Y. 1992. (Has lots of good, easy-to-do activities. Children in 4th grade on up could probably read it by themselves.)

Kirkpatrick, Rena K. *Look at Leaves.* Milwaukee: Raintree Children's Books, rev. ed., 1985. (Appropriate for children K–4.)

Lauber, Patricia. *From Flower to Flower: Animals and Pollination.* New York: Crown, 1987.

Muller, Gerda. *The Garden in the City.* New York: Dutton, 1992. (K–5.)

Overbeck, Cynthia. *Carnivorous Plants.* Minneapolis: Lerner, 1982.

Patent, Dorothy H. *Flowers for Everyone.* New York: E.P. Dutton, 1990.

Pohl, Kathleen. *Morning Glories.* New York: Bantam Skylark Books, 1987.

Prochnow, Dave and Kathy. *Why? Experiments for Young Scientists.* TAB Books, 1993. (See Part 5—The Young Biologist. For children who are able to read.)

Rahn, Joan Elma. *Plants Up Close.* Boston: Houghton Mifflin, 1981.

Rahn, Joan. *Nature in the City: Plants.* Milwaukee, WI: Raintree, 1977.

Sabin, Louis. *Plants, Seeds, and Flowers.* Mahwah, NJ: Troll, 1985.

Selsam, Millicent E., and Joyce Hunt. *A First Look at Leaves.* New York: Scholastic Book Services, 1972.

Selsam, Millicent E., and Joyce Hunt. *A First Look at the World of Plants.* New York: Walker, 1978. (Appropriate for children in grades K–4.)

Selsam, Millicent E. *Play with Plants.* New York: Wm. Morrow, 1978.

Tresselt, Alvin. *Gift of the Tree.* New York: Lothrop, 1992.

Tresselt, Alvin. *Autumn Harvest.* New York: Morrow, 1990.

Watts, Barrie. *Mushroom.* Morristown, NJ: Silver Burdett, 1986.

Watts, Barrie. *Potato.* Morristown, NJ: Silver Burdett. 1987.

Wellnitz, William R. *Science in your Backyard.* TAB Books, 1992. (See Part II—Plant Experiments. For children who are able to read.)

Wexler, Jerome. *Flowers, Fruits, Seeds.* Englewood Cliffs, NJ: Prentice-Hall, 1988.

Wexler, Jerome. *Flowers, Fruits, and Seeds.* New York: Simon & Schuster, 1987.

Wood, Robert W. *Science for Kids: 39 Easy Plant Biology Experiments.* TAB Books, 1991. (Plant experiments for children who know how to read.)

Wyler, Rose. *Science Fun with Peanuts and Popcorn.* New York: Julian Messner, 1986.

Selected resource books for more ideas

Brockman, C. Frank. *Trees of North America.* New York: Golden Press, 1968.

Brown, Robert J. *333 More Science Tricks and Experiments.* TAB Books, 1984. (See Chapter 5, Biology and Psychology, for additional plant activities to do. Adult.)

Brown, Robert J. *200 Illustrated Science Experiments for Children.* TAB Books, 1987. (See Chapter 9, Biology, for additional plant activities to do. Adult.)

Cohen, Joy, and Eve Pranis. *Grow Lab: Activities for Growing Mind.* National Gardening Association, 1990.

Damon, Laura. *Wonders of Plants and Flowers.* Mahwah, NJ: Troll, 1990.

Marcus, Elizabeth. *Amazing World of Plants.* Mahwah, NJ: 1982.

Peterson, Rodger Tory. *Wildflowers.* Boston: Houghton Mifflin, 1986.

Petrides, George A. *A Field Guide to Trees and Shrubs.* Boston: Houghton Mifflin, rev. ed., 1973.

Van Cleave, Janet. *Biology for Every Kid.* New York: John Wiley, 1990.

Zim, Herbert S., and A. C. Martin. *Trees: A Golden Nature Guide.* New York: Golden Press, 1987.

Selected literature connections for younger children:

Howard, Ellen. *The Big Seed.* New York: Simon & Schuster, 1993.

Krauss, Ruth. *The Carrot Seed.* New York: Scholastic, 1971.

Lobel, Anita. *Alison's Zinnia.* New York: Wm. Morrow, 1990.

Lobel, Arnold. *Frog and Toad Together.* New York: Harper and Row, 1972.

Silverstein, Shel. *The Giving Tree.* New York: Harper and Row, 1964.

Zemach, Margot. *Little Red Hen.* New York: Viking, 1983.

Zion, Gene. *Harry by the Sea.* New York: Harper and Row, 1965.

General community enrichment activities

There are many opportunities in most towns to see plants growing. When you bring children to observe plants, help them notice the cultivation techniques that are obvious: the arrangement of pipes in the field for watering and irrigation, the harvesting technique, the insecticides that might be used, and the tools and special equipment that are used to make taking care of plants easier.

Help children observe fruits growing and the different stages of development of a fruit, insects that might be damaging leaves, the texture of the soil, the temperature in the field or greenhouse. Below is a list of places for observing plants. These are available in most locations.

- A botanical garden.
- A farm that grows fruits, vegetables, or flowers.
- A local florist or garden nursery with a greenhouse.
- A tree nursery or fruit orchard.

8

Ecology

Objectives

The objectives of this chapter are for children to develop an awareness of the following:

- Their environment.
- The interdependency between populations that live within a community.
- The variety that exists within populations.
- That living things grow and change and adapt to their environment.
- That the earth has many different biomes (large environments or regions), each of which has distinct characteristics that animals and plants have to adapt to in order to survive.
- That animals depend on green plants for food and that green plants depend on the sun's energy.
- That all living things are eventually food to other living things. (Even predators are "eaten" by decomposers when they die.)
- Terms such as: predators, prey, food chain, consumer, producer, food web, balance of nature, environment, biome, pollution, poison.
- What pollution is and what causes pollution.
- The varieties of life, its delicate balance, and our responsibility as humans to care for the other living things with which we share the planet.

General background information for parents and teachers

This chapter contains a lot of enrichment vocabulary for children as well as for yourself. As adults, please use your discretion as to how much vocabulary a younger child is ready for. It is more important for younger children to become aware of a big concept. For example, some animals hunt and catch other animals, and some animals are always hunted by other animals; don't expect younger children to remember such words as: predator, prey, and decomposer. It is good for children to be introduced to appropriate words, but please do not expect them to memorize the vocabulary.

Ecology The study of relationships between animals and plants, and the relationships between organisms and their physical environment.

Organism Any living plant or animal.

Environment The surroundings of an organism. The physical conditions that affect and influence the growth and development of organisms.

Habitat The place where a particular species of a plant or an animal usually lives.

Niche The area within a habitat occupied by an organism.

Territory A specific area that one or more animals will defend.

Population The total number of any one species of a plant or an animal living in a community.

Community All the living things that live together in a particular place.

Competition The striving or vying between animals for the things needed for survival.

Cooperation Animals working together toward a common end or purpose. (Animals that live in herds or colonies cooperate.)

Survive To remain alive or in existence.

Variety A different sort or form of something of the same general classification.

Adaptation A characteristic that makes an organism particularly well suited for survival in its environment.

Protective adaptation Adaptation that organisms have developed to protect themselves. Examples are coloration, special anatomical features, very keen senses, speed, and agility.

Characteristic A distinguishing feature or attribute.

Biosphere or ecosphere The total environment of the earth. It is the largest of the ecosystems. It includes all other ecosystems on earth.

Biome A major community that covers a large area of the earth. A biome contains several ecosystems within its territory.

Ecosystem A complete ecological community together with its physical environment. An ecosystem is considered a unit that can be studied. An ecosystem consists of producers, consumers, and decomposers.

Producers Green plants that make their own food and release oxygen into the air through photosynthesis. Animals eat the food that producers produce. Producers are the first living things or link in a food chain.

Consumers Consumers are animals. Consumers eat producers. Consumers depend on producers or other organisms for their food.

Decomposers Many fungi, bacteria, and some animals (such as worms, crustaceans, and insects) are decomposers. A decomposer rids the ecosystem of dead producers and consumers by digesting them and breaking them up.

Fungi Yeasts, molds, and mushrooms that live on dead plants and animals or living organisms.

The major biomes on earth Arctic—tundra; Taiga—evergreen or coniferous forest, deciduous forest; Savannah—grassland, desert; Tropical rain forest—jungle.

Rain forest The rain forests on our planet cover less than ten percent of the land surface; however, approximately fifty to seventy percent of all plant and animal species live in rain forests. Rain forests are an important link in the oxygen, carbon, and water cycles, which affect the world's climate. The trillions of leaves in the rain forest convert carbon dioxide to oxygen. Fifty percent of the world's rain forests have already been destroyed. They continue to be cut down at an alarming rate.

Balance of nature Populations in an ecosystem are balanced. An equilibrium is established by the plant and animal populations within a given area.

Endangered species An animal or plant whose numbers are so small it could easily become extinct.

Food chain Consists of a series of animals that eat plants and other animals. It is a "picture" that shows the foods that producers produce and consumers consume.

First-order consumer Eats first animal in food chain.

Second-order consumer Eats second animal in food chain.

Third-order consumer Eats third animal in food chain.

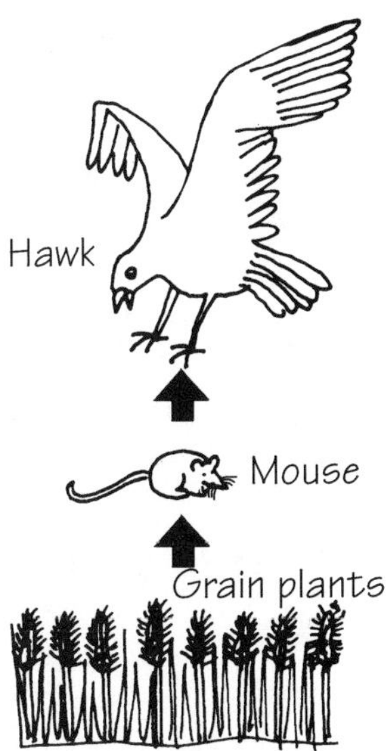

8-2 *A food chain.*

Food web A food web consists of many food chains within an ecosystem. A food web is a "picture" of the food that is produced and consumed in an ecosystem. It shows how the numerous food chains are interwoven to form a weblike pattern.

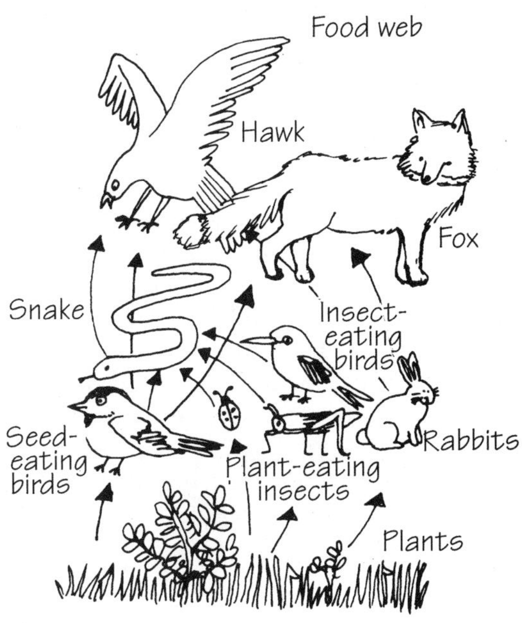

8-3 *A food web.*

Food pyramid A broader "picture" that shows the transfer of food energy that takes place in every web and food chain. The pyramid shows the consumers, producers, and decomposers in an ecosystem. There are more decomposers than producers. There are more consumers than producers.

Predator Animals that eat other animals.

Prey Animals that get eaten by predators.

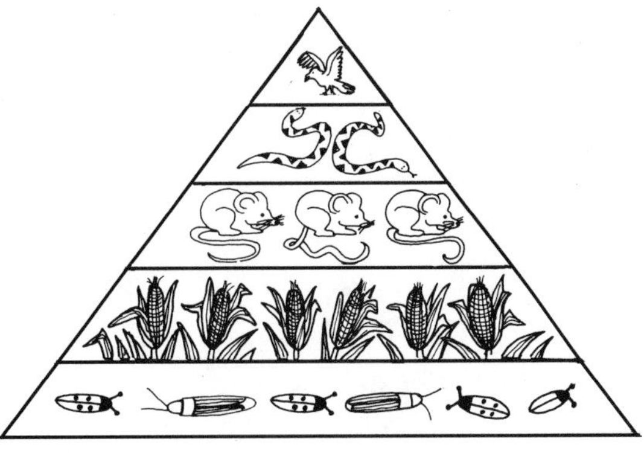

8-4 *A food pyramid.*

Unstable population The size of a population that changes from year to year.

Population explosion A sudden or great increase in the size of a plant population or an animal population. It is usually caused by a change in the ecological balance of an area.

Overpopulation Too many of one kind of an organism are in competition for the available resources.

Herbivore Animals that eat only plants. They are often prey to predators.

Carnivore Animals that eat only meat. Carnivorous animals are predators.

Omnivore Animals that eat both plants and animals.

Scavenger Animals that eat dead animal flesh or other decaying matter.

Parasite An organism that lives on other organisms that are still alive. Example: fleas on a dog, mistletoe on a tree.

Symbiosis When two different kinds of organisms live together in a common space so that each will benefit. Example: lichens consist of algae and fungi living together.

Pollution Something that appears in an environment that is unwanted and does not belong. It means "dirtying" the environment. There are several kinds of pollution.

Air pollution Air pollution sometimes results in smog—dirty air caused from too many fuels being burned from factories, furnaces, and cars. Sometimes raindrops touch polluted air as they fall. The rain is then called acid rain. Some types of air pollution cause acid rain. Acid rain is detrimental to the environment, particularly bodies of water.

Water pollution Dirty water caused by detergents, insecticides, chemicals, oil spills, and sewage that is added to our rivers and streams. Water pollution can affect the ecosystem by poisoning food chains. It also might cause low oxygen content, which is generally harmful to aquatic animals.

Pesticides Kill insects, but also add poisons to the atmosphere. The poisons seep into food chains. The food chains eventually affect some of the future consumers.

Solid waste Plastics, trash, junk, and litter that are not biodegradable. The solid waste is unpleasant to look at, and difficult to dispose of.

Noise pollution Too much noise. It is unpleasant to live near it because it drowns out all the natural sounds in nature.

Recycling Reusing materials that are normally thrown away. Recycling helps reduce solid waste and conserve or save some of our natural resources.

Conservation Using natural resources carefully and wisely.

Conservationist A person concerned that the earth has limited resources and who believes that the resources should not be wasted or used needlessly.

Greenhouse effect Caused by too much carbon dioxide in the atmosphere. Carbon dioxide is produced by fossil fuels when they are burned. Carbon dioxide traps the sun's heat. That is why it is called the greenhouse effect. The trapped heat causes global warming.

Global warming Scientists are concerned about global warming due to the greenhouse effect. If the atmosphere continues to get warmer, there is a concern that the polar ice caps could melt and that a new ice age could begin.

Note: If the polar ice caps were to melt, the water level in the oceans would increase and the majority of cities located on coastlines of all the continents would be flooded by coastal waters (possibly submerged under the ocean). In order to survive, major portions of the human population would need to relocate and change their lifestyle to adapt to the new environmental conditions. The world's climate and agriculture would also be greatly affected. (These changes would occur gradually over time.)

Environmentalist A person who seeks to protect the natural environment from air and water pollution, wasteful use of resources, and excessive encroachments by humans.

Note: As you do these activities with your children, try to encourage them to keep a science journal of their observations and their thoughts.

Activities and procedures

I. Observing our environment

1. Ecology

Materials

The word "ecology" printed on a large word card.

Procedure

1 Ask the children if they know what the word says and if they know what it means.
2 Discuss what ecology means. "Eco" comes from the Greek word *oikos*, which means household. "Ology" means the study of something.
3 *Explain:* Ecology is the study of households, or more precisely, the study of households in nature. Nature is our environment or our surroundings. Plants and animals are members of nature's households. Some of nature's households are very tiny and can live in a drop of pond water. Other households in nature are larger and are contained under a rock or a log; and some households include many households, like a large city. The biggest household in the world is the whole planet. Everyone, including all plants and animals, lives in the world together.

Individual households, like the one you live in with your family, are called ecosystems. Ecosystems can be very tiny, or they can be very large and include the whole world. It is a little bit like living in an apartment building with your family. Your family has a space in the building, along with several other families in the building who have different spaces. You all live on the same block, on a space of the block. Several other families live on the block too in other buildings that occupy other spaces on the block. The block is one of many blocks that make up your community. Each building is made up of many possible ecosystems. Each building is like an ecosystem; so is each block, and so is the entire community like an ecosystem. An ecosystem can be as large or as small as you want it to be.

An ecosystem includes the immediate environment or surroundings and the plants and animals that live in those surroundings. An ecosystem must include plants that produce food, animals that consume food, and bacteria to destroy and eat dead and rotten things. We all share the earth together, and we depend on each other. When we live in an apartment, we live in an incomplete ecosystem.

Could you survive by yourself in an apartment building with your family? (Your food comes from outside your building and from outside your block. You probably could not survive by yourself, even with your family. You depend on the farmers who grow food outside your building and outside your block. Even though your food can be purchased at a grocery store, it might have been shipped from far away, and it does not grow in large enough quantities on your block to feed everyone who lives in your apartment house, or on your street.)

4 *Explain:* Ecology is the study of the interdependency of households in nature. Ecologists are scientists who study the interdependency and relationships of nature's households to one another.

2. Nature walks

Materials

Paper bags for each child.

Procedure

1 Ask the children the following question:

What does environment mean? (Environment means the surroundings a living object is in.)

8-5 *Take a walk to observe and collect objects.*

2 Record the childrens' responses on a chart.

3 Discuss what the surroundings are like inside. (There is a roof, a floor, walls, and windows. The temperature can be adjusted, the lights can be turned on or off, and windows and doors can be opened or closed.)

4 Tell the children you are all going to go outside to observe the environment and to find plants and animals that live in the outside household.

How is the outside environment different from the inside environment?

5 Ask the children the following kinds of questions:

Can the temperature be adjusted outside? (If you stand under a tree, it's cool. If you stand in the sun, it is warmer. But the temperature cannot be controlled.)

Can the lights be turned on and off? (No, the sun comes up and the sun goes down, and clouds sometimes block the sunlight.)

Is there a roof or a floor outside? (Yes, but a different kind of roof and floor. The ground is the floor and the sky, or the thick trees are the roof.)

Are there any walls outside? (Only natural walls. They do not look like walls. But a pond is like a wall. Animals that cannot swim cannot go into the pond. It becomes a natural barrier for some animals.)

If we lived outside, would we be comfortable? (We would probably have to make some adjustments to adapt to living outside.)

6 Take the children outside. Advise them to be quiet so that they can listen for sounds in the trees and in the grass. If they place their ears on the ground or on tree trunks, they might be able to hear sounds nearby. Help them to identify the sounds that they hear.

What other senses can you use on your walk? (See Table 3-2, Some other observations that can be made on a nature walk.)

How many of nature's colors can you find?

7 Pick some pine needles, some bark from the ground, an aromatic flower, and so on, and have the children smell the aroma of each. As you come across things on the walk, see if they have odors. Help the children label or identify the odors as earthy, or floral, or sweet, or putrid. As the children smell odors, have them use their hands to touch the different textures. Help them label or identify the things they feel as being something that feels: wet or dry, prickly, smooth or rough, sticky, warm or cool, moist or damp.

8 Have children look under rocks, leaves, and logs to see what lives underneath, and replace whatever items they disturb or turn over so that the animals that live under them will not be disturbed.

9 If the walk is taken in the fall, have the children collect the colorful autumn leaves that have fallen on the ground. Have them place the leaves in their paper bags. When they arrive back inside, have them sort the leaves by size, color, width, or length. Have them look for textures on the leaves or places on the surface of the leaves where insects took bites or caused other damage.

10 Ask children to collect small things that interest them on the walk. When the children are indoors again, have them make scrapbooks or collages of things they have gathered on their walk.

3. Watering the soil

8-6A *Water a plant and observe what happens to the water.*

8-6B *Water leaves and observe what happens to the water.*

8-6C *Water unprotected soil and observe what happens to the water.*

Materials

Water in a small sprinkling can for each child.

Procedure

1 Take the children outside to a wooded area where the foliage is very thick and where a path is available so that they will not be walking through poison ivy.

What do you think happens to the trees and the soil when it rains?

What do you think happens to the trees and soil when it rains lightly?

2 Stop in front of some foliage near the path. Tell the children to use some of the water from the sprinkling can (which they are each carrying) to water the leaves and to pretend that they are a cloud raining on the plant's leaves.

3 Have the children observe what happens to the water after it comes out of the can. (The water will stick to the leaves and will run from one leaf to the next. Not everything will get wet. Chances are that, unless there is a heavy downpour, the ground will receive only a little bit of moisture. The leaves will keep most of the water from reaching the ground.)

4 Have children water the soil directly and have the children observe what happens. (If the dead leaves are watered, the leaves will protect the soil. If the soil is watered directly, some of the soil might wash away.)

5 Ask the following kinds of questions:

Does everything get wet? (Some things get less wet than others. Trees protect some things from getting as wet as those things that are exposed to the rain without any protection.)

Does water get absorbed by the soil? (Yes. The leaves on the surface help absorb some of the water and keep the soil from washing away.)

If the rain is very light, will water reach the soil? (Some of it will, but most of the water will be caught by the leaves on the trees, and some of the moisture will be absorbed by the loose dead leaves on the ground.)

How do the dead leaves protect the soil? (They help absorb moisture like a sponge, and they keep the water from washing away the soil.)

4. Seasonal nature walk

Materials

Paper bags for each child.

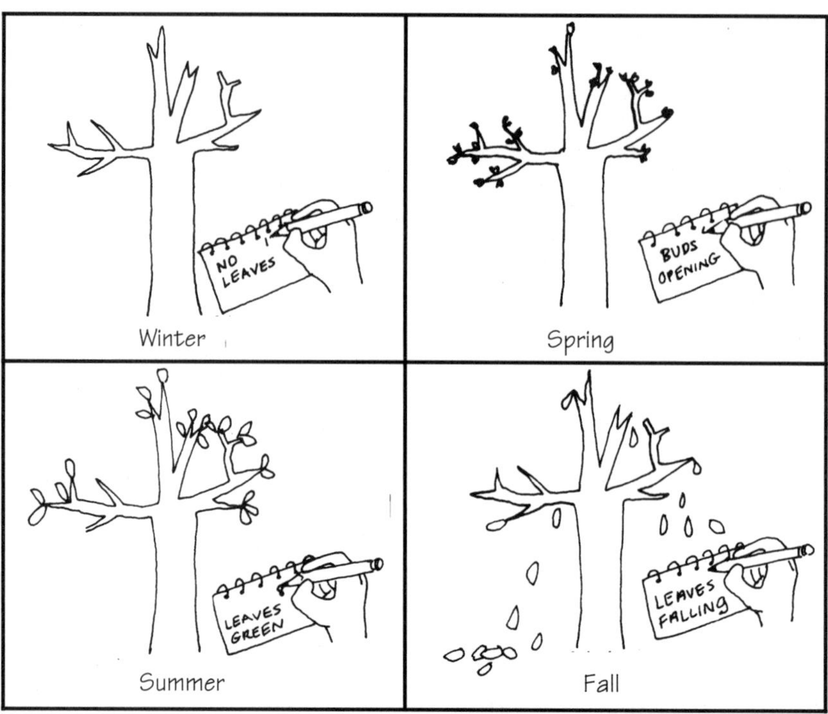

8-7 *Take a seasonal nature walk to observe and record changes.*

Procedure

1 Take the same walk that you took in Activity 1, Procedure 2 as the seasons change. Take the walk in the fall when the deciduous leaves begin to fall, and again in the middle of winter when everything appears to be asleep or dead, and again in the beginning of spring when the buds are opening up, and later when all of the buds have opened.

2 Have the children observe some of the changes that are taking place as the seasons change. In the fall, many birds are migrating south. In the autumn, the plants are storing food, making and scattering seeds, losing their leaves, and making and forming waxy coats on their buds. In the spring, the rains fall, the days become longer, the buds swell, sap begins to run through the trees, bulbs bloom, birds migrate north, and insects emerge.

3 Have the children collect interesting materials in paper bags for nature collages or scrapbooks about their nature walk; have them either write experience charts or write in their science journals about their observations.

5. Adopt a tree

Materials

A deciduous tree.

Procedure

1 Have the children adopt a tree outside and observe the seasonal changes that happen to it in the course of a year.

What animals live in or off the tree?

What insects make their homes near or in the tree?

Do birds nest in the tree or use its branches to perch on?

What birds use the tree?

What do the leaves look like?

Where do the biggest leaves grow?

Where do the smallest leaves grow?

How much new growth took place on the branches?

When are the seeds and fruits made by the tree?

What happens to the seeds and fruits?

2 Decorate the tree with seasonal decorations (such as paper pumpkins, hearts, or colored eggs). Take in the dead wood and leaves from the tree to observe.

3 Force budded twigs from the tree to sprout in the winter by soaking them in water.

8-8 *Decorate and collect objects from an adopted tree.*

6. Seed-collecting walk

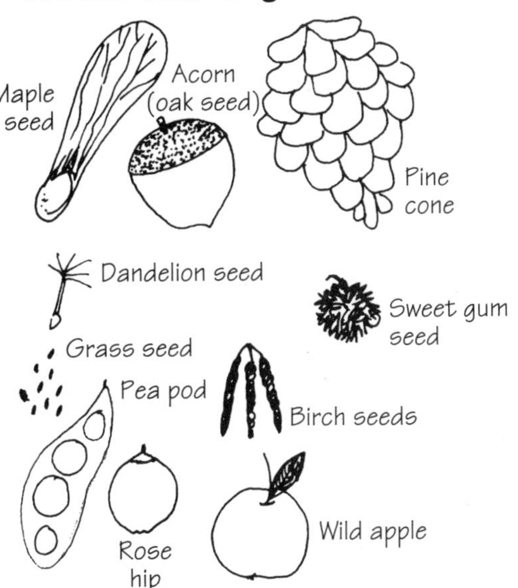

8-9 *Seed cases and seeds.*

Materials

Paper bags for each child.

Procedure

1 In the fall, take the children on a seed-collecting walk. Try to identify the various seed cases and seeds, where they came from, and how they got where they got (by water, wind, animal, or by popping out of a pod and falling).

2 Have the children collect assorted seeds they find in their paper bag.

3 Have children put their found seeds into moist soil to try to sprout them.

Note: Not all of them will sprout. Some need to be exposed to a cold winter before they sprout. (See chapter 12, Plants, Activity VI, Experimenting with seeds.)

4 Discuss why some seeds have a delayed sprouting.

How does a delayed sprouting help the plant? (If it sprouted before winter set in, it would die.)

7. Animal track walk

Materials

A nature guidebook that has labeled pictures of animal tracks.

Procedure

1 Take the children along a path that is frequented by animals, near a pond where there is mud, on a field, or to the seashore.

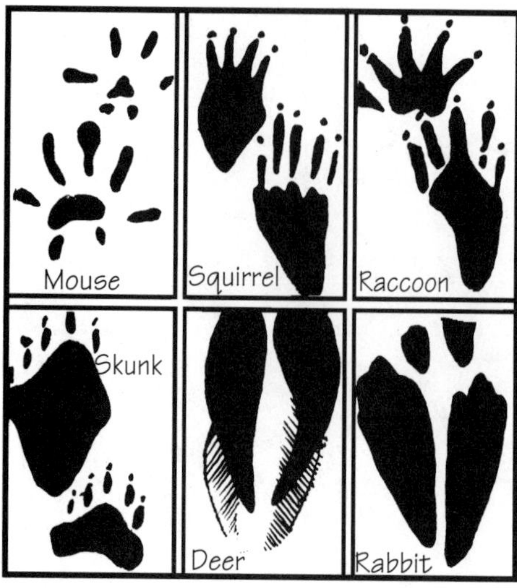

8-10A *Animal tracks.*

2 Have them look for animal footprints in the mud or along the sand, or in the snow if it snows.

3 Use a nature guidebook to help children identify the animal that made the tracks.

Going further

Help children make plaster casts of animal footprints that are found in mud or sand. (The directions for mixing plaster are on the side of the package.)

II. Populations

1. Cooperation in populations

Materials

Pictures of ants, bees, and wasps living in a colony; pictures of wolves together in a pack, of animals that live in herds, and of a flock of birds.

Procedure

1 *Explain:* When plants and animals live together in the same area, the area is called a community. A community is made up of several households. Households are made up of many populations. A population is made up of the same kind of plant or animal that lives in the community. For example, in a farm community, on one farm there might be a population of horses, a population of cows, a population of people, a population of corn plants, a population of hogs, a population of ants, and a huge number of other insect populations.

Can you think of other populations that could live on a farm?

2 *Explain:* Some populations help each other and cooperate. They form societies, colonies, herds, or flocks. Show children the pictures of ants, bees, and wasps living together, and of wolves in a pack hunting together, of animals that live in herds to protect each other. Different members of the population are given different jobs to do. Discuss the different pictures and how they show that the animals are cooperating with each other.

How do human beings cooperate when they live together?

3 Discuss different forms of cooperation among people that live in families, in communities, and in the world. Some people produce food; others produce buildings and machinery; other people help run the government, write laws to

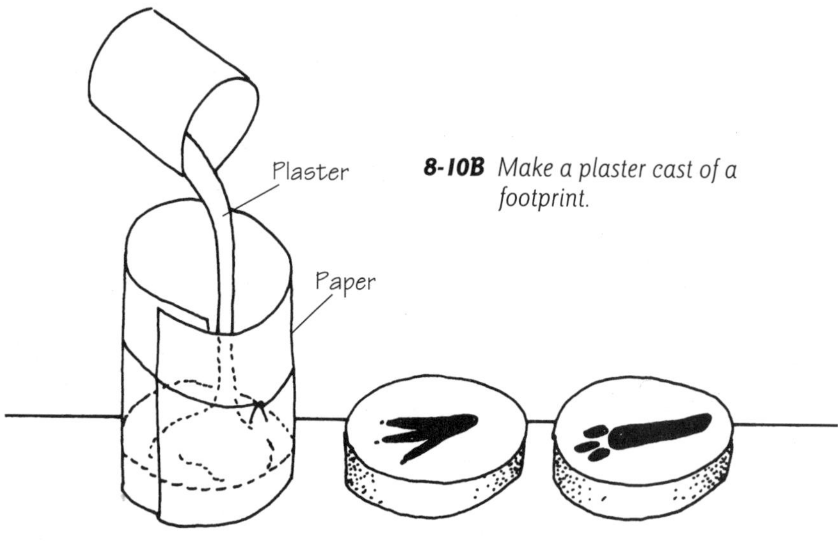

8-10B *Make a plaster cast of a footprint.*

live by, keep order, plan for disasters, teach others, cook for others, etc.

2. Population survey

Materials

Paper and pencil.

Procedure

1 Have the children go outside and make a list of the plants and animals that make up the community of their yard. For example, some birds, many insects, six trees, thirty flowers, two squirrels, lots of grass.

2 Ask the following kinds of questions:

How many of each population is in the yard?

How many varieties of plants grow in the grass? (Usually, several varieties of plants like dandelions, clover, chickweeds, and grape ivy, to name a few).

Which plant or animal population is the largest?

Which plant or animal population is the smallest?

Is there a relationship between the size of the plant or animal and its population? (Usually there is less of a large thing and more of a small thing. For example, there are more grass plants than trees. There are more insects than squirrels.)

3. Variety in human population

Materials

Rulers, measuring tape, a yardstick, a scale, pencil, paper.

Procedure

1 *Explain:* A plant or an animal is called an organism. Organisms that belong to the same population vary. No two organisms from the same population are ever exactly alike. Even twins are not alike. Each organism has properties or traits that make it alike or different from other organisms in the population.

2 Tell the children that you are going to conduct a study of children with them. *Note:* As a group, they are a population

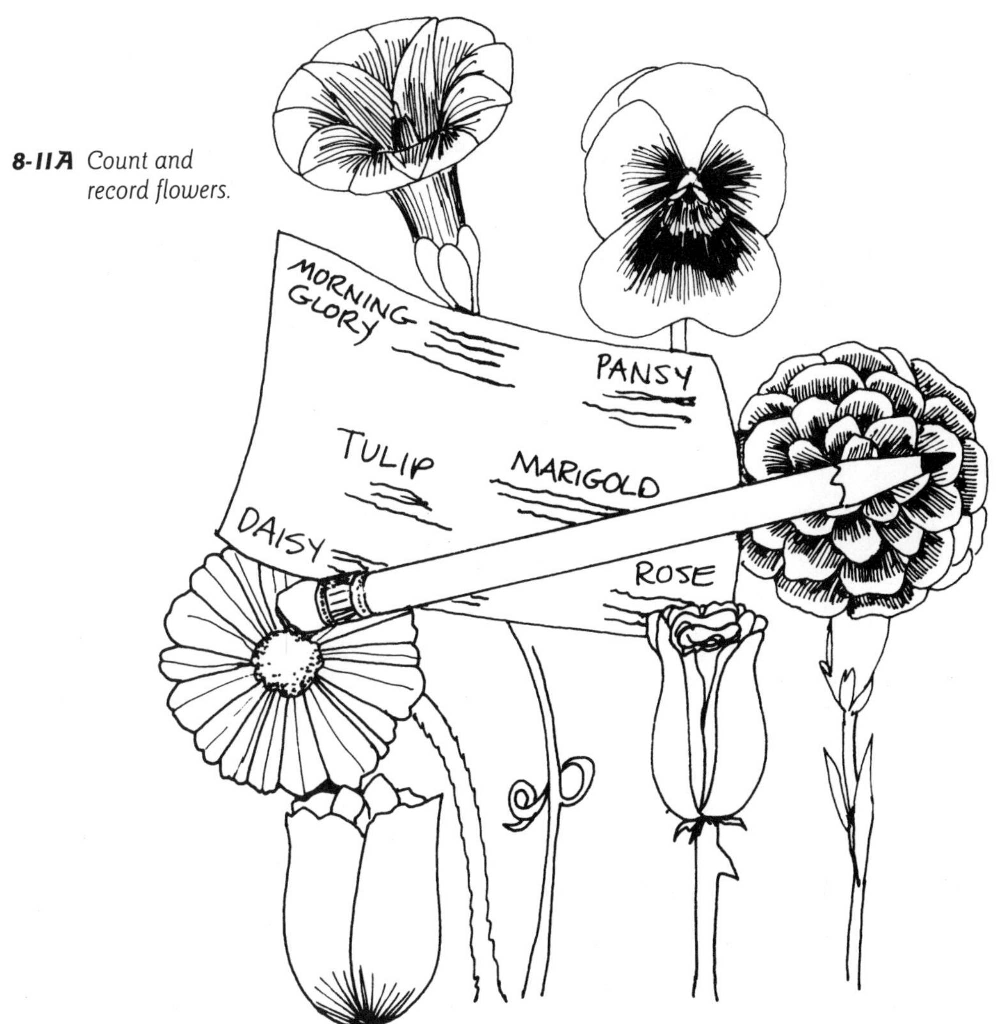

8-11A *Count and record flowers.*

8-11B *Count and record birds.*

of children. Children have properties or traits that can help describe their bodies.

3 Ask children the following kinds of questions:

How tall are you?

Is everyone here the same size?

How much do you weigh?

Will everyone weigh the same amount?

What color is your hair?

What color are your eyes?

How large is your head?

How old are you?

When is your birthday?

How many of you are boys?

How many of you are girls?

How many of you have freckles?

Do you have naturally curly hair?

Do you have straight hair?

How long are your feet?

How long are your legs?

How long are your hands?

How wide can you spread your fingers?

Can you curl your tongue?

Are your earlobes attached to the side of your face or do they hang free?

4 Have the children examine and measure themselves and each other. Record the statistics they find out about each other. Make a chart so that they can see the differences for each child.

5 Compare the statistics on each child with the children.

6 Ask children the following kinds of questions:

Do any two children have the exact same traits or properties? (Probably not).

Which trait or property is shared by the most children? (Probably age).

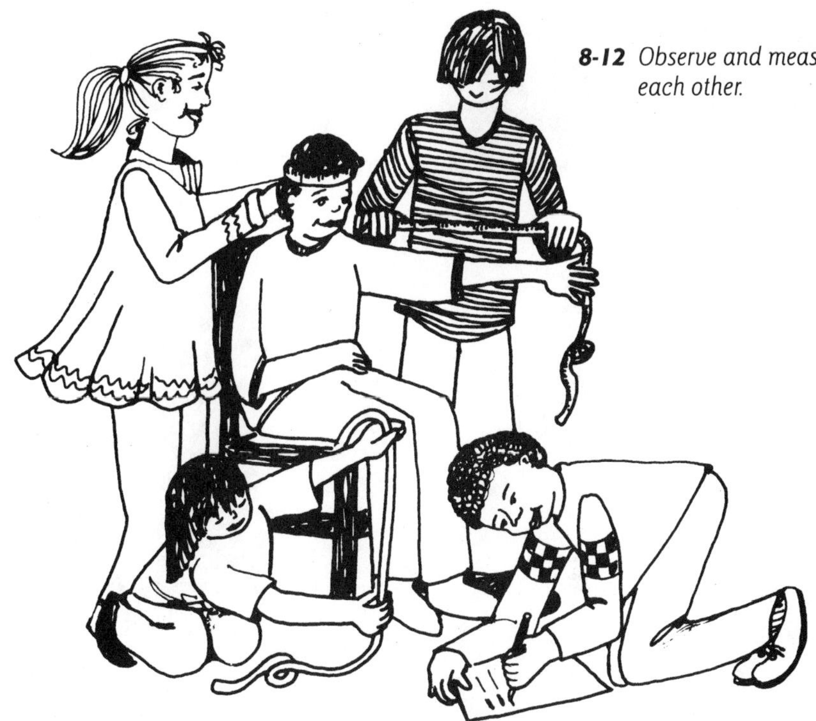

8-12 *Observe and measure each other.*

Which trait or property is shared by the fewest children?

Do the children with shared traits look alike?

7 Have each child find another child in the population who is most like him or her.

4. Other varieties in human population

Materials

None.

Procedure

1 *Explain:* Besides looking slightly different from each other, human beings also vary in their interests, hobbies, and the places where they live and were born.

2 Ask the children the following kinds of questions:

What is your favorite book, movie, or cartoon?

What is your favorite sport, game, or toy?

What is your favorite song, television show, or place to be?

What is your favorite food or color?

Where were you born?

3 Have children notice their differences and the varieties of interests within their population. Help them understand that they are each unique and are like no other individual within their population. Even though each of them belongs to the human population, they each are also quite distinct from each other and special to the world.

5. Human fingerprints

Materials

Ink, ink pad, paper, magnifying glass.

Procedure

1 Have children roll their fingers on the ink pad, and then press their fingerprints on to a separate piece of paper (for fingerprints). Have them examine their fingerprints and the other children's fingerprints with a magnifying glass to see the similarities and differences between the prints. Discuss the uniqueness of each print.

2 *Explain:* Everyone in the world has a set of fingerprints. Fingerprints are unique to the individual. No two people have the exact same fingerprints. Fingerprints come in four basic patterns. These four patterns are called the arch, the loop, the whorl, and the composite. They appear on the tips of everyone's fingers and thumbs. (See Fig. 8-13.)

3 Have the children divide the sets of fingerprints they have made on the separate pieces of paper into the four basic patterns.

8-13A *Roll your finger in ink.*

8-13B *Make a print of your fingers.*

6. Variety among tree population

Materials

Measuring tape, pencil, paper.

Procedure

1 *Explain:* Just as each human is unique, so are all other organisms. Take the children outside to where several trees are growing. *Note:* The trees can be of the same or varied species. A variety makes it easier to make distinctions.

2 Have children measure the circumference of the tree trunks. Then have them count how many branches grow off the trunk. Have children pick several leaves off each tree and compare the leaves.

3 Tell the children to record their findings and compare the statistics about each of the trees. Have them look for similarities and differences between the trees. Have the children see if any of the leaves are exact matches of each other.

Note: Even though leaves might look alike because they are the same shape or color and come from the same tree, they never match exactly. Leaves are like fingerprints; each leaf is unique. The veins, sizes, and the weights of leaves vary.

8-14 *Look for similarities and differences in leaves in the same tree.*

7. Competition in a population

Materials

Picture of cars in traffic during rush hour, picture of a crowded beach, pictures of people standing in line.

Procedure

1 Show children the pictures.

Have you ever been in traffic that was not moving or on a beach that was very crowded, or at an amusement park with very long lines to stand in? How did you feel standing still in traffic, or standing still in a long line at an amusement park?

2 *Explain:* When a population of anything in a community becomes too large, it becomes unpleasant to live in the environment. Sometimes people become frustrated, cross, and angry with each other because they do not have enough space, or because people cut in front of them on line. People begin to compete with each other for space and position. When this happens to a population of plants or animals in a community, it becomes difficult for that population to live. Not all of the members of that population will survive in the community. Only the

strongest, fastest, smartest, most flexible, and hardiest will survive in the community. Those animals that are able to move on to another community or are able to live on a great variety of foods will also survive.

Animals and plants that cannot survive the change in the population or in the environment will become extinct, like the dinosaurs.

Note: There are three kinds of extinction. Biological extinction is like the dinosaurs; there are none left. Ecological extinction is like the American bison; there were too few left in the population to live without protection. However, with laws to protect them, their population has increased. Regional extinction occurs when a plant or animal no longer exists in an area where it once had a large population.

8. Effects of overpopulation

Materials

Four paper cups, potting soil, about 30 to 35 bean seeds, a marking pen, water, a sunny window.

Procedure

1 Tell children that they can observe the effects of overpopulation by planting too many seeds together and watching the population of seeds grow.

What do you think will happen to the plants if 15 seeds are planted in one cup? (As the seeds sprout, they will begin to compete for: space, their roots, position for the sunlight, and the available water).

2 Fill four cups with potting soil. Plant about 15 seeds in one cup, about 10 seeds in another cup, about 5 seeds in the third cup, and 2 seeds in the fourth cup. Place all of the cups on a sunny window sill, and water each cup with the same amount of water every day. Label the cups so that you will know how many seeds were planted in each cup.

Note: This experiment will take about two weeks. Have children keep a record in their science journal of how many seeds sprout each day in each cup. Remind children not to give the seeds too much water.

3 Have children discuss the end results of their experiment by asking the following kinds of questions:

How does the appearance of the plants in the four different cups differ?

Why do you suppose this is so?

Which cup has the tallest bean plant?

Why do you think this happened?

Which cup has the bean plant with the most leaves?

Why do you suppose that happened?

What effect did overpopulation have on the bean plants?

Did all of the bean plants sprout? Why not?

Which cup has the healthiest-looking bean plants? (Probably, the one with only two seeds.)

Which plants grew best in the overpopulated cups? (The strongest or hardiest, or the ones that were most fit for survival.)

III. Adaptations

1. Living things grow and change

Materials

Old photographs of children or their families.

8-15 *Overpopulation of seeds will affect their growth.*

Procedure

1 Show children the old pictures of themselves or of their families.

2 Discuss how the people in the pictures and they themselves have changed since the pictures were taken. (They have probably grown up or changed since the pictures were taken.)

3 Discuss how they are not able to wear some of the same clothes they were wearing in the picture because their bodies have become larger, and they wear a different size now.

4 *Explain:* All living things grow and change. When animals and plants change, it is called adaptation. Adaptation means that a plant or an animal changes to fit into its environment so it can survive. If a plant or animal cannot change and adapt to its environment, it might mean that the plant species or animal species will die, and that it might become extinct as a species. The more versatile and flexible a plant or animal is with its growth, the more likely it is to survive.

2. Adaptability of dandelions

Materials

A cut lawn with dandelions and a field of tall grass with dandelions.

Procedure

1 Have the children observe the dandelions growing in the two places—the lawn and the field of uncut grass. They will observe that the flower stalk is much longer on the dandelions in the tall grass than it is on the dandelions growing on the cut grass. In the cut grass, the dandelion grows with a very short flower stalk, and the leaves spread out flat. In the tall grass, the leaves grow upward towards the sun.

2 Ask the children the following question:

Why does a plant grow differently in different places? (Many plants like the dandelion are versatile or flexible and can adapt and change. Many plants can change their sizes and their forms as they grow.)

3. Specialized body parts for protection

Materials

Assorted pictures of animals with protective parts like claws, teeth, beaks, armor, feet with hooves (from wildlife magazines or picture books).

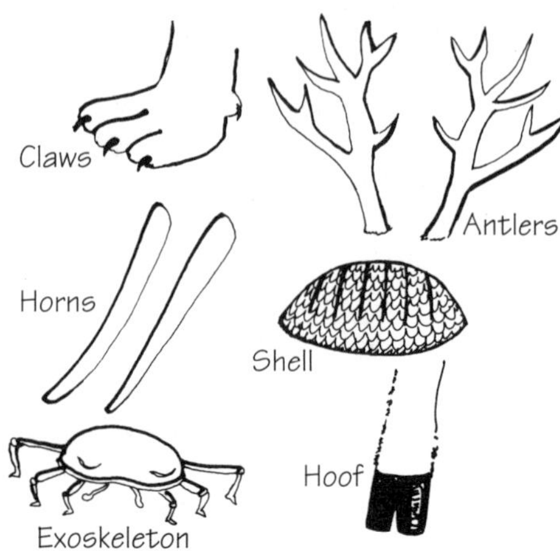

8-16 *Protective body parts.*

Procedure

1 Show children the assorted pictures of the animals and discuss the special parts each animal has to protect itself from its enemies.

2 Discuss the following: claws for scratching and climbing; feet with hooves for kicking and climbing rocks; armor or shells that protect animals like turtles and armadillos; teeth for digging, tearing, cutting, grinding, and puncturing other animals; horns for stabbing and digging.

3 Have the children identify a part on each animal that helps protect it from other animals. Or you can describe to the children how each animal or set of animals protects itself from its enemies. For example:

This animal has a very sharp beak. What animal is it?

This animal gives off an unpleasant odor. What animal is it?

This animal has sharp teeth. What animal am I thinking of? (Any carnivore.)

This animal can fly. What animals can do that? (Many insects, along with most birds and all bats.)

This animal has very sharp claws.

This animal swims very fast.

This animal has sharp spines.

This animal has horns.

This animal stays in large groups or herds of its own kind.

This animal has large and powerful legs.

This animal has tough, scaly skin.

This animal has eyes placed on the sides of its head so that it can see all around its body. (Rabbit, horse, cow.) *Note:* Mammals that only eat plants often have their eyes located on the sides of their heads.

These animals are hard to see because they blend into their surroundings.

This animal becomes very still when it senses an enemy is near. (Rabbits, squirrels, snakes.)

This animal becomes very noisy when it senses an enemy is near. (Monkeys, some birds, and rattlesnakes.)

4 Have children create a make-believe animal and describe its parts and special adaptations.

4. Specialized protective survival tricks and habits

Materials

Pictures of migrating birds in flight, of bears in caves hibernating, of animals that play dead like the opossum and hognose snake, animals that mimic others like the viceroy and monarch butterfly or the coral snake and the king snake. (These kinds of pictures can usually be found in nature magazines.)

Procedure

1 Show the pictures to the children.

2 Discuss the special tricks or adaptations that the children might know of that these animals in the pictures make or have made in order to survive. Possible methods of protection and adaptation to the environment to discuss are: mimicry of color or behavior, hibernation and migration for protection from extreme temperature changes, playing dead, and hiding in a shell.

5. Camouflage and toothpicks

Materials

A box of colored toothpicks.

Procedure

1 Have children sort out the toothpicks into different piles according to their color. Have them count each pile and record how many toothpicks are in each pile. Then have the children mix all the toothpicks together again and toss them outside on a grassy area.

8-17 *Find the colored toothpicks in the grass.*

2 Tell children you are going to give them five minutes to find and collect as many toothpicks as they can find. After the five minutes are up, tell children to sort out the toothpicks they have found and to count each colored pile. Ask the following kinds of questions:

Which color was the hardest to see in the grass?

How many toothpicks were found?

What color was the easiest to see in the grass?

If birds are looking for insects in the grass, which color would be the hardest for the bird to see? (Green, brown or black, yellow.)

Would color help protect an insect from a bird? (It depends on the color of the insect and the background it is on.)

What color is a protective color? (A color that blends with the surroundings.)

How does a protective color help an animal adapt to its environment? (By helping it hide out when it has no place to hide.)

6. Beak and feet adaptations on birds

Materials

Pictures and models of various birds.

Procedure

1 Have children observe pictures or models of birds.

2 Guide them to observe the different kinds of beaks that birds have.

3 Help children see the differences between the kind of beak that a woodpecker has, and the kind of beak that a duck has. (The woodpecker's beak is useful in trees for drilling to obtain insects in the wood, and the duck's beak is useful in the water as a shovel to find food in the mud.)

4 Have them compare the long spoon bill on a flamingo with the short, strong beak on a sparrow.

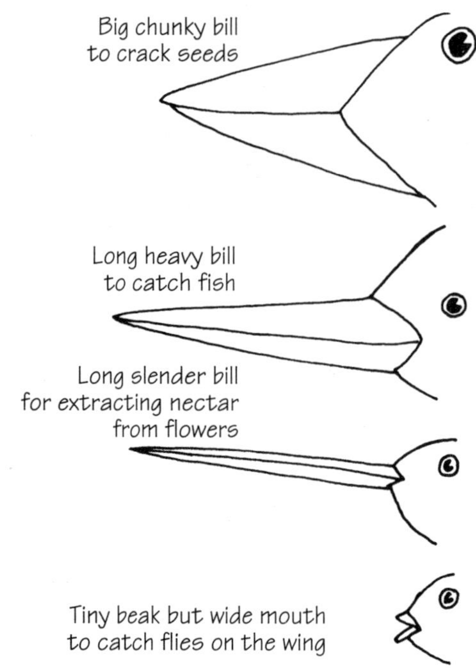

8-18A *Adaptation of birds' beaks.*

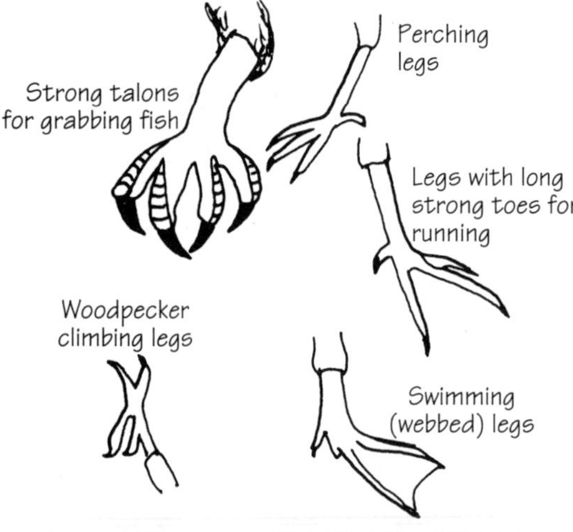

8-18B *Adaptation of birds' feet.*

Which beak is useful as a strainer to separate food from the mud?

Which beak is useful for cracking nuts and seeds?

5 Have children observe the different kinds of feet that birds have. *Note:* Birds can have feet that are adapted for wading, climbing, perching, or grasping.

6 Either ask questions that elicit from children what they think the assorted feet tell them about each of the pictured bird's feeding habits, or explain: Birds that swim and live near water have webbed feet (like the duck). Birds that live in trees and need to perch on branches have feet with three toes in front and one long toe in back. Birds that climb trees (like the woodpecker) have two toes in front and two toes in back. Owls and hawks are animals of prey. They have claw-like talons on their feet for attacking animals that they eat. (See Fig. 8-18.)

7 *Explain:* Birds can be divided into groups. They can be grouped by the way their bodies look, by their size, by where they live, by whether they migrate, or by what they eat.

Note: Some birds (like vultures) only eat dead animals. Others (like the hawk) eat other animals and small birds. Some birds (like the woodpecker) live on insects, and other birds (like sparrows) live on seeds. Some birds hunt fish with their spearlike beaks. Birds eat a wide variety of foods and have many adaptations to survive. They can live in different climates by migrating when the temperature does not suit them. Most birds that migrate go to warmer places in the winter and migrate back to cooler places in the summer.

Going further

"Take a Closer Look," a science program on public television, suggested letting children manipulate simple household tools like: a nutcracker, a pair of needle-nose pliers, an awl, spaghetti tongs, and a fork. Then, compare the kind of work that these household tools can do with the kind of work a bird's beak is adapted for. This will help children become aware that the different species of birds can eat the kinds of food they like to eat because of their special adaptations. For example:

- Seed-eating birds (like the cardinal) use their short, thick beaks to crush their food like a nutcracker crushes nuts.
- Insect-eating birds like the woodpecker use their long, hard beaks like an awl to bore holes into trees to reach insects with their tongue; other insect eaters (like the warblers) use their long, thin plier-like beaks to catch and hold onto their food.
- Water fowl (like ducks that eat plants) use their spoon bills to strain water like a pair of spaghetti tongs.
- Fish-eating birds (like heron) hold their fish between their long beaks like a fork that holds meat.
- Meat-eating birds (like the hawk) use their hooked beaks to tear meat apart.

7. Adaptations for extremes in temperatures

Materials

Pictures of animals that live in the desert and pictures of animals that live in the Arctic.

Procedure

1 Have children compare the adaptations that plants and animals have to make in a desert with those that plants and animals would have to make in the Arctic.

2 Discuss how the temperature in a desert is very hot and how the temperature in the Arctic is very cold.

How do you cope with a very hot day or with a very cold day?

How do the clothes you would wear in the middle of winter on a snowy day differ from the kinds of clothes you would wear if you were planning to go swimming?

3 *Explain:* Reptiles live in the desert. Reptiles are cold-blooded animals. Having cold blood means that the animal's body temperature changes with its surroundings. These animals would not be able to survive in the Arctic. They would freeze to death. Polar bears have extremely thick fur. They even have fur on their feet. They would roast to death in the desert.

Note: When animals are raised in a zoo, the zoo regulates the temperature for the animals so that they can survive. The zoo keeps the environment at a temperature that the animals have adapted to in their natural surroundings.

IV. How environments differ

1. What is an environment?

Materials

None.

Procedure

1 Ask the children the following question:

What is an environment? (Record their responses on a chart. How do their responses compare to the responses they gave when you asked a similar question before taking a Nature Walk (Activity I, Procedure 2 of this chapter)?).

2 *Explain:* An environment is all of the conditions that act on a plant or an animal. An environment is the physical conditions like the amount of water, sunlight, temperature, and condition of the soil. It is also things like population within the area and the communities of other living and nonliving things.

3 Discuss with children their environment at home, their environment at school, and the environment outside in the yard or inside of a car. Ask the children to think about how these environments differ and how they are alike. Remind children that plants and animals have adapted to certain environments. Ask the following kinds of questions:

How does our environment differ from the kind of environment other animals would experience, such as: an alligator, a whale, a frog, a penguin?

What are some of the conditions that keep all kinds of plants and animals from being able to live in your house, at school, outside, and in your car? (Temperature, amount of water, sunlight, soil, space.)

4 *Explain:* There are various kinds of environments. They differ from one another. Not all environments have the same temperature, rainfall, or sunlight. Biologists disagree as to how many different kinds of environments exist. But, there are at least six. These large environments or regions are called biomes. A biome covers a large area or region of the earth and contains many communities with many populations. The amount of rain, the amount of sunlight, the temperature, and the soil are similar throughout most of a biome's territory, which makes it possible for certain specific animals and plants to live in them.

2. The major biomes on land

Materials

Pictures of: an Arctic-tundra area, a taiga-evergreen area, a deciduous forest, a grassland or savannah, a desert, a tropical rain forest. Also: old nature magazines; paper; crayons; a physical relief globe of the earth; a prism.

Procedure

1 Show children the pictures and tell them that these pictures represent the different environments on the earth.

2 As you show children the pictures, ask them:

8-19A *A polar bear adapts to its environment.*

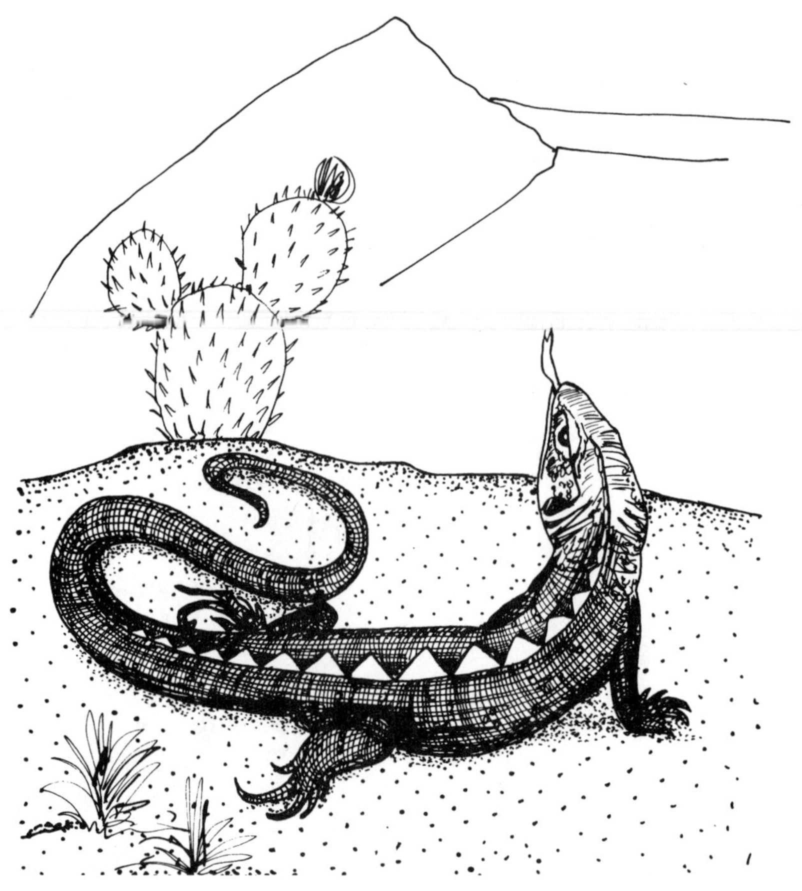

8-19B *A lizard adapts to its environment.*

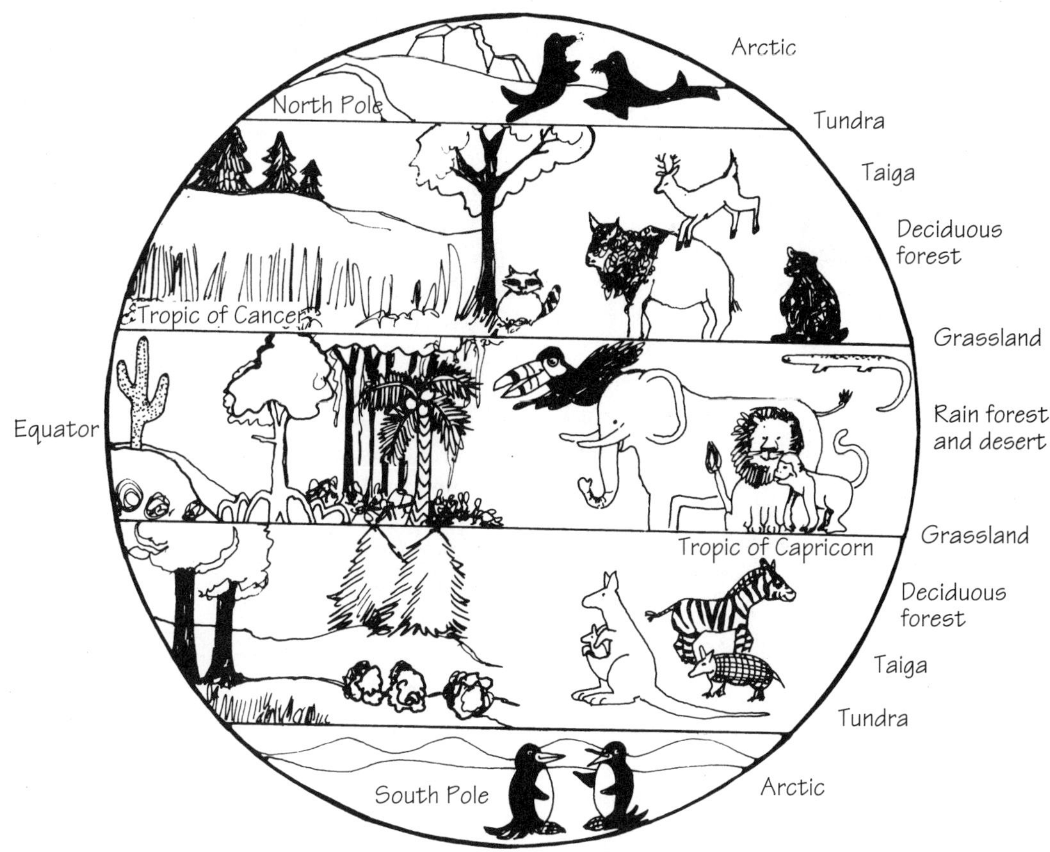

8-20 *The major land biomes.*

What kinds of animals would live in each of these environments?

3 Have them draw pictures of some animals or cut animal pictures out of magazines. Have the children place their animal pictures on the appropriate environmental picture. Ask them which kind of environment probably has the most variety of living things.

Which environment would be easiest for them to live in?

Which kinds of plants and animals seems to live in the most environments? (Simple plants and animals like insects, algae, and moss.)

4 Show them the globe of the earth.

What is a globe? (The globe is a model of the earth.)

5 Help them find the imaginary line that is called the equator.

6 *Explain:* It is very warm on and near the equator. Point to the "top" and the "bottom" of the earth. The top is called the North Pole and the bottom is called the South Pole. These are the polar regions.

Note: The region known as the Arctic is located around the North Pole. It includes the Arctic Ocean and parts of three continents (Europe, Asia, and North America). The Antarctic is on the South Pole, and it includes the continent of Antarctica and parts of three adjoining oceans (Atlantic, Pacific, and Indian).

What do you think the climate is like on the ice caps? (Both poles of the earth are very cold.)

7 Show them the deserts, the oceans and lakes, and the mountainous areas of the earth on the globe. The environments of the earth take up large areas.

8 *Explain:* These environments change gradually. They do not go from one extreme to another. Tropical rain forests and the Arctic poles are far away from each other. The environments in the different biomes change gradually. Some environments on the edges of two distinct areas blend together. Their boundaries intermesh so that it is hard to know when you have left one environment and entered another. The animals and

plants that live in boundary areas are adapted to both environments. For example, ponds and woods often appear together, as do grasses and trees.

9 Show the children the prism. Have a child catch a light beam with it.

10 *Explain:* Biomes are like a color spectrum made from a prism. The various colors appear side by side, and though the colors might blend at the edges, each of the bands of color still has its distinct hue. The hues tend to be more intense in the center of the bands and become less intense on the edges. On the edges, the colors blend. Each hue is like a biome. At the edges of biomes, biomes blend together, as the colors do in a spectrum. The rainbow or spectrum of colors consists of many bands or parts. Each color represents a part of the spectrum, just as each biome represents a separate kind of environment on the earth. All of the biomes are part of the whole. Each biome affects all of the other biomes.

3. The tundra

Materials

A globe of the earth; pictures of Eskimos, caribou, lichen, huskies, polar bears, and other forms of Arctic life; ice; thermometer; fresh lichen on a rock or on a piece of bark.

8-21 *Very few trees can grow in the tundra.*

Procedure

1 Show children the globe.

What do you think the climate and environment would be like at the North Pole?

2 Ask the following kinds of questions:

Would the snow and ice ever melt? (Yes, briefly in the summer, but the soil that is six inches below the surface is permanently frozen.)

Would the summer be warm? (The temperatures are still near freezing in the summer.)

How long would the summer last? (Very briefly. Plants grow for two months all year.)

How cold would it get in winter? (Extremely cold, below freezing.)

Is there a lot of food? (Food is scarce because the soil is frozen most of the year.)

How do plants and animals survive in Arctic winter? (Animals survive by migrating south to warmer climates, or by staying and growing a white fur for camouflage, and an extra thick coat of fur for protection from the extreme cold. Plants remain small. There are no trees in the tundra.)

What would human beings have to wear in the winter? (Eskimo-like clothes or other warm outfits.)

3 Pass the ice around for the children to feel. Place a thermometer in the ice so they can see how cold the temperature of ice is on the thermometer. Have them hold the ice until their fingers sting.

4 *Explain:* When our skin is not protected in cold weather, we can get frostbite. Frostbite stings like a burn and numbs our sense of touch. Animals in the tundra have to adapt to the tundra to survive.

5 Have the children study the photographs of animal and plant life in the tundra and discuss the adaptations that each form of life has had to make in order to survive.

6 Show the children the lichen.

7 *Explain:* A lot of lichen grows in the tundra. A lichen is really two plants: an alga and a fungus growing together. The fungus holds water, but cannot make food. The alga can make food, but has no roots. So the alga uses the water from the fungus. When two organisms live together and are useful to each other, they have a symbiotic relationship. Very few trees can grow in the tundra. The ground is too frozen for roots to grow. Only a few birds live in the tundra, but many birds migrate to the Arctic from other biomes for the short summer.

4. The taiga or evergreen forest*

* Also known as the coniferous forest.

Materials

For each child or group of children: freshly cut twigs from spruce, pine, fir, and cedar trees, and their seed cones. Pictures of: moose, cross-bill birds, red-backed salamander, porcupine, mink, wolverine, black bear, lynx, rabbit, beaver.

8-22A *Norway spruce.*

8-22B *White pine.*

8-22C *Balsam fir.*

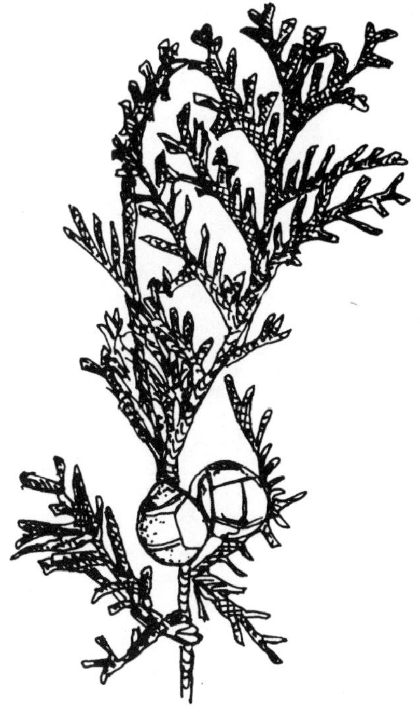

8-22D *White cedar.*

Procedure

1 Show children the twigs from the freshly cut trees.

2 Have them notice the differences in the needles of each kind of tree, and the differences in their seed cones. Ask the children to open up or shake a cone so they can see the seeds.

3 *Explain:* Forests of evergreen trees border the tundra area. These evergreen forests are sometimes called coniferous forests because most of the trees grow their seeds in cones. The taiga area has very cold winters and a small amount of underbrush that grows near the ground. As the needles of the trees fall to the ground, they form a layer of new soil. The needles make the soil very acidic. Evergreens grow well in the acidic soil. The evergreen trees are very narrow and grow very close to each other. They lose their bottom branches because the bottom branches do not receive much light. A canopy of leaves (needles) forms on top of the trees and prevents most sunlight from reaching the ground. The largest animal that lives in this biome is the moose. There are different niches in the forest. A niche is a place where an animal lives and feeds.

Different kinds of animals live in the different horizontal zones.

8-23 *Horizontal levels of life in the forest.*

4 Show children the pictures of animals as you talk about them. Some animals (like the salamander) live on the cool, damp ground. Other animals (like birds) divide the forest into vertical parts. Some of the species of birds live in the treetops, while other species of birds live on the mid-branches of the trees, and still other bird species live off the low scrubs. The cross-bill birds have a beak designed for eating seeds from cones. Some animals come out only at night, while others come out only during the day. Some animals are herbivores and eat only plants or seeds, while other animals are carnivores and eat only other animals like insects, worms, and small mammals. Some of the animals are scavengers and eat only dead things that are left. Each population of animals has a different menu of food to eat. There are a great variety of animals that live in the taiga biome, but they do not all compete with each other for the same food.

5 Have children discuss any physical adaptations they might have noticed about the animals as they are discussed.

What makes it possible for each of these animals (pictured) to adjust or to survive the winter? (Remember: some of the animals migrate or hibernate.)

5. The deciduous forest

Materials

Pictures of: deer, black bear, fox, raccoon, mice, squirrel, chipmunk, opossum, turtle, toad, frog, owl, hawk, crow, blue jay, woodpecker, assorted insects, assorted decomposers on a log, the remains of a forest fire, a pond, a meadow.

Procedure

1 *Explain:* Deciduous forests are found in most of the eastern half of the United States. The temperature and the rainfall vary with the four seasons. However, the amount of rainfall is usually plentiful, and a huge variety of plants and animals live in this biome. Deciduous forests are found between the evergreen forests and the grasslands or oceans. Most of the trees in a deciduous forest shed their leaves in the fall and stay dormant and lifeless-looking all winter. Most of the animals in a deciduous forest live there all year, except for some of the birds that migrate to other biomes, and some of the animals that hibernate.

2 Have the children think of all of the animals they can that live in a deciduous forest. Show them the pictures of animals that live in a deciduous forest. Then have them compare those animals with the ones that live in the tundra and in an evergreen forest. Talk about their differences.

3 *Explain:* There are a few evergreen trees that grow in the deciduous forest and a few deciduous trees that grow in the evergreen forest.

Can you explain why this happens? (There is no clear line between biomes. There are a few hardy plants that can survive and adapt in an alien environment, but their population remains small. If the environment in a biome changes, the plants will either die out or they will be able to produce seeds for more of their own kind with the special adaptations they have.)

4 Show the children a picture of a forest that caught on fire, and a large pond or swamp.

5 *Explain:* A deciduous forest often starts out as a swamp or rebuilds itself after a fire. Over time, the swamp evaporates and fills up with sediments and dead materials. Eventually, the swamp becomes a meadow. Seeds blow in from nearby trees, and the meadow becomes full of seedlings. Eventually, the trees become a forest. The whole process of change from burnt-out forest, swamp, or pond to forest takes place slowly and gradually over a long period of time—thousands and thousands of years. The process of change is slow and hard to see, but the surface of the earth is constantly changing.

6. The grasslands

Materials

A physical relief globe of the earth; pictures of animals that live in grasslands (mainly grazing animals, both wild and domestic), for each child or group of children: old nature magazines; paper and crayons; a hand trowel; a magnifying glass.

Procedure

1 Show children the globe. Have the children locate the ice caps, then show them the mountains and the grassland areas on the globe.

2 *Explain:* The grasslands are usually located between deserts and forests. They are usually flat and have soil that can produce good grasses and few trees. Many farms are located in the Midwest grasslands of the United States. The area is called the Great Plains. Sometimes a grassland biome is called a prairie. Grasses help prevent erosion of soil. The roots of grasses help hold the earth in place. In Africa, the large grasslands are called the savannah. Many animals that graze on grasses live in the grassland biome.

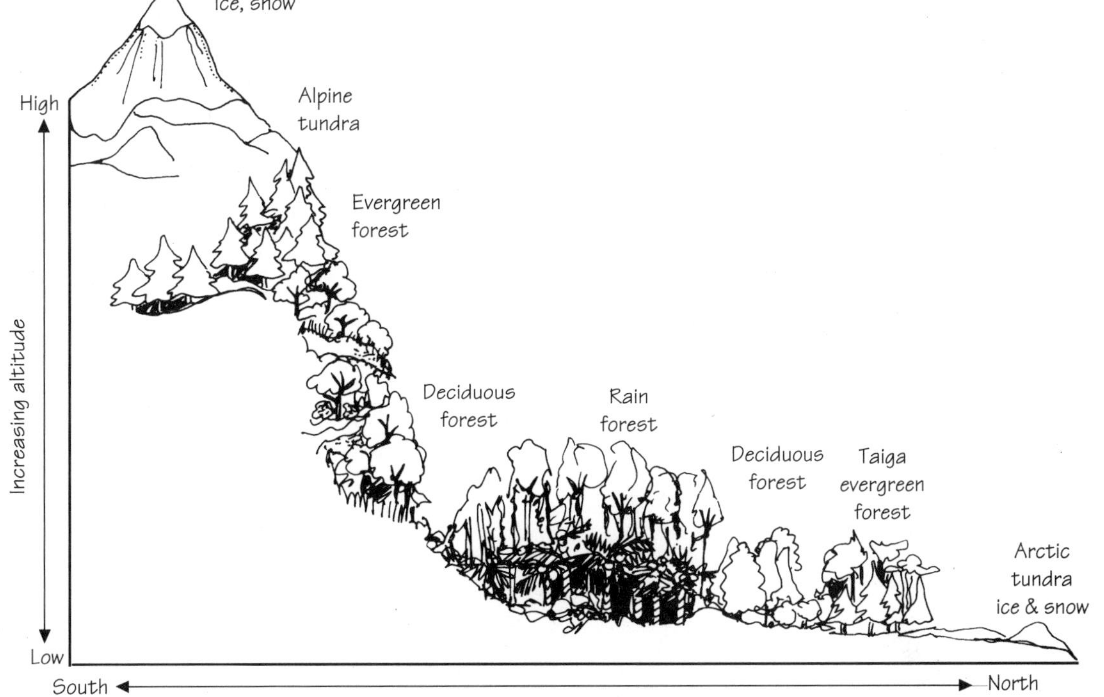

8-24 *The change from one biome to another is gradual.*

3 What kinds of animals do you think would live in the Great Plains of the United States, and which kind of animals would live in the African savannahs?

4 *Explain:* The Great Plains has a lot of farms, and a lot of the African lands are still natural and wild. Have children look at pictures of the kinds of animals that live in grasslands. Have them compare the differences between wild and domestic animals. (Discuss the importance of animals living in herds for protection.)

5 Have the children cut out pictures of animals from magazines or draw pictures of animals that live in the American Great Plains and those that live in the African and Indian grasslands.

Note: Examples of wild animals that live in the grasslands are bison, antelope, deer, zebra, ostrich, elephant, giraffe, snake, termites, grasshoppers, ants, prairie dogs, gophers, mountain lions, coyotes, fox, weasels, lions, and tigers. Examples of non-wild animals that live in the grasslands are: domestic farm animals like horses, cows, and sheep that graze on the land.

6 Take the children outside to a grassy area. Have them use a hand trowel to dig up some earth with grass and roots of grasses. Have them hold the grass and shake the earth loose. Tell children to observe how soil clings to the roots and how the roots help hold the soil together.

7 Have the children examine the blades of grass with a magnifying glass.

Do all of the blades of grass have the same kind of leaf, or is there a variety of grasses growing together?

What kinds of tiny animals are living in the soil under the grass in or near the roots of the grass, or on the grass?

7. The desert

Materials

Pictures of deserts and desert life; tiny cactus plants.

Procedure

1 Show children the pictures of the desert and of desert life.

How is a desert different from a forest or a grasslands or tundra biome?

2 Ask the following kinds of questions:

How often do you think it rains in the desert? (By definition, a desert receives less than 10 inches of rain a year.)

How do plants and animals get enough water to live? (They have adapted to make use of what water there is.)

What is the temperature like in a desert? (Extremely hot during the day and cool at night.)

What kind of soil is in a desert? (Sandy and rocky soil.)

3 *Explain:* Because it is so hot during the day, most desert animals rest during the heat of the day and look for food in the evening or at twilight. Most desert plants store water in their stems and have tiny leaves. Some desert plants have very deep roots that seek water from deep beneath the ground. Most desert plants also have a tough waxy coat and thorns or prickly parts to help protect them from harm. Animals that live in the desert get most of their water from eating other plants or animals. The camel can store water in its hump. As it uses up its water, its hump becomes smaller.

4 Show children the small cactus plants and have them observe the special adaptive features that the plants have for living in the desert.

8. The rain forest

Materials

A globe, pictures of jungle life.

Procedure

1 Show the children the globe.

2 *Explain:* The area around the center of the earth near the equator has a very warm climate. When a region is very warm and receives a lot of rainfall, it is called a tropical rain forest. A tropical rain forest has a huge number of plants and animals. The climate is warm and moist and steamy every day of the year. Animals do not have to adapt to the extremes of temperatures as they do in other biomes. They just have to adapt to warmth and rain. The biome is like a giant greenhouse.

Note: It is strongly recommended that you take the children on a field trip to a greenhouse that grows tropical plants and to a zoo or pet store that has tropical birds or fish. The rain forest biome is difficult to experience without feeling the temperature and humidity of the biome, seeing how bright the colors of the animals are, or observing how big the leaves are on some of the plants. The rain forest is such a lush and exotic biome that pictures alone are not enough.

3 Show children the pictures of jungles.

4 *Explain:* Life exists at lots of different vertical levels in the rain forest: on the ground, in the low bushes, and in the lower and upper canopy of trees. A tropical rain forest has a larger variety of living things growing and living in it than any other biome. It is the most populated of all the biomes.

It is fairly easy to walk on the ground in a rain forest because there is very little underbrush growing on the ground. The plants and vines and the canopy of trees block most of the sunlight. Some smaller plants grow on taller plants so that they can receive sunlight. These kinds of plants never touch the soil. They have adapted to grow without soil because there is so much moisture, sunlight, and warmth in the rain forest.

The plants in a rain forest grow to an enormous size. They compete for sunlight. Most of the larger animals that live in the rain forest live in the trees above the ground. Most of them have adopted a protective coloration that helps them hide from their enemies and blend with their surroundings. Often, the limbs and tail of a monkey or the hanging body of a snake can look like a thick vine. The spots on a leopard can look like the shadows of leaves. Many insects look like twigs, flowers, or leaves.

Going further

Create a terrarium for each kind of environment.

Materials and preparation Materials will vary according to what kind of terrarium is created. (Visit a botanical garden or a pet supply store to find pamphlets and books about creating terrariums, supplies to use, and creatures to buy or collect on your own. Either buy the supplies at the pet store or improvise when you know what is needed.) For more details see: *New Unesco Source Book for Science Teachers*, pp. 164–166.

You will need the following materials: large, empty, clean "UTZ" pretzel jars, or commercial-sized pickle jars are ideal to use for terrariums. Terrariums can also be made from clear (non-green) empty, plastic liter (soda) bottles. Take the bottom piece of hard plastic off the bottom of the plastic bottle. (If you run hot water over the bottom, it will be easier to pry off.) Cut the top off and use the bottom piece of hard plastic for the top. (See Fig. 8-25.)

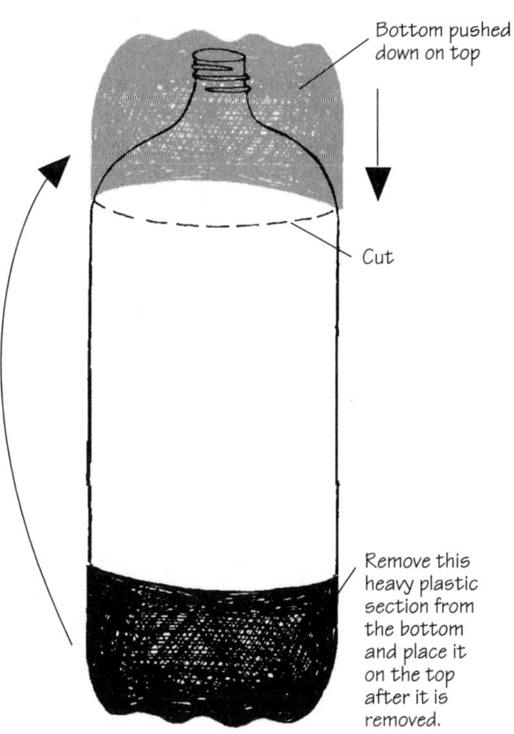

8-25 *Remove top and bottom of a plastic bottle to make a terrarium.*

Procedure

1 Take a field trip to a local pet store or zoo. After the trip, suggest that the children create their own terrarium that represents a miniature habitat for animals and plants.

2 Brainstorm about the possible kinds of terrariums that could be made. (Some possibilities are: a desert community, a grassland or meadow community, a forest floor community, a rotting log community, a freshwater pond community.)

3 Discuss with children what supplies would be needed to create an adequate environment for the various kinds of environments.

4 Allow children to choose a habitat to study and to create an appropriate environment in a terrarium for the habitat they choose.

8-26 *A desert community.*

8-27 *A grassland or meadow community.*

8-28A *A forest floor community.*

8-28B *A woodland habitat.*

8-29 *A rotting-log community.*

8-30 *A freshwater pond community.*

V. Food chains and webs

1. What did you eat today?

Materials

None.

Procedure

1 Ask the children the following questions:

What did you eat for breakfast and lunch?

What do you think you will eat for supper?

2 Discuss with the children where their food came from. Have them trace where the food was before it arrived at their house or at the grocery store.

3 If they ate a cereal for breakfast or a bread for lunch, talk about how the cereal or bread became cereal or bread. Ask children the following kinds of questions:

Where did the flour come from?

How did the wheat or grain become flour?

Where did the wheat or grain come from before it became flour?

4 *Explain:* Green plants are called producers. Green plants are able to produce their own food supply from the sun's energy. Green plants provide food or energy for animals. Animals cannot produce their own food. Animals are consumers or users and choosers of food. Not all animals eat plants, but some animals do. Animals that eat other animals are eating animals that grew from eating plants. So, all animals are dependent on plants, even if they do not eat plants. If it were not for the green plants, the herbivores or plant-eating animals would not grow up to be food for the carnivores or meat-eating animals. Meat-eating animals eat other animals for food.

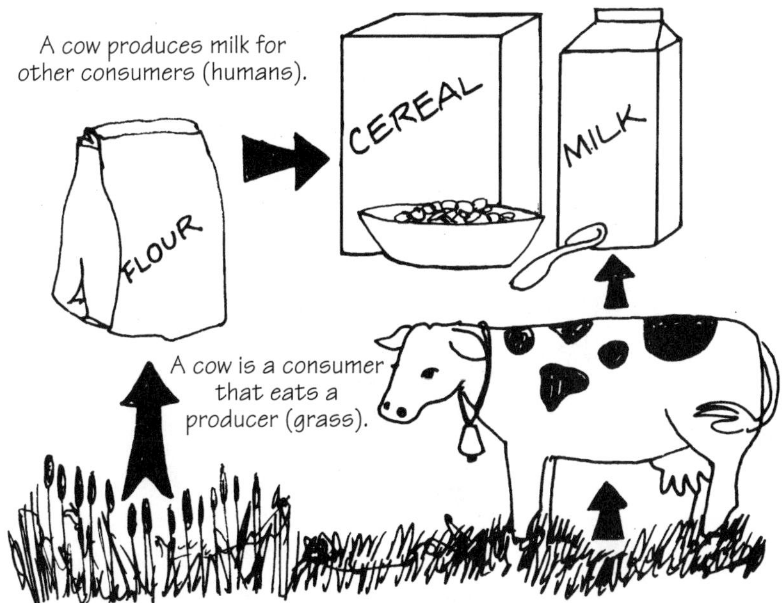
A cow produces milk for
other consumers (humans).
CEREAL
MILK
FLOUR
A cow is a consumer
that eats a
producer (grass).

8-31 *Green plants are producers; animals are consumers (they eat producers or other consumers).*

Do you eat meat? (Discuss where the meat they eat comes from.)

5 *Explain:* When you eat fish, chicken, lamb, pork, or beef, you are eating animals that have died.

What kinds of food do chickens, sheep, and cattle eat? (These animals eat plants.)

What kinds of food do fish eat? (Most fish eat small plants, other fish, or small animals.)

2. Food preferences and niches

Materials

A fruit fly, a housefly, a jar, raw meat, a banana, a butterfly net.

Procedure

1 Catch a housefly and a fruit fly. Place them in a jar with a piece of raw meat and a banana. Have the children observe which fly prefers which food. Ask the following kinds of questions:

What do houseflies like to eat? (Generally, garbage and putrid-smelling materials.)

What do fruit flies like to eat? (Rotting fruit.)

Why are flies considered a nuisance? (They tend to fly around garbage and land on rotting or dirty things. Most people consider them a nuisance because they believe that flies spread diseases.)

How do flies help the environment? (They help clear away nature's garbage. They lay their eggs in decaying things like dead animals, and when the eggs hatch, the larvae eat the dead animal.)

2 *Explain:* Animals have their own niche or territory in an environment. A niche is a special place to live that belongs to a population of animals. The two flies are not in competition for the food supply in the jar. They each prefer eating a different kind of food.

When there is a large variety of plants and animals living in a biome such as in a jungle, there tends to be less competition for food. The great diversity allows each animal to have its own niche or territory to live in. Animals in a jungle rarely need to compete for the exact same foods. There is a plentiful supply of food in a jungle or rain forest biome because of the immense diversity. In the Arctic or tundra (where food is scarce in the winter) there is a lot of competition, but there are also fewer animals to compete with. Each healthy biome is balanced.

3. Predator and prey

Materials

Pictures of assorted animals that are eaten by other animals and of the animals that might eat them—for example: insect and frog, antelope and lion, bird and cat, toad and snake, snake and hawk, sheep and wolf, chicken and person, rabbit and fox.

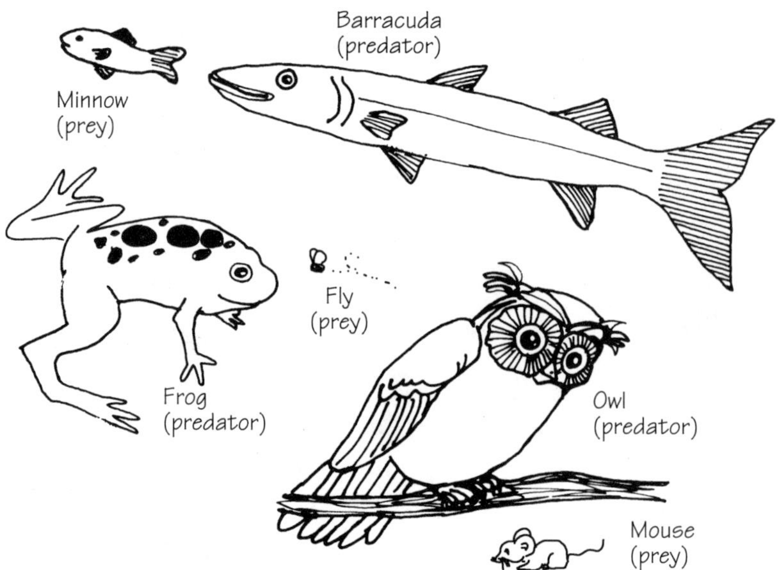

8-32 *Some predators and their prey.*

Procedure

1 *Explain:* All animals need food. Most living things eventually become food for other animals, or become food for bacteria and fungi when they rot.

2 Show children the pictures of the assorted animals.

Can you guess what kind of food each of the animals eats?

3 Have them sort the pictures so that all of the animals that eat only plants are in one pile, and all of the animals that eat only meat are in another pile.

Do any of the animals from the meat-eaters group also eat plants? (If so, place those pictures into a separate pile.)

4 *Explain:* When an animal eats only meat, it is called a carnivore. Animals that eat both plants and animals are called omnivores. Animals that eat only plants are called herbivores. Ask the children the following kinds of questions:

Which animal group eats the largest variety of foods? (Omnivores.)

Which animal group probably has the best chance to adapt to foods in a new environment? (Omnivores.)

What animal group do we as human beings belong to? (Omnivore.)

5 Have the children look at the sorted pictures and guess which of the carnivores would eat which of the herbivores. Help them become aware that the carnivores do not restrict themselves to just one kind of animal to eat. For example, foxes can eat rabbits, squirrels, mice, and birds, and so can hawks.

6 *Explain:* When an animal is eaten by another animal, it is called the prey or the animal that gets caught and eaten. The animal that does the eating is called the predator. Predators attack other animals and help keep the population of the prey down. If foxes and hawks did not eat rabbits, there would be too many rabbits. The rabbits would destroy the balance of the biome by eating too many green plants so that other animals would not have enough to eat.

4. Food chains

Materials

A picture of a grasshopper, a frog, a snake, and a hawk; some paper; glue; a marking pen; old nature magazines; scissors.

Procedure

1 Show the children the pictures.

2 *Explain:* The grasshopper eats grass. It is a primary consumer. A primary consumer is the first animal in a food chain that eats a plant.

Can you think of other primary consumers? (All herbivore animals are primary consumers.)

3 *Explain:* The (other) animals in the pictures listed in materials above can also eat grasshoppers. If these animals eat a grasshopper, they would be

secondary consumers in a food chain. If the frog eats the grasshopper and is then eaten by a snake, the snake would be the third consumer in the food chain. The snake is a predator, but the snake has enemies. The hawk could eat the snake. The hawk would then be the fourth consumer in the food chain. The hawk has no enemies. It is at the top of the food chain. When the hawk dies, other animals eat it. The dead hawk eventually decays with the help of bacteria and fungi that help turn the remains of the dead hawk into soil. The soil then becomes rich in minerals and nutrients to grow new plants.

4 Draw a picture of the food chain described above for the children so they can see how the arrows move from the first consumer to the fourth consumer. (See Fig. 8-33.)

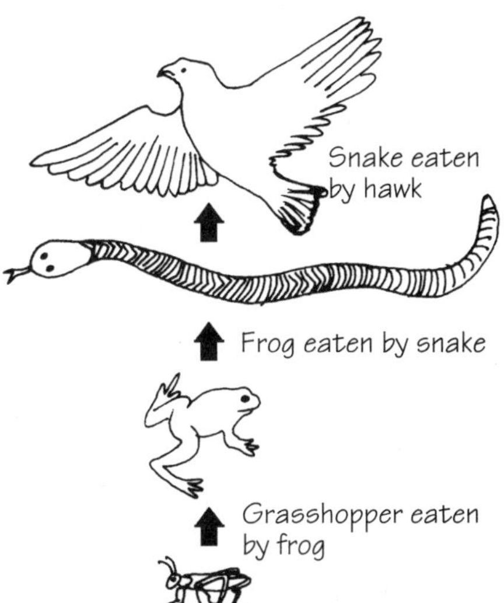

8-33 *A food chain.*

5 Have the children cut out pictures from magazines that could make up a possible food chain. Ask them what the first picture would have to be. *Note:* All food chains start with the sun, and the first living thing in a food chain is a green plant. Then the consumers have to be added in.

6 Have the children arrange the cut pictures on a piece of paper before they glue them down and then add a pencil arrow mark to show the direction of the food chain to show what eats what.

Do you know what a food chain is?

7 *Explain:* A food chain traces the chain of energy that transfers from plants that produce food to animals that consume food to other animals that consume other animals. Every time an animal eats food, energy is used. It takes energy for an animal to digest food, but the food gives the animal energy. Animals need food to keep their bodies working.

8 Have the children jump up and down, blink their eyes, feel their heart beating, and notice their ribs going up and down when they breathe.

9 *Explain:* All these activities that go on in our bodies use energy. Food gives us the energy to keep going. Food is our fuel. As our bodies work and exercise, they use up or burn the fuel. The energy is consumed and changed. Food to animals is like gasoline to a car. Without energy from fuel, nothing in the car can function; likewise, without food, nothing in an animal's body can function.

10 Ask children to think back to the different kinds of animals that lived in the different biomes. Have them think up various food chains for the different biomes discussed in Section IV of this chapter. They might want to use some of the reference books listed at the end of this chapter.

5. Food webs

Materials

A spiderweb, a toothpick, a diagram of a food web.

Procedure

1 Take the children outside to look at a spiderweb. Have the children notice the pattern. Touch the web with a toothpick. Ask the following kinds of questions:

What happens when you shake the spiderweb? (It bounces around, but stays together.)

What happens to the shape of the spiderweb if one small strand in the spiderweb breaks? (The shape of the web changes slightly.)

What happens to the web if a major spike or thread breaks? (The web is destroyed and needs to be repaired and rebuilt by the spider.)

2 *Explain:* A food web is like a spiderweb. It is a complex system in which animals can be in more than one food chain. For example, rabbits, squirrels, and mice all eat plants. Rabbits are eaten by foxes, hawks, and

mountain lions. Squirrels are eaten by foxes and hawks. Mice are eaten by snakes, foxes, and hawks. The food chains are interlocked and interwoven like a spiderweb. (See Fig. 8-34.)

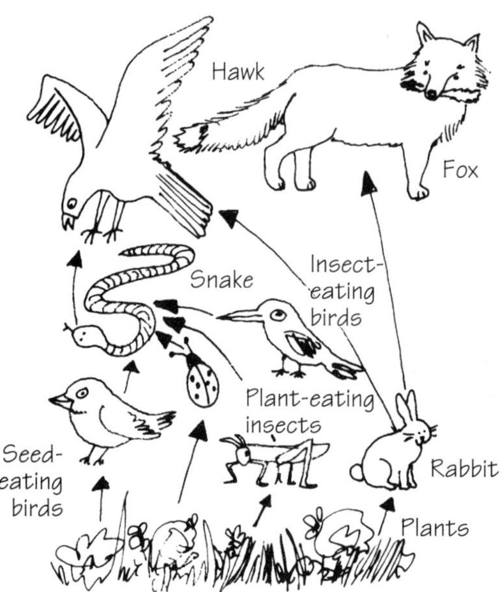

8-34 *A complex food web.*

Many food chains make up a food web. Each biome has a food web that is as delicate as the spiderweb. If one small chain in the food web breaks, not a lot of damage is done, but the shape of the web might change slightly. If a major part of the chain is broken, a lot of damage can occur. The whole food web could collapse.

What would happen if there were no mountain lions around to eat deer? (If there were no mountain lions around to eat deer, the deer population would increase. There would be too many deer. The deer would eat all the grasses, and the soil would start to erode because there would be no more roots from the grasses to hold the soil in place. Eventually, all the deer would die of starvation because they would not have any food.) *Note:* All of these changes would take place gradually over many years.

How can an unbalanced change in a food web cause damage? (Any change in a food web can bring about a disaster if it is not a balanced change.)

Note: When foreign insects like the Japanese beetle arrived in our country, they caused much damage to plants because the Japanese beetles had no natural enemies, and they were able to multiply. Farmers and gardeners used poisonous sprays like DDT to kill them, but the poisons began to get into the food chain and also poisoned parts of food webs, causing much harm and destruction. Eventually, when the effects of the poisons were understood, the spraying of some of the poisons was outlawed.

6. Poisons in a food chain

Materials

Pictures of oil-soaked beaches, polluted water, and dead fish.

Procedure

1 Show the pictures of oil-soaked beaches to the children and ask them whether or not the animals look healthy.

What do you think might have caused their problem? (Discuss the apparent pollution in the picture and how it affected the environment and the food chains and the whole food web.)

2 *Explain:* If birds eat fish from polluted water or insects that have eaten poison, the birds eat poison too by eating the sick animals. If the birds eat too many sick animals that are poisoned, the birds eventually become weak.

Note: Scientists discovered that eagles were laying eggs with thin shells. The thin-shelled eggs cracked easily before the birds hatched, and the babies died. The population of eagles became smaller because the birds were eating other animals in their food chain that had eaten poison.

3 *Explain:* Poisons in food chains have caused some animals to be in danger of becoming extinct. Animals in danger of becoming extinct as a species are called endangered species.

4 Have the children find out what animals in their biome are endangered, and how these animals are important to the food web. Information about endangered species can be obtained from: Fish and Wildlife Service, U.S. Department of the Interior, Washington, D.C. 20240.

VI. Pollution

1. What is pollution

Materials

Pictures illustrating air, water, and land pollution. (They can be found in nature magazines or library books.)

Procedure

1 Show the children the pictures of polluted areas. Discuss what pollution is and what causes it.

2 *Explain:* Pollution occurs when something appears in an environment that is unwanted and does not belong. For example, litter on a street or in the park spoils the natural beauty. Old, abandoned cars left on streets and in yards are ugly to look at. Garbage looks okay in the trash can and old, abandoned cars look okay in a junk yard, but it is unpleasant to see this litter of garbage and old rusty non-workable machinery around where you live. Pollution also causes damage to water and air.

What kinds of pollution are there? (Air, water, land, noise, toxic chemicals.)

What causes pollution?

3 *Explain:* Air becomes polluted when too much fuel is burned improperly by factories, furnaces, and cars. The winds can blow away some of the pollution in the air. Sometimes in large cities there is too much polluted air for the wind to carry it away, and the polluted air stays still and trapped in the city. (Particularly when there is no wind!)

Large bodies of water, rivers, and streams become polluted when chemical waste from factories (such as detergents, oils, and treated and untreated sewage) are emptied into them. The land becomes polluted when it becomes littered with garbage. The levels of noise sometimes pollute a nice, quiet place by creating unwanted sound. Poisons and insecticides poison our air and water. They also contaminate food chains. *Note:* Emphasize to children that we need to take care of our environment. We all share it together, and we are all responsible for its care.

Going further

The Native American Science Education Association had a wonderful activity in its Spring, 1984 issue.

1 The article suggested cutting up an apple into quarters. The apple represents the earth and its land surface.

2 Take away three of the quarters. These represent the land underneath the oceans.

3 Slice the remaining quarter in half. Take away one of these pieces, as it represents the land that is inhospitable for people to live on (the polar regions, deserts, swamps, high, rocky mountainous terrain). The remaining one eighth slice is the land that people live on.

4 Slice the remaining ⅛ into four sections, which will give you four 1/32 pieces. Take away three of these pieces. These represent the land surface that is too difficult to grow food on because it is too dry, too rocky, too wet, too cold, too steep, and/or the soil is too poor. These three 1/32 pieces also represent the land that could produce food, but it is buried under concrete highways, buildings in cities, suburban housing developments, shopping centers, and parking lots.

5 That leaves one 1/32 section of the earth's land surface to produce food for the earth's entire population of human beings!

Note: We must help the younger generation realize how important it is to protect the environmental quality of our air, our water, and our land. The children we are reaching today will be the future caretakers of the earth.

2. Air pollution

Materials

A picture showing a smoggy, dirty-looking skyline in a city; two styrofoam meat trays; petroleum jelly; a branch from a tree near a highway; a branch from a tree on a quiet street; a dirty furnace filter; a clean furnace filter.

Procedure

1 Show the children the picture of the polluted air in a city. Discuss what in the picture makes the air dirty.

2 Show the children two branches of trees, preferably from the same kind of tree. Tell them that one of the branches was taken from a tree that grows on a busy highway; the other was taken from a quiet street.

Can you see the difference in the way the leaves look?

How does the dirty air affect the leaves on the tree? (Discuss how the leaves from the tree on the busy highway are covered with

8-35 *Collect the results of polluted air.*

oil and grime from the car exhaust that passes by constantly.)

3 You are going to do an experiment to find out whether the air is dirty outside. Show the children the two styrofoam meat trays. Spread a layer of petroleum jelly on the two meat trays.

4 *Explain:* The jelly will hold any dirt that lands on it from the air. Take the children outside to find a place where they think the air might be dirty. This would most likely be near a highway or under a car exhaust. Place one of the trays where the air is dirty. Place the other tray inside the house or classroom. In a few days compare the two trays to find out which one is dirtier.

5 Show the children filters from a furnace. Have them notice the difference between the old and the new filters.

Where does the dirt and grime come from that is in the old filter? (The air that goes through the furnace becomes dirty. The filter helps trap some of the dirt. The furnace needs to have its filter changed when it becomes dirty. When the filter becomes too dirty, it prevents the furnace from working efficiently.)

6 Have the children breathe in and out.

7 *Explain:* We all need air to survive. If the air we breathe in is dirty, it can cause illness. Some people have become sick because the air where they live was so polluted.

3. Water pollution

Materials

Two clear plastic glasses filled with tap water; detergent; oil; some sand or loose soil; coffee filters or paper towels; cotton; wool; a wide-mouth jar; pictures of polluted water; a potted coleus or impatiens plant.

Procedure

1 Show the children the two clear plastic glasses filled with water.

Where does the water come from and how did it get to be in the faucet?

2 Have the children trace the source of their water supply by discussing where water comes from and how it gets to the plumbing system in buildings.

3 Add some detergent, oil, and loose soil or sand to one of the glasses of water. Have the children watch the ingredients mix with the water.

Is the water with the mixture in it suitable for drinking?

4 Show children the coffee filters and the cotton wool.

5 *Explain:* If you pour the dirty water through the filters, some of the pollutants will be removed from the water. Sometimes water can be filtered before it makes other water dirty. Pour the dirty water through the filters and through the cotton wool into the wide-mouth jar. (See Fig. 8-36.)

6 *Explain:* Many communities have water filtration plants to clean pollutants and sewage from the water before it is dumped into a river. *Note:* Even though this dirty water might look cleaner after filtration, it is still not suitable to drink.

7 Show children the pictures in the experiment of polluted water.

8 *Explain:* When water is polluted, the animals that drink the polluted water and that live in the polluted water become sick and sometimes die. When water is filtered before it is dumped

8-36 *Water can be filtered.*

into a lake or river, it helps keep the water cleaner. When accidental pollution occurs due to oil spills into the ocean from an oil tanker, the oil slick settles on the shore lines. The oil slick at the shore kills birds, fish, and plants that live on and near the shore line.

What do all living things need in order to live? (Food, shelter, air, and water)

Note: There are three kinds of water on the earth: fresh water, salt water, and water frozen in glaciers. Ninety-seven percent of the earth's water is salt water. Two percent of the water is frozen in glaciers. One percent is left for us to use! This one percent is continually recycled in the water cycle. (See Chapter 4 (Weather), Activity III (Water Cycle).)

9 *Explain:* All living things need water in order to live and survive. Green plants use water when they make food in their leaves. Most animals can survive for a while without food, but most cannot survive without water.

Going further

Allow a potted plant like a coleus or an impatiens plant to become dehydrated, then water it. Have the children observe the change in the plant after it has been watered.

4. Getting rid of trash and garbage

Materials

Assorted paper, plastic, and metal waste products used for packaging products; gloves; paper bags.

8-37 *Plants need water.*

Procedure

1 Show the children the assorted leftovers of products. Ask the children the following kinds of questions:

What do we call this stuff? (Garbage or trash.)

What do we call it when we find it outside on the grass or along a highway? (Litter.)

Where does garbage belong? (In trash cans.)

Where does the garbage go after it is stored in a trash can? (The can goes to the street, and the garbage truck takes the trash away.)

Where does the garbage truck take the garbage? (To a dump, an incinerator, or a site called a landfill, where the trash gets buried beneath the ground.)

2 *Explain:* Garbage and trash are called solid waste. When solid waste is not disposed of, it looks ugly and it becomes smelly. When solid waste is burned, it often pollutes the air. When it is left in the open air in a dump, it becomes smelly, looks ugly, and attracts insects and rats. When it is buried and untreated, dangerous chemicals can drain into water that flows under the ground and contaminate the water. When it is buried before things are taken from it that can be recycled, valuable materials are lost. For example, paper comes from trees. If paper is recycled, fewer trees need to be cut down.

3 Tell children to become litter collectors around the house and school. Give each of them a glove to wear and a paper bag in which to collect trash. Examine the trash that is collected. Ask the following kinds of questions:

Which kind of trash would decay outside? (Paper products.)

Which kind of trash would take a long time to decay outside? (Metals, plastics, and glass.)

What kinds of things can be recycled? (Metals, glass, and paper.)

How does recycling help reduce the amount of solid waste that builds up? (It eliminates a lot of solid waste by putting trash back into circulation as material that can be used in a new product.)

5. Things you and the children can do to improve the environment

Materials

See the books listed in the Bibliography at end of this chapter.

Procedure

1 Read to the children one of the following: *It's My Earth Too: How I Can Help the Earth Stay Alive* by Kathleen Krull, *Dinosaurs to the Rescue!*

8-38 *Litter is not pleasant to see.*

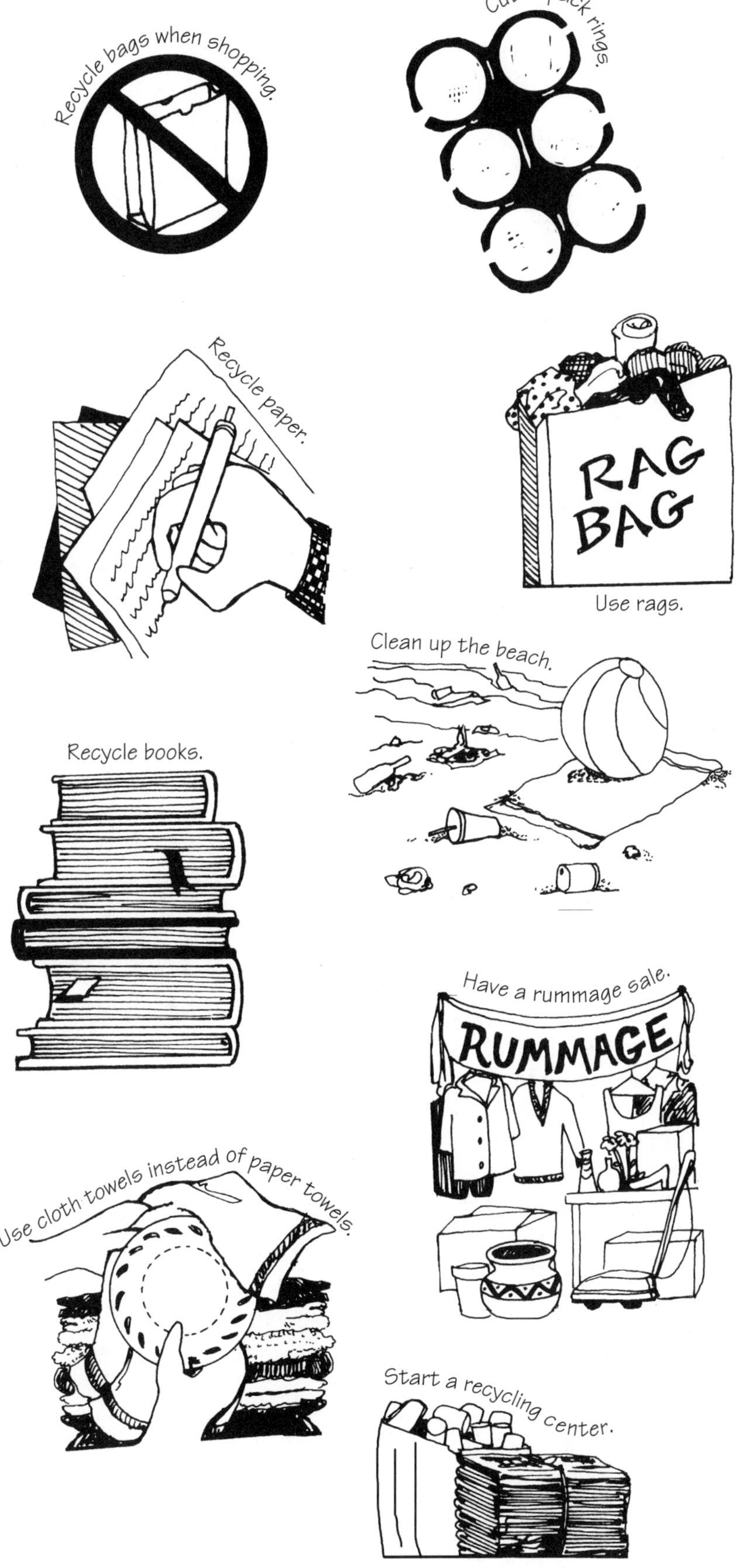
Recycle bags when shopping.
Cut 6-pack rings.
Recycle paper.
RAG BAG
Use rags.
Clean up the beach.
Recycle books.
Have a rummage sale.
RUMMAGE
Use cloth towels instead of paper towels.
Start a recycling center.

8-39 *Things you can do to help the environment.*

by Laurie and Marc Brown, or one of the books listed in the bibliography. Discuss the ideas mentioned in these books about what they can do to improve the environment.

2 Have them make a list of things they can do around the house, in their gardens, and at the store when they buy things. Some of the ideas suggested in these books are:

1 Walk or ride a bike because cars pollute the air.

2 Make your own compost pile from vegetable peelings, tea leaves, coffee grinds, leftover pieces of fruit, and grass clippings. Use the compost as a fertilizer.

3 Visit the recycling center in your community. Sort out the cans, newspapers, and bottles that can be recycled at the center from your garbage and bring them to the recycling center.

4 Use less paper by using reusable sponges or cloth rather than paper towels. Write on both sides of paper. Use blackboards for messages.

5 Find new uses for things rather than throwing them away.

6 Grow your own organic garden. Do not use any pesticides or chemical fertilizers; instead, mix the compost into the soil. (Your compost pile is a fertilizer.)

7 Buy glass bottles rather than plastic. Glass bottles can be recycled. (If you buy plastic, be sure to read the label to see if it can be recycled.)

8 Do not buy products that have too much extra packaging around them.

9 Save shopping bags from the store to use again.

10 Do not buy drinks that come in "no deposit, no return" bottles, unless you plan to recycle the glass.

11 Conserve water when possible by repairing leaky faucets, using only as much water as necessary, turning off water while brushing teeth, and taking shorter showers.

12 Conserve electricity and energy by not keeping lights and electrical appliances on when no one is benefiting from them.

13 Keep air and water clean by not pouring insecticides or poisons down drains or spraying poisons and chemicals into the air.

Going further

1 Discuss the greenhouse effect that takes place inside a closed automobile on a hot day. The heat is trapped inside. An animal or child left inside of a closed automobile is in danger from the extreme heat that builds up.

2 Robert Gardner, in his book, *Celebrating Earth Day*, suggests simulating the greenhouse effect by letting children experience a water level rising. He suggests marking off the water level in two glasses of water that are about half full. Float an ice cube in one glass of water. Place a funnel on top of the other glass of water with an ice cube in the funnel. Observe whether the water level increases in the two glasses after both ice cubes have melted. Discuss how the floating icebergs in the oceans as well as the melting glaciers on poles of the earth would lead to an increase in the overall water level on the earth.

Going further with older children

Surface versus Volume Adapted from an article by Michael Lyden entitled "The Strange Silos," which appeared in *Science and Children*, October, 1985 (Vol. 23, No. 2).

Materials

For each child: two 3-inch-by-5-inch index cards, scotch tape, two empty film canisters filled with corn kernels, a paper plate, a container of salt packaged in a cylinder, Quaker Oatmeal Cereal packaged in a cylinder, another brand of cereal with the same content weight packaged in a rectangular box.

Procedure

1 Help each child create a cylinder from each of the 3"-x-5" index cards. Make one cylinder long and tall and the other short and wide. (See Figs. 8-40A and 8-40B.)

2 Help each child tape the index card cylinders together without overlapping the seam where the edges meet. Place a piece of scotch tape or masking tape down the entire seam so that there are no openings in the seam.

3 Tell children to place the taller cylinder on a paper plate on a flat

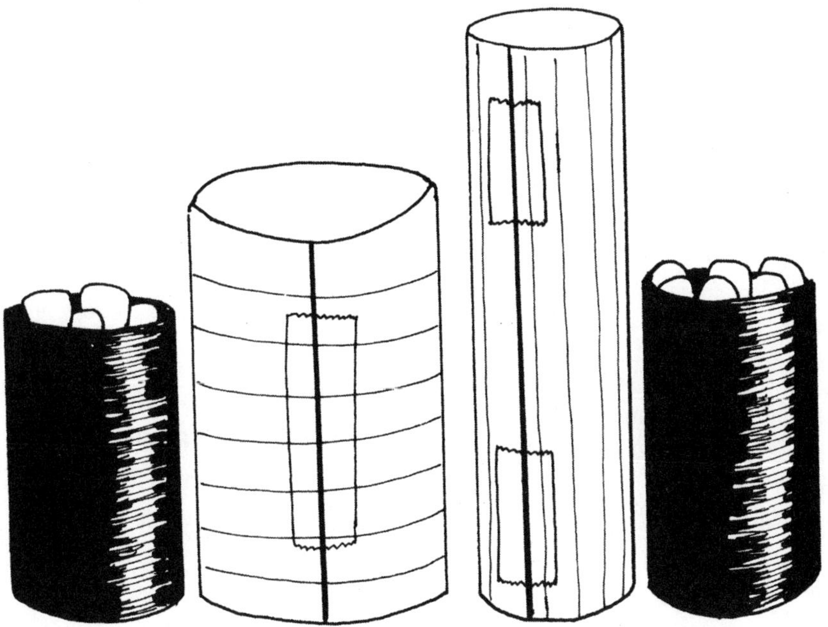

8-40A *Surface area versus volume. Film canisters with corn; two index cards.*

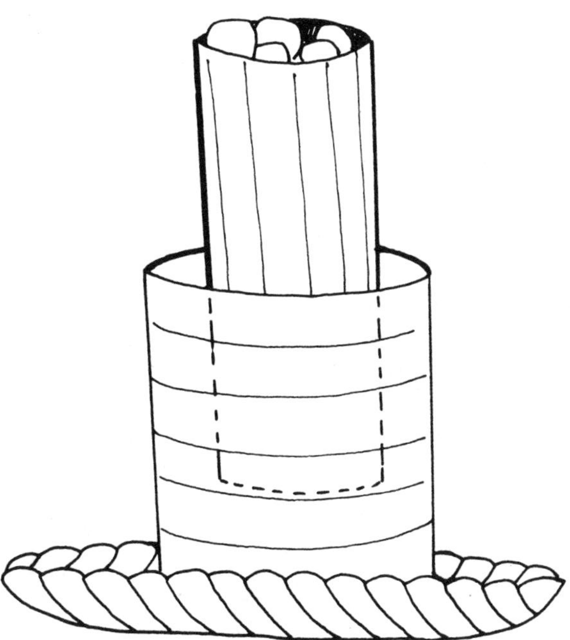

8-40B *Put the corn from the tall tube into the short tube. Which cylinder will hold more?*

table. Have children fill this taller cylinder all the way to the top with the corn from the two film canisters that have been filled with corn kernels.

4 Tell children to slip the shorter, fatter index card cylinder over the taller, thinner filled cylinder.

5 Tell children to lift the filled, tall cylinder up and remove it so that the corn kernels will remain behind in the short, fat cylinder.

Fine point to discuss with older children

The preceding is called a discrepant event. The unexpected occurs. At first, it appears to be unexplainable. But it creates a reason to think and to solve a problem. A cylinder's volume is equal to the area of the base times the height. (The large difference comes about due to the difference in the size of the radius being squared.)

Volume = 2 π R squared times height

($V = 2\pi r^2 h$)

The fat silo has a much larger base.

How many tall thin cylinders can be stuffed into the base of the fat one?

Questions to ask children

Is there still room left for more corn kernels in the short, fat cylinder? Can you explain why?

Where are cylindrical shapes found in real-life situations?

What shape are veins in animals and plants?

What shape are tree trunks and stems?

What shape are pipes and pipelines, storage tanks, and tank trucks that transport liquids?

Are round shapes more energy efficient then square shapes?

What shapes are animal bodies?

What shape are air conditioning and heating ducts?

What shape do coins from banks come in? Why?

Explain: In general, the round or cylindrical shape is more energy efficient and more space efficient. It is found in most forms of life and has other uses in tools and machines. Other examples of cylinders: liquids like soda come in bottles; most table salt containers and Quaker Oatmeal cereal are packaged as cylinders; gas and milk are shipped in horizontal cylinders on tank trucks. Ask children if they can name other things that have a cylindrical shape.

Extension questions raised in the article "Strange Silos" by Michael Leyden:

Can a cereal box be designed to hold more? "If 40 percent of the paper used in a given cereal box can be saved by using a different design, why, then, do food producers not reduce their overhead (as represented by the cost of paper) by using a (different) design? Might there be some consumer manipulation going on here? Are there considerations other than volume per area in designing a box? . . . Would a cube be as satisfactory of a cereal box as a rectangular prism? . . . Does a cylinder with the same height and surface area as a rectangular prism always have a larger volume? . . . What implications do the economy of cylinders have for 'packaging' in the natural world? Can you think of other organic forms that are cylindrical? Why might it be important in trees or arteries to get the most volume with the least surface area?" (page 33).

What can you and the children do about the paper that is wasted in packaging? (See the Bibliography at the end of this chapter for: Lewis, Barbara, *The Kid's Guide to Social Action: How to Solve the Social-Problems You Choose—and Turn Creative Thinking into Positive Action*; Miles, Betty, *Save the Earth: An Action Handbook for Kids*; Schwartz, Linda, *Earth Book for Kids: Activities to Help Heal the Environment*.

Further resources

Dewey Decimal Classification Number for ecology is: 574; 363.72 (pollution), 628.4 (waste, refuse and recycling).

Selected books for children

Amos, William H. *Life in Ponds and Streams*. Washington, D.C.: National Geographic Society, 1981. (Large color photos.)

Burnie, David. *Tree*. New York: Knopf, 1988.

George, Craighead. *One Day in the Tropical Rain Forest*. New York: Thomas Y. Crowell, 1990.

Gibbons, Gail. *Recycle! A Handbook for Kids*. Boston: Little, Brown and Co.: Boston, 1992. (Explains the process of recycling from start to finish and discusses what happens to paper, glass, aluminum cans, and plastic when they are recycled into new products.)

Johnson, Sylvia. *How Leaves Change*. Minneapolis: Lerner, 1986.

Krull, Kathleen. *It's My Earth Too. How I Can Help the Earth Stay Alive*. New York: Doubleday, 1992. (Text and illustrations pay homage to the earth and its resources. Includes suggestions that children can follow to help preserve the environment.)

Lewis, Barbara. *The Kids Guide to Social Action: How to Solve the Social Problems You Choose—and Turn Creative Thinking into Positive Action*. Minneapolis, MN: Free Spirit Press, 1991. (A primer for adults and children who want to bring about social action to initiate or change laws affecting the environment.)

Leyde, Michael. The Strange Silos. *Science and Children*. Washington, DC. Vol 23, No.2, October, 1985.

McLaughlin, Molly. *Earthworms, Dirt, and Rotten Leaves*. New York: Atheneum, 1986.

Miles, Betty. *Save the Earth: An Action Handbook for Kids*. New York: Knopf, 1991. (Filled with success stories about how kids can bring about an environmental change and influence government.)

Nagel-Fischer, Heiderose and Andreas. *Fir Trees*. Minneapolis: Carolrhoda, 1989.

Patent, Dorothy Hinshaw. *Buffalo*. New York: Holiday House, 1986. (This book is a photo essay detailing a year in the life of an American bison today. The buffalo almost became extinct. They have been a source of food, clothing, and shelter for the Native Americans of the Great Plains. Indians respected, appreciated, and admired buffalo.)

Pratt, Krisren. *A Walk in the Rainforest*. Nevada City, CA: Dawn Publications, 1992.

Russell, Naomi. *Tree*. New York: Dutton, 1989.

Schwartz, Linda. *Earth Book for Kids: Activities to Help Heal the Environment*. Santa Barbara, CA: The Learning Works, 1990. (This book has lots of great activities for children who can read.)

Selsam, Millicent, and Ezra Jack Keats. *How to Be Nature's Detective*. New York: Harper and Row, 1966.

Shepard, Elizabeth. *No Bones*. New York: Macmillan, 1988.

Showers, Paul. *The Listening Walk*. New York: Harper and Row, rev. ed., 1991. (Nature walk.)

Sisson, Edith A. *Nature with Children of All Ages*. Englewood Cliffs, NJ: Prentice-Hall, 1990.

Taylor, Barbara. *Rain Forest: Look Closer Series*. New York: Dorling Kindersley, 1992. (Has beautiful illustrations.)

Tresselt, Alvin. *The Dead Tree*. New York: Parent's Magazine Press, 1972. (About the organisms in a dead tree that decompose it.)

Sterry, Paul. *Nature Search: Rain Forest*. Joshua Morris (*Reader's Digest*), 1992. (The book comes with a magnifying glass.)

Yolen, Jane. *Welcome to the Green House*. New York: Putman, 1993. (This book has beautiful, colorful illustrations.)

Selected resource books for more ideas

Alvin, Virginia and Robert Silverstein. *Recycling: Meeting the Challenge of the Trash Crisis*. New York: G.P. Putnam, 1992. (Discusses different methods of recycling waste, associated advantages and problems, and the possible future. This book has few pictures; it is better suited for older children or adults.)

Caduto, Michael. *Pond and Brook: A Guide to Nature in Freshwater Environments*. Hanover, NH: University Press of New England, 1990.

Caduto and Bruchac. *Keepers of the Earth*. Golden, CO: Fulcrum, 1988. (Contains Indian legends that explain how and why nature acts the way she does. There are also many creative activities to help children become more aware of their environment.)

De Vito, Alfred, and Gerald H. Krockover. *Creative Sciencing*. Greenville, IL: 1980.

Earthworks Group Staff. *Fifty Simple Things That Kids Can Do to Save the Earth*. Boston, Mass: G.K. Hall, 1991.

Eustice, V., and C. Heald. *Outdoor Play: Bright Ideas for Early Years*. Warwickshire, UK: Scholastic Publications, 1992.

Frith, Michael. *Some of Us Walk, Some Fly, Some Swim*. New York: Random House, 1971. (Animal adaptation and defense.)

Forsyth, Adrian. *Journey Through a Tropical Jungle*. New York: Simon & Schuster, 1988.

Gardner, Robert. *Celebrating Earth Day: A Sourcebook of Activities and Experiments*. Brookfield, CT.: Millbrook Press, 1992. (Contains activities about environmental education and earth day.)

Gutnik, Martin J. *Experiments That Explore Recycling*. Brookfield, CT: Millbrook Press, 1992.

Harlow, Rosie, and Gareth Morgan. *175 Amazing Nature Experiments*. New York: Random House, 1991.

Herman, Marina Lachecki, Joseph F. Passineau, Ann L. Schimpf, and Paul Treuer. *Teaching Kids to Love the Earth*. Duluth, MN: Pfeifer Hamilton, 1991.

Javna, John. *25 Simple Things Kids Can Do to Save the Earth*. Berkeley, CA: The Earth Works Group, 1992

Johnson, Rebecca L. *The Greenhouse Effect*. Minneapolis: Lerner, 1990.

Katz, Addrienne. *Naturewatch*. Reading, Mass: Addison-Wesley, 1986.

Langone, John. *Our Endangered Earth: What We Can Do to Save It*. Boston: Little, Brown and Co., 1992. (Discusses the environmental crisis, focusing on such problems as overpopulation, the pollution of water, air, and land, ozone depletion, global warming, and disappearing wildlife in the 21st century. This book has no pictures; it is for older children or for adults.)

Lingelbach, J. *Hand on Nature: Information and Activities for Exploring the Environment with Children*. Woodstock, Vt.: Vermont Institute of Natural Science.

National Wildlife Federation. Rainforests: Tropical Treasures. *Ranger Rick's Nature Scope*. Vol.4, No.4, 1989. Washington, D.C., National Wildlife Federation. (An activity book with a helpful bibliography.)

Petrash, C. *Earthways: Simple Environmental Activities for Younger Children*. Mt. Rainier, Md.: Gryphon House, 1992.

Pringle, Laurence, and Jan Adkins. *Chains, Webs, and Pyramids: The Flow of Energy in Nature*. New York: Thomas Y. Crowell, 1975.

Pringle, Laurence. *Antarctica: The Last Unspoiled Continent*. New York: Simon & Schuster, 1992. (Has beautiful photographs and text about the earth's most southern continent.

Pringle, Laurence. *Global Warming: Assessing the Greenhouse Threat*. New York: Arcade, 1990. (Grades 4–7)

UNESCO. *New UNESCO Source Book for Science Teaching*. The UNESCO Press: Paris, 1976. (This is a classic; it should be read by everyone who wants to teach science. It was written for people in undeveloped countries who have no money for supplies.)

Selected state curriculum recycling programs (that can be ordered)

A-Way With Waste
Washington State Department of Ecology
4350 150th Ave, NE
Redmond, WA 98052

Recycle Alaska: Activities Handbook
Alaska Litter Reduction and Resource Recovery Program
Alaska DEC, Pouch O
Juneau, AK 99811

Recycling Study Guide
Wisconsin Department of Natural Resources Education Programs
Bureau of Information and Education
PO Box 7921
Madison, WI 53707

Super Saver Investigators
Division of Litter Prevention & Recycling
Ohio Department of Natural Resources
Ohio Academy of Science
445 King Avenue
Columbus, OH 43201

The Conserving Classroom
Waste Education Clearing House
1350 Energy Lane
St. Paul, Minnesota 55108

Selected literature connections for younger children

Blake, Robert. *The Perfect Spot*. New York: Philomel (Putnam), 1992.

Brown, Ruth. *The World That Jack Built*. New York: Dutton Children's Books, 1991. (Summary: A book of few words with stunning illustrations of the earth's fragile wonders and a warning that humans are endangering it.)

Brown, Marc, and K. Laurie. *Dinosaurs to the Rescue! A Guide to Protecting our Planet*. Boston: Little, Brown, 1992. (Introduces children to our environmental problems and suggests ways to help out.)

Cherry, Lynne. *The Great Kapok Tree*. San Diego: Gulliver Books (HBJ), 1990. (Summary: The many different animals that live in a great kapok tree in the Brazilian rain forest try to convince a man with an ax of the importance of not cutting down their home.)

Foreman, Michael. *One World*. New York: Arcade, 1990. (Beautifully illustrated story about two children who create a miniature habitat for marine life in a bucket. They clean up the real tidal pool of its pollution, and then return the creatures they have collected back into the repaired tidal pool.)

Geisel, Theodor Seuss. *The Lorax*. New York: Random House, 1971. (Summary: The Once-ler (a character in the story) describes the results of the local pollution problem.)

Geraghty, Paul. *Stop that Noise!* New York: Crown, 1992. (Summary: A story about the rain forest.)

Halpern, Sheri. My *River*. New York: Macmillan, 1992. (Summary: Animals along a river state their need for the river and plead for the river to be protected.)

James, Simon. *Sally and the Limpet*. New York: Macmillan, 1991. (A story about a little girl who picks up a limpet. The limpet sticks to her finger, and she cannot remove it. The story tells about her plight and how she finally solves the problem.)

Latkin, Patricia. *Jet Black Pick Up Truck*. New York: Orchard Books, 1990. (Summary: A little girl tells about her ride to the dump with Granny.)

Lyon, David. *The Runaway Duck*. New York: Morrow, 1987. (A story about an unexpected trip of a child's favorite toy.)

McDonald, Megan. *Is This A House for A Hermit Crab?* New York: Orchard Books (Watts), 1990. (A story about a hermit crab that has outgrown its shell.)

Payne, Emmy. *Katy No-Pocket*. New York: Houghton Mifflin, 1972. (A story about a mother kangaroo who has no pocket to carry her baby joey.)

Rand, Gloria. *Prince William*. New York: Holt, 1992. (A story about baby seals living in polluted water.)

Rice, Eve. *Peter's Pockets*. New York: Greenwillow, 1989. (A story about Peter who has no pocket in his new pants.)

Thompson, Collin. *The Paper Bag Prince*. New York: Knopf, 1992. (Summary: A wise old man visits the town dump every day. He moves into an abandoned train at the dump and watches as nature gradually reclaims the polluted land.)

General community enrichment activities

The following is a list of many local places that most of us probably take for granted and that children could benefit from visiting with an adult. It is just a matter of visiting these places with a different point of view. Try looking at these places as a scientist interested in the environment and discover and observe what is located at each of these sites. Do a population study of plants or animals; record the variety and number of plants and animals you observe at each site. Try to figure out what happens to the garbage in your town. Where does it go? What happens to it? How is the sewage treated? How is the water treated? What happens to landfills when they are full? Does your town make money on recycling? What happens to junk? How is it used?

- Wooded area.
- A lake.
- A dam.
- A river.
- A park.
- Local sanitation department.
- A landfill.
- A recycling center.
- The town dump.
- A water treatment plant.
- A junk yard.

Bibliography

The American Heritage Dictionary of the English Language. Morris William, ed. Boston: Houghton Mifflin, 1976.

Brainard, Audrey, and Denise H. Wrubel. *Literature-Based Science Activities, an Integrated Approach*. New York: Scholastic, 1993. (Appropriate for grades 1–4. This book is filled with creative and innovative science experiences using children's literature as a springboard for science investigations and activities.

Bruner, J.S. *The Process of Education*. Cambridge, Massachusetts: Harvard University Press, 1960. (See especially chapter 2, "The Importance of Structure," and chapter 3, "Readiness for Learning.")

Beakman's World. A Universal Press Syndicated television program, distributed by Columbia Pictures for the Learning Channel. Various programs.

Children's Television Workshop. 3, 2, 1, Contact. Educational Television Series. Various dates.

Davis, Barbara. Science Supervisor, Virginia Beach City Public Schools. Making Inferences about Animals. A lecture given in her course: Topics in Life and Physical Science for Kindergarten Teachers, Spring, 1993.

Fee, Sally. A Child's Real World-Developing Science Within the Program. A workshop presented in Washington, D.C. at the National Association for the Education of Young Children (NAEYC), Washington, D.C., November, 1982.

Gagne, Robert M. *The Conditions of Learning, 4th edition*. New York: Harcourt, Brace Jonovich, 1985.

Hewitt, Paul G. *Conceptual Physics, 7th edition. A New Introduction to Your Environment*. Boston: Little, Brown & Co., 1992.

Merrit Student Encyclopedia. New York: Macmillan Education Co., 1991.

Tryon, Bette. Science, A Practical Approach. A workshop presented in Washington, D.C., at the National Conference of the National Association for the Education of Young Children (NAEYC), Washington, D.C., November, 1982.

Williams, David, "Science" for Young Children—Gathering Experiences. 16th Annual Conference sponsored by the Maryland Council of Parent Participation Nursery Schools, Montgomery College, Rockville, Maryland, March 7, 1984.

World Book Encyclopedia, 1979 ed. Chicago: World Book-Childcraft, 1979. (See especially: Weather, Volcanoes, Atoms, Animals, Plants, Leaves, Flowers, Ecology.)

Series

Audubon Society Field Series. New York: Knopf, (various dates).

Doubleday Nature Guides. New York: Doubleday (various dates).

Golden Nature Guides. New York: Golden Press (various dates).

Great Explorations in Math & Science, (GEMS) Teacher's Guides. Berkeley, CA: Lawrence Hall of Science (various dates).

How and Why Wonder Books. New York: Grosset and Dunlap (various dates).

Ladybird Natural History Books. London: Ladybird Books (various dates).

Life Nature Library. New York: Time-Life (various dates).

National Geographic, Books for World Explorers. Washington, DC: National Geographic Society (various dates).

Nature Scope. Washington, DC: National Wildlife Federation, (various dates).

Peterson Field Guides. Boston: Houghton Mifflin (various dates).

Spotter's Guides. London: Usborne (various dates).

Selected generic resource books for parents and teachers

Brown, Sam Ed. *Bubbles, Rainbows and Worms: Science Experiments for Preschool Children*. Mt. Rainier, MD: Gryphon House, 1981.

Druger, Marvin, ed. *Science for the Fun of It: A Guide to Informal Science Education*. Washington, DC: National Science Teachers Association, 1988.

Exploratorium Teacher Institute Staff. *Exploratorium Science Snackbook: A Teacher Resource for Hands-on Science Exhibits & Activities*. San Francisco: CA, 1991.

Goldman, Jane F. *The Curiosity Shop: A Sciencing Sampler for the Primary Years*. Minneapolis: T.S. Denison, 1988. (Has an extensive list of free and inexpensive materials, as well a chart listing assorted small creatures and how to care for them.)

Milford, Susan. *The Kid's Nature Book: 365 Indoor/Outdoor Activities and Experiences*. Charlotte, VT: Williamson, 1989. (Despite the title, it is more suitable for parents or older children. The book suggests a nature experience for every day of the year.)

Mastusiak, C. *Seasonal Activities Spring & Summer: Bright Ideas for Early Years*. Warwickshire, UK: Scholastic Publications, 1992.

Nature Education Kits. Newton, Kansas: Young Naturalist Co. (Nature kits: What leaf is it? What Seed is it? What twig is it? Packaged with real "pieces" of nature.)

Ontario Science Center Staff. *Science Express*. Reading, Mass.: Addison-Wesley, 1991.

Ontario Science Center Staff. *Scienceworks*. Reading, Mass: Addison-Wesley, 1986.

Ontario Science Center Staff. *Sports-works*. Reading, Mass: Addison-Wesley, 1989.

Poppe, Carol A. and Nancy A. Van Matre. *Science Learning Centers for the Primary Grades*. West Nyack, N.Y.: The Center for Applied Research in Education, 1985. (Instructions for setting up learning centers, plus 40 activities to do at the learning centers. Better suited for beginning teachers than parents.)

Strongin, Herb. *Science on a Shoestring*. Reading, Mass: Addison-Wesley, 1992.

Wolfgang, Charles H. and Mary E. *School for Young Children: Developmentally Appropriate Practices*. Needham, Mass.: Allyn and Bacon, 1992.

Additional generic science books for children and their parents

Althea. *What Makes Things Move?* Mahwah, NJ: Troll, 1991.

Ardley, Neil. *The Science Book of Gravity*. New York: Gulliver Books (HBJ), 1992.

Ardley, Neil. *The Science Book of Energy*. New York: Gulliver Books (HBJ), 1992.

Bourgeois, Paulette. *The Amazing Apple Book*. Reading, Mass: Addison-Wesley, 1991. (Great after-school enrichment activities or for special school projects done at home to share with classmates. (Ages 6–11).

Bourgeois, Paulette. *The Amazing Dirt Book*. Reading, Mass: Addison-Wesley, 1990. (After-school enrichment activities for children 7–11.)

Burnie, David. *How Nature Works*. New York: Reader's Digest, 1991. (Great photographs.)

Challoner, Jack. *The Science Book of Numbers*. New York: Gulliver Books (HBJ), 1992.

Cobb, Vicki, and Kathy Darling. *Bet You Can! Science Possibilities to Fool You*. New York: Avon Books, 1983.

Cobb, Vicki, and Kathy Darling. *Bet You Can't! Science Impossibilities to Fool You*. New York: Lothrop, 1980.

Cobb, Vicki. *Chemically Active!* New York: Harper and Row, 1990.

Cobb, Vicki. *More Science Experiments You Can Eat*. New York: Harper and Row, 1979.

Forte, Imogene. *Science Fun: Discovering the World Around You*. Incentives Publications, Inc., Nashville, Tennessee, 1985.

Gardner, Robert. *Kitchen Chemistry*. Morristown, NJ: Silver Burdett, 1988.

Grant, Lesley. *Discover Bones: Explore the Science of Skeletons*. Reading, Mass: Addison-Wesley, 1991. (After-school enrichment activities for children 7–12.)

Hann, Judith. *How Science Works*. New York: Reader's Digest, 1991. (Better for older children.)

Hazen, Robert M. *Science Matters*. New York: Doubleday, 1991.

Herbert, Don. Mr. *Wizard's Super Market Science*. New York: Random House, 1980.

Herbert, Don. Mr. *Wizard's Experiments for Young Scientists*. New York: Doubleday, 1990.

Jennings, Terry. *Bouncing and Rolling*. New York: Gloucester Press, 1990.

Kenda, Margaret and Williams, Phyllis S. *Science Wizardry for Kids: Authentic, Safe Scientific Experiments Kids Can Perform!* Hauppauge, N.Y.: Barrons Educational Series, 1992.

Mandell, Muriel. *Simple Science Experiments with Everyday Materials*. New York: Sterling, 1990. (For older children.)

Mandell. Muriel. *220 Easy-to-Do Science Experiments for Young People: 3 Complete Books*. New York: Dover, 1985.

Mollenson, Diane, and Sarah Savage. *Easy Science Experiments*. New York: Scholastic, 1993.

Penrose, Gordon. *Dr. Zed's Science Surprises*. New York: Simon and Schuster, 1989.

Rockwell, R., E. Sherwood, and R. Williams. *Hug a Tree and Other Things to Do Outdoors with Young Children*. Mt. Rainier, MD: Gryphon House, 1983.

Penrose, Gordon. *More Science Surprises from Dr. Zed*. New York: Simon & Schuster, 1992.

Penrose, Gordon. *Magic Mud and Other Great Experiments*. New York: Simon & Schuster, 1987.

Ross, Catherine, and Susan Wallace. *The Amazing Milk Book: Two Dozen Fun Proj-ects for Home or School.* Reading, Mass: Addison-Wesley, 1991. (Great after-school enrichment activities, or for special school projects done at home to share with classmates. Ages 7–11.)

Stein, Sara. *The Science Book.* New York: Workman Publishing, 1980.

Stetten, Mary. *Let's Play Science.* New York: Harper and Row, 1979.

Van Cleave, Janice. *Biology for Every Kid.* New York: John Wiley, 1990.

Van Cleave, Janice. *Earth Science for Every Kid.* New York: John Wiley, 1991.

Weiner, Esther. *Dirt Cheap Science: Activity-Based Units, Games, Experiments & Reproducibles.* New York: Scholastic, 1992. (Great activities for an after-school science program).

Wyler, Rose. *Science Fun with A Homemade Chemistry Set.* New York: Julian Messner, 1987.

Index

About the Author

Elaine Levenson brings a rich blend of professional and life experiences—and her own unique educational perspectives—to *Teaching Children about Life and Earth Sciences*. An early childhood educator, Elaine has held a variety of teaching assignments: in New York, Maryland, Virginia, and the District of Columbia, working in nursery school through graduate-level venues.

As a Projector Director for the National Science Foundation, through the University of the District of Columbia, (1985–1987), she trained and assisted teachers in grades K–6 to be more confident and effective in doing science activities with young children.

Her higher education began at San Diego State College, then continued at Boston University and New York University. She completed her B.S. in Elementary Education and her Masters Degree in Early Childhood at Queens College, City University of New York.

Elaine's teaching career began in a second grade, at P.S. 50, an inner-city, special-services school in the Bronx, New York City. (Subsequently, she took a ten-year leave of absence after her children were born.)

Later, in 1977 when her youngest entered The Franklin Montessori School in suburban Washington, D.C., she was asked to become that school's art and science teacher. The director, Lynn Oboler, knew that Elaine had majored in early childhood, and Lynn was anxious to develop a science teacher for her school. Lynn Oboler suggested that Elaine study some children's science books in the belief that Elaine would surely know more than enough to answer the questions of four-year-olds. The Director of the Montessori school, as well as the parents and other teachers, realized that Elaine had a natural talent for teaching early childhood science, and so they encouraged her to take additional science courses. After completing a series of graduate-level science classes in life, earth, and physical sciences, Elaine was able to start her own visiting science teaching service, known as Science-on-Wheels. For six years, Science-on-Wheels offered weekly sequenced science lessons at private schools and day-care centers throughout the Washington, D.C. suburbs.

Today Elaine continues to enjoy developing awarenesses in children and extending their curiosity. She relishes open-ended activities and likes to ask lots of questions, as well as to play.

Her first book, *Teaching Children about Science: Ideas and Activities Every Teacher and Parent Can Use* (first published in 1985), attracted widespread notice—in reviews, college and university education departments, museums, and in the media. That book went through four printings and is used in college classes and in many homes across the country.

Elaine currently resides with her husband, Hal, a media consultant, in Virginia Beach, Virginia. She teaches kindergarten at Linkhorn Park Elementary School, a public institution.

Other Bestsellers of Related Interest

Nature through Science and Art

Susie Gwen Criswell

A how-to book for teachers, parents, and other educators who spend time exploring nature with children. Instills a deep awareness of the environment in children in grades 3-6 through hands-on science investigations and art activities.

Paper 0-8306-4576-4 $12.95

Hard 0-8306-4575-6 $22.95

The Little Scientist;: An Activity Lab

Jean Stangl

This book encourages young children to view the world around them as a giant experiment in progress, to explore their surroundings in search of knowledge about how and why their environment works. Forty stimulating hands-on science experiments physically involve children ages 4-6 in the learning process. Projects include measuring temperature, caring for small animals, studying insects, and recycling garbage. Safety icons.

Paper 0-8306-4102-5

Hard 0-8306-4101-7 $17.95

A Teacher's Science Companion

Dr. Phyllis J. Perry

A carefully researched bibliography, organized by topic, of more than 2,000 children's science and math books in print. Includes step-by-step activities that provide instant "lessons" on the subject. Perfect for teachers of grades K-6.

Paper 0-07-049519-X $14.95

Hard 0-07-049518-1 $24.95

Teaching Children About Physical Science

Elaine Levenson

Companion science survival guides for teachers and parents, with activities for grades K-3. These idea-filled editions incorporate the latest teaching techniques to stimulate kids' interest in science.

Paper 0-07-037619-0 $16.95